Psychedelic Chile

Psychedelic Chile

Youth, Counterculture, and Politics
on the Road to Socialism and Dictatorship

· ·

PATRICK BARR-MELEJ

The University of North Carolina Press Chapel Hill

© 2017 The University of North Carolina Press
All rights reserved
Set in Charis and Lato by Westchester Publishing Services
Manufactured in the United States of America

The University of North Carolina Press has been a member of the Green Press Initiative since 2003.

Library of Congress Cataloging-in-Publication Data
Names: Barr-Melej, Patrick, author.
Title: Psychedelic Chile : youth, counterculture, and politics on the road to socialism and dictatorship / Patrick Barr-Melej.
Description: Chapel Hill : University of North Carolina Press, [2017] | Includes bibliographical references and index.
Identifiers: LCCN 2016045887| ISBN 9781469632568 (cloth : alk. paper) | ISBN 9781469632575 (pbk : alk. paper) | ISBN 9781469632582 (ebook)
Subjects: LCSH: Chile—Politics and government—1970-1973. | Counterculture—Chile—History—20th century. | Hippies—Chile—History—20th century. | Youth—Political Activity—Chile—History—20th century. | Chile—Social conditions—20th century.
Classification: LCC F3100 .B356 2017 | DDC 983.06/46—dc23
LC record available at https://lccn.loc.gov/2016045887

Cover illustration: Photograph of young man at the 1970 Piedra Roja festival in Las Condes, Chile (© Paul Lowry, used with permission).

Portions of chapters 1, 4, and 5 were previously published as "Hippismo a la chilena: Juventud y heterodoxia cultural en un contexto transnacional, 1970–1973," in *Ampliando miradas: Chile y su historia en un tiempo global*, ed. Fernando Purcell and Alfredo Riquelme (Santiago: RIL Editores, 2009), 305–25. Used here with permission.
Portions of chapter 6 were previously published as "Siloísmo and the Self in Allende's Chile: Youth, 'Total Revolution,' and the Roots of the Humanist Movement," *Hispanic American Historical Review* 86, no. 4 (2006): 747–84, doi:10.1215/00182168-2006-049. Republished by permission of Duke University Press, www.dukeupress.edu.

For Melissa, our children,
and my parents.

Contents

Illustrations

Acknowledgments

. . . .

I may not have gone where I intended to go, but I think I have ended up
where I needed to be.
—Douglas Adams, *The Long Dark Tea-Time of the Soul*

Ending this book's journey brings with it reflection from which deep gratitude and heartfelt emotions spring. My debts are many, and the following
few paragraphs only begin to express my appreciation to those who were
with me on the trek.

Tulio Halperín-Donghi, my dissertation adviser at Berkeley in the 1990s,
was a brilliant and world-renowned historian—and he had a big heart. Soon
after my first child's birth nearly twenty years ago, Tulio invited me to lunch
at Berkeley's faculty club to discuss turning my dissertation into what became my first book. When I arrived there, he was waiting for me in the
lobby, with a wrapped package in hand. Inside was a stuffed animal—a gift
for my newborn daughter, Eva. With a smile, he remarked that the gift came
with a caveat: that my wife and I never call her "Evita." (Those who knew
Tulio will most appreciate the Argentine's quip.) It just so happens, we never
have. My other—and first—graduate mentor was Arnold J. Bauer, whose er-
udition, kindheartedness, sympathetic soul, and humility were even larger
than his imposing frame. Arnie's deep love for Chile and its people is evident in what he wrote, and it also appeared in his eyes when he spoke of
that beautiful land on the edge of the earth. Arnie saw a historian's work
not as a vocational pursuit but rather as a pilgrim's sojourn into the lives of
those who wait patiently in the past to teach us something about our humanity. Both Tulio and Arnie passed away while I was writing this book.
I am immensely fortunate to have been their student and to have experienced their kindness.

When working to finish this project, few things were as motivating as
friends and colleagues repeatedly asking: "When is that book coming out?"
As many authors know, the question can get old—really fast—but it springs
from genuine comradeship and support. I warmly thank Claudio Robles Ortiz, James Cane-Carrasco, Valeria Manzano, Eric Zolov, William Skuban,

Brenda Elsey, Jaime Pensado, Francisco Barbosa, Anadelia Romo, Daryle Williams, Mary Kay Vaughan, Claudio Rolle, Fernando Purcell, Alfredo Riquelme, J. Pablo Silva, Eduardo Devés, Sergio Grez, Margaret Power, Juan Luis Ossa, Iván Jaksic, Oscar Ortiz, Lessie Jo Frazier, and Fabio Salas Zúñiga for their encouragement and feedback as I researched, thought about, and wrote these chapters. I also extend thanks to my Ohio University colleagues Robert Ingram, Katherine Jellison, and Michele Clouse, and to the university's Office of the Vice President for Research for its financial support.

I am indebted to Gary Fritz, Julián Burgos, Pía Figueroa Edwards, Carlos Lowry, and Mario Luis Rodríguez Cobos for their tremendous help in my efforts to piece together the stories herein. Of great assistance, too, was Pink Lizard, the *nom de hippie* of an American whose recording of short interviews at a momentous Chilean rock festival is the kind of source about which historians dream. It saddens me that he did not live to read about his youthful exploits in this book. Former students of mine at Ohio University, Chile's Pontifical Catholic University, and the University of Concepción also have my gratitude for helping me work through many of the ideas at the heart of this study. I especially thank Sebastián Hurtado Torres, Brad Eidahl, Jared Bibler, Carla Rivera, Marcelo Casals, Diego Mundaca, Róbinson Lira, Leslie Perera, Anne Allman, and Christina Matzen. I also thank Michael Elliot, Amanda Roden, Paul Relstab, and Leah Graysmith for their assistance. Jaime Román and Liliana Montesinos at Chile's National Library brought smiles to long days of work, and the staffs at the Library of Congress and National Administration Archive in Santiago have my gratitude. Special thanks go to Chile's National Historical Museum and to Paul Lowry for permitting the use of their photographs. To the crew at Donkey Coffee in Athens, Ohio: thank you for providing the best possible space for sitting down with a laptop, some thoughts, and a decaf iced mocha.

My wife, Melissa Barr, and our children, Eva Gabriela, Emilia Violeta, and Nicolás Abraham, have taught me volumes about life's simple joys and love's indefatigability. Despite my many shortcomings, they make me better every day. In the mid-1960s, my parents, Roger Barr, a Wisconsinite by birth, and Cinthia Melej, a *santiaguina*, met in La Serena, Chile, not very far from where my father served as a Peace Corps volunteer in Guanaqueros—then a poor fishing village, now a vacation hot spot. I am forever grateful to my parents for making Chile my second home, just as I am blessed to have my loving godparents, Silvia Bullezú Melej and Walter Bufadel, always waiting for me in Santiago. Violeta González Ossandón, my grandmother to whom I dedicated my first book, passed away before I could share this one with her. She was a strong woman with a powerful spirit and inexhaustible love, and I find solace in thinking that when I write about Chile, in a way I'm writing about her. I also lost my paternal grandmother, Dorothy Barr, while on this academic journey. I take with me her beaming smile and love.

This book could not have happened without the spirited support and colossal patience of my editor at UNC Press, the incomparable Elaine Maisner. She has the capacity of calming the stressed and assuring the doubtful. Thank you, Elaine. My appreciation also goes to the press's editorial, production, and marketing staffs; Annette Calzone, who steered the manuscript through editing; and to the peer reviewers whose suggestions made for a better book. All errors that remain are mine and mine alone. As Luther is known to have said when addressing Charles V, "Here I stand. I can do no other. God help me."

Abbreviations in the Text

BEC	Brigada Elmo Catalán (Elmo Catalán Brigade)
BRP	Brigada Ramona Parra (Ramona Parra Brigade)
CODEH	Comité de Defensa de Derechos Humanos (Human Rights Defense Committee)
CRM	Comando Rolando Matus (Rolando Matus Command)
CUT	Central Única de Trabajadores (Central Workers' Union)
DICAP	Discoteca del Cantar Popular (Popular Song Record Library)
FECh	Federación de Estudiantes de la Universidad de Chile (Student Federation of the University of Chile)
FESES	Federación de Estudiantes Secundarios de Santiago (Federation of Santiago Secondary-School Students)
FEUC	Federación de Estudiantes de la Universidad Católica (Federation of Students of the Catholic University)
FEUT	Federación de Estudiantes de la Universidad Técnica (Student Federation of the State Technical University)
FLN	Frente de Liberación Nacional (National Liberation Front)
FNPL	Frente Nacionalista Patria y Libertad (Fatherland and Liberty Nationalist Front)
IC	Izquierda Cristiana (Christian Left)
IJ	Iglesia Joven (Young Church)
JDC	Juventud Demócrata Cristiana (Christian Democratic Youth)
JN	Juventud Nacional (National Youth)
Jota	Juventudes Comunistas (Communist Youth)
JS	Juventud Socialista (Socialist Youth)
MAPSA	Movimiento Antipololeo Solo Atraque (No Dating, Just Linking-Up Movement)

MAPU	Movimiento de Acción Popular Unitaria (Unitary Popular Action Movement)
MIR	Movimiento de Izquierda Revolucionaria (Movement of the Revolutionary Left)
PCCh	Partido Comunista de Chile (Communist Party of Chile)
PDC	Partido Demócrata Cristiano (Christian Democratic Party)
PDI	Policía de Investigaciones (Investigations Police)
PH	Partido Humanista (Humanist Party)
PN	Partido Nacional (National Party)
PR	Partido Radical (Radical Party)
PS	Partido Socialista (Socialist Party)
SNJ	Secretaría Nacional de la Juventud (National Secretariat of Youth)
SNM	Secretaría Nacional de la Mujer (National Secretariat of Women)
UP	Unidad Popular (Popular Unity)
VOP	Vanguardia Organizada del Pueblo (Organized Vanguard of the People)

Psychedelic Chile

Introduction

· ·

Live, let live, and help live.
—Ralph Waldo Emerson, 1838

Live, let live, and help live.
—A Chilean hippie, quoted in *El Mercurio*, 1970

I sat next to Jorge Gómez Ainslie as the lights dimmed inside the sold-out Teatro Nescafé de las Artes (née Marconi), a historic theater in Greater Santiago's municipality of Providencia. We were among a thousand or so ticketholders and special guests who had gathered on that mild evening in the austral spring of 2011 to await the premier of the documentary *Piedra Roja*, which had received the coveted distinction of kicking off the capital's eighth annual In-Edit Film Festival. Looking younger than his sixty years and somewhat nervous, Gómez was about to see a chapter of his young adulthood flash before his eyes, so to speak, as were many others in the crowd who, like Gómez, had been protagonists in an exceptional and revealing moment: the Piedra Roja festival of October 1970—Chile's version of Woodstock. The work of first-time filmmaker Gary Fritz, and conferee of an honorable mention from In-Edit's panel of critics, *Piedra Roja* captures *criollo* (homegrown) counterculture as it was generated, lived, and has been remembered, focusing on the intent, meanings, and consequences of the three-day festival that drew thousands of young people to Los Dominicos, a hilly and grassy sector of the capital's municipality of Las Condes. There, festivalgoers listened to the music of local rock bands like Los Jaivas and Los Blops; many smoked marijuana, and some made love freely and openly. While most everyone there contributed to the atmosphere in one way or another, the festival would not have occurred without Gómez. Piedra Roja was his idea, after all, and it embroiled him in a brouhaha that grabbed a nation's attention. He garnered more than his fair share of notoriety and public scorn as the media, the state, and a range of sociopolitical actors transformed him from an anonymous teenager into a poster child for a generationally specific malady.

At the time, Gómez was nineteen years old. An unassuming and some-what reserved but clever student sitting in on classes at Liceo No. 11, a public high school in affluent Las Condes, he had been living many of the common joys, complications, and bouts of angst of young adulthood. But he had also faced significant adversity in his schooling that soured him to most every manifestation of authority. Inspired by New York's Woodstock, transnational counterculture, and a love of rock music, Gómez and a hand-ful of Chilean and American co-organizers (including Gary Fritz), most all in their late-teens, managed to pull off an episode that remains a locus of nostalgia, and perhaps even legend, in Chile today. "I organized the festival with a lot of faith, a lot of conviction, as an idealist," Gómez recalled nearly four decades later. "We believed that we could make changes. We were all searching for our personal selves."[1] He and his assistants succeeded in mak-ing Piedra Roja happen, but at great cost to the mastermind, as any challenges in organizing the event paled in comparison to the enormity of what befell him in the festival's wake. Just days after Piedra Roja came to a trou-bled end, Gómez's life, which had already seen many twists and turns over the years, swiftly went upside down. With his name and deeds appearing in all the major newspapers of the capital and across the country, the Ministry of Education banished Gómez permanently from his high school—and all high schools in the country—for the rest of his life. Meanwhile, the young man's parents, who were deeply angry, publicly embarrassed, and ulti-mately responsible for many festival expenses, kicked him out of the house.

Gómez's festival was a sociocultural inflection point that coincided with a momentous episode in Chilean and Latin American history: the rise of the ill-fated "Chilean road to socialism" (1970–73), spearheaded by the Marxist-led Popular Unity (Unidad Popular or UP) coalition led by Socialist presi-dent Salvador Allende Gossens. This confluence of circumstances amplified and sharpened public reaction to Piedra Roja in significant ways, all within the global context of the late 1960s and early 1970s, which saw Cold War antagonisms and a transnational surge of young people's rebelliousness and heterodox ways of being in the world. Counterculture and various questions fundamentally related to it, smatterings of which had reached Chilean news-papers and magazines before October 1970, entered public discussion most forcefully and starkly as reports and images from Piedra Roja appeared in the media. Indicative of an emerging vernacular counterculture and the first festival of its kind in Chile, Piedra Roja threw issues associated with youth and the counterculture, some of which had not yet become ubiquitous in the public sphere, into sharp relief, provoking responses from across society that laid bare mainstream cultural attitudes and practices and gave further resonance to serious sociopolitical conflicts. Public interest in counterculture persisted during the early seventies, as concerns about sexual liberation, the consumption of marijuana, the length of men's hair, and the purported prevalence of many lazy, lawless, and otherwise lost young people (to mention only some complaints) were in plain view and were the nuclear material of a range of discourses.

This book is about what happened when some Chileans in their teens and twenties thought and behaved in ways a great many others found repulsive. Those youths wanted to lead lives that were different, in all or some aspects, from the ones the majority of their generational peers and older folks were living in the late sixties and early seventies. In a culturally rigid society and during the most conflictive period in Chile's modern history, highlighted by the rise and fall of a democratically elected and pluralistic Marxist government, a cross section of the younger generation discovered and partook in a counterculture they quickly made their own. Its contributors did so to have fun, flout authority, and even seek personal enlightenment to accomplish nothing short of humanity's total transformation. Whether manifested as having sex openly at a rock festival, smoking marijuana, adopting nonconformist hair and clothing styles, or engaging in Transcendental Meditation, the cultural heterodoxy of these youths was revolutionary amid the making of a vehemently contested Marxist social revolution. Criollo counterculture, which arose in relation to transnational and domestic trends and circumstances, provoked well-publicized and politicized responses from those who realized that some young men and women were becoming protagonists in the making of new and unsanctioned values. The counterculture "problem" reached its peak under Allende and the Socialist- and Communist-led UP, exposing the inner workings and conduits of mainstream culture in the context of severe social and political turmoil. It also accentuated the relevance of youth and "generation" in a democratic and developing country where class and political ideology (and party) largely defined one's identity. The present study thus examines a collision involving countercultural sensibilities and practices of the Age of Aquarius and the prevailing values, ideas, and expectations of the "Age of Allende."

The Scene

Allende's historic election in September 1970 drew the eyes of the world. Unique among Marxist governments, UP's project was a democratic, incrementalist, and pluralistic "Chilean road to socialism" that adhered to the country's tradition of constitutionalism and civilian government. As the victorious Left exuded an optimism and vivacity that rallied supporters and infuriated opponents, young men and women became consequential actors in both the making and unmaking of Allende's national project.[2] Youth groups tied to the major political parties, including the Communist Party (Partido Comunista de Chile, PCCh) and the conservative National Party (Partido Nacional, PN), were particularly conspicuous in everyday politics, as were student federations and many other associations and interest groups. They organized, marched, fashioned propaganda, and got into more than a few street brawls. Although young people had been lively players in national politics for many decades, the scale of youth mobilization in the late 1960s and early 1970s was exceptional. Constituencies from every corner of the sociopolitical landscape had good reasons to see youths as pivotal actors, not the least of which were their sheer number, vitality, and the fact that the minimum voting age dropped to eighteen in 1970.[3] Indeed, it was essentially a social expectation for "good young Chileans" in their teens and twenties to have political commitments—and act accordingly. But they received contradictory messages. Their politicization rested on a presumption of maturity and agency that constrained the idealism, voluntaristic tendencies, and the innocence of youth; they also were to toe party lines, obey their elders, and operate within the confines of dominant discourses.

In that environment, young leftists were active participants in the cultural affairs of UP and the nation. The PCCh's youth branch, for example, became known for its colorful and striking murals in support of the road to socialism, and the Nueva Canción (New Song) movement, with many young performers, set the Marxist revolution to music. Among UP leaders and constituencies who endeavored to end the socioeconomic power of the bourgeoisie (through bourgeois democratic means, as some more radical Marxists lamented), there were those who nevertheless toted and touted what otherwise were conventional bourgeois cultural values. Upon criollo counterculture's emergence at the end of the 1960s, many of the Left's leading voices joined those of moderate and conservative sectors—often in outbursts that blended moral panic and political opportunism—to decry modes of cultural heterodoxy and agency that were generationally and historically specific to the era. Such indignation exposed salient aspects of mainstream culture that were jointly safeguarded by forces from across the sociopolitical landscape otherwise engaged in fierce ideological combat. At the same time, in the broader fields of political discourse and practice, resisting counterculture became an instrument in class and party struggles, with elements of UP and their opponents blaming each other for the coalescence and development of youth cultural dissent and the threats they claimed it posed to morality, the family, and the nation. For Chile's Marxists, counterculture's emphasis on the self and personal freedom negated the imperative of social consciousness (notwithstanding counterculture's communalist inclinations), ignored the reality of class struggle, and evinced the egoism of capitalism. Thus, the immorality of countercultural youths lay not only in what they did, but also in what they did not do. Concurrently, culturally heterodox young people ran afoul of the Right because counterculture—like Marxism—disregarded traditional forms of authority and because its emphasis on personal freedom did not center on the imperative of private property (although it could).

Countercultural youths were caught in this crossfire for "doing their own thing" during a period marked globally by innovation and the power of possibility. The sixties and early seventies saw extraordinary human ambition combined with great anxiety. Ideas once considered implausible if not impossible, such as humankind's exploration of space, not to mention the thought of walking on the moon, became the stuff of nonfiction, with Jules Verne giving way to Neil Armstrong. Such realizations reflected, reinforced, and propelled the belief that momentous earthly advances were within reach. Revolutionary movements pledged to end exploitation in short order; communitarian experiments (including hippie communes) sprang up across the West; and the rapid spread of spiritualism and esoteric philosophy transcended the Cold War's seemingly inelastic framework. Realizing utopias of many kinds—from the personal to the collective—became a matter of individual or combined will, not merely imagination. At the same time, thermonuclear annihilation was a bona fide threat, a devastating war raged in Indochina, poverty and disease were ubiquitous in the developing world, and postwar consumerism and prosperity had not solved pressing social and environmental problems in capitalist societies. In that world, young people in places like Berkeley, Mexico City, Buenos Aires, London, and Santiago generated counterculture linked by a transnational culture industry and mass media, while also existing in relation to the family lives, socioeconomic realities, and political cultures of counterculture's progenitors and protagonists.

Mexican sociologist Ricardo Pozas Horcasitas, when discussing young people around the globe during the sixties, explains that youths, and student movements in particular, took their frustrations and complaints from private to public spheres, from homes to the streets, and from campuses to society, exerting such agency in the face of crackdowns by states and the vitriol propelled by dominant social and generational forces. Even though youth movements had distinctive attributes from country to country and region to region, to be young (and urban, especially) meant being aware of, if not sympathetic to, or directly involved in pursuits that valued "a world outside hegemonic conceptions of it" and produced "a cultural and ideological diversity that constitutes the richness of the 1960s."[4] Pozas also observes that a confluence of international circumstances—crises afflicting predominant political ideologies, a surge in radical cultural and political ideas, and scientific and technological advancement, coupled with ample measures of utopianism and ambition—made the 1960s extraordinary.[5] U.S. historian David Farber put it this way: "By the sixties local customs and local power elites were being challenged and often radically subverted by national and international forces."[6] Such was a decade of youthful rebelliousness unmatched in modern times.

With greatest focus on the years 1968 to 1973, bookended by a spike in youthful activism in the Americas and Europe and the military coup that shattered Allende's road to socialism, this study centers on two currents at the heart of Chilean counterculture: *hippismo* (or hippie-ism) and Siloism ("see-low-ism"). Hippismo emerged principally in Greater Santiago (this study's geographical emphasis) and larger provincial cities at the end of the 1960s, and it was, as the term indicates, about hippies—what they thought and did and what mainstream interests believed hippies thought and did. There were hippies who saw in their conduct the sincerity of a rebelliousness spawned from angst and alienation; conversely, there were hippies who engaged in self-reflection only when putting on headbands or bell-bottom pants (also called *patas de elefante* or "elephant's feet") in front of their mirrors. In practice, hippismo could include smoking marijuana, disregarding society's sexual mores, and taking in some Jimi Hendrix, Cream, and the rock of such local bands as Los Jaivas, Los Blops, and Aguaturbia. Male hippies often grew out their hair, making them *melenudos* (young men with *melenas* or "lengthy manes") and thus symbols of hippismo for its practitioners and their detractors. Such melenudos and so-called *palomas*— "doves" or teenage girls—gathered in homes, at concerts and festivals, and on the streets to socialize and share the *hippista* vibe. Providencia Avenue, the main thoroughfare of Greater Santiago's upscale municipality of Providencia, and Parque Forestal (Forest Park), a large space in the capital's downtown area, were preferred hangouts, with wealthier hippies traversing the former and lower-middle- and working-class hippies populating the latter. Indeed, hippismo crossed class lines in a classist society—a fact the Left was hesitant to admit at first—but it did not constitute an organized movement. Rather, it was ad hoc, improvised, and decentralized, though shaped by particular national and transnational circumstances and trends.

As hippismo coalesced toward the end of the presidential administration of Eduardo Frei Montalva (1964–1970) of the Christian Democratic Party (Partido Demócrata Cristiano, PDC), young Marxists and many student-federation activists (and those who were both) were often in the streets; they marched, protested, and sometimes fought it out—literally—with their foes over international and domestic hot-button issues. In 1970, a periodical published by the Marxist-led Student Federation of the University of Chile (Federación de Estudiantes de la Universidad de Chile, or FECh, founded in 1906) drew a sharp distinction between what it called transnational hippismo's "primitive expression of youth rebellion" and the outlooks and actions of "the vast majority of young people" in Chile, especially students and working-class youths, who had developed a mature and genuinely revolutionary consciousness.[7] Ubiquitous among the counterculture's critics, such formulations reveal an understanding of "the political" that essentially dismisses a multitude of cultural gestures that otherwise qualify as meaningful forms of political agency.[8] Chilean hippies practiced a species of cultural politics that was countercultural and antipolitical, and while unorganized, diffuse, and inconsistent, counterculture nevertheless burst into the nation's political life, just as it came up against mainstream sociocultural values. In short, hippies had certain ways and looks about them. For this, they faced accusations involving most every indiscretion, were threatened and physically attacked in the streets by leftist and rightist youths, were spat upon, and were mocked publicly in the media.

Unlike hippismo, Siloism was an organized movement, revolving around the teachings of the Argentine spiritual leader known as "Silo" (Mario Luis Rodríguez Cobos), a middle-class and well-educated native of Mendoza who spent much time in and around Chile's capital in the sixties. In 1970, the followers of Silo in Santiago formed the group Poder Joven (Young Power), which recruited young men and women, including disaffected hippies and Marxists, and published numerous books during the Allende years. Melding Eastern thought, anarchism, Western Marxism, and other features, Siloism offered young people defined and elucidated epistemological and philosophical passageways to individual emancipation, humanity's enlightenment, and the making of a just world—what Poder Joven ambitiously called a "total revolution" realized by young people against the ruling generation. Overturning prevalent political, social, and economic structures was but one aspect of such an overhaul; true liberation from authority, tyranny, want, violence, classism, racism, and other afflictions was contingent on fundamental change in the cultural, moral, and psychological configurations of the self.[9] Siloists, then, shared with hippismo emphasis on the self and liberation (and the liberation of the self), a generational identity, and disdain for the powers that be, but they also articulated a body of guided practices, including precise meditative processes, which structured their heterodoxy. Silo's followers, moreover, looked askance at casual sex, the use of drugs, and patterns of (capitalist) consumption inherent in hippismo.

The fact that Poder Joven was an esoteric countercultural movement with defined convictions, printed books and pamphlets, a discernable membership, and a penchant for provocative graffiti, made it an eye-catching and irresistible target for its mainstream adversaries. All the while, few observers and critics of Poder Joven demonstrated an appreciable understanding of it, either due to Siloism's complexity or its detractors' will to ignorance (or a combination thereof), Siloists concluded. Amid intense public scrutiny of other countercultural tendencies, Poder Joven's participants found themselves targets of ridicule and harassment, and they were publicly accused by the media and in popular culture of abductions, sexual offenses, and satanic ritualism (among other things). In response to specific claims made by parents whose children allegedly were kidnapped by Siloists, police jailed prominent members of the movement in 1971. Some Siloists were also arrested a few years later—after September 11, 1973—under much more daunting circumstances. Broadly speaking, the treatment and pressures that Siloists and many hippies encountered only furthered their sense that behind the façade of pluralism and democracy of the Allende years lay the cultural, social, ideological, and psychological structures of intransigent authority managed by *los viejos* (the old people).

Some Propositions

Resting on an evidentiary base that includes newspapers, magazines, oral history, archival documents, music, films, and literature, three principal and interrelated propositions frame this book. First, entering Chilean history of the 1960s and 1970s by way of criollo counterculture tells just as much about the phenomenon's foes as it does the youths who holistically or selectively lived it. As the body politic polarized further during the Allende years, formidable adversaries defended certain mainstream cultural assumptions and frames of reference in their condemnations of hippismo and Siloism, but not necessarily for all the same reasons. For the Right, led by the PN, to do so was consistent with its conservative credentials, elitist pedigree, and some measure of Church influence, while the moderate Christian Democrats, also with Catholic foundations but with more progressive political and cultural inclinations, saw in the counterculture many of the same general threats and disruptions to the nation, culture, and family values that conservatives did. Notwithstanding the pertinence of those reactions, and given the extraordinary rise of UP to power in 1970, this study focuses more on the Left's complicated position in regard to cultural change in the sixties and early seventies.

The Chilean and Latin American Lefts changed dramatically in the sixties—with the triumph of the Cuban Revolution and its youthful air, the application of Ernesto "Che" Guevara's *foco* strategy (fatal for the Argentine *guerrillero* in 1967), and the sharpening of Cold War tensions—as there emerged a New Left wed to revolutionary vanguardism over democratic incrementalism.[10] In Chile, the original infrastructure and ongoing leadership of UP were those of an "Old Left," forged during the Popular Front years from the 1930s to 1950s and behind Allende's four bids for the presidency between 1952 and 1970. As such, both the PCCh and Allende's faction in the Socialist Party (Partido Socialista, PS) were steadfastly committed to party politics and democratic elections. In other words, the Old Left was "old school" in some elemental ways, and the ideological inclinations of UP's chiefs toward emergent strains of Marxism reflected that posture. A case in point, the works of Freudian Marxist Herbert Marcuse, a principal pillar of the New Left and the sexual revolution of the 1960s in Europe and the United States, encountered slight tolerance, at best, among UP's elders. Moreover, Chile's New Left*ish* impulse, the Movement of the Revolutionary Left (Movimiento de Izquierda Revolucionaria, MIR), was more interested in Marxist-Leninist and Guevarist vanguardism than Marcusean propositions.[11] Owing to its tradition of persistent sociopolitical mobilization and electioneering, and in the face of New Left alternatives, Chile's Old Left rose to power in 1970 with a democratic-revolutionary agenda, a coalition whose far-from-monolithic composition included many young people in its ranks, and with elemental conceptions of what revolutionary behavior, liberation, and cultural transformation were and should entail.

The Left's responses to counterculture also reveal some of UP's internal problems that were consequential enough to impede the road to socialism, as leftists were sorely in need of unity despite cooperation between Communists and Socialists in coalitions since the mid-1930s. They could easily agree that capitalism was bad, but there were competing ideas for bringing about its end and about the nature of the social order that would replace it. Some on the Left, led by the PCCh and Allende's wing of the PS, believed in pluralism and competition against the Right and the PDC, while others, especially the MIR and the more radical PS contingent headed by Senator Carlos Altamirano Orrego, advocated for their outright destruction. Anticounterculture discourse provided Marxists a point of much-needed commonality—with a baseline standard framed by leftist conceptions of the "good young Chilean." Even then, generational dissonance among and between Marxists complicated the Left's response to youth-driven cultural change in the late 1960s and early 1970s.

When many in UP subscribed to "cultural transformation," they were not typically referring to altering a particular cluster of sociocultural values they shared with more conservative sectors in regard to such matters as family relations, gender, and sexuality—positions that counterculture helped throw into question. Such mainstream Marxists and others were alluding predominantly to pedagogical, intellectual, artistic, literary, and related initiatives to "lift the cultural level" of the masses, all areas to which the UP government dedicated considerable resources and in which the Marxist-led coalition made significant headway. In Allende's words, the revolution would realize "the right for all people to obtain a proper education and culture" and "the right to well-being, health, and culture" and would ameliorate the shared plight of those who "have practically no access to culture."[12] UP leaders, supporters, and detractors alike shared this conceptualization of "culture," and the Left's cultural outreach to the masses and the cultural politics of the Chilean road to socialism furthered cultural democratization and growth in the areas Allende underscored. Yet, governing Marxists and UP nevertheless preserved certain mainstream and bourgeois cultural outlooks and impressions that fell under the rubric of "family values," existing in conjunction with an otherwise antibourgeois, anti-imperialist, and anticapitalist revolutionary cultural-political project that saw public murals by young Communist artists, the massive publishing campaign of the state-owned publishing house (Editora Nacional Quimantú), the songs of Nueva Canción, expansive volunteer and "revolutionary" pro-literacy efforts on the part of young activists, and other pursuits.[13]

The second proposition is that as criollo counterculture percolated through the youth scene, some attitudes and values it embodied seeped into mainstream sectors of the younger generation that otherwise rejected most of what amounted to counterculture's vibe. Shifts in viewpoints with respect to sexuality and aesthetics, for instance, were especially evident by the second half of Allende's presidency. Important here is that youth factions of the leading political parties worked in line with the ideological frameworks and platforms of their elders, but, at times, members veered in matters of culture. I argue that much of the Left's leadership demonstrated a palpable degree of cultural conservatism in such areas as gender, sexuality, and physical appearance—sounding and acting much like their more politically conservative antagonists—as the counterculture "problem" pushed such issues into clearer view. At the same time, within the Left there were rumblings from some young activists who sought greater cultural leeway in their lives, thus underscoring the makings of a generationally informed cultural fissure. In the case of the Communist Youth (Juventudes Comunistas, colloquially "la Jota," or "the J"), some activists who were attracted to particular expressions of cultural heterodoxy ran up against Marxist apparatchiks and officials who sought to blunt them. The resulting debate brought generational and cultural dissonance within revolutionary ranks into the open, with the Left's elders and youths at times expressing divergent positions on manifestations of cultural change that most everyone understood were connected, in some way or another, to counterculture. As historian Alfonso Salgado, who has looked at shifts in the Jota's cultural sensibility in the early 1970s, points out, "To understand the relationship between the Old Left and the different social and political movements that emerged in these years, historians need to start paying more attention to the counterculture trends that shaped this entire generation."[14]

Third, the media, especially newspapers and magazines, were critical in swaying as well as reflecting public opinion regarding counterculture. For the most part, accounts of criollo and foreign counterculture were ideologically driven, bombastic, and hasty, and therefore constitute a rich repository of prejudices, falsehoods, and insight, with the onslaught building in earnest upon the realization of Piedra Roja. Sex, drugs, and rock culture had never before been on such conspicuous and public display as they were over a holiday weekend in October 1970, and the media firestorm that Piedra Roja touched off set the tone for the ways parents, political parties, educators, police, soldiers, and many others came to identify and interpret both hippismo and Siloism. This created particular problems for countercultural youths during the Allende years—problems that only became graver with the 1973 military coup. Meanwhile, mass communication, mass culture, and the global-capitalist marketplace funneled the aesthetics, sounds, and news (via international wire services) of transnational counterculture to young Chilean consumers and observers.[15] As a result, international media accounts of everything from the brazenness of New York's Woodstock to the exploits of Charles Manson, whom Chilean press outlets referred to as the "American hippie," flowed into the country. In other words, the national media complained about and attempted to contain a force they played a crucial role in unleashing. Thus, criollo counterculture, with a particular morphology and context, existed in relation to transnational conduits of information and representation that influenced public opinion and provided fuel for moral panic and heavily politicized anticounterculture barrages. Together, these propositions form the substrate for approaching Chilean history of the sixties and seventies, the tumultuous UP years, and the complicated relationship between culture and politics from alternative thematic and analytic angles, including "generation" and cultural heterodoxy.

Where We Are

In his reflections on the historiography of the "long 1960s," historian Eric Zolov observes, "We are finally reaching a point where more *historia* than *memoria* is being written."[16] It is apropos that the shift to which Zolov alludes is a generational one. He explains that young scholars—"unencumbered by the ideological baggage carried by those who witnessed and participated in the political struggles and artistic exuberance of the 1960s"—have pursued "a new conceptual approach to understanding local change within a transnational framework, one constituted by multiple crosscurrents of geopolitical, ideological, cultural, and economic forces." This new generation of historians working on the "Global Sixties," Zolov adds, has helped us question long-held dichotomies (communism/capitalism and First World/ Third World, for instance), understand better the internal workings and diversity of the Left (including Old Left–New Left dynamics), and decipher the political engagement and implications of global counterculture.[17] The present study joins—but also deviates from—the recent wave of historical scholarship on Latin America's involvement in the Global Sixties and the political and cultural agency of young people, with the Chilean case adding new dimensions to the thematic and analytical approaches underpinning that body of research.

Works by Zolov, Jaime Pensado, and Elaine Carey on Mexican youths facing off with the ruling Institutional Revolutionary Party; studies by Victoria Langland and Christopher Dunn on intrepid young Brazilians living under military dictatorship; Valeria Manzano's close reading of Argentine young people's pivotal roles in political and cultural conflicts from Perón to the Dirty War; Vania Markarian's research on students, the Left, and counterculture in Uruguay; and other contributions have deepened our knowledge of postwar popular culture, generational identity, gender and patriarchy, and the transnationalism of youth-related phenomena.[18] For the Southern Cone in particular, Chilean experiences with counterculture differ from what Manzano and Markarian have revealed about the long 1960s elsewhere in the region. The Argentine and Uruguayan Lefts, for instance, generally were more open to aspects of counterculture as revolutionary gestures than were Chilean leftists before and during the Allende years. In the case of Argentina, left-wing Peronists were suspicious of counterculture but nevertheless saw in rock culture an anti-authoritarian streak that fit in with revolutionary politics. Right-wing Peronists and conservatives would accept nothing of the sort and repressed rock and counterculture upon Perón's return to power in 1973. The Left in Uruguay was far more receptive to the revolutionary potential of cultural heterodoxy, with the nation's leading Communist newspaper providing its younger readers a weekly supplement—*La Morsa*, or "The Walrus," à la the Beatles' 1967 hit "I am the Walrus"—with a patently hippyish flavor.[19] In Chile, some young Marxists forged spaces to enjoy certain countercultural ways of thinking and being that they found attractive. However, such interstices were few, as elder Marxists and many others staked out and defended mainstream sociocultural positions.

Broadly speaking, said scholarship on Latin American young people in the era of transnational counterculture has tended to reflect two interests that inherently overlap: the history of youths under authoritarian governments—critical in light of the prevalence, diversity, and cruelty of authoritarian regimes in the region during the Cold War—and the aims, grit, mistakes, and gains of student activists, many of whom were killed by police and soldiers at such sites as Tlatelolco in Mexico City and Brazilian campuses in the late 1960s. This study neither focuses primarily on authoritarianism nor on university-student movements, although these concerns figure into its interrogation of youth, counterculture, and politics. Instead, the following chapters emphasize Chilean circumstances that provide atypical pathways of investigation involving how generational conflict and cultural heterodoxy played out in a pluralistic and deeply divided democratic society amidst socialist revolution.

In the field of Chilean historiography, this book is an oddity, as counterculture is largely absent from a body of literature that prioritizes young people's participation in class-related party politics. There is no dispute that class and political ideology have been extremely powerful centers of gravity in culture, identity, organization, and interaction in everyday Chilean life, especially since the early twentieth century, when working- and middle-class movements and parties rose to challenge the traditional elite's power in politics, economy, and culture.[20] It therefore stands to reason that studies on Chile's young people have tended to focus on political mobilization, with emphasis on their involvement in consequential organizations.[21] I engage both class and traditional politics, to be sure, but insofar as they were connected to generational phenomena that force us to rethink conventional assumptions about culture and what constituted "the political" at a significant juncture in Chilean, Latin American, and global history. Only recently has Chile's counterculture drawn some interest from historians, but no one has provided a close reading of criollo counterculture in its own right or as a means to reassess the history of class, ideology, gender, sexuality, and other important fulcrums in the lives of the young and older.[22]

Coming to Terms

For the scholar, identifying counterculture often seems like an adventure on the stormy waters of approximation. Some of counterculture's essential characteristics—its amorphousness, flexibility, creativity, spontaneity, individualist subjectivity, and contradictions—make it a challenge to pin down. If that is true for the historian operating in retrospect, one can imagine how elusive, and perhaps even impenetrable, it was for observers who gazed upon counterculture's manifestations in its heyday. A superficial but indicative example of this problem involved the way counterculture's detractors looked upon hippies' dancing, which tended to lack rhythmic discipline and convention. A lot of flailing went on, essentially. For one critic writing in Chile's largest newspaper, it did not register that such movement could reflect freedom and individuality (traits certainly not allowed in the time-honored ballroom, for sure), much less constitute something culturally relevant. Rather, it was a cross between uncontrollable convulsion, contortionism, and stupor brought on by marijuana.[23] How, then, might we identify countercultural currents if their very personalities were nebulous and swirling—in a word, psychedelic? How might we connect one young person's cultural heterodoxy to another's when so many of counterculture's manifestations were ad hoc and improvised? Ludwig Wittgenstein's concept of "family resemblance," though originally applied by the Austrian-British scholar to the study of language, is a valuable way to conceptualize entwined webs of thought and practice that made counterculture what it was. Wittgenstein defined family resemblance as "a complex network of similarities overlapping and crisscrossing: sometimes overall similarities, sometimes similarities of detail." He explained, "I can think of no better expression to characterize these similarities than 'family resemblances'; for the various resemblances between members of a family: build, features, color of eyes, gait, temperament, etc. etc. overlap and crisscross in the same way."[24] Wittgenstein's concept—perhaps better conceptualized as "community resemblance" for our purposes—works well in combination with scholarly definitions of counterculture, together providing the historian some bearing for close analysis of the variances and commonalities that were characteristic of phenomena like hippismo and Siloism. Far from being what Grateful Dead frontman Jerry Garcia evidently described as "the plain old chaos of undifferentiated weirdness," counterculture may be identified and delineated in workable and pliant ways.[25]

In 1960, the sociologist J. Milton Yinger, who coined the term "contraculture" (which later became "counterculture"), wrote, "I suggest the use of the term contraculture wherever the normative system of a group contains, as a primary element, a theme of conflict with the values of the total society, where personality variables are directly involved in the development and maintenance of the group's values, and wherever its norms can be understood only by reference to the relationships of the group to a surrounding dominant culture."[26] Embedded in Yinger's formulation are conceptualizations—conflict with values, personality variables, dominant culture, and so forth—that also inform Theodore Roszak's influential *The Making of Counter Culture: Reflections on the Technocratic Society and Its Youthful Opposition* (1969). Roszak counted a range of actors as contributors to counterculture, including hippies and the New Left, and anchored the term in a specific temporal and spatial context: the 1960s in the West. He explains, "It strikes me as obvious beyond dispute that the interests of our college-age and adolescent young in the psychology of alienation, oriental mysticism, psychedelic drugs, and communitarian experiments comprise a cultural constellation that radically diverges from values and assumptions that have been in the mainstream of society at least since the

Scientific Revolution of the seventeenth century."[27] Needless to say, asserting that anything is "beyond dispute" invites dispute, but Roszak's argument, like Yinger's suggestion, does provide a bevy of traits with which to go about locating and outlining counterculture through family or community resemblance. "Counterculture," itself a knotty category of analysis, is indelibly tied to an array of slippery terms and concepts—"youth," "generation," and "mainstream," among others—through which we might get a better handle on counterculture's manifestations and implications in political and cultural affairs during the 1960s and 1970s.

The relationship between youth and age "is something that is fought over in all societies," as sociologist Pierre Bourdieu tells us. "My point is simply that youth and age are not self-evident data but are socially constructed, in the struggle between the young and old."[28] In other words, the threshold at which a "young" person becomes "not young" is relative and subjective—a matter of identity and discourse, essentially—for the young and not-so-young alike. So, too, is the threshold between childhood and "young person."[29] For the historian, this means that youth is a moving target begging for context and scrutiny. Consequently, the same goes for phenomena that particularly correspond to "youth." The category "youth culture" is of greatest relevance here. Sociologist Talcott Parsons, who popularized the term in the 1940s, observed that "youth culture is not only, as is true of the curricular aspect of formal education, a matter of age status and such but also shows strong signs of being a product of tensions in the relationship of younger people and adults."[30] A way to get at such tensions is to bring "generation" into view as an analytic tool. As a concept and category, "generation" functions in much the same way as "youth," but the former does have an empirical quality in the microenvironment of one's family, as it pertains to not only one's lineage but also the parent-child relationship. Matters become more complicated when discerning a broader generation from the prior and the next because generation is not merely a function of being born in the same ten- to twenty-year span as others. Like youth, "generation" entails contingency and identity, but it risks being conflated with a calendric "cohort."[31]

In the 1920s, Spanish philosopher José Ortega y Gasset saw generation as a driving mechanism in historical development, with an ongoing younger-older generational dialectic involving distinct characteristics.[32] Hungarian sociologist Karl Mannheim, a contemporary of Ortega y Gasset credited with popularizing "generation" in academia, shared the Spaniard's conviction. "The phenomenon of generations is one of the basic factors contributing to the genesis of the dynamic of historical development," Mannheim wrote in 1928, noting that generation becomes most elusive "at the social and cultural level, where its effects can be ascertained only by great difficulty and by indirect methods."[33] Much later, Bourdieu and other scholars warned of clumsy "generationalism," a problem with roots in the nineteenth century (in Auguste Comte and Wilhelm Dilthey, for instance), which presupposed and reified "generation." Ortega y Gasset and Mannheim were among the culprits, as historian Robert Wohl observes, in giving rise to a priori notions of generational groupthink.[34] It is imperative, then, to carefully apply "generation" without such reductionism and in combination with other categories of analysis, such as class and gender, to maximize its methodological value.[35] This is perhaps even more crucial in the case of Chile in the late sixties and early seventies, not just because of the country's characteristically class-centric social and political life, but in light of UP's explicitly class-centered transformative agenda.

"Mainstream," which, like "youth" and "generation," cuts across analytic categories, also comes with methodological challenges and opportunities. What constitutes "mainstream" in a changeful society? This study uses the term as an adjective and noun—that is, "the mainstream (something)" and "the mainstream"—but with some caution, given that the general concept runs the risk of meaning practically everything and nothing, as some scholars have reminded us.[36] It is fair to say that the idea of mainstream often turns up in contemporary scholarship even when the term is not employed. For example, in studies on the "subaltern," the "marginal," and the "Other," the mainstream essentially appears as hegemony, with those aforementioned categories applicable only in relation to someone not subaltern, marginal, or "othered."[37] In that vein, Florencia Mallon contends that hegemony is an ongoing and contested process between social actors, as well as an outcome.[38] Mainstream operates in the same basic fashion. What makes any particular mainstream powerful—and indeed hegemonic— is that it may at once be intransigent and malleable, capable of warding off or absorbing and reconfiguring the most disparate cultural elements in the ongoing creation of a broadly shared "common sense." The definitional elements of mainstream are many and complex, involving social, political, and cultural movements, the state, identity, mass media, mass politics, and the culture industry, among other factors. Such components change over time, and thus mainstream culture and politics do as well. That is why, as culture scholar Alison Huber explains, if "we think about the *specificity* of mainstream and the particularities of its practices and processes, then mainstream becomes an historically contingent category that usefully refers us to modes of dominant (or dominance-producing) behaviors, discourses, values, identities, and so on."[39]

Fearing the snare of generalization, I hoped to refrain from using "mainstream" when I began researching criollo counterculture. However, it became increasingly evident, notwithstanding haziness surrounding what makes something mainstream or not, that perceptions, declarations, and contestation vis-à-vis what was mainstream and out-of-the-mainstream were deeply embedded in Chilean politics and culture during the late sixties and early seventies. The UP coalition essentially portrayed itself—and accurately so—as revolutionary and mainstream at the same time, emphasizing the *chilenidad* (Chilean-ness) of its Socialist- and Communist-led *revolución de empanadas y vino tinto* (revolution of meat pies and red wine), which had deep-rooted nationalistic and folkloric underpinnings. The Right and many centrists, meanwhile, moved to delegitimize UP's cultural-political project by arguing that Marxists were out to destroy mainstream values and contributed to tragedies like vernacular counterculture and a crisis gripping the nuclear family and nation. Marxists charged their opponents with the selfsame offenses, which, the former argued, were indicative of the mechanisms and repercussions of capitalism, imperialism, and "bourgeois immorality." As they did so, many Marxists, centrists, and rightists reinforced some fundamental facets of mainstream culture that counterculture played a vital role in revealing and disputing. As mainstreamers accused each other of not being mainstream, countercultural youths understood and lived their heterodoxy in relation to the orthodoxies that provoked them, with many young people cutting through the discursive and rhetorical clutter by focusing on generation as a definitional element of their reality.

The Road Ahead

This book's opening chapter finds us at Piedra Roja and focuses on the voices and agency of those who gathered at Los Dominicos during a landmark three-day weekend in October 1970. One person in particular, Jorge Gómez, is the chapter's principal figure. His experiences and proclivities as a teenager point to why the festival happened, and the people and goings-on at Piedra Roja speak to criollo counterculture's coalescence, attributes, and allure. My choice to begin with Piedra Roja reflects its significance in the stories of criollo counterculture and the antagonism heterodox young people encountered, while also asserting this study's broad imperative: to foreground countercultural Chileans as actors who shaped alternative forms of sociability, trends, and values. Obviously, neither the festival nor criollo counterculture came about in a vacuum. Indeed, they were deeply interconnected with the world around them, evincing and contributing to the subject of chapter 2: the "youth question." An amalgam of circumstances and phenomena, including intergenerational distrust and outright rebelliousness, the "youth question" of the 1960s and 1970s was a complex substantiation of a generation gap with period-specific ideational and behavioral qualities and transnational manifestations.[40] In Chile, the period saw student movements, outbreaks of street violence, and widely shared consternation about perils threatening the nation's social and cultural footings, with the era's main combatants instrumentalizing the youth question to admonish rivals.

Chapter 3 fleshes out Chile's youth question by looking at gender norms and sexuality, drug use, and music—important signifiers of identity, sociability, and agency. In popular parlance, "sex, drugs, and rock 'n' roll" often prompts thoughts of hippies practicing free love while stoned and listening to Jimi Hendrix. A lot of that happened. But the adage also serves as a doorway into a broad range of sensibilities, innovations, and conflicts that lay bare cultural contestations—with generational overtones and sociopolitical implications—during Chile's road to socialism then dictatorship. Sex, drugs, and rock music were part and parcel of a generation's Zeitgeist, as many young people searched for things ethereal and new at a unique time in modern history.

Initiating the book's closer reading of counterculture, chapter 4 looks at hippismo's people, spaces, and expressions, spotlighting what hippies thought about their lives and the heterodoxy to which they contributed. It shows that while hippismo was of foreign origin, its Chilean practitioners made it theirs in everyday and pronounced ways. The chapter also maps hippie hangouts in and outside Greater Santiago, including the usual haunts of both affluent and working-class criollo hippies, as well as small-scale experiments in collectivism and communitarianism. Class is of particular importance in this discussion, as hippismo had the capacity to blur its inherent distinctions. Yet class remained a potent determinant of sociability that complicated young people's generational identity, just as generation complicated class. Chapter 5 details the highly politicized moral panic that exploded onto the scene in response to hippismo—beginning with the public outcry over Piedra Roja—and emphasized such matters as sexual liberation and the use of marijuana as countercultural menaces to the Chilean family and nation. I argue that as morality politics exposed values shared by leftists, centrists, and rightists alike, these groups also exploited such anxiety to score political and cultural points against their adversaries as the body politic polarized further.

Chapter 6 shifts our line of sight away from hippismo and toward the esoteric counterculture of Siloism. The chapter unpacks Siloism's call for young people to focus their youthful energy inward, peer deeply into their own psyches, experience fully the connection between mind and body, and realize *socialismo libertario*, or libertarian socialism. Such undertakings would effectively transform the individual, his or her immediate surroundings, and the world. These and other aspects of Siloist thought and practice raised quite a ruckus among those pledged to protect culture and public morality, thus motivating authorities to repress what many identified as Poder Joven's depravity.

The imperatives of censuring and limiting the cultural heterodoxy of young people, in combination with the polemical barrages being exchanged among sociopolitical foes over criollo counterculture, accorded particular utility to the subject of chapter 7: the "good young Chilean." There were, in fact, many "good young Chileans"—from the pious member of a conservative youth group to the Jota *compañera* who volunteered her summer to harvest onions on a state-managed farm, all of whom demonstrated the discipline and sacrifice that political parties, the Church, labor unions, and other bodies expected. The era's foremost political factions each defined their own activist youths as good young Chileans who stood in contrast to both countercultural youths and their opponents' young militants. For the Left, projections of the good young Marxist were particularly useful in discerning what properly revolutionary conduct was or should be in light of the revolutionary pursuits of Siloists and other heterodox youths. But intergenerational friction arose within UP's ranks as some young radicals gravitated toward forms of personal agency and expression that typically were associated with counterculture.

Chapter 8 refocuses our attention on many of the subjects and subjectivities discussed in previous chapters, but does so through the eyes of novelist Enrique Lafourcade. His *Palomita Blanca* (Little White Dove), the best-selling novel in Chilean history, tells of counterculture, class, love, and heartache, with hippismo and Siloism making their marks in the lives of the story's two young protagonists. Published in 1971, *Palomita Blanca* reflects the combination of lucid observation, misreading, and media-roused hogwash that characterized much of mainstream responses to both the youth question and counterculture. It is, of course, a work of literature, with all the leeway that grants. But the novel's reach, including its extensive use in secondary schools, has done much to shape how more recent generations in Chile have come to understand the late sixties and early seventies.

Finally, an epilogue briefly casts our view forward in time, into 1974, when countercultural youths faced very different conditions put upon them by a military regime whose leaders were familiar with anticounterculture discourses, especially those of the Allende years. Upon the military coup that ended UP and democracy in September 1973, matters turned from troublesome to dismal for many hippies, Siloists, and countercultural youths in general.

1 The Opening Set

Young Jorge and the Criollo Woodstock

. . . .

Some five thousand or so young people—many wearing bandanas, sunglasses, bell-bottom pants, and garments emblazoned with peace signs and carrying marijuana and contraceptive wares of one kind or another—gathered over the holiday weekend of October 10–12, 1970, on a private parcel of land in what now is a posh sector of Greater Santiago's eastern reaches.[1] A good number of them pitched large tents as well as their clothes, made both bonfires and love, and took in marijuana's smoke and the electrified sounds of local rock bands such as Los Jaivas and Los Blops. As one festivalgoer later recalled, "Anybody of that age who wasn't, oh, I don't know, particularly stuck in a different world, was out in that sort of expressive [environment] of experimenting with new ideas, new ways of being. . . . I think it was kind of a radical movement of free expression and so forth, so I was certainly doing that as much as anybody else was."[2] For many, the festival was a deeply formative experience, as they forged enduring relationships, fell in love, enjoyed the feeling of having bucked parental authority, and learned more about themselves. To numerous young people who missed it, the festival nevertheless became a symbol of the potential, promise, and consequences of pursuing different ways of thinking and acting in their society. At the same time, Piedra Roja provoked an outpouring of dismay and anger from foes of hippismo and counterculture, as families, the media, politicians, and others depicted what the festival was and meant—or what they thought it was and meant.

Piedra Roja's very existence essentially questioned the cultural conventions and broader sensibilities of an older generation in power, and as an expression of the criollo counterculture's emergence, it revealed that a growing number of youths in the sixties and seventies found meaning in ideas that were recalcitrant, amorphous, contradictory, nondoctrinal, spontaneous, and expansive—and therefore quite attractive. The organizers, musicians, the so-called *marihuaneros* (potheads), and the vibes of Piedra Roja revealed "revolutionary" dispositions and new values through inference and practice rather than a totalizing theory. Shared outlooks, like smoke, wafted in the air. The stories of Jorge Gómez Ainslie and his festival provide us inceptive peeks into what countercultural young people were thinking, hoping, wanting, and doing, and they bring forth some attributes of the society, mainstream culture, and political culture in which those youths lived. Gómez and others found themselves the targets of widespread rebuke (and sometimes punishment) even though the festival fell quite short of the grooviness envisioned by its protagonists, including the very rock music groups that made Piedra Roja a rock festival. Just as the festival began with young Jorge, our discussion shall as well.

Young Jorge

Jorge Gómez was a disillusioned adolescent in the late 1960s, but hardly an apathetic one. Born to a Chilean father and Scottish mother (hence the matronymic "Ainslie") in Santiago in 1951, he had returned to Chile's capital in 1967 after having lived in England for a dozen years—the England of John, Paul, Ringo, and George, not to mention the Rolling Stones, the Kinks, and many others. He was sixteen, fresh from a boarding school in Surrey, and experiencing "culture shock," he explained, in a society both foreign and familiar to him, and where the clock of cultural change seemed to be running slow. Some three years after arriving in Chile, young Jorge returned the favor of a culture shock, and he did so, in part, due to what he later called his "long and sad" history in Chilean schooling. "I was bored with it all," Gómez described.[3] His story is largely unique among Chilean youths of the 1960s and early 1970s; the vast majority never lived abroad or, for that matter, never organized a momentous rock festival. Yet, young Jorge and a good many of his generational brothers and sisters shared similar sentiments—boredom and rebelliousness, for instance—that drew the attention of figures in government and academia, among other circles.

After departing Surrey in his fifth year of secondary school, Jorge was wondering what to make of a new life in Santiago. To his family's dismay, the Chilean Ministry of Education declared it would not fully accept and credit Jorge's secondary-school years in England, citing differences in educational emphases and scope. The ministry ordered Jorge to begin secondary schooling almost anew. "I had arrived in Chile with all the certificates and documents from my [English] school," Gómez recalled. "I practically lost four years." The experience weighed heavily on Jorge as his resentment grew toward authority and institutions, especially the one that negated his English credits. His thoughts wandered. In 1969, after Jorge's nearly two years of playing catch-up in high school, and amid his growing rebellious-ness, his parents dictated two options: enter a Chilean boarding school (quite possibly the Barros Arana Boarding School, where his father had studied) or join the armed forces. "It wasn't going well for me in my house with my parents. They were very strict and I was feeling beaten down by society," Gómez remarked. The thought of attending Barros Arana was "terrible" enough for Jorge to choose entry into the Naval Academy at Valparaíso, even though the academy would only reinforce and intensify his ongoing frus-tration regarding institutions of authority. Soon, Jorge butted up against the state's intransigence once again. What his parents viewed as a step for-ward in Jorge's maturation was, they came to find out, another academic leap backward: the Naval Academy did not recognize Jorge's two years of coursework that he had undertaken—in a Chilean high school, no less—in order to make up for the years of schooling in Surrey that had been lost thanks to the Ministry of Education.[4] Almost eighteen at the time, he was back to square one. Once at the academy, young Jorge realized (unsurpris-ingly) that military life was not for him: "I made them throw me out [in late 1969] because I couldn't stand it," Gómez explained. His academy days were positive in at least one respect: Inspired by news of the 1969 Woodstock fes-tival, he and some fellow cadets formed an ephemeral rock band, with Jorge the lead singer.

Expelled from the Naval Academy in 1969, Jorge was to resume public secondary schooling at the behest of his concerned parents. However, news from the Ministry of Education again left the Gómez family exasperated: the ministry did not accept the academic credits Jorge earned at the acad-emy. Once more, a bureaucratic sinkhole had swallowed Jorge. "From the time I arrived from England, I was confronted by the bureaucracy," Gómez noted. Dismayed and gripped by deepening alienation, Jorge understood his ongoing conflict with the state's bureaucracy in generational terms more than anything else, very much like he understood his growing conflicts with his parents.[5] With his options dwindling, he began attending Liceo No. 11 in Las Condes (now called the Liceo Rafael Sotomayor) as an *oyente*, or auditing student. At nineteen, then, Jorge was sitting in on classes and bored out of his wits by lessons that were years behind his intellectual ca-pacity. One consolatory aspect of the Liceo No. 11, however, was its reputa-tion as "the aerodrome of Las Condes—for its joints, and many of them," Gómez remembered. And while breathing the air of Liceo No. 11, young Jorge pondered and coordinated an event, a spectacle, which would be long remembered—by Jorge and by a society. Indeed, more than four decades

Jorge Gómez at seventeen, in his Navy cadet uniform (1969). His subsequent expulsion from the academy marked yet another difficult chapter in his relationship with "authority." Courtesy of Jorge Gómez Ainslie.

after his criollo Woodstock, Gómez, who remains a loyal fan of Jimi Hendrix, Bob Dylan, and other icons of the 1960s and early 1970s, routinely fields telephone calls from journalists and radio stations seeking interviews about a weekend in the spring of 1970 that left an indelible mark on the shared memory of a generation of Chileans. "It ended up being a unique phenomenon," Gómez explained. "It never happened again and, obviously, today they wouldn't give permission for such a thing."[6]

For all intents and purposes, Jorge was a hippie by 1970, although his hair was not as long as it would be in subsequent years, when he took up residence in a hippie community in the foothills of the Andes Mountains. In the months before Piedra Roja, he hung out with fellow hippie types— "people who'd get together and thought about things differently [than the mainstream]," Gómez recalled—at countercultural haunts in Greater Santiago's municipality of Providencia and elsewhere. Jorge was, in short, a "hippie by heart" rather than a "weekend hippie," or the type who feigned hippismo in order to fit in with a hip crowd. Strongly influenced by foreign counterculture and having witnessed beat- and rock-music scenes firsthand during his final months in England, Jorge also immersed himself in Santiago's expanding rock sphere, elements of which appeared on a rickety stage at Piedra Roja. The music of such criollo rock groups as Los Jaivas and Los Blops dovetailed with the young man's admiration of the Rolling Stones and Jimi Hendrix, billowing and mixing in his mind with imaginings of a festival that, Gómez reminisced, came to pass by way of faith, conviction, and idealism.

Setting the Stage

Much of the inspiration to hold a criollo Woodstock struck the intrepid young Jorge and some friends while they were at the movies. During September and October of 1970, the well-known documentary about New York's festival, *Woodstock: Three Days of Peace and Music*, appeared in some of Santiago's cinemas, including the Cine Las Condes on Apoquindo Avenue, not terribly far from the Gómez home on Vitacura Avenue and Liceo No. 11.[7] Young Chileans who were curious about counterculture, in addition to youths who already were living it as best they could, sat in those local theaters and together witnessed the unfolding drama that was the Woodstock extravaganza, with naked men and women, drugs of all kinds (including LSD), and tens of thousands of communing hippies in living color. Sources of inspiration did not stop there. Since the late 1960s, Chilean magazines and newspapers had been commenting, here and there and usually in negative or ambivalent ways, on what countercultural youths were up to in other Latin American countries and around the globe, thus bringing that world closer to readers young and older. Moreover, less than a week before Piedra Roja took shape, and with timing that was as perfect as it was coincidental, one of the Woodstock film's (and festival's) performers, Country Joe McDonald of Country Joe and the Fish, arrived in Santiago to participate in the production of a new film—part spy story, part musical, part documentary—called *¿Qué Hacer?* (What Is to Be Done?) which was co-directed by U.S. filmmaker and political activist Saul Landau.[8] Country Joe did not make an appearance at Piedra Roja, but his arrival made news in periodicals that young people riffled through at any curbside kiosk. In a manner of speaking, Woodstock became three dimensional upon Country Joe's arrival.

With Woodstock, frustration, boredom, and hippismo on his mind, Jorge found motivation in September 1970 to create a modest event that would bring together perhaps five hundred or so young people who were drawn, like Jorge, to local rock and counterculture. With friends Andrés Lewin and Roberto Cherit, Jorge asked Liceo No 11's Student Council to sponsor a festival. Their pitch failed, likely due to doubts among student leaders that Jorge could pull it off. Undeterred, Jorge, Andrés, Roberto, and others, including a few American friends and friends of friends (some the children of Methodist missionaries), decided to go it alone. Not yet grasping the challenges that lay ahead, Jorge began searching for an open space, away from the hustle and bustle of the city but close enough for young people to reach. Fortunately for Jorge, he was dating the niece of Luis Rosselot, president of Santiago's Hippodrome and owner of a large *fundo*—a rural estate—up a road called El Alba in the Los Dominicos sector of Las Condes. The location was ideal. Not far from where the San Carlos de Apoquindo soccer stadium stands today, it was countryside dotted with rocks and the usual shrubbery of the Andean foothills. It was close enough to urbanity for youths to journey there from most every part of the metropolitan area, and, as it turned out, it was far enough out to escape the attention of Carabineros (national police)—for a while. Jorge visited with Rosselot, and, with his girlfriend's help, obtained the landowner's permission, with one proviso: that a blank check be left with Rosselot in case damage came to fencing or anything else on his property. Jorge asked his mother, an upright Scottish woman (Constance Ainslie Walker) who found the idea of a musical gathering innocuous, to provide the guarantee, and she kindly did.[9]

The organizers lacked money needed for putting down security deposits on various types of infrastructure and accoutrements. Jorge's mother again came to the rescue, giving her son the second of what would be ten blank checks for use as security deposits, all without knowing the kind and magnitude of festival that would come to pass. Jorge and fellow planners did not know either, for that matter. As the infrastructural arrangements, as they were, slowly came together, the organizers set out to secure bands and advertise the festival. In the context of a relatively small rock music scene, a web of contacts and friendships made it fairly easy for Jorge's helpers to reach bands and convince them to show up on Rosselot's fundo. There were some groups, such as High Bass (becoming increasingly known as Los Jaivas at the time) and Los Blops, which the organizers feared would not agree to play at an event without any official sponsorship or money. To Jorge's surprise (and, really, to everyone else's) the organizing party managed to line up leading criollo rock groups as headliners: Los Jaivas, Los Blops, Aguaturbia, Escombros, Lágrima Seca, Los Ripios, and Los Trapos. At the time, the rock music scene was maturing and its bands mostly played in small indoor venues, including *casas de cultura* (neighborhood cultural centers) and high schools in Greater Santiago's many municipalities. Thus, the enticement of playing an open-air festival, especially as the documentary *Woodstock* was playing in Santiago, was quite a pull even for the very well-known and popular bands. As Los Bops vocalist and guitarist Eduardo Gatti noted, "It was like Woodstock, and Woodstock was very present, very, at that moment. I think for everyone it was very important because Woodstock had a virtue that no one expected: that 500,000 people got together and there were no major problems. Quite the contrary. They were days of a lot of tranquility and a lot of peace, of a lot of sharing, of having a good time, and that was an enormous precedent. I think Piedra Roja was our opportunity [to do the same], one could say."[10] All the bands that promised to play at Jorge's festival agreed to perform for free—a convenience because organizers had very little money. Likewise, Jorge charged no entry fee to festivalgoers, thus underscoring the event's countercultural impulse in a consumerist society.[11]

The responsibilities of advertising and promotion fell to two Americans: Pink Lizard, who was nearly twenty, living in Santiago, and using the moniker as his *nom de hippie* (he asked that his real name not be used in this study), and Gary Fritz, then seventeen and a student at the affluent Nido de Aguilas International School in what is now the municipality of Lo Barnechea. Essentially constituting the propaganda wing of the Gómez-led circle of friends and acquaintances that collectively imagined and carried out the criollo Woodstock in Los Dominicos, Pink Lizard's principal charge was to draw up attractive flyers with explicitly countercultural images. Featuring cartoon characters in the style of San Francisco's underground and edgy comic artist Robert Crumb, Pink Lizard reproduced the handbills on a mimeograph machine, the use of which Fritz secured thanks to his connection with its possessor: his father, a Methodist missionary and rector of the Methodists' Santiago College, an elite, English-speaking secondary school. Pink Lizard and Fritz handed out flyers "by the dozen," mostly in Providencia, and "to anyone who looked like they'd be receptive to the festival," Fritz reminisced.[12] The two also were in charge of getting local radio stations to publicize the upcoming festival. Their success in that regard actually worried them and sowed some consternation among Piedra Roja's other planners as well. "I do remember back then worrying about 'Uh-oh, now that they said it you can't retract it,' [and] so many people had heard about it that if we did retract a lot of people wouldn't hear it. So there would be swarms of people on those dates going up the hill," Fritz expounded.[13] Pink

Created by Pink Lizard, the flyer for what became known as Piedra Roja reflects the event's countercultural inspiration and intentions (1970). Courtesy of Gary Fritz.

Lizard's handbill also points to a lesser-known detail: Piedra Roja was not "Piedra Roja" when organizers were conjuring it. Billed originally by Pink Lizard and his cadre as the "Festival Media Luna" (Half-Moon Festival), the event was being called "Piedra Rajada," or "Cracked Rock"—the name of an imposing rock formation on the festival's grounds—by the crowds who began to gather in Los Dominicos well before the scheduled start. By the end of the fateful weekend, the media had coined the name "Piedra Roja" (Red Rock), used first by the conservative newspaper *El Mercurio* for no stated reason then widely adopted in and outside journalistic circles. Gómez and his co-organizers were and remain puzzled by the misnomer.[14]

While co-organizers like Pink Lizard tended to important details, Jorge pursued authorization from the local government, as the law required, in preparation for the event. The paperwork he submitted to the municipality of Las Condes proposed a "youth song festival," and it included a note from Rosselot that confirmed the landowner's permission to use his land in Los Dominicos.[15] After Las Condes officials gave their quick approval, Jorge ventured to the offices of the intendancy of Greater Santiago and the Carabineros, both of which gave their consent as well. It was, in short, an uneventful process. "The officials would say, 'Yeah, sure, a music festival in the mountains. It sounds nice, picturesque,'" Gómez remembered. "We had everything, all the documents."[16] In the aftermath of Piedra Roja, however, government officials found nothing innocuous or quaint in Jorge's "youth song festival." To Las Condes Mayor Ramón Luco Fuenzalida, for instance, what unfolded on his municipal turf entailed "a concentration of delinquents from many *comunas* [municipalities in Greater Santiago] that tarnished the prestige of Las Condes."[17] He added, "We were tricked in an infamous way."[18] Luco also designated Jorge's description of a "youth song festival" as an inventively conceived cover story, a ruse, for what was immorality at its most brazen. But neither premeditated underhandedness nor delinquency was in play, as Gómez and other organizers recalled decades later. The festival's scale, trajectory, and power astonished them all.[19]

With only a few weeks of planning behind it, what became Piedra Roja was to happen on Sunday (October 11)—a one-day event, or so its founders thought. Eagerness, however, got the best of many hundreds of young people (perhaps more than a thousand) who arrived on Saturday while organizers were busily installing the little infrastructure they could muster, including a small wooden stage and lighting, which amounted to a single incandescent bulb nestled in a tin can.[20] The stage (about twenty-four square meters) materialized due to a quid pro quo agreement that Jorge has arranged with the Andina Coca-Cola Bottling Company. Andina provided the stage, and Jorge allowed the vendor to set up kiosks to sell soft drinks on the festival's grounds. A stage for musicians with electric guitars, organs, amplifiers, and the like would be useless without power. Thus, with a blank check from his mother in hand to serve as a security deposit, Jorge managed to secure a lengthy electrical cable from Chilectra, the country's main utility company, given that the nearest power pole was thousands of meters away. Volunteers hooked up the costly main cable on Saturday evening, and power began flowing to the stage, but without utility poles fixed between the faraway source and the stage, the cable sat dangerously on the ground or rested on shrubbery. Complicating the situation, thieves cut away a portion of the cable that night, leaving festival organizers scrambling to find a replacement before the music was to begin on Sunday.[21] With most organizational matters under control by Saturday night, the stage was set—figuratively and literally—but hundreds of young people had already taken it upon themselves to get Chile's Woodstock rolling.

Moments in Los Dominicos

At least a thousand young people were milling about under the springtime glare on Saturday afternoon. Festivalgoers had erected a white flag with an inscribed peace sign as well as sizable tent within which youths sought shelter from the sun and found privacy for varying manifestations of coupling. Meanwhile, marijuana was abundant, beer and wine made the rounds, and, at times, stoned and drunken youths made for interesting conversations and occurrences. Young men with shoulder-length hair, others with striped pants, and a few with rounded sunglasses in the style of John Lennon, chatted with and wooed young women—palomas. Some palomas sported turtlenecks, a staple of the era, and joined with many young men in wearing headbands and bead necklaces. Outnumbered significantly by the opposite sex, the festival's young women certainly received a great deal of attention, including one paloma with whom Jorge became acquainted during the eventful weekend—and later married. Meanwhile, circulating in the crowd were a few clean-cut youths, no more than thirteen or fourteen years old, of both sexes, who were witnesses to the conspicuous hippismo of those a bit older. More rare still was anyone over thirty, with the vast majority falling somewhere between their mid-teens and early twenties.[22]

In the crowd, which ebbed and flowed during the weekend, were youths of varying socioeconomic means. Although Jorge and his assistants were from the more prosperous sectors of the capital, Piedra Roja was by no means a uniquely bourgeois affair. "More than [organizing] a musical encounter," Gómez explained much later, "the intention was to unite the authentic hippie communities, those who lived down the way from Plaza Italia [toward the working-class neighborhoods of the metropolis] and those who lived in the more affluent parts of the city—the ones who gathered at the Coppelia café [a famed hippie hangout in Providencia]."[23] Class differences—the fountain of intense political conflict in Chile—divided those groups in sociological and socioeconomic terms, but Jorge reasoned that they nevertheless shared generational attributes, especially in manners of thinking and acting that were countercultural. Indeed, they shared a fondness for rock music and more-than-cordial relations with marijuana, which at Piedra Roja were the bridges that realized Jorge's goal, if only for a short time.

Among those "authentic" working-class hippies Jorge mentioned stood Jaime Román, a self-described "former Parque Forestal hippie" for whom the festival's setting—Las Condes—was a region of the capital much further away conceptually than it was geographically from his home in a working-class

With a child in one arm, a hippie shares in the social life of Piedra Roja (1970). Courtesy of Paul Lowry.

municipality west of downtown Santiago. Word of a festival "like Woodstock" spread speedily through his high school and inspired young Jaime and his friends to venture into the metropolitan region's eastern suburbs. Decades later, Román explained that he and his pals from Liceo Integral No. 1 in Quinta Normal happened to share a public bus with others youths who were heading to Piedra Roja and fortunately seemed to know precisely where to go. After a long bus ride, he and his companions disembarked, only to face a long, uphill walk to the event's grounds. Trudging alongside them, as Román recollected, were "wealthy young people wearing blue jeans with marijuana leaves, 'LSD,' 'Acid,' and names like Jimi Hendrix and Santana painted on them." He added, "Guys had flowers on their shirts, which, where we came from [in working-class neighborhoods], would have people calling you gay. But Piedra Roja and hippismo were about the freedom to do what you wanted to do."[24]

Still a resident of Quinta Normal, Román was fifteen when he went to Piedra Roja, and he remembers noteworthy experiences that say much about class and, to some extent, racial dynamics. He said that upon arriving at the festival he became aware, as did most others, of differences in class among those assembled near the giant *piedra rajada*. Yet, awareness of those differences receded, or was superseded, as youths of different socioeconomic and geographic origin united in their appreciation for, and self-celebrated use of, marijuana. They also plainly shared an affinity for the festival's rock music, which was slow in coming to the event and hampered by infrastructural problems, but eventually took center stage. As Román remembered it, he and his friends, upon arriving to the festival grounds, were met by odd expressions on the faces of hippies who obviously were from the *barrio alto* (high neighborhood) of the capital. Many were tall, blond, and dressed in the latest fashions, while young Jaime was a short, dark-haired, and working-class hippie who tried to imitate barrio alto counterculture as best as he could on an extremely limited budget. Initially, Jaime and friends were virtually ignored by affluent hippies, and especially by the beautiful young women among them. Yet, barriers between classes collapsed when his working-class companions introduced and shared their marijuana—a poor-quality hemp or cannabis, in reality—with the well-to-do youths. "We all got along very well after that," Román noted in our interview. "We all smoked—the men and women—and some blond women [*rubias*] took a liking to some darker men [*morenos*] and some blond men liked darker women [*morenas*]."[25]

On Saturday—nearly a full day before the festival was to kick off with the sounds of Los Jaivas and others—festivalgoers, whether they were moneyed and drove Austin Coopers or Peugeots to Piedra Roja or those of more humble origin who hitchhiked and took buses, together provided their own, improvised entertainment, thus propelling and reinforcing the festival's hippismo. Without any introduction or coordination, young people broke into music and song—mostly covers of popular English-language hits—on the stage and in the audience. A young woman was the first to perform off the cuff, belting out a few lyrics from Canned Heat's "Goin' Up the Country," which the California-based band played at New York's Woodstock. A harmonica player and an acoustic guitarist then joined in as she sang, in somewhat of a shrieking voice, "Let It Be," "Love Me Do," and "Hey Jude" by the Beatles. Later, a crowd of youths apparently "looking for adventure" began belting out the recurring chorus of Steppenwolf's "Born to Be Wild," while severely muddling the remaining words in light of a palpable language barrier—and perhaps some alcohol or marijuana.[26]

After a night of bonfires and with many festivalgoers having slept in tents or directly under the stars, dawn broke on Sunday morning. The crowd began to swell, reaching three to five thousand by the afternoon. But before the headliners arrived, improvisation took center stage once more—this time, electrified—at around midday. An organist, Víctor Rivera, arrived

Dancers enjoy the improvisational sounds of the rock bands Lágrima Seca and Los Ripios on the festival's first day (1970). Courtesy of Paul Lowry.

first, having hauled his heavy Hammond organ in the back of a small, burdened pickup truck. After a prolonged warm-up, Rivera pleased the crowd with sounds that would have impressed any fan of the Doors. Members of Los Ripios and Lágrima Seca then joined Rivera in an impromptu jam session, providing revelers with the best music they had heard since stepping onto Luis Rosselot's land. Unfortunately, the two small amplifiers on the stage could barely meet the power needs of the organ, much less anything else.[27]

Later that afternoon, with attendees and organizers alike wondering when the festival might realize its potential, other bands began showing up. The music of Los Jaivas and Los Blops, among others, lasted well into the night, amid a darkness interrupted only by the stage's solitary light bulb and bonfires dotting the grounds. "I remember an eerie image of Eduardo Gatti [of Los Blops] standing in front [on the stage] with a red guitar, and he was barely being illuminated by this light in a tin can," recalled Carlos Lowry, a Chilean rock aficionado and another of Gómez's helpers. "And nothing was cranked up real loud."[28] As described in a subsequent chapter, Los Jaivas and Los Blops were up-and-coming rock bands whose members were becoming local rock luminaries, and they and the festival were part and parcel of an emerging rock culture that evinced a particular sensibility—an audio, aesthetic, and thoughtful one which was more serious than some perceived—that effectively defied normative conceptions and practices of cultural production set forth by their critics, including

Festivalgoers socialize and listen to rock music under a bright October sky. Tents and a Coca-Cola stand are visible in the background (far right) (1970). Courtesy of Paul Lowry.

those orchestrating the *allendista* agenda. Audience members with harmonicas and bongos, individual amateurs riffing on an organ or a bass guitar, and professional groups like Los Jaivas and Los Blops contributed to rock music's grip on the criollo Woodstock and its celebrants. Their performances reflected the tastes and cultural demands of many young people who embraced a genre for which an older generation allowed little space and about which it offered much ridicule.

After the bands played, packed up their equipment, and departed, festivalgoers did not want to follow. They remained, again building bonfires in the darkness and continuing with the revelry that many had enjoyed since Saturday. By the time the sun rose on Monday morning, the crowd had thinned to under a thousand, but as Fritz noted, it carried on, with festivalgoers wanting to extend, as much as possible, a shared experience and camaraderie that Piedra Roja tapped and furthered.[29] However, the weekend's togetherness and peacefulness would not last. Sunday's complications, including the acute intoxication of revelers and scheduling issues, were, by Monday, eclipsed by other problems, some more severe than others. During the morning hours of Monday, a holiday (the *Día de la raza*, Chile's version of Columbus Day in the United States), a band of young thieves stole

The Opening Set   35

valuable musical and electrical equipment, a loss in addition to that of the first main power cable, which disappeared sometime Saturday night. They also relieved many revelers of purses, backpacks, and other belongings, in addition to picking fistfights. Moreover, Gómez recalled that prostitutes began showing up, hoping to sell their services in the festival's crowd, which included young people who had been smoking marijuana and drinking since Saturday. Moreover, young people had ransacked the Coca-Cola kiosks on Sunday night, taking sodas, breaking bottles, and using wooden crates for bonfires.[30]

By midday on Monday, as the festival was winding down and after the morning newspapers had reported on Sunday's partying, Carabineros entered the festival grounds for the first time, subsequent to having patrolled the nearby area since Saturday. Gómez recalled the arrival of a Carabinero who took him aside and announced the nullification of the municipality's consent due to evidence that underage drinking was afoot. It was a bit late. Moreover, the Carabinero made no mention of the consumption of marijuana, which was ubiquitous, or any other activity happening at that moment, nor did he point to anything that had taken place during the festival's two previous days.[31] Instead, the Carabinero seized on what was, in the broader scope of things, a minor issue at Piedra Roja. "I just remember Carabineros, you know, fellows in green uniforms, coming up the hill and basically shutting us down. Everyone started leaving," Fritz explained. "I don't think anyone had a clue about what was happening up there until it came out in the newspapers."[32] Witnesses maintained that the robberies, fights, and other sour happenings on Monday were the doings of delinquents from outside the hippie community and reflected social problems that onlookers should not ascribe to hippismo.[33] Others explained that such incidences were common at large gatherings of any sort, especially soccer matches. But some lamented that the festival's regrettable final hours did much to damage criollo counterculture's image, legitimizing the idea circulating in mainstream circles that festival participants were, in fact, delinquents.[34] To many of hippismo's critics, there was little practicality in differentiating between perpetrators and victims when everything about Piedra Roja was beyond the pale, as a later chapter will illustrate. Hippies or not, the behavior of some antisocial youths at Piedra Roja took a financial toll, to say nothing of its effect on families, including Jorge's.[35] And Monday's circumstances, including the intervention by the Carabineros, did not bode well in terms of the vibes emitted by media outlets regarding Jorge's "youth song festival."

The press gave young people in attendance at Piedra Roja an opportunity, though limited, to offer their perspectives on the festival and hippismo. Those points of view were framed, for the most part, by overtones mocking and stigmatizing whatever countercultural notions festivalgoers embraced and expressed. Fortunately, however, other voices were recorded (quite literally) that weekend in the hills of Las Condes, without discursive addenda brought to bear by and in newspapers like the conservative *El Mercurio* or the Marxist *Clarín*. A twenty-year-old hippie from the United States had a reel-to-reel audio recorder with him and sought to capture the voices and sounds of the weekend's fun. The only one of its kind, the off-and-on, one-hour-forty-minute recording includes questions the American hippie asked of his Chilean coreligionists, the answers of young people intent on experiencing a criollo Woodstock, some impromptu singing, a great many bongos and harmonicas, and the overall bustle of a countercultural event in the making. It is a recording done by a young person, about young people, and for young people, and it provides the listener invaluable and unusual access to what youths were thinking and doing as those striking few days in October 1970 played out.

Voices of Piedra Roja

An *El Mercurio* correspondent covering the festival came across a young countercultural fellow from the United States with a rather peculiar and convincingly hippista name: Pink Lizard. The young man, as the reporter described in print, was dressed as if he were a character in the film *Easy Rider* (translated into Spanish as *Busco mi destino*, or *I Search for My Destiny*). When asked about the goings-on around him, Pink Lizard explained, "I've participated in events like this in my country and I believe that youths all over the world today share many of the same ideas in common." Pink Lizard—the hippie who recorded nearly two hours of Piedra Roja on his reel-to-reel machine and, unbeknownst to *El Mercurio* was a festival co-organizer—told readers of the conservative daily that similarities among Chilean hippies and his hippies back home transcended dress and style; hippies everywhere shared a common experience as young people and, he suggested, thought about the world in similar ways. But any morsel of sympathy Pink Lizard may have garnered from *El Mercurio's* readers probably faded when they came across the hippie's seemingly ambivalent description of Charles Manson, who the newspaper identified as an "American hippie." When asked about the homicidal maniac whose depraved deeds were in the news most everywhere in the world at the time, Pink Lizard noted that Manson had "psychic energy, is very intelligent, but you can't agree at all with his actions."[36] Pink Lizard believed, or so *El Mercurio* inferred, that Manson had some redeeming qualities, as evidenced by the "but" in the festivalgoer's statement. Putting Manson aside for a moment, one gathers from Pink Lizard's general outlook that hippismo was not merely an expression of a transnational cultural industry with its homogenizing music, hairstyles, and so forth; it was a new cosmology, however vague it may have been.

To Pink Lizard, it was obvious why *El Mercurio* chose him for an interview. "I may have had a moustache and a beard. I certainly had hair hanging down my back and, you know, the usual suede boots with fringe, the tie-dyed T-shirt," he recalled decades later. "Anybody who was more extreme looking [than most everyone else at the festival] would stand out and I think that may have been one of the reasons that the newspaper approached me for a conversation. On the day of the festival, if you were to wander the grounds I was probably one of the most colorful people out there. I would have been a natural to approach for an interview." When reflecting on *El Mercurio*'s line of inquiry, Pink Lizard explained, "As it turned out, I knew full well what *El Mercurio* was all about in those days. And [the reporter] asked a series of leading questions like 'Hey, how about that Charles Manson, huh?' So what do you say to a leading question like that? And so I didn't want to give him a fed response either positive or negative, so you can see from the [published] interview, which I believe quoted me accurately, I kind of came down the middle on that one. He was hoping that I would say something positive and [the people at *El Mercurio*] would come back and say 'See? I told you that all of those young people are bloodthirsty!'" Knowing that his words would likely appear in *El Mercurio* (and they did—on the front page, no less) was partially behind the use of his distinctive nom de hippie, which came to him as he pondered, well before the festival, some nomenclatural options that spoke to "the times we were living in." In other words, it was to be "far out." But the name also had a more practical application: it served to protect the U.S. citizen's friends and relatives in Chile—the latter were Methodist missionaries—from any derision resulting from his appearance in the public eye. "I'm fairly sure that [the festival] was the first public use of it [the moniker]. Post festival, I continued to have other adventures in that guise," Pink Lizard recollected, chuckling.[37]

Pink Lizard's role at Piedra Roja went much further than providing testimony on behalf of hippismo. He made the aforementioned recording. The American's tape endured the passage of time and bestows upon us an auditory peek at a moment in Chilean cultural history that afforded posterity few photographs and only poor snippets of video taken by the Catholic television Channel 13. The recording opens with the assorted sounds of Pink Lizard's bus ride to Los Dominicos—with the mumbles of passengers and the din of a struggling engine. He interviewed a young man and some companions also en route to the Media Luna Festival—soon to become Piedra Roja—before they both, and many others, made the final leg of the journey by foot: up a winding road into the hills, into a revolutionary environment in the making.

Pink Lizard: Where are you going?

Young Man: To Los Dominicos, to the festival.

Pink Lizard: To the festival? What do you think you'll find there?

Young Man: Music, tranquility, and peace.

Pink Lizard: And how long do you think you'll stay?

Young Man: Two days. Hope so, and during every weekend for the rest of the year.

Once off the bus, Pink Lizard chronicled his trek to the festival grounds, where a gatekeeper estimates that seven hundred people had already gathered—all well before any music was slated to begin. As Pink Lizard made his way through the assembling crowd, he came across a young man engaged in one of the festival's defining experiences.

Pink Lizard: Would you mind telling me what you are doing?

Young Man: I'm smoking a marijuana cigarette.

Pink Lizard: Is it nice?

Young Man: Nice.

Pink Lizard: Do you think there's going to be a lot of that here at the festival?

Young Man: Whew! Tons of it will be going around.

Yet another young man, when asked about his opinion of what was happening in Los Dominicos, responded with a very clear understanding that the festival's premise was as transnational as it was enticing.

Young Man: That's a good thing, to have a festival, because it will show that the Latin American youth are like those in the United States and in Europe.

Pink Lizard: Is that a good thing?

Young people sit amid the grass and bushes on Luis Rosselot's land (1970). Courtesy of Paul Lowry.

> *Young Man*: It is a good thing.
>
> *Pink Lizard*: Why?
>
> *Young Man*: Not [like the U.S. and Europe] in everything, but [we want to show] that we here in Latin America want friendship, [that Latin America] isn't aggressive, it's none of those things that gets said [about us] in other countries.
>
> *Pink Lizard*: Do you think there are lots of people in Latin America who think the same way you do?
>
> *Young Man*: Yes, I think so. Many.

Pink Lizard recorded other brief exchanges as well, including the words of one young woman whose mother was not aware of her daughter's adventures. When asked by Pink Lizard about what her mother would say, the teenager simply quipped: "To each her own."[38]

As the interviewees' allusions to peace, their playful and open approaches to marijuana, their concrete affirmations of youth and youthfulness, and their defiance of generational authority suggest, festivalgoers not only understood and embraced some typically countercultural outlooks and ways of being, but were aware of counterculture's transnational roots and dimensions. While the young woman's "To each her own" was as sweeping as it was telling, staking out her independence in addition to gendering it, there were revelers who were more specific and explanatory (though not necessarily more revelatory) regarding their worldviews as they experienced and contributed to what was happening at Piedra Roja.

In an interview with an *El Mercurio* correspondent, a twenty-year-old identified simply as "Raúl" diagnosed hippismo as a "transitional stage between two cultures: one moribund and one that is about to be born." He added, "And all who have taken part in transitions have been persecuted," including Jesus Christ and Buddha. Spearheaded by young people, this process of sociocultural change had far-reaching spiritual implications in addition to any structural effects, Raúl signaled.[39] As another festivalgoer affirmed nearly twenty-five years after Piedra Roja, many hippies at the rock event understood hippismo's spiritual dimension as a utopian spiritualism that stressed unity and freedom and that overshadowed the materialism and certain patterns of consumption that partially defined the counterculture.[40] Raúl's description of hippismo essentially identified its sensibilities as revolutionary—just as Christianity revolutionized the West and Buddhism revolutionized the Far East. Thus, while a cogent and collective revolutionary *political* ideology was absent from Piedra Roja, there were people in the throng who apparently had a grip on what hippismo meant to them and what its historical significance would be. The media representing constituencies from the Left to the Right, despite including in their reports some brief ruminations on hippismo uttered by festival attendees like Pink Lizard and Raúl, seemed more interested in detailing the apparently audacious practices—mostly the illegal ones—of Piedra Roja's hippies than pausing to seriously assess any of hippismo's cosmological and epistemological components.

Seizing on Sunday's circumstances, the media shrewdly used the words of Piedra Roja's youths to accentuate the argument that the festival was an immoral fiasco. For instance, a disappointed hippie named Ángel Francescone, reportedly with tears in his eyes, described Piedra Roja's downward spiral to a writer for *El Mercurio*: "The festival did not reach its objective of love and peace and, quite the contrary, was transformed into a hive of many delinquents who practiced violence and abused some of the youths. In my case, eight people assaulted me . . . then they robbed my watch, my ring, and all the money I had with me."[41] While young people like Francescone complained of having lost cash and jewelry, some hippies bemoaned their loss of a specific form of material culture—of the illegal variety. A young man who went by the initials P. H. M. was obviously shaken, like Francescone, by things he witnessed on that eventful Sunday: "Everything was perfect until a gang of delinquents arrived. I don't care that they robbed me of my backpack and my sleeping bag. What I am most upset about, and I say this truthfully, is the loss of my bag of marijuana. For me material things are always easier to get than the one thing that really makes me understand who I am: a joint. Unfortunately, our motto of 'Peace and Love' didn't happen." P. H. M., whose frustration about his stash apparently stimulated a less-than-positive assessment of Piedra Roja, then proclaimed the festival "was deformed and transformed into a veritable brothel that wasn't short on wine and loose women [*niñas de vida airada*]."[42]

In light of how often elected officials and others used "delinquents" and "hippies" interchangeably, it is interesting that P. H. M. deployed the term "delinquents" when describing outsiders whose brutish behavior brought the festival to a halt. That usage had the effect of casting others—and not necessarily countercultural young people, notwithstanding P. H. M.'s denunciation of the festival—as the bona fide delinquents that authorities should pursue, investigate, and punish. Additionally, it is reasonable to speculate that P. H. M. may have confused mainstream readers when he lamented the presence of alcohol and sexual improprieties at Piedra Roja and, in the same breath, fretted about the loss of his cherished bag of marijuana. P. H. M.'s assumption, moreover, that marijuana somehow was not a "material thing" that countercultural youths consumed—that it was, in effect, outside the world of material culture—is patently problematic yet endemic in the counterculture of the 1960s and 1970s in Chile and elsewhere.

The Piedra Roja rock festival did not create the Chilean counterculture; it drew on it, reflected it, and thrust it forward. What occurred in October 1970 greatly accelerated the criollo counterculture's conversion from a phenomenon mostly indigenous to the private lives and sociability of some young people to a very public and publicized spectacle with repercussions well outside Santiago. Less than a week after the happenings in Los Dominicos and enthused by the reports of what transpired in the capital, a group of young people in the major southern city of Concepción announced their intention to organize their own festival—in the Plaza Independencia, a popular hangout for young people in the center of town—slated for Christmas Day. Local officials were not keen on the idea, to say the least, noting, "The trafficking of drugs and the moral transgressions that occurred in Santiago give pause about what could happen in our city." Youths behind the initiative sought to soothe qualms by clarifying that, unlike youngsters in the capital, Concepción's young crowd had no interest in LSD. This might have helped their case—if they had not then argued that marijuana was another thing entirely. *Pitos* (joints), they said, helped a person "see the world in a more natural and beautiful way" and are "irreplaceable." Concepción authorities denied permission, explaining that such an event "would be detrimental to public health and good manners."[43] Mayor Guillermo Aste Pérez explained, "These [young] people don't have any concerns; they only want to kill time doing something, and they believe that killing time listening to soul music [a term interchangeable with 'rock' at the time in Chile], or so they say, and smoking marijuana, free love, and a series of other crap, all for style, are sure ways of creating one's own destiny." He added, "I believe it's a national embarrassment that a gathering of this nature was authorized in Santiago." The directors of the Concepción Boy Scouts, YMCA, and Rotary Club, as well as local school officials, expressed similar views.[44] Mayor Aste, as we shall later see, was but one voice in an enormous chorus that jeered young Jorge's festival and criollo counterculture.

By the beginning of the 1970s, it became clearer than ever that countercultural matters no longer were pertinent only in faraway places like the San Francisco Bay area, Amsterdam, Mexico City, or Paris. The phenomenon was close by, and such an explosive manifestation of it—Jorge Gómez's "youth song festival"—coincided with Popular Unity's rise to power. As a result, the criollo counterculture became a lightning rod of interest in government circles and among the general public. The historic change in presidential administrations in late 1970, overlapping with Piedra Roja and the brouhaha it caused, brought with it energetic and continuing efforts on the part of the state and powerful groups in civil society to discredit and restrain a recognizably countercultural being-in-the-world. Criticism of hippismo and counterculture reflected concerns shared in many sociopolitical circles about certain young peoples' disassociation from normative forms of sociability and culture, and most public commentary and initiatives that emerged in response to criollo counterculture surfaced after Piedra Roja. Moreover, the media, which had broached the subject of counterculture from time to time toward the end of the 1960s, became enthralled in the festival's aftermath by criollo and transnational counterculture, which many viewed as outrageous, insolent, and dangerous. Although violence, acts of larceny, the arrival of prostitutes, and the eventual actions of Carabineros cut the long weekend's festivities short, Piedra Roja's organizers and young people who hitchhiked, walked, took buses and taxis, or drove their parents' cars into the hills to partake in what they expected would be a colloquial Woodstock, remember the event largely as a testament to peace, love, and freedom.

Making sense of Piedra Roja and criollo counterculture requires an examination of transnational and local conditions unique to the sixties and early seventies. Doing so provides a way to get one's head around what criollo counterculture entailed, the reasons why young people adopted some or many of its outlooks and practices, and the complexities of the mainstream reaction that ensued. Our discussion, which returns to Piedra Roja from time to time, must turn to the "youth question" in Chile and abroad before we engage more specific themes—namely, sex, drugs, and rock music—that also were intimately intertwined with the emergence, development, and reception of criollo counterculture. The youth question involved an expansive array of problems, concerns, gestures, and initiatives that, while transnational, had vernacular manifestations during the period under consideration here. The concepts of "youth" and "generation" mattered, not merely as conceptual categories but as markers of identity with epistemic value.

2 A Bad Moon on the Rise?

Coming to Grips with the Youth Question

On the heels of being sworn into office and receiving the presidential sash, Salvador Allende stood behind a podium with more than 100,000 supporters watching in the capital's National Stadium. Allende's inaugural address in November 1970 outlined his coalition's project for the nation, breaking ground for the "Chilean road to socialism" and, as one would expect, focusing on the present and future of the working class whose cause and historical role the new Marxist government pledged to champion. But the Socialist physician went beyond "class"; he paused to speak to his nation's young people in generational terms, outlining their responsibilities to the *patria* (Fatherland) and their collective revolutionary promise. Identifying himself as a formerly "rebellious student," Allende told his compatriots in the grandstands, "I will not criticize [youthful] impatience, but it is my duty to ask [young people] to think calmly." Allende explained, "Young people, yours is that beautiful age during which physical and mental vigor enable you to undertake practically any endeavor. For that reason you are duty-bound to help us advance. Turn your eagerness into more work, your hopes into more effort, and your impulsiveness into concrete accomplishments. Use your drive and energy to be better—the best—students and workers." He then went on to proclaim, "Thousands upon thousands of young people have demanded a place in the social struggle. Now they have that place. The time has come for all young people to participate in that action."[1] Many thousands of young people already had responded to the Left's calls to action before the ascendance of Allende's Marxist-led coalition, Popular Unity (or UP). Thousands also rallied behind the opposition.

Most every political party had a youth faction, and together they shared a generational milieu with numerous youth-related organizations, such as student federations, that existed separately but in relation to the parties. In the heated political environment of the sixties and early seventies, active engagement in politics became a marker of a young person or of a youth organization's legitimacy. Groups like the Jota (Communist Youth), the Socialist Youth (Juventud Socialista, JS), and some rivals had long histories, beginning shortly after the formation of the parties to which they were fused. The Jota came together in 1932, and over the decades it included such renowned members as the poet and Nobel Laureate Pablo Neruda, Violeta Parra, Víctor Jara, and Ángel Parra, while the JS, founded in 1935, boasted Allende as its most famous member. Within the Jota and JS, moreover, there were subgroups, often called *brigadas* (brigades), such as the Jota's Ramona Parra Brigade (Brigada Ramona Parra, BRP), which, aside from its powerful muralism, also acted as if it were a street-level enforcer of the Chilean road to socialism. The right-wing National Party (Partido Nacional, or PN), meanwhile, had its Rolando Matus Command (Comando Rolando Matus, CRM), which went about its business much like the BRP but on behalf of starkly different political principles—and minus the murals. The belligerent Fatherland and Liberty Nationalist Front (Frente Nacionalista Patria y Libertad, FNPL) was independent of the PN but, like the CRM, worked openly to harass young and older leftists alike, often getting into street scuffles. Positioned somewhere between the forces of Left and Right (with some cozying up to each during the Allende years) were young reformers, affiliated largely with the PDC (Christian Democratic Party). Youths in their teens and twenties also acted on campuses and in the streets by way of the FECh (the Student Federation of the University of Chile) and the Federation of Santiago Secondary-School Students (Federación de Estudiantes Secundarios de Santiago, or FESES), among others. The federations collaborated with the Jota, the Christian Democratic Youth (Juventud Demócrata Cristiana, JDC), and other groups, with members commonly belonging to more than one body at a time. By the 1960s, elections within these and other student associations were closely watched by the media and politicians as barometers of electoral trends, evincing just how important the organizations had become. Such groups and others like them were, quite simply, tuned in; they were politicized and part of political machineries.

Meanwhile, a portion of Chile's youth embraced ways of being in the world—ideational and behavioral—that were countercultural, shunning the rallying cries of student groups, parties, and other organizations at the heart of the political milieu. They did so at a pivotal moment, when political activism was at its apogee. Of course, to be young did not necessarily entail either being countercultural *or* taking part in the CRM, the Jota, the FECh, and so on. An array of personal and situational factors were at play in the lives of young individuals, and many went about their days without the types of engagements and modes and means of expression that are this study's main focal points. Regardless of their political and cultural dispositions,

Salvador Allende receives the cheers of young supporters at a rally in Santiago in 1972. The president often spoke publicly to and about young people. Courtesy of the Colección Museo Histórico Nacional (Santiago).

young people lived at a unique moment in modern history during which youth and youth culture had global reach and resonance. Indeed, "youth" and "generation" consumed quite a bit of ink and framed a good many conversations, as conservatives, centrists, and leftists grappled with the ascendant "youth question" during the presidency of Christian Democrat Eduardo Frei Montalva (1964–1970) and the subsequent Allende years. The youth question entailed particular and historically contingent manifestations of generational agency as well as an array of consequences, conjectures, and calls to action in response to the restlessness and rebelliousness of young people.

In an intense electoral environment and in the course of social strife, assessments of the youth question were highly politicized, with leading sociopolitical actors deploying attribution and blame instrumentally in volleys of condemnation showered upon opponents. Conceptually, the youth question was contested discursive terrain with real-world effects among individuals, in the family, and in society. In advance of considering the youth question's salience, which will provide substrate for subsequent chapters, we must pause to survey what Chileans were seeing in terms of youth movements and youth-related problems around the world amid the rapid globalization of means of communication. Any Chilean paying some attention to the news was apprised of student movements and youth-related problems and issues that were unfolding globally in dramatic and, at times, tragic ways. Such reports, in addition to manifestations of youthful unrest in their own country, impelled the recognition among young and older Chileans that their society was not at all isolated from generational tremors and profound cultural change occurring elsewhere.

A Transnational Question

The youth question was transnational and was understood as such during the 1960s, with 1968 constituting a critical year in the United States, Europe, and Latin America. Young people's mobilizations of most every sort underscored the youth question's transnationalism, the power of global means of communication, and the pertinence of "youth" and "generation" as social and cultural (and often political) markers of identity. As a result, existing literature—academic and otherwise—on the 1960s devotes much attention to the student movements of 1968, to the overall upsurge in youth activism around the world, and to what may be called the Zeitgeist of 1968. Journalist and writer Mark Kurlansky, for instance, identifies 1968 as "the year that rocked the world," with young people at the center of events worldwide—from the Prague Spring to a bloody autumn at Tlatelolco—who fomented and reflected transnational bonds of generational identity, ideational convergence, and straightforward activism.[2] That year was, in the words of renowned Mexican novelist and essayist Carlos Fuentes, "one of those constellation-years in which events, movements, and personalities that were unexpected and separated by space coincided without an immediately explicable reason."[3] As Kurlansky also notes, nostalgically, "The shrinking of the globe will never be so shocking in the same way that we will never again feel the thrill of the first moon shots or the first broadcasts from outer space."[4] Whether or not the world shall ever again shrink so quickly is obviously debatable. More relevant is the notion that the 1960s constituted an unquestionably crucial decade in light of 1968 and other watershed instants and trends.

In Europe and the United States, reflections on 1968 encompass numerous episodes involving young people engaged in direct action against prevailing political, social, economic, and cultural actualities. That activism, driven in part by what Paul Berman describes as young peoples' "utopian exhilaration" in the so-called First World (and behind the Iron Curtain as well), demonstrated the potential and promise of counterhegemonic agency in the proverbial lion's dens of hegemony and authority.[5] Thus, cracks appearing in a metropole's hegemonic architecture unquestionably emboldened young people outside that metropole, confirming, reinforcing, and further propelling their desires and demands in diverse contexts. In his reflections on 1968, Fuentes locates such interconnectivity in Paris, Prague, and Mexico City, as have other interrogations of the 1960s.[6] In addition to publishing news of the profoundly influential student riots in Paris, the Chilean press brought attention to student unrest in such places as Italy, Japan, Poland, Portugal, West Germany (including West Berlin), New York, and Yugoslavia.[7]

In Latin America, the October 1968 massacre of students at Tlatelolco by Mexican security forces loomed and looms large, often overshadowing the memories of other important events and circumstances involving youth in the region. The killing of hundreds of young demonstrators on the eve of the Mexico City Olympics was part of a larger generational conflict—replete with public protests by youths and also characterized by the emergence of counterculture—brewing in Mexico since the 1950s. As Eric Zolov notes, many young people became disillusioned with the hegemonic Institutional Revolutionary Party and its conception of a united and stable "Revolutionary Family."[8] In September and August of 1968, when Mexico's student movement picked up momentum on Mexico City campuses and others elsewhere, the Chilean press began following those circumstances by way of reports from the Associated Press, United Press International, and Reuters.[9] *El Mercurio*, as one would expect, was less than sympathetic toward the students in Mexico City, even after Tlatelolco. Equally unsurprising is that the Chilean Left's treatment differed.

A year and a half after Tlatelolco, *Punto Final*, published by the MIR (Movement of the Revolutionary Left), a Marxist-Leninist and vanguardist organization founded in 1965 and opposed to incrementalist paths to socialism, recalled the massacre as a "traumatic scar," arguing that the Mexican government showed "its internal crisis, its sclerosis, and the incapacity to absorb and accept the petitions of young people."[10] Less iconic than events in Mexico but significant nonetheless were other examples of direct conflict between Latin American governments, including military regimes, and young people pursuing student-related goals. In Brazil, for instance, a student movement bravely challenged the policies of a dictatorship that had overthrown progressive President João Goulart in 1964.[11] Again, the Chilean press, including its most widely circulated newspaper, *El Mercurio*, followed events as they unfolded in Brazil, as it did in the cases of student unrest in Argentina, Uruguay, and even the faraway Dominican Republic.[12] Such reports appeared along with media accounts of similar problems in Chile, especially in Santiago, which saw its share of student unrest.

Chile's student-led university reform movement, which began in 1967 and spilled into 1968, was an upwelling of agency that, to a considerable degree, informed youth activism in subsequent years. The movement exemplified youthful action that was focused, disciplined, and driven by policy pursuits. It commenced in mid-1967 at the Pontifical Catholic University when its Federation of Students (Federación de Estudiantes de la Universidad Católica, or FEUC, founded in 1938), led by members of the reformist PDC's youth faction, seized the main building on the institution's central campus. Their demands focused on democratization and shared governance, clashing with Church leadership. The latter relented. The university's rector was sacked, and a new procedural landscape for university governance emerged, giving power to students and faculty in the selection of administrators. The FEUC's actions touched off a wave of student activism that swept through the country's major institutions of higher learning over the next year. Meanwhile, some original leaders of the reform at the Pontifical Catholic University, including the movement's chief, Miguel Ángel Solar, became disaffected with the PDC, which had given the reform only tepid support. They left to form the Unitary Popular Action Movement (Movimiento de Acción Popular Unitaria, MAPU), which joined UP. In sum, the reform movement empowered young people and faculty in the administration of top universities, but just as important was the morale boost the movement gave to youths who successfully flexed their power, or witnessed peers doing so, on the eve of the eruptions of student protests in Paris in 1968.[13]

As the university reform movement waned in Chile, it became increasingly common for observers of the youth question to locate an array of unfocused and undisciplined outlooks and modes of agency that contributed to the younger generation's problematic image. In fact, one voice that originally was an ardent critic of the university-reform movement—*El Mercurio*—seemed to wax nostalgic about it in an October 1968 editorial that ostensibly regretted the passing of such dignified forms of youthful agency. The newspaper had come to accept the reality of "young power" and the promise of improving academic institutions of higher learning in the country. That progress arose from the student movement's apolitical, policy-minded, and nonviolent focus. However, since the beginning of the university reform movement, more and more students had taken to street demonstrations and run-ins with police—"marches" and "provocations" that "we also see in other countries." The result was not the strengthening of young power but its corrosion and transformation into "revolutionary frivolity," *El Mercurio* concluded.[14] The conservative newspaper's admonishment came after a large October 4 demonstration by university and high-school students in downtown Santiago in response to the deeply troublesome situation facing Mexican youths in the wake of the Tlatelolco massacre, political instability in neighboring Peru, and the suspension of civil liberties in Uruguay. Such "grave disorder," to quote *El Mercurio*, involved hundreds of young people—many associated with the FECh—who threw stones through the windows of businesses and the nearby U.S. and Uruguayan embassies.[15] Some sixty young people were arrested and six were injured when Carabineros intervened. One of the injured, an engineering student at the University of Chile, suffered a gunshot wound, according to a hospital spokesperson. The Carabineros denied any involvement in the shooting. As the situation developed, Frei's Christian Democratic administration lashed out against the demonstrators. Interior minister Edmundo Pérez Zujovic declared that "the government respects all manifestations of opinion that the citizenry wishes to express as long as they are done legally, but it cannot tolerate or condone any manifestations of violence." Gabriel Valdés Subercaseaux, minister of foreign relations, argued, "It is evident that those who supposedly act to show their support for democratic institutions adopt measures that are incompatible with their stated objectives."[16] *El Mercurio* chimed in as well, adding, "There exists clamor among citizens for their protection [by the state] against delinquency."[17] Meanwhile, the University of Chile's rector, Ruy Barbosa Popolizio, struck a more conciliatory note, calling for restraint on the part of police and urging young people to engage in public discourse in an "orderly and respectful" manner.[18]

The October disturbances were among the many in Greater Santiago during the second half of 1968. In one episode, leftist students ("extremists" in the words of the rightist media) at the University of Chile's Pedagogical Institute—a hotbed of student activism, which earned it the nickname "Piedragógico"—cast rocks (*piedras*) at police for nearly three hours and built barricades during a demonstration in support of a momentous strike of *campesinos* (rural workers) at a well-known Central Valley hacienda, the Fundo San Miguel de Los Andes. Carabineros responded with water cannons and tear gas. Sixteen students were arrested and all those involved were reprimanded publicly by the Frei administration and in the government-owned newspaper. The conservative media condemned the violence and also criticized students for littering the walls of the institute with posters of the late Ernesto "Che" Guevara and the flag of North Vietnam, which gave a demonstration in support of local campesinos a more internationalist flavor.[19] The leftist media was rather forgiving, to say the least.[20] In another incident, hundreds of mostly university students brought the western reaches of downtown Santiago to a halt when they erected barricades in front of the Estación Central, a principal rail terminal. Unrest had surfaced days earlier, with some violent confrontations between students and Carabineros. This time, the young demonstrators were calling for a larger budget for the State Technical University. According to the Ministry of the Interior, the demonstrators numbered no more than 500 and dispersed when Carabineros arrived.[21]

One deduces from such episodes and public reactions to them that young Chilean activists, their critics, and other observers and commentators understood that young peoples' inquietude on the streets and campuses of Greater Santiago and elsewhere in the country in 1968 was connected to a transnational upwelling, in addition to domestic issues.[22] By the end of the sixties, the general state of youth affairs generated increased attention among older folks and young people alike. Public discussion often became pointed. The conservative press, for instance, explained, "Young people today do not concern themselves with the opinions of others, nor does criticism bother them. . . . They give the impression that they vehemently seek, with near desperation, a premature maturity."[23] In the minds of many, counterculture joined other forms of youthful agency, including student protests, as a defining characteristic of a transnational youth question. Countercultural young people very rarely were afforded legitimacy, especially after the Piedra Roja music festival in October 1970. To further contextualize counterculture's coalescence and meaning, we must turn to conceptualizations and interpellations of the youth question as it arose and became a subject of much debate during the late 1960s and early 1970s.

Articulating the Question

In 1971, the author Esther Huneeus Salas de Claro, better known by her nom de plume, Marcela Paz, published yet another installment in her popular children's book series about a young Opie Taylor-like boy named Papelucho.

Mi hermano hippie (My Brother the Hippie), was her tenth in a string of twelve Papelucho books—many of which are read in Chilean primary and secondary schools today—which helped earn Paz the country's coveted National Literature Award in 1982.[24] The book follows Papelucho's investigation of the disappearance of his older brother, Javier, who earlier had returned home from vacationing with friends, sporting long hair and recognizably hippie apparel while also smelling like someone who had gone without bathing for too long. Papelucho, the narrator, describes the problematic homecoming: " 'I can't condone this!' father said, pulling at his own hair. 'A child of mine a hippie!' he exclaimed as he pounded his fist on the table. He had to suck on his fingers due to the pain from striking the table and to keep from swearing."[25] As Papelucho details, his mother faints at the sight of Javier's hippismo, their domestic servant, Domitila, was bowled over, and their father spends the evening punching furniture while uttering unflattering epithets about Javier's unexpected and strongly bemoaned countercultural turn. The fact that Javier had been a naval cadet only makes his transformation more stupefying and egregious in a palpably bourgeois household, with a commanding and intransigent father, an affectionate mother, and a nurturing maid who was a de facto member of the family. The eventful homecoming of Javier the hippie takes place on a Sunday. By Wednesday, the young man is nowhere to be found; it was as if Javier had "turned into smoke," Papelucho noted.[26]

As fears abate that his brother had been kidnapped, Papelucho comes to believe that Javier had instead run away from home, and he understands the reason for the hippie's departure: the reception Javier had received. After all, the gregarious and insightful Papelucho observes, "He hadn't done anything wrong. He had let his hair grow like I let my ears grow. His hair is his and my ears are mine. And when someone has been a cadet and obeying and obeying for such a long time, he has to get the urge to do whatever occurs to him."[27] Later, Papelucho finds a note left by Javier imploring his family to not search for him, which affords Papelucho some relief because it means Javier had not fallen victim to foul play. Still worried and energized by the challenge of the hunt, Papelucho searches for his hippie brother anyway, accompanied by his faithful dog, Nerón, and some friends. Papelucho soon discovers that scruffy-looking Javier had been arrested, though mistakenly, which also brings consolation to the young sleuth. Released shortly thereafter, Javier returns home and cleans himself up, shaving off his straggly beard and ostensibly reentering the family a different young man. Their father then shakes Javier's hand and pats his eldest son on the back; everything, it seems, was back to normal, almost eerily. "The famous reception of the hippie prodigal son seemed as if his disappearance had never taken place and all spoke about anything but what had happened," Papelucho explains. "Even the happiness brought on by his return wasn't noticeable and I started to feel sad for myself because I had searched for the hippie throughout the world."[28]

Far from a playful children's book, Paz's story is layered and complex, bringing to light shock, fear, and even denial in a society experiencing the heterodoxy of hippismo, counterculture in general, and the emergent and contextually specific youth question. Disgusted by his appearance, Javier's parents reject him, but Papelucho is more curious and understanding, which suggests a real generational gap existed between parents and children. But all were worried sick by Javier's disappearance, given the young man's apparently questionable capacity for making good decisions. Even Javier's father desperately wants his son to return home, Javier's hippismo notwithstanding. And when Javier does return, he is a changed young man, a better young man, allowing life to go on normally. Javier, the hippie who frightened his family, was redeemed—perhaps by his time in jail—just as all hippies were capable of redemption, or so Paz hints. But Paz also affirms that hippies were not necessarily criminals, regardless of dress and hairstyle, and that there existed a certain logic in counterculture and its rebelliousness, which Papelucho identifies when alluding to his brother's years of unquestioning obedience. All the while, Paz hints that Javier's angry and petulant father was too rough on his child, forcing Javier's flight from home instead of engaging in reasonable dialogue.

As *Mi hermano hippie* and what one might call the "Papelucho paradigm" suggest, many Chileans—and parents in particular—were not short on worry when it came to the doings and sensibilities of young people in the late 1960s and early 1970s. Aside from intrinsic concerns related to the banalities of everyday life, and beyond a prevailing nervousness rooted in unfolding (and notably historic) political, social, and economic circumstances and transformations, there existed a palpable disquietude in the public sphere and in government toward what appeared to be the extant restlessness, disinterestedness, and sociocultural heterodoxy of a good many Chileans in their teens and twenties. Indeed, as the presidential election of 1970 neared, a visit to any news kiosk in Santiago would afford the prospective reader a wide range of publications that included reports and commentaries about young people. Such views were mixed. Reports about the use of marijuana appeared near stories about young volunteers repairing shanties, while scathing indictments of sexual liberation and unkempt hippies, with photos included, shared newsprint with articles praising studious and pious youths.

Among the popular periodicals of the era, those produced for young readers regularly published articles on musical trends and other expressions of *farándula* (entertainment or showbiz). In this mediatic environment, a prominent and emblematic pop culture magazine, the largely apolitical *Ritmo de la Juventud* (Rhythm of Youth, or simply *Ritmo*, as it was known), delved into serious generational matters that, for our purposes, certainly fell under the rubric of the youth question. Mere weeks after Allende's inauguration, *Ritmo*'s María Yolanda González, a media fixture at the time, explored a complex question that rapidly was becoming quite relevant: "Does a generational war exist?" While the author opined that it did not, she nevertheless identified serious problems in intergenerational relations created by an abject failure to communicate. González pointed to the case of a fifteen-year-old girl who lived alone and was involved in the trafficking of marijuana. The young woman's life, González explained, would be much different—for the better—if she and her father merely conversed regularly. "The tragedy had presented itself," the journalist explained. "It's one in a long list. There was no friendship and perhaps not even a minimum amount of sincerity necessary for her and her parents to come down from their ideological and generational pedestals." The relational distance between Papelucho's brother, the hippie Javier, and his obstinate father brings to bear this very point. But hope was not forsaken, González affirmed. While conducting interviews in the capital's downtown, she came across an elderly gentleman and a young man sharing a bench and some conversation at the Plaza de Armas. When González inquired about the quiddity of intergenerational discord, the older man responded, "What's happening is that most every old person like myself, before getting to know a young person, already finds him ridiculous because he has long hair, lazy because he likes to listen to music that's all the rage, and dirty because he wears whatever he feels like wearing. It seems to me that everyone should do what they like." González concluded, "When two people decide to come down from their pedestals, it is much easier to talk."[29]

González took up a similar subject nearly a year later, again in the pages of *Ritmo*. Her interviews at high schools and with university students in the Santiago metroplex exposed a generational divide that largely pertained to conceptions of freedom and being "real." Jaime Bolados, eighteen, a student at the affluent Liceo José Victorino Lastarria in Providencia, assured the reporter, "[Young] people today are more genuine because they have more liberty, because they dare to disagree with their parents; in general, they say what they feel without being as calculating as before." A student at the University of Chile's School of Fine Arts, María Luisa López, twenty, echoed the sentiment: "Now there is more liberty and that gives you more of a chance to become your own person, to become authentic." But such liberty, according to María Oróstica, the principal of Santiago's Liceo No. 1 de Niñas (Girls High School No. 1), entailed "an impulsiveness that hinders their comprehension of the values of previous generations." Oróstica went on to declare that young people demonstrated "a rush to judge other points of view" and that most youth-related problems could be addressed through "a continual dialogue" between parents and their children.[30] The concerns expressed in González's article about intergenerational communication and what amounts to the perception of a cognitive gap between parents and children were common in Chilean society during the late 1960s and early 1970s. *Ritmo* was a mainstream *farándula* magazine at heart, and its editors and reporters quite obviously found these and other aspects of the youth question important enough, journalistically and in terms of marketability, to merit the space allotted to them. If one also considers Paz's book on Papelucho's hippie brother, it becomes evident that young people, in one form or another, were just as aware of the "youth question" as were adults—a supposition supported by academicians, as we shall see. Obviously, young people were divided regarding the promise or perniciousness of the youth question. So, too, were older Chileans, who, while largely united in their rejection of counterculture, found some instances of young people's agency acceptable, depending on circumstance, ideology, and scope. The far Right, for instance, found the belligerence of the FNPL perfectly reasonable, while Marxists embraced Jota activism, which, at times, was undeniably petulant.

Although right-wing Chileans had numerous periodicals on their side, including the often-peevish *Tribuna*, no rightist publication was as powerful and conspicuous as *El Mercurio*, the giant daily newspaper published in Santiago by the Edwards clan. Serving the interests of the conservative PN, it pointed to moral problems—primarily those related to the nuclear family—when discussing the youth question. In a telling 1970 editorial, the newspaper argued that the notion that mothers could leave their homes and enter the labor force was an utter blunder, with grave generational consequences for children and youths. "The weakening of paternal authority [is] a phenomenon seen in all social strata," it claimed. The rupture of the family unit—upon the departure of the woman to work outside the home—

left youths with prolonged periods of idleness, the writer continued. Free and unsupervised time, therefore, drove youths to fill hours (and their bodies) with such things as marijuana.[31] Another *El Mercurio* intervention argued that bored and restless youths found respite in manifestations of cultural decadence—like Andy Warhol and the "underground" film culture in the United States—unless adults intervened to stimulate and develop the capacity of youngsters to relate with the outside world.[32]

The Catholic Church, which set a moral tone in civil society and, to a degree, was in league with rightist political groups and *El Mercurio,* also addressed the restlessness of young people. During the Frei administration, for instance, Santiago's Archbishop, Cardinal Raúl Silva Henríquez, recognized that young people in the sixties were living in a peculiar era that was fertile ground for "errors" and "the danger of excessiveness." As the cardinal observed, "One must realize that we are living in a very special time during which the rhythms of evolution and change are much more rapid and intense than those of any previous era. Immutable values remain and, in most cases, are even clearer; but no longer are artificial superstructures and anachronisms accepted." Silva then put responsibility on the shoulders of the older generation to orient youths toward a positive and Christian mentality. He stated, "To adults, then, I say: The new generations urgently need a greater commitment from you" and that "solidarity between generations was a pressing need." Every generation, Silva added, "restructures the patria and the Church; no single generation creates them from nothing."[33] This was a most pertinent statement in the age of Vatican II.

The Church had some firsthand experience with generational rumblings. In August 1968, a leftist revolutionary Catholic group called Young Church (Iglesia Joven, IJ) occupied the Metropolitan Cathedral in Santiago for most of one day. The ragtag IJ consisted of relatively young clergy from working-class neighborhoods and well-placed laypeople who protested the Church's lack of social action, arguing that it was dragging its heels instead of promoting social revolution in a changeful era.[34] Telling, too, is that IJ also protested the Church's stance against contraception, which more progressive elements of the Chilean clergy had questioned as early as 1964 in light of the country's soaring abortion rate.[35] In other words, IJ, with strong undercurrents of liberation theology, demanded that the Church keep up with changing social, cultural, and political circumstances in Latin America and elsewhere. The cathedral's occupiers sang songs, held Mass, and identified revolutionary figures, including Che Guevara and the dead Colombian guerilla-priest Camilo Torres, from which they drew inspiration.

One spokesperson announced, "We are hand-in-hand with our Marxist brothers, on the barricades of the people against capitalism, following the example of Camilo Torres. We are members of the Young Church."[36] The Vatican quickly and forcefully condemned as "arrogant and profane" the more than two hundred activists who occupied the cathedral.[37] Silva also blasted the radical young clerics and their lay associates: "They do not represent, in any way, what the Church in Santiago thinks. This small group, which seeks radical and sudden change, should know that their methods shall not be successful."[38] Indeed, IJ did not triumph over the Church's conservative leadership in Chile or at the Vatican, but it continued to champion, in a minor yet vocal way, revolutionary ideas during the Allende years, proclaiming, among other things, "The duty of every Christian is to be a revolutionary!"[39]

After his initial lambasting of IJ, Silva retreated, opting for a more cordial relationship with the cathedral's occupiers. Indeed, he visited the occupied cathedral and later explained that IJ's demands were not to be rejected outright; rather, the group's gripes were to be the subject of ongoing discussions within the Church. What is more, Silva became much more amenable to "revolution" after Allende's victory in 1970, pledging his support for the new government and claiming, "The basic reforms contained in the program of Popular Unity are supported by the Chilean Church. We look upon this with intense sympathy."[40] Silva and other Catholic leaders pledged allegiance to the country's long-standing democracy and embraced the idea of social reform in the name of Christian beneficence. It is clear, then, that IJ not only exemplified a more progressive element of the Chilean Church but also anticipated the Church's openness toward UP's road to socialism.[41]

Far less radical than IJ, but likewise Catholic, were the Christian Democrats, and Frei's Ministry of Education had much to say in the matter of young people and the problems associated with them. Ministerial publications made it quite clear that young people at the dawning of the Age of Aquarius experienced things and faced challenges unlike those native to previous generations. Máximo Pacheco, minister of education under Frei, was an outspoken critic of "restless" young people and their various forms of rebelliousness. As Pacheco explained in a March 1969 speech to open the school year, "A tremor among young people is being felt across the globe, provoking, at times, profound changes in the lives of nations. Speech, ways of dressing, accessories, hair styles, groups, ideas, attitudes, tastes, etc., frequently distinguish certain sectors of young people who desire to show their radical unconformity vis-à-vis anything they deem unacceptable." He blamed rapid modernization, the independence afforded to youths within the family, the "education" young people received on the streets and through the media, and "social, political, and economic deficiencies." He also lashed out against violence professed by "unscrupulous elements" that "mix with the younger population, deforming and orienting it toward negative slogans that have nothing to do with youthful idealism." Pacheco then praised the Frei government for devoting time and energy to combating youth-related "restlessness" and the presence of "violent elements," pointing to such statistics as a 90 percent increase in public university funding and an 81 percent spike in public-university enrollment since 1964. Pacheco proclaimed, "Without vacillation I can assure you that never in Chilean history has there been such an effort to tend to the needs of the country's youth."[42]

Six months later, Pacheco received a lengthy report produced by three teachers who were considerably more specific when bemoaning unfortunate, and sometimes violent, tendencies among the country's youth. To document signs of troubled times, the teachers pointed to, among other things, fifty-four strikes among university students during the first six months of 1969 alone, the emergence of young *guerrilleros*, and unrest at the University of Concepción—the latter two circumstances presumably related to the MIR. "Recently, the theme of violence among youths has constituted the source of passionate polemics in different circles in our society," they wrote. It had become the subject of "talks, forums, conferences, and writings; diverse intellectuals, sociologists, educators, and politicians have analyzed it extensively." But while adults appealed to young people to demonstrate "greater maturity, reflection, and realism," youths nevertheless maintained the notion that "adults should practice what they preach," the teachers explained. The result was a stalemate, leading to the use of policing powers "to control phenomena that cannot be controlled because they are still not understood." The study, titled "La juventud y la violencia" ("Youth and Violence"), avows that youths of the late sixties were experiencing what amounted to a collective form of psychosocial disruption resulting from accelerated change in all aspects of life, which produced alienation, angst, and rebelliousness. "Youths, with a capacity to respond to the situation they face and as conduits of social modernization projects, are struck by reality with greater force and consequence than any adult. They perceive the existence of coercion that comes from within and from outside their society, and they react in ways adults consider to be violent," the teachers argued. Harboring contempt for the "system," or simply isolating themselves from it, constituted a coping mechanism and the consequence of "the notable potentiality of insecurity and anguish that young people may accumulate." Whereas in traditional agrarian society, "young people were completely beholden to adults, sometimes parents, other times religious leaders and so forth," modern urban society sees youths gain their "liberty at a much younger age and, therefore, are more vulnerable to whatever influences there may be." Thus, many young people gravitate toward "the severe criticism of existing ideological formations as well as the search for a new youth culture that is distinct." In line with Frei's "Revolution in Liberty"—a reformist capitalism, essentially—the report suggests that Pacheco adopt two (vague) measures to lessen social and generational conflict: installing a new system of social relations that would truly put power in the hands of the majority and be committed to economic development (in line with the PDC's communitarianism) and making certain that young people would have a place in that system that transcended "mere protest and agitation." Ideally, a continual and broad "dialogue of social participation" would ensue. The report concludes, "To the strong gestures of young people we must respond with the strength of responsibility and with the solidity of commitment, with the steadfast-ness of a great, valuable, and serious task."[43]

Adding to this unfolding conversation among educators, Juan Gómez Millas, a renowned pedagogue, social and cultural reformer, past rector of the University of Chile, and former Minister of Education for Frei and President Carlos Ibáñez del Campo, reflected on what he called the "youth problem" during the final months of the Frei administration. In an article focusing on university-age youths that appeared in the Minis-try of Education's *Revista de Educación*, Gómez pinpointed a number of failings in Chilean society and culture, including the bureaucratization and "depersonalization" of education, the weakening of familial and social cohesiveness, the proliferation of television and the massification of com-munication, and the low levels of motivation and poor study habits among university students who, in general, felt like "conscripts." One obvious sign of "depersonalization," Gómez explained, was the fact that high schools and universities—bent on economic modernization, one infers—were mech-anistically producing "potential executives and managers" rather than providing learning environments designed for the "personal growth" of young people. More and more students, especially in the universities, were, in effect, tuning out; they were becoming jaded, distant, and rebel-lious.[44] Complicating matters further, Gómez wrote elsewhere, were signs of "youth violence and other forms of aggressive expression" that were becoming evident in secondary and primary schools, not merely at universities where rebelliousness and frustration were most conspicuous.[45]

PDC figures outside the field of education also addressed the youth question. One such official was Dr. Patricio Rojas Saavedra, Minister of the Interior (in charge of policing and domestic security, among other things). Rojas, who later became Minister of Defense for President Patricio Aylwin, spoke to the Lion's Club in the southern city of Valdivia in April 1970 about what he called "youth and commitment" and "generational harmony." Published by Frei's Ministry of Education, the speech was notably positive in many respects, with the main theme being that although a "breach" existed between generations, the possibility of intergenerational concurrence in the country remained. In other words, the youth question had a solution. With praise for the work of his friend, Juan Gómez Millas, in matters of youth and education, Rojas reflected on differences between a relatively passive 1950s and exploding youthful rebelliousness around the globe during the 1960s. While the university reforms of the latter 1960s addressed some concerns voiced by the younger generation at the time, the "youth crisis," as Rojas puts it, nevertheless intensified due to rapid modernization and the "wearing out of the many different systems and ways of life." Thus, the 1960s were a conceptual "crossroads in human history similar to (or even more effectual than) the spread of the Hellenistic spirit in ancient times, the diffusion of Christianity, and the Renaissance." And although Chilean youths experienced different social, political, economic, and cultural realities than rebellious and anxious young people in the developed world, Rojas affirmed, "there exist common roots of youth rebellion that are apparent all over the earth." Such roots, he explained, included young people's profound dissatisfaction with their parents' inability to end war and poverty. He then called on educators, in particular, to become "moral and intellectual leaders" for youths to see, hear, and emulate, rather than merely serving as conduits of scientific and other forms of knowledge. Rojas, moreover, implored the older generation, working in conjunction with dedicated young people, to found a new society—one that values the individual—and for every citizen to set aside ego and instead "awaken the grand sentiments of effort and sacrifice" to produce "the minimum conditions of a dignified life."[46]

The call for a more dignified life was not unique to Frei's Christian Democrats. In a 1972 interview with the Jota's magazine, *Ramona*, Allende warned of problems affecting youth in the modern world, explaining to the publication's young readers, "You know and all of Chile knows the conditions facing youths that have been created by the capitalist system, not only here but in many countries. It seems to me that, in light of their fear of young people, [capitalists] have steered youths toward the consumption of drugs, they don't provide young people with educations or work, and they do not open any doors to the future." The Socialist emphasized that his government was busily addressing the economic, social, and cultural needs of children and young adults. He then told the *Ramona* correspondent, "If copper is Chile's salary and the working class decisively Chile's first and foremost strength, young people are one of the engines of our advancement. We are making this revolution while thinking of the fatherland's future, and its future indubitably is the youth of today. Young people are more than witnesses to this historical moment and are not merely waiting statically for the coming of a new society. Instead, they are participating in the building of a new Chile."[47]

The pro-Allende news magazine *Onda*, produced by the state-owned Quimantú publishing house, cast a bit of a shadow on the government's intent to control and harness youthful energy. In 1971, youths with seemingly progressive-revolutionary dispositions expressed frustration and disillusion vis-à-vis the Allende government's plans and programs, especially those orchestrated by the Presidential Youth Secretariat (Secretaría Juvenil de la Presidencia), a short-lived arm of the executive branch devoted to youth-related matters. Founded by presidential special decree soon after Allende took office, the Secretariat essentially was an extension of the Popular Unity Youth Command (Comando Juvenil Unidad Popular), a medley of pro-Allende youth groups from the coalition's parties and union support. One of the six Allende-appointed directors of the Secretariat, Francisco Díaz, explained the unit's role as being "about the total incorporation of young people in the building of a new society."[48] Likewise, Allende described the Secretariat as a mechanism for the insertion of young people into initiatives identified by his government—including home construction, reforestation projects, and literacy campaigns—for the betterment of the laboring masses.[49] Regardless of this revolutionary call to action, a sixteen-year-old interviewee named Alberto complained, "I don't think there is a politics [on the part of the state] directed toward young people." Indeed, Alberto essentially signaled that the UP coalition's plans and goals for youths were not entirely about young people—members of a distinct social category with both a subjectivity and identity; instead, those plans and goals seemingly were for the benefit of Allende's government and the working class. Indeed, the *Onda* contributor went on to deride young people for succumbing to the habit of waiting for someone—someone older—to organize them, suggesting that good-hearted and properly ideological youths could and should help build the road to socialism without being carefully controlled (or "incorporated," to use Díaz's term) by a coalition spearheaded by agents of the older generation.[50]

As the UP government's attention to the youth question indicates, Marxists seemingly viewed the totality of youth-related problems as an epiphenomenon—the expression of more deeply rooted problems inherent in capitalist development. In the words of one columnist in the Communist newspaper *El Siglo* in October 1970 (ten days after Piedra Roja), while there was no doubt that youths from all social classes were threatened by a generational maelstrom with structural antecedents, one class in particular was the begetter of its most grave manifestations:

> For that past few years, a sector of our youth has become accustomed to a harmful way of life that clashes with the lively impulses of our young people. As for the more modest classes, the causes are rooted in the incongruence and contradictions of the political, economic, and social system under which we live as well as the examples provided by the youths of North America and Europe who suffer from the same ill. . . . The destiny of our country, social peace, the happiness of families, and the wellbeing and progress of the patria will largely depend on young people.[51]

The contributor then explained, "The political, economic, and social system under which we live is going through a heightened crisis of values. . . . In this crisis of values we see the germination of the seeds of dissatisfaction among our young people that not only manifests itself against the deficiencies of our educational system, which falls behind in terms of social, scientific, and technological advancement, but also against their parents and teachers whom they accuse of not understanding the needs and necessities of young people."[52]

As political actors found much to say about the youth question, a number of academicians and other figures were hard at work on the issue in the sixties and seventies. Studies gauged young people's opinions on an array of subjects pertinent to their lives and the life of the nation, in addition to identifying what they were or were not doing, politically, socially, and culturally. The studies also addressed issues of identity and subjectivity and how youths perceived their peers and adults. Although far from panoptic and not without some drawbacks, such inquiries provide the historian some empirical information regarding pressing issues that were associated with the era's youth question.

Studying the Question

Belgian sociologist Armand Mattelart and his French sociologist partner, Michèle Mattelart, conducted a survey of youths in 1968 as part of a long-sustained research agenda on Chilean social relations.[53] The resulting *Juventud chilena: Rebeldía y conformismo*, which appeared in 1970, peers across class lines and into many issues, questioning and compiling responses from four hundred young people, equally divided between males and females and all between fourteen and twenty-four years old. They represented four "social stratifications," as the authors identified them, in equal numbers: university students (enrolled at either the Pontifical Catholic University or University of Chile), white-collar workers (also called *empleados*), blue-collar workers, and rural laborers (campesinos and campesinas). All were residents of Greater Santiago except for the rural respondents.[54] Among many other areas, the investigators probed matters of organizational involvement and perceptions of young people's conduct. Interested in the sorts of activities in which youths were engaged, the Mattelarts prompted respondents to rank, from most to least important, their organizational commitments, including political ones. A minority of respondents placed their participation in a "political organization"—such as the Jota, the JS, MIR, JDC, and so forth—at the top of their lists. Other options included participation in syndicates, student federations, religious associations, and sports clubs. Twenty-four percent of university-enrolled young men and a mere 6 percent of women ranked activity in a political organization at the top of their lists. Among white-collar males, 26 percent placed political activity first, while 6 percent of white-collar young women did the same. Perhaps most surprising is that only 4 percent of campesinos and not a single campesina ranked membership in a political group as number one, at a time when limited agrarian reform was underway as part of Frei's "Revolution in Liberty" and rural unionization was spreading (among peasant men, mostly). Also, fewer blue-collar youths than one might expect—10 percent of men and 6 percent of women—prioritized such membership.[55] Of course, membership in a party-affiliated group is not necessarily a leading indicator of political participation, especially when other organizations, such as unions and student federations, were rather active in politics. What is more, one can be a member of a political organization and do little or nothing for it.

Another theme of interest to the Mattelarts and others was the socio-cultural phenomenon known as *colerismo*. In common use in public debate by the early sixties, "colerismo" entailed aping everything from clothing trends to modes of rebelliousness that originated abroad, mixed with a certain degree of slothfulness and detachment.[56] As one young female university student explained, "*Coléricos* are young people who follow the styles, go-go dance, etc., and the majority of young people do it." Other respondents argued that colerismo was confined to a minority of youths who had the time and money to practice it. One white-collar young man put it this way: "There are young people who don't have the time to dedicate themselves to it [colerismo]; they study and they work, and colerismo becomes something secondary and they ignore it in their daily lives." A male university student hit a similar but more class-conscious note (with a revolutionary tone) when he declared, "[The coléricos] are a small group from the higher class that aren't representative of all Chilean young people." Another university student, a young woman, concurred, noting that colerismo "affected only the higher class" and that "all young people don't have the money to spend on clothing styles and diversion."[57]

In 1966, conservative commentator Antonio de Pérdigo published a book that described coléricos (the vectors of colerismo) as "young people who lack a comprehensive education [in the "cultured" sense], they are without ideals, disoriented, strangers in society and to the norms that prevail in it, instinctive, rebellious, and violent with a wrath that overflows from a kind of primitive brutality." Colerismo demonstrates "the attitude of sustained rebelliousness, inhibition in the face of moral and social norms, a thirst to live but live without control and against control, and an indifferent pose regarding their own offenses and misdeeds." To Pérdigo, the United States was colerismo's contemporary epicenter, followed closely by Britain and France; but far from being a novel trend, colerismo was a condition detectable in the distant past in addition to Pérdigo's present, and traces could be identified in all modern societies, socialist ones included. Young men and women showed their colerismo by running away from home and committing criminal acts, from the egregious to the relatively innocuous, he adds, noting that any solution must go beyond simple policing to get at the problem's cultural roots. The media and other cultural conduits should therefore suppress images and information, especially that coming from abroad, which serve to incite young people to engage in colerismo, in one form or another. Pérdigo calls on strict government supervision of cultural "traffickers" who, through (unidentified) novels, magazines, radio and television programs, and films sow nothing but the seeds of immorality and corrupt otherwise "innocent" young people. He then concludes that religion provides the most effective elixir, and the aggressive expansion of Catholic schooling and other means of teaching and instilling the Church's moral teachings are the only adequately conceived solutions to colerismo.[58]

Complementing the work of the Mattelarts, sociologist Darío Menanteau-Horta studied what urban youths were thinking immediately before and during UP's road to socialism. For a paper presented in 1973 to Chile's pre-coup Ministry of Education, Menanteau-Horta collected data from surveys in 1969 and 1972. Of the 2,460 respondents in the 1969 sample (surveyed just as they were finishing secondary education), 460 were randomly selected for the 1972 inquiry. In regard to familial affairs, Menanteau-Horta found significant change between the 1969 and 1972 inquiries in matters of parent-child relations. For instance, in 1969, 43.9 percent of respondents agreed that "children should always follow the advice of their parents," while only 24.2 percent agreed in 1972. In addition, 49.3 percent responded in the positive in 1969 when asked if it is better to live near their families even if it meant sacrificing good opportunities elsewhere. The 1972 survey registered 13.7 percent in agreement.[59] Notwithstanding its relevance, the study has some pitfalls. Changes of opinion among youths over a three-year span do not necessarily indicate a generational shift in outlook, nor do they simply reflect the process of maturation. Nor do they allow for any conclusion as to the impact of contextual variance between 1969, near the end of the Frei administration, and 1972, at the height of UP's road to socialism. Moreover, the report does not provide a breakdown by gender or geography, although it is inferred that the samplings were gender-balanced and took place in Greater Santiago. A combination of many factors may very well be at play, and precisely gauging the impact of any or all of them is impossible. Yet, broadly speaking, the surveys indicate that notable change was afoot in the lives of young respondents, just as it was among the rest of their generation and across their society.

Far less empirical, but nevertheless "academic" in its treatment of the youth question, is Eugenio Velasco Letelier's *Algunas reflexiones sobre la juventud actual* (1971), based on a speech he delivered upon his induction into the Academy of Social, Political, and Moral Sciences at the University of Chile. Velasco was a professor of law, one of the foremost legal minds of late twentieth-century Chile, dean of the faculty of Legal and Social Sciences, member of UP's Radical Party, and a former ambassador to Tunisia and Algeria. Having devoted much of his professional life to teaching university students, he was motivated to share observations of what he called "the attitude, conduct, and proceedings that young people have adopted in the past few years and have worsened most recently."[60] Firmly situating Chile among other countries experiencing the rebelliousness of youths, including France, the United States, Japan, Indonesia, Czechoslovakia, and Argentina, Velasco argued that the younger generation was unlike any generation before it; it emerged amid rapid modernization, the likes of which had never before been seen. As a result, the differences between the young and older generations were greater, deeper, and more obvious than those inherent in any process of generational turnover in the past. And generational conflict—the innate struggles of generational turnover—was the "motor of history" and "pushes progress along," he explained, mirroring the generationalism of José Ortega y Gasset and Karl Mannheim.[61] Velasco went on to assert, "There exists a clear and consequential attitude of contempt—and even scorn—toward adults and mature persons. All of the negative things in humanity's inventory are considered the faults of the preceding generation." Yet, youths did not promote specific ideas to rectify the mistakes of the past. Instead, he argued, "There is a cloudiness in their ideas and, above all, in their goals. Youths look for a 'new world' or the 'new university' but don't explain what those are, what their characteristics would be, and are even less apt to be precise about how and by what means we could arrive at their concretion." And regardless of any political proclivities youths may entertain, all seem to share that profoundly generational sensibility—one rife with rebellion and protest.[62]

Chileans were well aware of the transnational youth question and its particular, local manifestations during the late 1960s and early 1970s, and student movements at home and abroad constituted a mode of collectivity and agency that directed considerable attention to the concerns and wishes of a younger generation coming of age. By and large, student activism was policy-driven and fundamentally political, which made it laudable or lamentable, depending on the onlooker's ideological disposition. When young Chileans channeled their agency through organized politics, the looser fabrics of movements, or more heterodox ways of being in the world, they sparked and participated in meaningful public discussions on the nature of "youth" and "generation" in a developing society seeing profound change. Many observers, especially those with political bones to pick, conveyed sentiments ranging from dismay to ire when describing the youth question. Was, then, Chile's youth question simply a discursive and rhetorical straw man? I submit that the youth question was "real" even if only perceived as such. However, it was real in a more tangible sense, as evidenced by student protests or hippies getting stoned at a momentous rock festival or bivouacking in a downtown Santiago park. In short, the youth question was a blend of perception and agency.

The youth question's protagonists and observers made reference to outlooks and practices that one may consider countercultural. I say "may" because a telling characteristic of counterculture was that its features were in flux; they were as malleable as they were contingent, especially in the case of hippismo. Moreover, there existed no impenetrable divide between countercultural and more mainstream ways of being or appearing; a well-coiffed, politically committed, and otherwise straight-laced young person could easily and privately sneak a joint, enjoy a premarital dalliance, or love the Rolling Stones. Notwithstanding counterculture's amorphousness, a criollo variant coalesced at the end of the 1960s, generating responses on the part of Chileans of different ideologies and ages. Put succinctly, numerous young "malcontents" were behaving badly, and when various mainstream actors pondered, criticized, and endeavored to account for such disorderliness, they revealed as much or more about themselves than about hippies, Siloists, or any other youths living life differently. In the context of the sixties and seventies, and if we are to take young people's social and cultural heterodoxy seriously, we must look to "sex, drugs, and rock 'n' roll"—an idiom that encompasses a great deal more than what its use in common parlance suggests. These important and contested spheres of sociability throw light on the youth question and provide additional footings for our examination of criollo counterculture.

A Lot of Searching for the Magical

Sex, Drugs, and Rock ('n' Roll)

· ·

In September 1968, the film *New Love* (also known as *La revolución de las flores* or *The Revolution of Flowers*) marked the first cinematic rendering of a nascent criollo counterculture. Directed by Álvaro Covacevich, it depicts disaffected and defiant countercultural teens engaging in "liberating" activities, including sexual encounters (portrayed with a good measure of on-screen nudity), smoking marijuana, and absorbing the rhythms and lyrics of rock music. So unfiltered was Covacevich's portrait of an emergent counterculture that government censors barred young people under age twenty-one from seeing it, leaving many in the cast unable to publicly witness the final product of their creative work.[1] Later, after the 1973 coup, the military regime banned *New Love* for its supposed depravity and exiled Covacevich for having *allendista* leanings, and the film went without another public screening until the return of democracy in 1990.[2] *New Love* most certainly has a lot of sex, drugs, and rock 'n' roll going on, but not as affectations, provocations, or gratuitous plot devices. Instead, sex, drugs, and rock music are meaningful in the lives of characters who know love—a "new" and genuine love, with genuine intentions, experienced by and among young people freed from (or at least mutinying against) the sociocultural repressiveness and political norms toward which most Chileans, and especially older ones, are deferential.[3]

New Love emphasizes generational, sociocultural, and emotional disconnects between countercultural young adults and their elders. As representatives of the older generation, government officials appear particularly averse to the protagonists' deeds, and not merely those involving sex, drugs, and rock 'n' roll. For instance, a sequence of scenes involves countercultural youths at the beach-resort city of Viña del Mar painting their bicycles white to nullify difference; a bicycle becomes just like any other bicycle and for all to share, as their former owners put into action communalist and collectivist aspirations. The movement grows and more items get white paint, alarming the generation in power and provoking a government crackdown.[4] Needless to say, mainstream Chileans—in the film or otherwise—who were also interested in collectivism (of the Marxist sort, especially) found no inspiration in rebellious, bourgeois adolescents who donned loud shirts, wore body paint, and whitewashed their bicycles to wage a "revolution of flowers." In a prerelease interview, a writer for the Communist *El Siglo* asked Covacevich, "Isn't *New Love* about expressing a form of escapism in the face of real problems and their solutions?" The director responded, "No, it's a new form of revolution. . . . It's a critical attitude. Youths have discovered a new strength—that of love—to disarm you, the guerrillas."[5]

As Covacevich's interview foreshadowed, *New Love*'s audiences noticed the director's palpable sympathy for Chile's embryonic counterculture. Soon after the film's release, *El Siglo* called Covacevich's settings and young characters "pretentious and ill-fated," claiming that *New Love* represented "everything the national cinema should not be." Only eighteen months earlier, *El Siglo* had concluded differently about Covacevich's art-house documentary, *Morir un poco* (To Die a Little), which counterposes the pastimes and indulgences of the financially secure with images of the poor and disenfranchised to drive home the country's glaring socioeconomic inequities. That film received accolades in the Marxist press (and from then-Senator Salvador Allende) for its interrogation of socioeconomic conditions that would bring about social revolution.[6] Undaunted by attacks on *New Love*, Covacevich addressed his critics—especially those of the Left—in a defiant tone in the weeks following the film's release. "Youths put forth a formula against which neither force nor violence can fight: love, silence, and doubt. That is enough to destroy the system and to give young people the most powerful and unbeatable of weapons in their struggle," Covacevich declared. "That attitude is the only truly revolutionary one. [It is] neither capitalism nor communism, which are traditional positions, but rather a sincere search for essential human values, for love in its purest and most primitive form."[7]

In Covacevich's *New Love*, in the lives of young Chileans, and in the public imagination, criollo counterculture was intimately entwined with matters of "sex, drugs, and rock 'n' roll." Yet, while in popular culture "sex, drugs, and rock 'n' roll"—an expression absent from Chile or anywhere else until Englishman Ian Dury's 1977 song "Sex and Drugs and Rock 'n' Roll"—became closely tied to the "Global Sixties" ex post facto, a young person who identified herself or himself as a hippie or, in some fashion, as countercultural, could do so while not having practiced free love. Another could stake claims to counterculture without smoking marijuana or limiting his or her musical tastes to the Rolling Stones, Cream, et al. In short, there was no "typical" countercultural youth other than he or she who existed in the collective imagination, but the perspectives and doings of a culturally heterodox young person often shared a family or community resemblance with those of other youths in and outside their country. This chapter surveys new values and practices that emerged in relation to sexuality, drug use, and music in the sixties and early seventies to provide additional thematic and analytical footings for our examination of criollo counterculture and of the broader field of youth culture. As one mainstream women's magazine declared in 1970, "The new generations have placed in doubt the many values that were unquestioned for centuries."[8] Sex, drugs, and rock 'n' roll presented a range of sensations for the body and mind with meanings that were contingent and consequential—not to mention vigorously contested.

Engendering Liberation

When reminiscing about her experiences as a countercultural teenager in the early 1970s, María Ester Lezaeta, with a smile, noted, "There was a lot of searching in Chile—a lot of searching for the magical."[9] To many young people, sexual relations potentially offered such enchantment and otherworldliness. On the eve of and during the UP years, broaching the issue of sexuality and, more specifically, the sexual emancipation of youths, meant fostering or stepping into conversations about women and gender, with considerable debate involving virginity, the family, femininity, and masculinity.[10] Generally speaking, and from a transnational perspective, "women's liberation" and "sexual liberation" practically became synonymous in the 1960s for two basic reasons. First, women—and feminists in particular—deemed and pursued the subjects as interrelated phenomena. Secondly, it was apparent that heterosexual men already enjoyed a "liberated" sexuality, in relative terms, so men rarely figured into "sexual liberation" except as actors either condemning or embracing women's sexual emancipation. In light of the women's liberation–sexual liberation link, it serves to briefly delve into conceptualizations of the former before more closely examining the latter. A broad front of sociopolitical actors defended conventional understandings of propriety and family values in the face of alternative mores and cultural attitudes. The expressed obligation to mitigate promiscuity was among the priorities underpinning mainstream discourses on sexuality and sexual liberation. As historians Margaret Power and Jadwiga Pieper-Mooney have shown, Catholic canon provided clarity for such matters to the pious, and centrist Christian Democrats and the Right reinforced family values through such mechanisms as Mothers' Centers (*Centros de Madres*), which offered women vocational training to strengthen the family household's economic security while also remaining *dueñas de casa* (housewives).[11] The Left exhibited a notable degree of cultural conservatism, but intramural dynamics involving generation and gender led to negotiated outcomes affecting how its family values, including sexual mores, played out before the 1973 coup.

In early 1969, Malú Sierra, writing in the *Cosmopolitan*-like magazine *Paula*, declared that Chilean women were experiencing a "great emancipation" with wide-ranging legal, social, and cultural implications. "It has always been said that the Chilean woman is one of the most emancipated on the continent," she began. That was the good news. The bad news was that while single women enjoyed such emancipation, married women were—by law—deemed "relatively incapable" and thus subject to their husbands' wishes.[12] (Per the Civil Code of 1855, a married woman's standing was comparable to that of a minor aged twelve to twenty-one or to someone found mentally incapable of managing his or her personal affairs.[13]) Sierra added, "Even though [men] also speak of equality [for women], the majority of Chileans maintain a certain mental feudalism."[14] Published by the conservative and market-savvy Edwards publishing clan (of *El Mercurio* fame) for a mainstream, middle-class readership, *Paula* offered its audience information, commentary, and readers' forums focused on women's issues—with perspectives many would consider "liberating"—during the late sixties and early seventies.[15]

Any perusal of the era's partisan media finds opinions of women's liberation that were sharp and indelibly grounded in normative conceptions of femininity. On the far Right and never timid in its criticism of revolutions of all sorts, the newspaper *Tribuna* declared in 1971, "Sex appeal and femininity, the two mysteries that define a woman, are ways of being in addition to being a way of living." It noted that women were undergoing "radical change" brought on by a popular culture (film and television) that gave false impressions about proper femininity. The newspaper pointed to the films of Roger Vadim, the director of *And God Created Woman*, a sexualized and erotic film starring Brigitte Bardot as the sexually charged Juliette, an eighteen-year-old orphan involved in a love triangle. Hollywood's female "stereotype," as *Tribuna* put it, is "commercialized just like any other consumer product." It must be "countered with the real, everyday image of femininity assumed by the woman as a quality that is defined by her essence, by her human destiny." With sleight of rhetoric, *Tribuna* concludes by quoting French feminist and philosopher Simone de Beauvoir: "Let the women be just women and everything will come as a result, without anyone having to give them anything."[16] The newspaper obviously hijacked Beauvoir's statement to defend a traditional and static femininity: the proper Chilean woman isolated from the influence of "anyone," including advocates for women's liberation (foreign ones, presumably).[17]

On the opposite side of the political spectrum, Allende and UP made it a point to include women as part of the revolutionary front—in particular and some conventional ways. UP's directorate understood that women's issues would be addressed and ameliorated through a specific form of revolutionary change. Upon becoming UP's presidential candidate in the winter of 1970, Allende declared to many thousands of women in Santiago's Bulnes Plaza, "The woman comprehends that she is exploited more than a man under this system, the capitalist regimen, and for that reason her presence has the value of a profound conviction that transcends emotion." He added, "I am certain that the woman . . . will be with us to defend Chile's victory [over UP's foes], which shall be the victory of your children, the victory of the Chilean woman."[18] Leftist women who attended the event, including Jota leader Gladys Marín, embraced Allende's speech, as did the *allendista* press.[19] In a 1972 address, moreover, Allende proclaimed, "When I say 'woman,' I always think of the woman-mother. . . . When I talk of the woman, I refer to her in her function in the nuclear family. . . . [The] child is the extension of the woman who, in essence, is born to be a mother."[20] Meanwhile, Marxist women hoped—if not expected—that enormous gains would be realized by the revolutionary government's war on bourgeois patriarchy. In the pro-UP news magazine *Mayoría*, journalist Marcela Otero declared in 1971, "The Chilean woman now has the grand opportunity to be visible in the country's political, economic, and social life. With the Popular Government's triumph, her creative capacity now has the best possibility of development." She then adds, "In reality, the Chilean woman is looking for her own expressiveness and the equilibrium that should exist between her role as *dueña de casa* and the role she should play for the broader community." Later, Otero embraces the idea of a "Ministry of the Family"—suggested in UP's platform—to build "new structures that would permit a woman to live life to the fullest."[21] By distinguishing the revolutionary state as the solution to women's problems, Otero passes over feminism, the international women's movement, and Chilean women's groups as agents of change. Also of note, Otero does not conceptualize "womanhood" as something separable from the home—either symbolically or practically.

Regardless of what a woman might or might not do for the "community," she remains a *dueña de casa*, which necessarily connotes being married and rearing children.

What Allende and Otero conveyed, while part of UP's "official" discourse, did not reflect convictions about womanhood and liberation shared by all on the Left. The Communist feminist Virginia Vidal, for instance, challenged the expectations pushed onto women by mainstream actors, including fellow Marxists in and outside her own party. As Heidi Tinsman notes, the PCCh and UP leaderships marginalized Vidal, but she did not cease being a vocal exponent of Marxist feminism. She argued, "Not all women want to be mothers, nor do all women want to join their life with that of man. Many single mothers are happy, but [simply] need better economic circumstances. They are also entitled to [sexual] happiness."[22] Ideas like Vidal's found resonance among some young radicals.

The Jota's *Ramona*, a weekly news and culture magazine, often challenged prevailing leftist convictions. In early 1973, for instance, it decried "centuries of *machismo*" and embraced women's liberation. Praising feminist movements in the United States and Europe, *Ramona's* self-proclaimed *equipo femenino* (feminine team) declared, "Not long ago a woman was an artifact whose principal obligations consisted of: being beautiful, maintaining a good appearance, completely obeying her husband, and staying at home to care for children." As the proletariat's struggle developed, so, too, did "feminist struggle." These were separate but related struggles, or so the article suggests, with "the struggle for feminine liberation" entailing fair demands.[23] The piece, which identifies "Women's Lib." as "action" that includes male striptease, sexual equality, and saying "no" to marriage, then identifies two feminists who were to be appreciated: Kate Millett, the U.S. feminist leader known for the book *Sexual Politics* (1970), and Isabel Allende, a first-cousin once removed of the president, and, at that time, a writer for *Paula* magazine and correspondent for a national television station. Isabel Allende told *Ramona*, "Numerous feminists thought that all women were going to join the [feminist liberation] movement if simply presented with the idea. It's not that way. Women have not been taught to liberate themselves; they have been taught to depend on men. That's why they become frightened by the possibility of having to take responsibility and make their own decisions."[24] Many Marxists frowned upon the very sort of individualism—one not directed at a properly collective outcome—that made the pages of periodicals like *Ramona*. Armand Mattelart and Michèle Mattelart captured this disposition clearly when arguing, "A revolutionary

The outlooks and practices of young women in regard to sexuality were components of ongoing debates over rights and liberation. These teenagers look to be enjoying Piedra Roja (1970). Courtesy of Paul Lowry.

country should create a type of woman that is different from that which is produced by the liberal ideology regarding emancipation. . . . Liberal ideology regarding emancipation does not directly imply any social objective. In a revolutionary society, emancipation intercedes as an instrument of consciousness building. . . . Revolutionary emancipation does not isolate the feminine masses from other social groups; rather, it makes them a pressure group in the transformation of structures and mentalities of the old society."[25]

Outside Allende's coalition, the MIR, a youthful, Guevarist, and vanguardist Marxist alternative, expressed views on gender and liberation that were more radical than those of UP leaders—and in line with those expressed by some young people working within Allende's coalition. Indicative is a response in *Punto Final*, the MIR's periodical, to a June 1971 meeting of Communist women that focused on their responsibilities in Allende's project. As the Communist newspaper, *El Siglo*, reported, the assembly vowed to recruit female compatriots for "concrete tasks in the Chilean revolution" by way of Mothers' Centers, which had been steered toward political mobilization under and for UP, and through other institutions associated with the government. *El Siglo* added that in addition to opposing Allende's centrist and rightists enemies, revolutionary women were also engaged in "permanent combat against all of the erroneous opinions of the far Left [the MIR]."[26] *Punto Final*, in turn, energetically attacked the assembly (and the PCCH and UP) for promoting a narrow vision. The *miristas* charged that Communists, including female activists, had failed to consider that a woman's being in the world may, in fact, be defined by power relationships and other factors that cannot be explained or alleviated in the context of UP's theory and praxis, which reinforced unequal power in the household by, among other things, maintaining the tired concept of *dueña de casa* and working through, rather than against, the Mothers' Centers. In sum, the MIR grew tired of Marxists who merely pledged to *include* women as partners in a UP revolutionary process that miristas viewed as bourgeois and reformist.[27]

(Making) Love in the Time of Coléricos

The issue of women's liberation was inseparable from the question of sexual freedom, which took on added emphasis in the public sphere with the rise of counterculture amid the youth question. As was the case with women's emancipation and rights, *Paula* was a leading venue for articles on sex and sexual liberation during the late sixties and early seventies. In 1968, for instance, *Paula*'s readers found a multiarticle treatment of the "Lolita"—a largely derogatory term taken from the name of a sexually charged twelve-year-old girl, Lolita, in Vladimir Nabokov's edgy and erotic 1955 novel of the same name.[28] In Nabokov's story, the redundantly named narrator, Humbert Humbert, a French intellectual living in the United States, becomes infatuated with "nymphets," falls in love with Lolita (the nickname for character Dolores Haze), and plenty of sex, promiscuity, lies, and tragedy soon follow. Although the terms "Lolita" and "Lola" (and the male "Lolo") were not always employed in derogatory ways in Chile, "Lolita" had negative overtones if used in certain contexts. The correspondent, Constanza Vergara, describes local "Lolitas" as young women between ages thirteen and sixteen and highly sexualized: with miniskirts and boots "no matter the temperature," abundant eye makeup, and subject to the sexual advances of *chiquillos* (boys). Their world essentially is that of colerismo—"a small world," Vergara observes.[29] Lolitas of the affluent and working classes, Vergara continues, cared more about fashion trends (on London's Carnaby Street, the famed shopping strip in Soho) and music (the latest stuff by the Beatles) than about national or international politics.

Paula's treatment, overall, reflects an ascribed association between the Lolita image and sexual promiscuity. It comes as no surprise, then, that virginity among girls and young women was also a topic of considerable conversation.

From time to time, *Paula* included "Confidential Documents"—pamphlets for parents' eyes only because "children do not have the required maturity to read them"—in its editions. One such supplement, published in late 1970, focused on virginity. It flatly states, "The virginity of women (men's virginity is rarely discussed) is one of the values most debated. The pressure to remain a virgin until marriage has many supporters, but it also has adversaries. And, above all, there are those in doubt, that is to say, men and women who do not express opinions because they are not sure."[30] An eroticized environment, newfound liberties, widespread reactions against old forms of morality, and the spread of sexuality-related material in the public sphere influence young women's choices regarding virginity, according to the document. *Paula* reached such conclusions upon conducting a small, non-scientific poll of young *santiaguinos* attending secondary schools and universities. Opinions ran the gamut, from young women embracing premarital sex to young men pledging monogamy with their *pololas* (girlfriends). Among other things (and likely to the appreciation of readers), *Paula* deduced that "not all of the girls between the ages of thirteen and seventeen were 'Lolitas.' "[31]

In June 1973, *Paula* declared in the article "The Erotic Life of the Chilean Woman" that for an unmarried woman "there is nothing more important than sexual desire and love." *Paula* took to the streets of Providencia, where young women in their mid- to late-teen years commented on sexuality, premarital sex, and dating. Most observed that virginity was a "myth" and that preserving it until marriage no longer carried weight for "the woman in love." In fact, many young women explained that a preferred mode of interaction was the *atraque*, or sharing fleeting kisses and caresses ("linking up") with young men—perhaps leading to sex. So popular was *atraque* that some young women came up with a name for their collective commitment to *atracar*: the MAPSA (Movimiento Antipololeo Solo Atraque, or the No Dating, Just Linking-Up Movement).[32] Moreover, the correspondent found that young women were rebelling en masse against what they saw as the "imposition of men": virginity until marriage. Meanwhile, not a single young woman (of more than fifty interviewees) expressed that they would not marry, and none questioned "marriage as an institution." Thus, at least among the young women sampled by *Paula*, sexual liberation did not entail eschewing marriage and family, which remained normative modes of conduct despite the problematization of premarital virginity. *Paula* contributor Cecilia Domeyko then concludes that young women's attitudes toward sex, virginity, and relationships were, in fact, "natural and healthy."[33]

Sexual freedom's effects on family and marriage drew substantial coverage in the leftist press and elsewhere.[34] On a Sunday afternoon in late September 1970, just weeks after Allende won an electoral plurality, readers casually thumbing through the emblematic pro-UP periodical *Clarín*, founded in the 1950s, likely found reason to pause upon noticing the enticing headline "Sexual Liberation: Are There Limits?" Accompanied by a photo of a bikini-clad, curvaceous Natalie Wood and another shot of two couples sharing a bed, the article condemns the immorality of "bourgeois ideology" in the matter of sexual relations and marriage and briefly surveys recent research by renowned sexologists William Masters and Virginia E. Johnson. *Clarín*'s specific bone to pick involved the upcoming release in Chile of Paul Mazursky's controversial 1969 film *Bob & Carol & Ted & Alice*, a story of extramarital dalliances, partner sharing, and group therapy starring Wood, Robert Culp, Elliot Gould, and Dyan Cannon (the four personas appearing cozy and satisfied in the aforementioned bed). *Clarín* warned that Mazursky's film would have a morally deleterious effect in Chile, given that many viewers "will discover that many of their dreams are present in the film . . . and it will make them think in ways to convert those dreams into realities." Upon reflecting on Mazursky's story of sexual adventure and intrigue among married persons, the article explains that sex—not love—drove couples to marry in order to normalize their sexual relations in the eyes of bourgeois society. If, then, a marriage based merely on sanctioned sex led to little sex, infidelity and divorce would result, thus damaging innocent children in the process. As for Masters and Johnson, their research on birth control also revealed a fundamental tendency toward "bourgeois" immorality, or so *Clarín* contended. The birth control pill's appearance, it was thought, would do away with the "aberrant behavior" of anal intercourse during a women's menstrual period, according to the periodical, but that had not come to pass. More dangerous still, pleasurable effects of anal coitus during menstrual periods often inspired men to have homosexual affairs—one of many sexual "deformities," *Clarín* argued.[35]

The Marxist periodical *Mayoría* echoed *Clarín* on the issue of philandering and normative conceptions of marriage when it discussed the subject of women and "frigidity." In 1972, a *Mayoría* writer cited a study that found that 60 percent of Chilean women suffered from sexual irresponsiveness and only rarely were such women capable of reaching orgasm during intercourse. By turning women into mere objects for the satisfaction of their sexual desires (a symptom of bourgeois sexuality, ostensibly), reckless men were directly responsible for the coping mechanism that was frigidity, the article argues. The *Mayoría* contributor asserts, "For modern sexologists, the worst possible scenario is for women to convince themselves that they're frigid and that sex has nothing to do with them." For some women, moreover, mistreatment by shallow partners also led to affairs with more loving and respectful men, thus potentially posing yet another danger to the nuclear family. What is more, questionable men also were to blame for a profusion of pornographic magazines that objectified women and inspired deviant sexuality, the article explains.[36] Broadly speaking, for the average reader of mainstream leftist periodicals like *Clarín* and *Mayoría,* there was mounting evidence—amid the transnational sexual revolution of the late sixties and early seventies—that the makings of a sexual crisis, with psychological and social consequences, were at hand. As we shall see in chapter 5, the goings-on at Piedra Roja did much to invigorate and sharpen the Left's commentary on sexuality and morality, especially as it pertained to the behavior of young people.

UP's dominant discourse on gender, sex, and sexuality, which stressed morality, discipline, and women's domesticity, and associated loosened mores with grave consequences for the familial and social good, was not solely anchored in "conservative" cultural values. An additional factor was at play. Working-class and rural women of UP were concerned about wayward husbands and the effects of their philandering on their families. They believed that sexual liberation raised the specter of encouraging dalliances that would undermine their marriages and the economic stability of their households. Moreover, as Heidi Tinsman has shown, government-run literacy and adult-education programs encouraged men to be good husbands by respecting women's work in the home, including child-rearing. These programs primarily focused on rural men as part of Chile's Agrarian Reform, but Allende essentially suggested the very same when speaking publicly to urban crowds about women in the revolution. Concurrently, for many working-class and rural men—and many urban ones as well, one may deduce—multiple extramarital relations and political activism in meeting halls and in the streets were part and parcel of their manliness.[37] These complex tensions posed significant problems for the working-class household, which was at the center of UP's discourse on women.

Complicating matters within the Left during the Allende years were Marxist periodicals meant for (and produced by) younger radicals that ran numerous open-minded articles on young people's sexuality. The Jota's *Ramona*, for instance, published a piece in mid 1972 titled "From the Parental Perspective: What to Do Amid Our Children's Sexual Liberation?" Based on interviews (lifted from a wire service, presumably) of "bourgeois" Europeans, the article conveyed to readers, "Prohibition and punishment are useless; young people claim their rights to sexual liberation."[38] Elsewhere in the weekly publication, the subject of intergenerational conversation about sex took center stage, with an eighty-five-year-old woman (Marta), her daughter (Adriana, fifty-one), and her grandchild (Lucía, sixteen) openly discussing what contributor Patricia Politzer called the "thorny issue of sex." Marta, who purportedly never went to a party before marrying at age twenty-six, told of her "strict" upbringing—one that she apparently applied when raising her daughter. Adriana, meanwhile, explained that Marta never allowed her to venture from the house alone. Lucía, on the other hand, told *Ramona*'s reporter of enjoying weekend parties until 3 A.M. Such differences meant complexities in the relationship of "two generations who don't understand how she [Lucía] thinks in such ways, how she can have so many friends, how she conducts herself in that way, etc.," Politzer describes. Her article goes on to explain, "The subject discussed least in this family of three generations living together is sex." Lucía's mother, Adriana, affirmed: "I have no prejudice regarding sex. The opposite is true, in fact." But she then added, "I think today's youth are losing out on the real value of sex. To sleep around is terrible! I also think they are irresponsible. They have sex without understanding the responsibility of having a child." Lucía interrupted her mother: "That's not true!" Adriana replied, "Let me finish. I'm speaking. You can express your opinion later." A frustrated Lucía then shot back, falling deeper into her chair: "Fine. I won't say a word." Lucía did, however, later add that young women should be free to have sex after their first menstrual cycle, or so a physician allegedly told her. Politzer then asked Lucía if she approved of "free love." "No," Lucía responded, "because free love is about whoring it up freely," but "I find it perfectly acceptable to sleep with your boyfriend." The grandmother then added, "I think young people are totally crazy."[39]

Another review of young people's opinions on premarital sex appeared in the Marxist and youth-targeted *Onda*, which, like *Ramona* and many other leftist periodicals, was the product of the state-owned Quimantú publishing house. In the autumn of 1972, a fourteen-year-old young woman from Viña del Mar told a reporter that "the desire of every girl should be to take her virginity into matrimony." Other young women disagreed. "Those who think [women] shouldn't have sex [before marriage] are crazy," said "Alejandra," seventeen. Another observed, "Girls who have [sexual] relations with boyfriends have no reason to be called whores. I would go to bed with my boyfriend as long as he wasn't a younger guy because he would tell the whole neighborhood." And what of young men's outlooks? Most male interviewees expressed devotion to their girlfriends, including one young man who told *Onda* that out of respect for his *polola* he had not slept with her. Moreover, a twenty-year-old male explained, "It's not the same [to have sex] with just any girl. With your *polola* one has a more complete union. It's not about the moment; it's about the conjunction of everything you feel about her." Indeed, numerous youths whose views appeared in the Socialist-oriented *Onda* held that "true" love and affection—not the adventurism of "free" love—should underpin premarital sex, which most condoned.[40] Together, the *Ramona* and *Onda* articles examined here indicate that sexual liberation was a reality and that only through improved communication and understanding could intergenerational discussions of sex bear fruit. More specifically, they convey that premarital sex was neither considered taboo nor defended unconditionally by many young people. What made these and other similar articles unconventional was the paucity of heavy-handed and ostensibly "conservative" normative conceptions of sex, marriage, and family that otherwise characterized much of the leftist media's treatment of such topics.[41] Put simply, the publications in question reflected a significant degree of openness vis-à-vis the transnational sexual revolution of the 1960s and 1970s.

Juan Carlos Moraga, a Central Committee member of the Socialist Youth under UP, recalled variation within the Left in regard to attitudes toward sexual liberation and other forms of sociocultural heterodoxy. He noted that miristas and most Communists, especially older ones, were—in terms of "human relations," including sexuality—the more culturally conservative leftists, despite some evidence in the mirista press that suggested a more progressive stance. Moraga observed that a cultural narrow-mindedness among certain Marxists paralleled their political dogmatism. "A Communist was a [cultural] conservative like a Catholic," he described. "I was more conservative, but it was known that Socialists in general would dance the salsa, the cumbia, the cha-cha-cha—all those things—if they had a party. The Socialist was always unruly [*desordenado*], more liberal, and for those very reasons more permissive." Such unruliness was the case—at least politically—for the Socialist Party, which, unlike the PCCh, was mired in an internal dispute involving its support for Allende's incrementalist approach to revolution. Culturally, however, the Socialist-leaning *Onda* was no more "permissive" than the Jota's *Ramona*, for example. What is clear, overall, is that generational differences were pertinent among Marxists in determining cultural outlooks, with younger radicals running up against the values and practices of the older crowd.[42]

The Catholic Church, with a commitment to canon that Moraga likened to the dogmatism of elder Communists, expressed views on sexuality that were more nuanced than one might expect. In March 1968, a reporter asked Santiago's archbishop, Cardinal Raúl Silva Henríquez, if there existed any ongoing conversation in Chile's ecclesiastical hierarchy regarding the easing of the no-sex-before-marriage stipulation. "Absolutely not," Silva declared.[43] But not all clergy were so cut and dry. Then thirty-year-old Father Jaime Correa, who later became a leading cleric, told *Paula* readers that the Church's stance on premarital virginity reflected a "tradition" rather than a specific biblical doctrine. He pointed out, "The influence of certain Christian ideologues like St. Augustine, a converted pagan, who reacted violently against sexual disorderliness, was decisive. But, in general, there is a paucity of Church doctrine with respect to sex and marriage, even recently." In no way, however, did Correa condone men and women's "fornication"—a stance, he asserted, which had doctrinal mooring. Correa went on to explain, "I believe that the emancipation of women is a very positive phenomenon. . . . But the error and the danger is for women to be like men in terms of a cultural defect: Men have traditionally separated sex and love." He then declared, "A woman is now in the [empowered] position to ask a man to be faithful to her, just as she is to him." Sexual activity, then, brings with it certain responsibilities—mutual ones that overcome the "search for pure [physical] pleasure that is egotistical." Again, love was a necessary condition in the proper development of a woman or man's sexuality (as leftists also argued when they criticized "bourgeois morality" while also reinforcing important pillars of it). Indeed, losing one's virginity to a spouse deepens and "personalizes love," Correa concluded. Father Gonzalo Valdivieso, vicar of the parish Our Lady of Providencia, reaffirmed Correa's interpretations, adding that dedicating oneself to virginity would later translate into total commitment to a spouse and to one's children.[44]

Contraception and abortion were also important issues as liberated sexuality came to the fore in the sixties and early seventies. Notwithstanding the power and influence of the Catholic Church and strong currents of cultural conservatism in society and politics, pro-contraception policies and practices developed early in the twentieth century. The first state-orchestrated distribution of contraception, for instance, began in 1938 under the newly elected Popular Front government of Pedro Aguirre Cerda (for whom a young physician, Salvador Allende, served as minister of health).[45] However, rates of self-induced abortion were soaring by the 1950s, with physicians and public-health workers providing limited alternatives. By the early 1960s, approximately one-third of women who engaged in self-induced abortion required subsequent medical care. The advent of new and accessible contraceptive technologies presented additional opportunities for women, but a stubborn culture of silence with respect to sexuality and reproduction persisted in Chilean society.[46] Meanwhile, physicians at public hospitals continued to provide care in the cases of botched abortions and also extended their educational outreach regarding contraception. Advances in birth control and sexual education fell short of meeting the needs of working-class women in particular, according to *Ramona*.[47] In 1972, the magazine argued that poorer and less educated women unfortunately resorted to abortion as their main source of birth control. This contributed to an ongoing "massacre" of working-class women who perished from botched abortions.[48] The illegality of abortion remained in place under the UP government despite signs that Allende favored the loosening of abortion laws, and clandestine abortion clinics and self-induced abortions were widely recognized across the political spectrum as social maladies.[49] Yet, nonemergency abortions were performed in limited numbers in government hospitals, and other advancements under Allende, including access to childcare and lower food prices, improved the lives of women working in and outside the home.[50] Historian Jadwiga Peiper-Mooney explains that women strove for personal empowerment and control over their bodies, often clashing with medical professionals and others who viewed abortion as a public-health concern and contraception as a demographic matter tied to development during a population boom rather than as issues rooted in women's rights.[51]

As evidenced by *Clarín*'s abovementioned article on sexual liberation, issues associated with heterosexual intercourse were concomitant with concerns about homosexuality—male homosexuality, in particular—in an era during which sexual values were in flux. Powerfully masculine discourses cast male homosexuality as worse than premarital or loveless heterosexual sex, inherently dangerous, and even criminal. As some historians have pointed out, Allende's national project, in addition to that of the MIR and those of groups across the sociopolitical spectrum, oozed masculinity.[52] As the Left's dominant discourse on "liberation" essentially relegated (feminist) women's emancipation to the ideological penumbra, homosexuality went also without positive space in UP's agenda. In other words, UP projected normative conceptions of "woman" and "man" that often were as culturally traditional as others emanating from more politically conservative reaches of the body politic. In the context of heavily masculine discourses, UP publications routinely identified gays as anything from "abnormals" (anormales) who deserved the "rejection and disgust of the public" to being purveyors of "a sickness through and through." Readers, moreover, were asked to conclude if homosexuality was either a "vice or disease" and to accept that male homosexuality constituted a "social problem."[53] The media also associated male homosexuals with more specific social ills, including violence. In October 1971, for instance, an article in the Marxist *Ahora* described "the bloody end" to the lives of two homosexuals—both middle-aged, one a lawyer, the other an art teacher—at the hands of their former lovers. The report casts homosexuality as the strongly problematic phenomenon that brought together victims and victimizers.[54] That same month, the government-owned daily *La Nación* ran the story "Detective Shoots a Homosexual," which essentially depicts the dead man as an aggressive pervert who accosted a plain-clothed detective on a sidewalk along an avenue in the northwestern reaches of Greater Santiago. A scuffle ensued, resulting in the "accidental" shooting death of the "sodomite" and "transvestite," to use the article's terms.[55] Meanwhile, the socialist *Las Noticias de Última Hora* pointed to what it saw as a significant problem: "The crimes of homosexuals that have happened over the last few months continue to go on without solutions."[56] Amid such press, however, gays did not shy from taking to the streets conspicuously in the capital during the Allende years, drawing the equal ire of Marxist media and those of other political groups.[57] (Later chapters in this book touch on the "feminization" and "homosexualization" of the countercultural male by those in the mainstream, further illustrating the sociocultural milieu in which criollo counterculture and its detractors operated.)

Mainstream voices often hitched liberating approaches to sexuality to representations of melenudos and palomas with pitos in their mouths and rock music on their record players. The recreational use of marijuana and other drugs induced noteworthy responses on the part of police, the courts, politicians, and the media in the late 1960s, but such awareness intensified, to put it mildly, in late 1970—in Piedra Roja's wake. Marijuana received the bulk of public attention paid to illegal substances; it was easily available, inexpensive, and, according to contemporary studies, large numbers of young people consumed it, irrespective of class or gender. Pegged as a telltale imprint of counterculture, marijuana rapidly was becoming a prominent moral, public health, and political issue when Allende assumed the presidency just weeks after Jorge Gómez's festival. Critics argued that marijuana use evinced and yielded grave problems—among them, criminality, crises of religious faith, alienation, escapism, and the mechanisms and intentions of capitalist imperialism—with acute familial, social, and political repercussions. Fears circulated that smoking *la hierba* (weed) led to the breakdown of parent-child relations, stimulated sexual irresponsibly, and damaged the intellectual and political potentials of youths. Rock music essentially precipitated the same worries.

Getting High

In July 1969, the month during which a Saturn V rocket propelled Apollo 11 to the Moon's Sea of Tranquility, authorities in Greater Santiago's upscale municipality of Providencia brought a few high-flying young men down to earth. Police arrested Christian Pohlhammer, twenty; Eduardo Benavente, twenty-four; Francisco Correa, nineteen; and José Bernardo Yévenes, seventeen, for smoking pitos in public—the first such arrests in the country's history. The setting—"Provi," as young people called it— was not necessarily surprising; most of the initial roundups of *marihuaneros*, as pot smokers were called, occurred in the trendy barrio, where a nascent hippie culture was taking shape on the sidewalks and in the cafes and stores along Providencia Avenue (an extension of the capital's main artery, Liberator General Bernardo O'Higgins Avenue, or simply "La Alameda"). Authorities rounded up some one hundred young people shortly after Carabineros arrested Pohlhammer and his friends, beginning what would be ebbs and flows of drug-related arrests, largely for marijuana possession and trafficking, in the capital. "People started to realize that there were plantations of cannabis all over Chile and that it was easy to access it," Pohlhammer recalled thirty-five years later. In many cases, such availability meant easy highs and profound lows. "Many back then succumbed to excessive consumption, but others reinserted themselves [into society] and are [now] excellent professionals, politicians, and artists," he pointed out.[58]

Chile's marijuana law was a month old when police jailed Pohlhammer and company for fifteen days—some of that in solitary confinement, in Pohlhammer's case. Things got worse. "I blew off college," he explained. "I lost my girlfriend and I was under such pressure that I left my house so that no one would bother me. I wanted to disappear . . . my family took it hard."[59] Meanwhile, the media's interest was piqued, rife with moralistic criticism. The conservative *El Mercurio* reported nationwide "alarm" over marijuana. Thought to have originated within "intellectual circles in the capital" before spreading to university students, like Pohlhammer, and high schoolers, marijuana use was a vice "new to our country" and not more than six months in the making, or so the newspaper asserted.[60] The giant daily also interviewed the young men in custody. Pohlhammer reportedly explained that he was an introvert and that pitos rid him of inhibition, thus incorporating him into the social whole, while Correa described how marijuana made his "ideas become more lucid."[61] That same week, the leftist press found great pleasure in reporting that another well-to-do young man, Rafael Edwards Aguirre—of the *El Mercurio*–owning Edwards clan and the nephew of the newspaper's proprietor, no less—found himself in a similar predicament with law enforcement. Arrested in Providencia near a shopping galleria appropriately called El Drugstore, where Pohlhammer and company also had been caught, Edwards allegedly cried out for help while being subdued by police. Such young people from "high society," as the periodical *Clarín* explained, would have to mobilize "their dear fathers to use all the influence they have" to ensure their children avoided jail time.[62]

In the month prior to the arrests of Pohlhammer et al., the government had instructed police to target marijuana users and the Appellate Court of Santiago assigned a special prosecutor to get at the roots of the growing prevalence of marijuana use among young people, especially those in secondary schools, and bring "wayward" youths to justice. The prosecutor, Hernán Cereceda Bravo, later wrote that authorities had been relatively uninterested in marijuana before the late 1960s. He recalled that he took charge of the marijuana matter at a time when such deeds were "causing great alarm in public opinion." Cereceda explained, "I then became known in the press and the media in general as the 'prosecutor in the campaign against marijuana.'" His investigations began by way of visits to "nocturnal establishments [in Santiago] where [marijuana] was consumed" and to "places where this 'wonder' was produced," such as Los Andes and San Felipe, both farming towns a short drive from the capital.[63] Among other discoveries, Cereceda found widespread use of marijuana in high schools, and, as a result, rectors of more than sixty public and private high schools in Greater Santiago met to discuss the marijuana issue. The Liceo Manuel

Salas, an upper-class high school where officials found that marijuana was circulating widely, was of particular interest to *Clarín*. It made no bones about a supposed connection between the "scandal" that was marijuana use and the bourgeois lifestyle.[64] In another case, a circle of concerned teachers at a working-class high school in Valparaíso appealed to a local newspaper to stir "public opinion about the grave problem of drugs among students." Students often covered for each other or remained silent in the face of drug-related inquiries and, in general, made policing difficult, according to the teachers.[65]

A brief spike in the Chamber of Deputies' interest in the marijuana issue coincided with the arrest of Pohlhammer and company in July 1969. Members jumped on the subject as a public-health concern but not without politicizing matters as the country's body politic was fracturing. Pedro Antonio Jáuregui Castro, a Socialist physician who represented Osorno (in the southern Los Lagos region) and was a member of the Permanent Commission on Public Health, sketched out the situation for his fellow deputies in a July 22 floor speech. Marijuana, he argued, was a significant problem "with grave consequences for the physical health and especially the mental health of our youth" and that it is "one of those drugs" that "provides society with criminals and psychopaths—the former because it degrades the personality of the individual, and the latter because it germinates and puts into relief otherwise latent psychoses, especially schizophrenic ones, that many times accompany an individual." Jáuregui went on to reject notions shared by some in society that drugs like marijuana accentuated one's artistic and creative capacities when, in reality, they merely favored "decadent expressions of art." This finding fit well within the Left's broader discourse that linked drug use to a specific social layer: a "decadent" bourgeoisie. Indeed, Jáuregui pointed to "the high schools of the upper bourgeoisie and our country's moneyed classes" as the collective source of the marijuana problem, thus suggesting a sociological phenomenon rooted in a particular political economy.[66]

The roundups of some alleged marihuaneros like Pohlhammer can be construed as a public-awareness campaign to highlight the government's increased attention toward the general problem of "stupefying substances"—a legal term akin to "narcotic." In June 1969, the government had reformed the penal code (via Decree No. 17,155) to outlaw production, distribution, and consumption of such substances, thus falling into line with an international wave of antinarcotic legislation and enforcement. The penal-code reform gave Chile's executive branch the authority to identify what exactly constituted "stupefying" substances. One month later, the Ministry of Public Health issued a substantial list of such *estupefacientes,* including marijuana, which, it noted, produced the "effects of dependency," thus giving local authorities in Providencia legal cause to arrest Pohlhammer and his friends. The list crafted by the ministry included various forms of barbiturates, amphetamines, morphine, cocaine, heroin, lysergic acid diethylamide (LSD), mescaline, and hydrocodone (a controlled substance that could be administered by medical professionals), in addition to marijuana, hashish, and all members of the cannabis family. In the case of marijuana, it remained legal to cultivate the plant for industrial or horticultural purposes only.[67] Realistically, that caveat meant marijuana would be easy to obtain for plainly nonindustrial and nonhorticultural uses. It grew far and wide in the countryside and thus retailed for relatively little money. Its quality, however, apparently left much to be desired.[68] Piedra Roja coplanner Gary Fritz noted, "Now, it was nasty stuff, and I just don't remember anyone having to buy it, ever." He also observed that marijuana was "a common language of youth" during that time, even in Chile. "It was also used as currency to enter into conversations and into social groups. It gave you some base upon which to communicate," Fritz said.[69] What is more, outlawing marijuana's recreational use gave it a new meaning: to smoke a pito became an act of defying orthodoxy and authority.

Marijuana was linked—in concept and in practice—to the youth question. Such was the conclusion of a team of sociologists from the Pontifical Catholic University in Santiago, who conducted an extensive study in 1970 that revolved around a simple question (and also became the study's title): "Does the Chilean Student Smoke Marijuana?" The researchers distributed anonymous questionnaires in four Santiago-area high schools, resulting in a sample of 1,302 students. Based on such factors as parental education and profession, the team identified the young men and women as either "upper class" and "upper-middle class" or "lower-middle class" and "lower class." The study's most general finding was not earthshaking, per se: "The rumor that exists regarding the consumption of marijuana in high schools has a base in reality. It is a deed that is not rare and does not appear only in isolated cases; it affects an appreciable number of interviewed young people." That "appreciable" number, to be more precise, stood just shy of 35 percent of all respondents, who reported as of November or December 1970 that they had smoked marijuana at some point.[70] That total is a noteworthy statistic, especially if one considers the United States, where, in 1971, 14 percent of youths ages fourteen to seventeen reported having smoked marijuana at least once, according to one study.[71] Moreover, of those young Chileans who admitted to marijuana use, 23 percent reported having used other drugs (barbiturates, amphetamines, and hallucinogens of varying type). More specific and telling data came from the study's considerations of class, gender, and age when scrutinizing marijuana as a sociocultural phenomenon. Among upper-class and upper-middle-class students, young men reported using marijuana at a much higher rate (47 percent) than did young women (23.9 percent). Compared to those students, reported marijuana use was slightly higher among young men of lower- and lower-middle-class standing (48.5 percent) and a bit lower among the category's young women (17.3 percent). In other words, gender mattered more than class when accounting for varying rates of marijuana use among the youths polled, with consumption of pitos crossing boundaries of class in a relatively uniform manner.[72]

The researchers also found that many of the same elements understood as central to what we have called the "youth question" were very much in the picture when young people accounted for their marijuana use. While 65.2 percent of those who had tried marijuana at least once noted that such consumption was either "dangerous" or "very dangerous," a large number of respondents identified what they considered to be reasonable rationales behind the prevalence of pitos. Allowed to pinpoint more than one explanation, 27.2 percent of smokers and nonsmokers alike saw marijuana use as outright but unspecified "rebellion," 48.9 percent saw it as "an attitude of protest toward society in general," 35.9 percent perceived it as a "rejection of the adult world," and 31.9 percent agreed that marijuana use reflected "resentment toward the lack of parental interest" in young people's lives. What is more, the inquiry found that high schoolers overwhelmingly agreed that parents and teachers must do a better job of communicating with youths, which would entail hearing young people's daily concerns and complaints to gauge such problems as alienation and disaffection. Overall, then, the sociologists found that youths perceived sociocultural heterodoxy (in this case, marijuana use) in terms of generation and a generational-familial divide.[73]

The impression of intergenerational dissonance—with parents bearing considerable blame—reverberated in tragic stories about drug users whose affinity for pitos (and likely other substances) damaged, and purportedly sometimes ended, their lives. One victim was Julio Ibáñez Durán, who died in October 1970—a few days before Piedra Roja. As one newspaper put it, Ibáñez, a marihuanero, died under strange circumstances related to a pot "orgy" in the Parque Forestal, the public park in downtown Santiago known for the presence of marijuana. Police, while strongly hinting at the foul play of others, nevertheless diagnosed the cause of death as "an overdose of *Cannabis sativa*," with Ibáñez allegedly having smoked some ten pitos over the course of an hour or two. (It is unclear how authorities arrived at that assessment.) Buttressing that conclusion, the media observed that four youths who discovered Ibáñez's body noticed that the dead man's fingers still gripped a half-consumed marijuana cigarette. The death, as one periodical explained, "emphasized one of the most grave problems affecting our young people." The young man had been a dutiful, respected, and well-liked employee of the Ministry of Education and had uncharacteristically skipped out on work the day of his death. His mother argued that Ibáñez had suffered a heart attack as a result of a preexisting but unspecified heart condition. "It's unjust what the newspapers have said about him," she complained.[74] Less than a week later, the news magazine *Vea* criticized parents who naively believed their children were always at school or work and never involved in drug-related exploits.[75] Also within days of Ibáñez's death, detectives arrested "María," sixteen, and her boyfriend, "Panchito," nineteen, in a downtown Santiago apartment and transported them to a nearby hospital. They reportedly had smoked pito after pito, to the point of hallucinating and stripping off their clothes. Both were from bourgeois families, a pro-UP newspaper noted condescendingly, and "had everything but the tenderness and attention of their parents."[76]

The Jota's magazine, *Ramona*, delved deeper into what ostensibly lay behind the use of drugs among moneyed youths like Osvaldo, a seventeen-year-old marijuana smoker whose worldview had been reduced to cynicism and disgust. The young man reportedly had started with marijuana and then had become ensnarled in cocaine. Little patience did Osvaldo have toward the correspondent's opening words: "Osvaldo, tell me something." Osvaldo interrupted: "What should I tell you? That the world is really shit, that everything is bad, that the elders have destroyed the youth? Yes, everything is shit." When asked about his parents, who were married and maintained a stable and prosperous household, Osvaldo again interrupted, echoing the words of many young people in the press, on questionnaires, and circulating among a generation: "What parents? The ones who brought me into this world after sharing a few minutes of pleasure? The ones who are too preoccupied by their own concerns to know that they even had a child?" When his parents *were* tuned in to his concerns, Osvaldo notes, they denied him most everything he wished. Osvaldo told the correspondent of one argument about his future goals, during which Osvaldo's father, a businessman, grew alarmed by his son's intention to be a painter. "My father would say that being a painter was a job for faggots [*maricones*] or strange people." Osvaldo added, "He can shove his money and his house up his ass." The young correspondent, María Teresa Larraín, a self-identified friend of Osvaldo who went on to become a film director, then concludes with a warning: "Osvaldo is a real and hard testament about the path that many young people might take."[77]

Associated with what observers often described publicly as the "tragedy" of marijuana were other dangers, ranging from more potent drugs to pornography, prostitution, and murderousness. During the month that Pohlhammer and others were arrested for having pitos, for instance, *El Mercurio* noted, "The use of marijuana leads to other excesses," while the youth-focused and oriented *Ritmo de la Juventud* later reported on marijuana as a possible "passport to death" via harder drugs.[78] In that vein, *Vea* established a firm connection—rhetorical more than scientific—between marijuana use and opium, morphine, and LSD, the last of which raised considerable concern during the late 1960s, with news stories on the "dangerous truth" about LSD and birth defects evident in children of its users.[79] Though novel, by the UP years, LSD—under the street names "orange sunshine," "purple haze," and "window pane," among others—had become accessible enough to become politicized. Scuttlebutt and the Marxist media identified the U.S. Central Intelligence Agency, with the intent to "put young people to sleep in developing countries," as LSD's primary trafficker in Chile.[80] Former hippies noted that rumors tied LSD to the CIA's efforts to infiltrate the universities and harm young people who supported the UP government.[81] Moreover, law enforcement officials and the media were quick to publicize LSD- and marijuana-related arrests, including those of a "gang" of Chilean and Peruvian LSD traffickers who allegedly furthered the CIA's plan to flood the country with the drug for the purpose of creating a "dormant" generation without interest in political, economic, and social affairs. The press noted that the gang's LSD supply originated in the United States.[82]

The periodical *Punto Final*—published by the *guevarista* MIR—took the matter of a direct U.S.–LSD–Chile link further. It provided names of young U.S. citizens attending private high schools who, it was alleged, fostered the use of LSD and marijuana in Chile. Those American youths, *Punto Final* specified, had well-placed parents, including the rector of Santiago College, a prestigious English-speaking high school in Providencia; a NASA official posted to Chile; and the head of USAID (United States Agency for International Development) in Santiago. Among other things, the periodical told of a party in mid-1971 attended by American expatriates in their late teens who were students at Santiago College or the equally prestigious American school Nido de Aguilas (Nest of Eagles), nestled in the elite barrio of Lo Barnechea. The group included the young Gary Fritz—a Nido de Aguilas student and son of Santiago College's rector—whose name appeared at the top of *Punto Final*'s list. Speaking in English but really saying nothing of any import, or so the article explains, Fritz and forty other young people of his ilk danced, enjoyed marijuana (of Mexican origin and therefore of higher quality than the local product), consumed LSD, and, on the whole, reveled in debauchery. These "children of the empire" (the United States) were both users and traffickers, having brought such substances with them from visits to the U.S. In the case of marijuana, the Americans had seeded Chile with the drug—figuratively and literally; they had introduced the smoking of marijuana (and the use of LSD) to Chilean youths and had brought to Chile seeds of a higher-quality plant. Moreover, the article notes that parents of the scrutinized teens also enjoyed wild parties with plenty of drunkenness and repugnant behavior. Corrupted and immoral Americans—of any age—thus posed a significant risk to Chilean culture and normative sociability. *Punto Final* noted that ten or twenty American couples, apparently including Fritz's parents, often gathered to play bridge, chat, and "drink and drink and drink until drunkenness." What is more, the parents' jokes were all of a sexual nature because "it appears that these people have a sex complex" and "don't speak of anything but what lies below the navel." The mirista publication then concluded, "The origins of drug consumption in our country are quite clear."[83]

Nearly four decades later, Fritz described *Punto Final*'s account as "quite a hoot." He explained that he and his friends were not international drug traffickers or dangerous stoners, his parents were Methodists and thus shunned alcohol, and that tales of drunken depravity involving his parents or his friends' parents were "ridiculous."[84] Fritz also suggested that such hype over foreigners and drugs largely was a manifestation of Chilean domestic politics and left-wing anti-imperialist discourse run amok.[85] However, he recalled and did not necessarily discount the notion, which was circulating in Chile at the time, that the U.S. government was behind the emergence of LSD and other psychedelic drugs. Indeed, the suspicion was widespread, as is underscored by more than one interviewee in this book, including former Los Blops guitarist Juan Pablo Orrego.[86] The MIR was off target when it pinpointed some American teenagers, including Fritz, as actors in a hemispheric web of drug running based at CIA headquarters

Piedra Roja co-organizer Gary Fritz, who was identified in a *Punto Final* article as attending a drug-laced party, relaxes amid the hubbub of Piedra Roja (1970). Forty years later, Fritz called allegations of drug trafficking "ridiculous." His documentary on the festival won two international awards. Courtesy of Paul Lowry.

in suburban Washington, D.C. Yet, with its allegations, the MIR was tapping into inklings already present in youth circles and in the broader public sphere.

LSD was the subject of periodic comment in the media. For instance, *Paula* published a story in March 1968 on a Chilean physician who observed the effects of LSD in controlled experiments. The article's author, Isabel Allende, explained that Dr. Rolando Toro, a professor of psychology at the Pontifical Catholic University, had overseen and collected data from two hundred such experiences. In the case of a married couple (together for fifteen years), Isabel Allende pointed to their incoherent ramblings on anything ranging from shapes and colors to the married woman's hope that she would be transformed into smoke so that her husband could inhale her, thus "filling him to his fingertips." Toro, a Chilean version of U.S. LSD advocate Timothy Leary, also had experimented on himself and spoke in quite approving ways about the drug. "There are no serious scientific studies that show LSD produces organic alterations in the nervous system, in blood or in chromosomes," he noted. "No one has gone crazy from LSD." Toro went on to add, "Without a doubt LSD entails 'social dangers' in the structure of our Western Civilization"—a good and transformative thing, he declared.

In Chile, however, LSD was relatively scarce (as of 1968), or so Toro observed, and marijuana, in ample supply, was a poor substitute for the more powerful and mind-altering lysergic acid diethylamide.[87]

Worried folks in the mainstream, in addition to warning of marijuana's effects, also associated the use of marijuana and other drugs to illicit sexual activities and criminal violence. The press was particularly interested in identifying libertine, immoral, and sociopathic impulses allegedly brought on by la hierba.[88] For the tabloid *Vea*, marijuana became correlative of rape, prostitution, and pornography in such spaces as Quinta Normal, a working-class municipality in Greater Santiago's western reaches; there, by 1970, youths, especially young women, were subject to a "dangerous world," the periodical argued.[89] In another working-class sector, La Cisterna, a prison escapee identified as a thirty-year-old "ruffian," "delinquent," and "marihuanero" crashed a large, all-night party being enjoyed by young people on an October evening in 1971. *Clarín* reported that Osvaldo Sepúlveda Rojas (not the Osvaldo noted above) had smoked "more than one pipe of marijuana" and, consequently, he was "flying high at great altitude" when a scuffle ensued involving a young woman. Sepúlveda, having designs on the young woman, became enraged—too easily, thanks to the marijuana, or so the article suggests—when another man drew the young woman's affectionate attention. The fugitive opened fire indiscriminately, killing one and injuring four others, before his arrest by police.[90] Some Chileans thus concluded that youths under the influence of a "marijuana invasion" could very easily mimic the sociopathic fancies of, say, monsters like Charles Manson, who, *Vea* described, had assembled "a sinister 'family' of hippies" that was "a sub-product of marijuana"—a "disease for which there is no effective vaccine as of yet."[91]

By the end of 1970, the recreational use of drugs—especially marijuana—had taken on a rebellious profile in the public sphere. For its musicians and aficionados, rock's modes and means of expressiveness and individuality also were revolutionary. Criollo groups like Los Jaivas and Los Blops produced music and lyrics that captured imaginations, with improvisation becoming vital in the music of both groups, as it was with many young people who were drawn to counterculture. Like changing attitudes toward sex and drugs, rock music was a cultural marker of sensibilities and forms of being that were constituted generationally and, in many ways, were antithetical to the dominant aesthetic sensibilities of the era. Rock pushed the cultural envelope at a time when the folk-driven and mainstream Nueva Canción (New Song) movement—with its clear, cogent, and partisan political message—became the soundtrack of Allende's "road to socialism." Rock's critics questioned the genre's moral credentials, with some focusing on its alleged complicity (along with free love and marijuana) in precipitating degeneracy. Others held that foreign and foreign-inspired rock culture registered the power of bourgeois-imperialist hegemony. I argue that criollo rock had a counterhegemonic effect, for it busted through mainstream art and politics, including that of Nueva Canción. The older generation of movers and shakers largely ignored the revolutionary potential of rock culture, while also eschewing the genre's associated (real or imagined) ways of being and aesthetics.

Revolution's Soundtrack

The UP years saw an explosion of artistic creativity and production closely tied to the coalition's project for the nation. Such effervescence was played out through an array of mediums, including poetry, posters, murals, and, most especially, music—a sphere of cultural production inextricably tied to an ever-expanding culture industry. One's musical taste is not necessarily defined through the prisms of generational or political or even national identities, but if any genre constituted the official soundtrack from Allende's road to socialism, it was Nueva Canción.[92] Indeed, so instrumental (and instrumentalized) was Nueva Canción that any scholar writing about Chilean music during the period under consideration here cannot go without at least broaching the history and trajectory of a genre populated by such luminaries as Violeta Parra and Víctor Jara, among many. The movement is pertinent for its inseparability from the Left and UP, as well as its appreciable distance, in terms of aesthetic and ideational moorings, from the rock music integral to Piedra Roja and criollo counterculture.

When Nueva Canción figures recorded with the fecund record label of the Jota—the Popular Song Record Library (Discoteca del Cantar Popular, DICAP)—or with other labels during the UP years, they participated in the making of an "official" musical expression of their Marxism and UP. The government's support was critical (a 94 percent import tariff on foreign records under Allende didn't hurt, to be sure), but Nueva Canción had much gravitas outside its connections to Allende's road to socialism.[93] To its participants and primary constituents in and outside the state, Nueva Canción was authentically Chilean, properly revolutionary, and reflected what was best about a nation embarking on a profound transformation for the better. Its songs were about "the people," their struggle, and their hopes, dreams, and loves, while its well-wrought rhythms and melodies came from rural folk music and, to some extent, indigenous Andean sounds. Meanwhile, to many Nueva Canción artists and their patrons, capitalism, imperialism, and bourgeois immorality were at the center of a torrent of imported music—the pinnacle of which was rock—that lacked relevance, depth, and utility, and whose presence only accentuated and furthered the youth question.

With a strong but tranquil voice often paired with the simple elegance of acoustic guitar, Violeta Parra began forging a species of folklorism in the 1950s that later took the name Nueva Canción.[94] She became the country's premier folkloric performer—more than a decade before UP—upon the release of a multialbum work titled *El folklore de Chile*, released by Odeón-Chile, a branch of England-based EMI. The matriarch of a musical family that includes children Isabel and Ángel, both also Nueva Canción figures, Violeta's early success took her to Europe, where she broke ground with international audiences for future Nueva Canción performers, including the group Quilapayún. While early-century uses of folk music in Chile were also political and politicized, the Parra clan and numerous other Nueva Canción artists put forth and pursued—lyrically and aesthetically—a clearly revolutionary and Marxist impulse that reinforced what would become UP's fundamental principles and outlooks. Their songs about the countryside were songs about rural workers, for instance, as the subaltern subject took center stage in the cultural politics of Nueva Canción and in the discourse of Allende's coalition.

Violeta Parra's politics loomed large early in her recording career, as evidenced by such albums as *Todo Violeta Parra*, which appeared in 1960 (also released by Odeón-EMI) and included the song "Hace falta un guerrillero" (There Lacks a Guerilla Fighter). Shortly after Fidel Castro's victory in Cuba, Violeta Parra's composition called for the emergence of a revolutionary hero in Chile—one who would take up the banner of revolution once held aloft by Manuel Rodríguez during the independence wars of the early nineteenth century, but who would fight for social justice on behalf of, and in concert with, the working masses.[95] UP and Nueva Canción artists would recognize Allende as that revolutionary, although the coalition framed and pursued the road to socialism as peaceful and constitutional rather than insurrectionary and armed (à la *guerrillismo*). Chilean *guevaristas,* who called for armed insurrection in lieu of Allende's revolutionary formula, seized on Violeta Parra's song during the UP years, as if to declare that an authentic revolutionary had not yet appeared in their country. In particular, the MIR reflected on the Nueva Canción matriarch and embraced her work, with particular reference to "Hace falta un guerrillero," in the following terms: "When more than a few [including many bourgeois leftists, we might add] were frightened by the torrential eruption of the Cuban Revolution, Violeta Parra, solely with her indomitable courage as an artist and her consciousness as a Chilean and Latin American, composed 'Hace falta un guerrillero.' . . . Her songs circulate across the continent and revolutionary combatants in La Paz or Montevideo feel as though they appear in them." Miristas, who were outside Allende's coalition and opposed his constitutional and peaceful path to socialism, praised Violeta Parra for having the spirit of a guerrilla and for being a "truly revolutionary artist."[96]

Sister of noted poet Nicanor Parra (a friend of U.S. Beat Generation poet Allen Ginsberg), Violeta Parra amplified her presence and further established the makings of a legacy when, in 1964, she founded the Peña de los Parra (The Parra Circle)—a house in the capital's downtown area where musicians and friends, including Víctor Jara, gathered with the Parras to further develop what was a rapidly expanding community of artists grounded in folk music and firmly ensconced in the Left.[97] The Peña essentially became the epicenter of Nueva Canción, and remains in Chilean collective memory as a site of cultural heritage. The principal voice in the Peña fell silent in February 1967, when Violeta Parra committed suicide at age forty-nine. Her death came shortly after the appearance of what most would agree is her most striking and famous composition: "Gracias a la vida" (Thank You to Life), a song that looks back on life with fondness and gratitude. "Gracias a la vida"—imbued with a deeply personal message rather than a political one—has been performed over the years by artists ranging from Joan Baez to Michael Bublé.[98] The song marked the pinnacle of a career that has inspired performers and listeners within and well beyond Chile's borders for decades.

At the time of Violeta Parra's death, the next great Nueva Canción figure was on the rise, having produced his first album in 1966: Víctor Jara. Remembered as a prominent victim of the military regime that overthrew Allende in 1973, Jara joined the Peña in 1965 and reinforced his Nueva Canción credentials, artistically and politically, through such songs as "El aparecido" (The Ghost), a 1967 composition dedicated to Che Guevara (a "son of rebelliousness," as one stanza proclaims) and 1969's "Te recuerdo Amanda" (I Remember You, Amanda). A deeply melodious song, "Te recuerdo Amanda" tells of a working-class couple: Amanda and Manuel, the latter a factory worker who must endure the terrible conditions of his labor—and who, as Jara describes, dies the death of an exploited worker. (The song's protagonists shared the names of Jara's parents, thus underscoring Jara's own working-class roots.) On the same album as "Te recuerdo Amanda" appeared "Luis Emilio Recabarren," which remembers and celebrates the founder of the PCCh, further emphasizing a relationship between the exploitation of workers and those who, like Recabarren, have pledged and struggled to realize a better world for the exploited masses.

A central figure—along with Ángel Parra, Quilapayún, and a few others—in the catalog and creative operations of DICAP, Jara recorded three albums under that label, and often enabled and participated in the production of other albums from soloists and groups alike. Jara, in short, essentially helped make DICAP what it was—a powerhouse of Nueva Canción and an assiduous and overt cultural arm of the UP government—and gave Nueva Canción much of the meaning it had and continues to have. All the while, Jara's political commitments were sure. On the eve of Allende's assumption of power, for instance, Jara traveled to East Germany in celebration of that country's twenty-first anniversary of its founding. Musicians, painters, dancers, actors, and other performers from more than three dozen nations (either socialist or recently decolonized) gathered in East Berlin to, as Jara put it, "utilize a common language [art] and analyze problems we share" as they worked together to "see the authentic development of a culture with regard to the people in the building of socialism, which without a doubt is the only way to ground the people in their own culture—a grand experience that nowadays we're living."[99] Here, Jara suggests that he and fellow leftist revolutionary artists share a responsibility to both impart culture to "the people" and help build a consciousness among the masses regarding authentic culture. Elsewhere, Jara likewise spoke of "creating a new culture"—a "culture of and for all."[100]

Jara's creativity by no means was confined to the artistic parameters of DICAP, folk music, and Nueva Canción. He was a theatrical director, poet, and teacher, and even within the sphere of music he departed from the vast majority of his fellow Nueva Canción artists by actively engaging rock music as a fan and, at times, as a performer. Jara sometimes worked directly with the group Los Blops and enjoyed rock concerts at the Marconi Theater and other spaces in Greater Santiago where rock culture appealed to young people, like those who made their way to the Piedra Roja.[101] This put Jara at odds with many of his fellow Marxists, including those of Quilapayún, who, as we shall see in chapter 5, wanted nothing to do with rock and what many thought it unabashedly propelled: counterculture and bour-

Víctor Jara participates in a discussion at a meeting of the Communist Youth (1968). In addition to becoming a principal figure of the Nueva Canción movement, he also was an aficionado of criollo rock. He was murdered by the military within a week of the September 1973 coup. Courtesy of the Colección Museo Histórico Nacional (Santiago).

geois imperialism. Jara not only recognized rock as good music and Los Blops as good blokes but also saw revolutionary potential in the genre. As musicologist Carol Hess notes, "Jara called such compromises 'invading the cultural invasion,' and argued that even commercial culture could be elevated for the greater good of spreading Popular Unity's message."[102]

Beating a Different Drum

Rock in Chile, whether recorded abroad and imported or domestically produced, emerged in the late 1960s. It was an evolutionary consequence of rock 'n' roll, which stormed U.S. popular culture the previous decade and grew influential throughout the West. One need only recall the approving screams of young women (and the gasps of so many others) that met a gyrating Elvis Presley on the *Ed Sullivan Show* in September 1956 to come to some understanding of how different rock 'n' roll was from music anyone had heard before. Early Chilean rock 'n' roll—central to what was the *Nueva Ola Chilena* (the New Wave) of the fifties and sixties—reflected the power of a transnational cultural marketplace and a globalized mass media, bolstered on the home front by a booming middle class and fast-paced consumerism. In that context, criollo rock 'n' rollers proved formative in forging a new variant in local popular culture.

Borrowing much from Elvis, the teen sensation Peter Rock (Peter Mous-choulsky Von Remenic, of Austrian birth) and other figures of Nueva Ola, which spanned from the 1950s to the early 1970s, worked with famed producer Camilo Fernández at studios in Santiago owned and operated by RCA, the U.S.-based multinational recording, marketing, and sales giant. Bitten by the rock 'n' roll bug, Peter Rock first sang in English, as did most all Latin American rock 'n' roll performers at the time.[103] Many others joined in the popularity of early Chilean rock 'n' roll, including Nadia Milton, unique for her gender in a male-dominated genre during the late 1950s and early 1960s. She became a teen sex symbol after posing in a bikini in 1960 for the pop culture and humor magazine *Can-Can*—a deed that got her expelled from high school.[104] Like Peter Rock, many Nueva Ola acts used Anglo *nom de disques* in addition to launching their careers by singing North American rock 'n' roll in English. By the early 1960s, they were either translating and performing English-language songs or performing songs they composed originally in Spanish.[105] The same transition—from English to Spanish—later characterized the trajectory of Chilean rock, which was on the rise by the last third of the sixties. Moreover, like rock 'n' roll in the U.S., Nueva Ola tended to stay away from such subjects as angst, alienation, and rebelliousness despite the genre's subversive potential, as it focused instead on characteristically "innocent" references to love and dating. The same was true for Chile's ensemble of young crooners with ties to Nueva Ola, including José Alfredo "Pollo" Fuentes, who appealed across generations.

Arising out of the rock 'n' roll milieu in the early-to-mid-1960s, "beat" music created many of the artistic and aesthetic parameters that would characterize rock. With the Beatles and Beatlemania setting the tone, beat was critical in moving Chile's music scene past Nueva Ola and into a new era of creativity that featured such bands as Los Jockers, Los Beat 4, Los Mac's, Los Picapiedras, and Los Larks.[106] Los Jockers—"*chascones* [shaggy ones] made in Chile," as a popular music magazine called them—defended their music, longer hair, and beat antics as "genuine" in the face of constant harassment by police and disparaging quips from mainstream onlookers, chalking up such negativity to their spot on the cutting edge of youth culture.[107] Los Beat 4, though resembling Los Jockers in many ways, fared better in their relationship with authorities. On two LPs in 1967 (with the inaugural album titled *Boots a go-go*, produced by RCA-Chile), one in 1968, and another in 1971, Los Beat 4 performed very much in the style of the Beatles and other beat bands in Chile, but they soon broke the mold by producing one of the first Chilean rock songs in Spanish. "We wanted to sing only in Spanish because that way it was easier to reach the public, which has a right to know and understand what its hearing," the band noted. "Beat lyrics have great substance, and in Chile there's been the impression that they were totally incoherent and without meaning precisely because they were not understood."[108] Moreover, they also recorded Spanish translations of songs by the Beatles and such groups as the Kinks and the Rolling Stones, thus indicating a transition from beat to rock.

By 1968, Los Beat 4 were sporting longer hair and were clearly merging into, and further propelling, a nascent criollo rock scene, becoming more and more experimental along the way. "We had to let loose our imagination, get away from formality, and take flight a little," bassist Guillermo "Willy" Benítez reflected.[109] In 1970, that flight took Los Beat 4 to a loose association with the Jota's DICAP, though the band never produced a record for DICAP's catalog. But any association with DICAP generally smacks of some ideological linkage with the organized Left, which would have been especially rare among Chilean rock groups of the period—a subject to which we shall return. Any link to DICAP, according to the Marxist press, signaled Los Beat 4's intention of "deepening" the group's music and musical knowledge, thereby suggesting that groups without DICAP associations lacked a certain level of cultural depth and enlightenment. Moreover, according to *El Siglo*, the group's dedication to writing and singing songs in Spanish reflected Los Beat 4's solidarity with Chilean and Latin American young people who were "alienated by foreign musical currents" (notwithstanding beat's foreign origin, apparently).[110] Early on, Los Beat 4, like such groups as the Doors and Steppenwolf, spoke to issues that were central to the "youth question" in ways that could easily be considered rebellious but not necessarily revolutionary in the orthodox political sense of the term. In the 1967 song "Ta ta ta," for instance, Los Beat 4 reached out to young people harboring a palpable sense of discontent with the sociocultural and political status quo. The chorus "Ta ta ta ta ta" means nothing, but such phrases as "Te sientes a un lado de la sociedad" (You feel like you're on the outside of society), "Te dicen no puedes amar a tu edad porque aún muy joven estás" (They say you can't love at your age because you're still too young), and "No quieres ver guerra ni la destrucción y solo te enseñan a odiar" (You don't want to see war or destruction and they only teach you to hate) address matters ranging from generational dynamics to geopolitics.[111] Their social criticism drew the attention of the experimental theater troupe of the University of Chile's Theater Institute.

In late 1970, the curtain went up for the musical production *El degenéresis* (from the verb "to degenerate") at the university's Antonio Varas Theater.[112] It was to be "the most revolutionary and best work in recent years," as one leftist newspaper put it."[113] On the surface, *El degenéresis*, with eighteen songs, shared much in common with Broadway and off-Broadway musicals like *Hair* and the highly sexualized *Oh! Calcutta!* It offered audiences an eclectic score, biting social commentary, and a notable dose of nudity.[114] As experimental theater went, *El degenéresis* was very much that, borrowing its artistic approach from Bertolt Brecht, a favorite of Marxists who wed the popular with the avant-garde and experimental, and Antonin Artaud's fusion of actors and audience. With music arranged by Sergio Ortega of the Nueva Canción movement, lyrics by Nueva Ola's Jorge Rebel, and under the direction of Edmundo Villarroel, a Marxist with close ties to the Allende government, the production used farce, satire, and comedy to drive home messages rooted in class struggle, anti-imperialism (with one tune called "Yanki, Goodbye"), and the moral superiority of the working masses—and therefore that of UP. The show's main character—a petty bourgeois colérico— becomes the subject of considerable mockery hurled by members of the working class. But what made *El degenéresis* different than most any other pro-UP artistic production was the participation of Los Beat 4, whose perfor- mance defies any single identification in terms of genre, though it includes songs very much in the beat and rock veins. In one such beat-rock song, "Self- Made Man," and sounding much like the Doors, Los Beat 4 relay an unmis- takable and contemptuous indictment of bourgeois consumerism through lyrics in Spanish and English. They include (with original English lyrics in italics): "He says he's a *self-made man* / I'm going to tell you all the truth / If you gain prestige / By buying stupid things / They don't mean anything / And don't have value / He says he's a *self-made man* / And he feels proud when thinking / That everyone respects him / That he's someone important / So if he made himself / Then it resulted in someone outrageous."[115]

Conceived and produced by pro-Allende figures, the ideological-artistic framework of *El degenéresis*—in other words, the performative context— placed songs like "Self-Made Man" firmly within UP's discourse on class. The theater troupe essentially made Los Beat 4—whose members were not card-carrying members of any UP parties or groups—more respectable by turning the band's music against those who otherwise were much of the band's audience: young bourgeois types, or so the Marxist press suggested.[116] It was an unusual circumstance in the cultural and political environment of the time. Clearly, some young radicals saw in beat and rock a purpose, notwithstanding what leading voices on the Left generally identified as their definitional profile: bourgeois and purposelessness. Overall, the revolutionary-political potential of rock generally fell on deaf ears among the Left's leadership and much of its rank and file.

Rock(ing) Culture

There would have been no criollo rock, with its peculiarities and permutations, without rock's prior emergence and popularization elsewhere. It was, as many Chileans often (and pejoratively) reminded their compatriots, imported. Rock music's origin and trajectory in the United States, the fertilization provided by British musicians, and the postwar international marketplace of cultural commodities combined to produce a transnational phenomenon that quite rapidly developed vernaculars in terms of sound, lyrics, and general aesthetic qualities and imprints. Multinational recording corporations, international newswires, films, radio, television, and other factors allowed for the fluid flow of cultural consumables, news, and knowledge around much of the world, and rock culture briskly traveled such conduits. Young people were at the helm of that rock culture as producers and consumers, bolstered and molded by record labels, such as RCA-Chile and Asfona. As rock emerged in the West, various social constituencies in national contexts met it with generous doses of skepticism, animosity, and criticism, just as they had in the cases of sexual liberation and drug use. Although the youth question, which brought to the fore new attitudes regarding sex, sexuality, gender, and drugs, was patently transnational, people young and old nevertheless contributed to it, experienced it, and reacted to it in specific local contexts, just as rock was simultaneously transnational and local. In Chile, rock's coming of age occurred at a unique moment—the rise of UP to power—and amid the most polarized, contested, and splenetic sociopolitical climate in the country's history. That setting also saw the golden age of the Nueva Canción movement. These factors touched criollo rock in particular ways, just as they shaped the way many Chileans viewed larger phenomena to which rock was inextricably linked: the youth question and counterculture.

Today, if a Chilean who was tuned in to the criollo music scene—and especially to rock—during the late 1960s and early 1970s, were asked to reminisce, Los Jaivas, Los Blops, and Aguaturbia would likely populate his or her recollection. While dozens of rock groups recorded songs and LPs during the era, few reached the altitudes of those three, all of which drew international attention and were complicit, in one way or another, in the development of counterculture.[117] The groups were revolutionary collectively and separately, each bringing variances of rock culture to the stage. Through the Nueva Canción-influenced folkloric and Andean undertones of Los Jaivas, the rhythmic range and New Age-*ish* impulse of Los Blops, and the outright psychedelia of Aguaturbia, rock artists challenged listeners and their society to embrace ways of being that stood in sharp contrast to Nueva Canción and mainstream music in general. Chile's was a vibrant, if small, rock milieu—then and now largely overshadowed in mainstream popular culture, both nationally and internationally, by the productivity, layered appeal, and Allende-related air of Nueva Canción. But if Nueva Canción was subversive vis-à-vis conservative, bourgeois, and "traditional" Chile, rock flexed a measure of seditiousness vis-à-vis Nueva Canción, if only as a "revolutionary" option to what was essentially an official genre of the state between 1970 and 1973.

With roots in the coastal city of Viña del Mar, Los Jaivas pushed forward a developing rock scene during the late 1960s, generating new creative space away from the highly influential and popular Nueva Ola and beat. They began in the early 1960s—under the Anglophone moniker High Bass—as high school students performing songs well within the Nueva Ola framework, but not without some eclectic elements. The group soon morphed, in profound ways, into Los Jaivas, and the brothers Eduardo, Claudio, and Gabriel Parra, along with Mario Mutis and Eduardo "Gato" Alquinta, went on to become a collective criollo rock legend. Indeed, they became, as rock journalist and historian Fabio Salas Zúñiga notes, "the most enduring group in the history of Chilean rock."[118] In 1964, a year after its formation, High Bass appeared in a story in a Valparaíso newspaper with an accompanying photo of five young men—clean-cut, with white dress shirts, bow ties, and patches on their jackets emblazoned with "HB." It was good advertising for a group thrilled to be appearing at local hotels, clubs, parties, and schools on Saturdays—the only day of the week they performed in light of school and homework. Their musical tastes and goals were clear: to get people dancing and to enjoy themselves. The band, which played music and played with music when it formed, using makeshift instruments and often riffing, became a more serious venture once its members entered the Federico Santa María Technical University in Valparaíso. At the time, member Claudio Parra recalled, they played covers, some criollo rock 'n' roll, including that of Luis Dimas, and enjoyed changing the words of well-known songs. "The rhythm really didn't matter much," he said. "We could play a potpourri."

Moreover, in a sign that folkloric music would become engrained in the band's music, each performance of High Bass ended with a *cueca*—the celebrated folk music considered typically Chilean.[119]

By 1969, the quintet had shed their jackets and bow ties; they were hippies, having been influenced by "all of the [era's] movements for change."[120] High Bass, as Mutis recollected, had gone through what might be described as the very early onset of a midlife crisis: "We asked ourselves: 'Who are we? Where are we going? What do we want?' We discarded all that we had come to know up to that time, and we started to do music that was one-hundred percent improvisation, just improvisation—and a completely freestyle improvisation without any predetermined parameters."[121] They were fusing local rhythms, some Andean (and even Afro-Caribbean) elements, the unmistakably transnational sound of rock, and a good dose of improvisation, all of which, in addition to their shoulder-length hair, beards, use of marijuana, and overall aesthetic imprint, placed them squarely within the countercultural scene of the period. In short, they had become Los Jaivas (a play on the Chilean word *jaibas*, or crabs, and their original name, "High Bass"). As keyboardist and vocalist Claudio Parra explained, "Our hair and moustaches grew and we felt like we were in a new era: the era of improvisation. Our house was transformed into a musical laboratory: we stopped playing the piano keys and began to scratch directly onto its wires and take advantage of every resonance to extract sounds like echoes in the mountains."[122] Improvisation was something High Bass had done early in the band's career, but it would become a hallmark of Los Jaivas and other criollo rock acts when they performed live, just as improvisation and exploration were, in a very real sense, essential aspects of being countercultural. "When I first heard of them [Los Jaivas] they were still the High Bass. And they were hippies but they wore clothes like those from Chiloé [a southern island region]. There's nothing greater than to look at early pictures of the Jaivas," said Carlos Lowry, who was close to groups like Los Blops on the rock scene of the late sixties and early seventies. "The three brothers were all really tall, skinny hippies, which is really uncommon in Chile, so they were just beautiful to look at."[123]

Their commitment to improvisation and experimentation made for some hurdles, especially in the recording industry. "What happened is that we appeared to be the strangest group, as in the most vanguardist. What we were doing was very different than what the rest were doing; we didn't play songs," noted Claudio Parra.[124] But unorthodoxy proved alluring in late 1970 to a figure who became, de facto, the group's first producer: psychedelic rock artist Country Joe McDonald of Country Joe and the Fish, who gained fame at Woodstock. With connections in Chile and through mutual acquaintances he shared with Los Jaivas, Country Joe became aware of what the band was doing. Country Joe also had contacts at RCA and pushed Los Jaivas to explore a record deal with RCA's Chilean branch. The group then began to record numerous songs in Country Joe's presence, but an album did not materialize immediately. As Claudio Parra described, "Country Joe took that work to the United States, along with some photos of us in Parque Forestal for an album jacket." Nothing became of those materials, and the band did not have any further contact with Country Joe until the mid-1980s.[125] This outcome produced embitterment among Los Jaivas toward the industry.

By the time of their brief collaboration with Country Joe, Los Jaivas already were becoming better known in Santiago, having moved there from the coast in order to take advantage of the developing rock scene, and their reputation grew after they played the Piedra Roja festival in October 1970, which took place around the time Country Joe was in Chile. In that year, moreover, they appeared, along with Los Blops and others, at a concert in Viña del Mar organized by Víctor Jara.[126] The event received little media coverage and apparently only mild fanfare. Record labels were uninterested in late 1970 and into 1971, meaning that Los Jaivas had to foot the bill for studio time. "The famed Yamaha organ that we had imported had to be 'sacrificed,' and with the money we received for it, we bought time at RCA studios," Claudio Parra reminisced. Those recordings laid the substrate for the 1971 LP *El volantín* (The Kite), the group's self-produced and first album.[127] That year, in the wakes of Piedra Roja and *El volantín*, Los Jaivas began garnering significant attention from the *santiaguino* press, from newspapers to glossy magazines, and their particular brand of rock—improvisational and eclectic—and their hippismo were front and center.

The popular current-events magazine *Novedades* sent a contributor to one Los Jaivas concert in late 1971, where the group headlined a lineup at the large Caupolicán Theater that included Los Beat 4. As the young audience went "crazy" for the music, police were in full force with the primary goal of negating any marijuana use. Things were orderly enough—aside from some men going shirtless, youths gyrating wildly to the music, and some women wearing tiny tops with English words on them—that the writer concluded that the event, though suspiciously subversive, showed some of the "respect and order that are traditional among our people."[128] To *Novedades*, Los Jaivas's improvisation was a topic of interest, as it was in many other stories on the band published in the early 1970s. For instance,

Ramona, in addition to citing the group's loose musical style, found it interesting to convey to its readers in the winter of 1972 that the band was not politically committed, and therefore suspect. When asked about politics—that is, when asked about the Chilean road to socialism and events surrounding it—Claudio Parra simply noted, "Well, that's a whole other issue . . . it's a personal matter for the individual."[129] The fact that politics was not at the forefront of rock (nor Nueva Ola or beat), notwithstanding *El degenéresis*, not only distinguished it from Nueva Canción but also contributed to a less than positive general impression of countercultural music among those, especially on the left, who were embroiled in the political struggles of the era.

The group's second album, *Todos juntos* (Everyone Together), which appeared in 1972 under the label IRT (Industrias de Radio y Televisión, formerly RCA-Chile and nationalized by the Allende government), included a title track that became Los Jaivas's most famous song, which fused Andean sounds with rock's electric guitar and bass. Lyrics include: "For a long time I've lived asking myself / Why is the earth so round and one and only? / If we all live separated / Then what are the sky and sea for? / What is the sun that shines upon us for / If we don't even look at each other?"[130] Its allusions to alienation and community are in the countercultural vein, but its communalist vibe also could potentially appeal to young radicals as well, although, in large part, such attraction did not materialize until after the 1973 coup reconfigured what community and solidarity meant, especially among those in exile. Moreover, at the time of *Todos juntos*, which sold a remarkable 180,000 copies, Los Jaivas already were quite serious and more public about their hippismo, including their use of drugs and their evolving mix of regional sounds with the hallmarks of rock. As guitarist and vocalist Eduardo "Gato" Alquinta explained, "We didn't want to mimic hippies with the same music that was made in the United States. It's easy to be that type of hippie, to leave the house dressed in wool and play North American music, then return home and have your mom have everything prepared for you, your bed made and the food ready."[131]

Although UP was nationalist as it pursued a *Chilean* road to socialism, critical components of the coalition did not necessarily appreciate the chilenidad of the music and hippismo that Los Jaivas produced. In early 1973, the Jota's *Ramona* reflected on a New Year's Eve concert in Greater Santiago's comuna of La Reina, where Los Jaivas and Los Blops shared the lineup. The concert made for a "concentration of strange birds, lazy people, and marihuaneros," the writer noted. The article then captured tidbits from

Eduardo "Gato" Alquinta of Los Jaivas performs at Piedra Roja (1970). A founding member of the revolutionary rock group, Alquinta died in 2003. Courtesy of Paul Lowry.

an interview with the band, including an exchange about politics. "We can't say that we're not political, because that is impossible, but we don't identify ourselves with any party," said one unidentified band member. This sharpened the line of questioning. Finally, when asked if changing a world that both hippies and social revolutionaries agreed was unjust required a concerted struggle, another member answered plainly, "I don't think struggle is needed. I'm not going to fight for anyone. And I don't want other people to fight and therefore I don't fight." The writer then adds, "To converse with Los Jaivas does not leave one with high spirits."[132] It is clear that Los Jaivas, unlike, say, Víctor Jara and Quilapayún, were far from being poster children of UP. Los Blops, who also performed at Piedra Roja, were also targeted by much of the same criticism from more orthodox revolutionaries, being scolded as "bourgeois" and "imperialist."

In our 2007 interview, Juan Pablo Orrego, now an internationally known ecologist, reclined in his chair as he recalled the summer of 1968. His group, Los Blops, performed at the popular central coast seaside town of Isla Negra, where they played covers of Cream, the Rolling Stones, and the Doors. Or- rego noticed a rather eclectic audience—one that would not be replicated at later Los Blops concerts (or rock concerts in general, for that matter), espe- cially during the UP period. In the Isla Negra audience sat Pablo Neruda (Communist senator, renowned poet, and part-time Isla Negra resident), Án- gel Parra (the son of Nueva Canción matriarch Violeta Parra), Ángel Parra's wife, Marta Orrego (who happened to be Juan Pablo Orrego's aunt), and Nueva Canción icon Víctor Jara. Figures like Neruda, in Juan Pablo Orrego's words, were "the elite of the Left who during the evening would listen to the operas of Wagner." Yet, in that one summertime moment at Isla Negra, Ne- ruda and other important cultural figures of the Left maybe—just maybe— found something not entirely unappetizing in the sounds of Los Blops as the group played the songs of Jim Morrison and other foreign rockers of the era.[133] (Probably not.) What is clear, though, is that at least one figure—Víctor Jara—became a Los Blops fan, and went so far as to collaborate artistically with the group, despite being a key figure in the Nueva Canción movement, whose performers and sponsors on the Left, by and large, found much to criticize in Blops-like rock music, culturally and politically speaking.

Leaving covers behind by 1969, Los Blops (a name largely inspired by the comic magazine *Condorito* and its use of the onomatopoeic "plop!") formu- lated a unique rock sound and composed albums that included electric and acoustic guitar, some flute, piano, organ, and deep drum rhythms. After three iterations of its lineup between 1964 and 1969, Los Blops in 1970 fea- tured Juan Pablo Orrego (bass and acoustic guitar), Julio Villalobos (guitar and piano), Juan Contreras (keyboard and flute), and Sergio Bezar (drums). The last piece of the puzzle was vocalist and guitarist Eduardo Gatti, who joined that year after gaining a degree of celebrity fronting the seminal beat- rock group, the Apparition. Los Blops sound brought together various influ- ences, including folk and U.S. rock, with the latter's impact largely the result of stays by Orrego and Contreras in the United States during the late 1960s. They brought back to Chile rock albums, instruments, and images of what they had witnessed: a growing U.S. counterculture. Gatti had done the same.[134] Gatti's addition lifted Los Blops to new heights and helped fuel the substantial success of their first album, *Blops*. Their inaugural LP featured one track in particular, "Los Momentos" (The Moments), with lyrics and music by Gatti, that ostensibly became a generational anthem and stands today as one of the most iconic songs of late twentieth-century Chilean music.

The debut album appeared under the Jota's DICAP label even though the group was not pledged in any way to the PCCh or the Allende government.

In fact, *Blops* was the first and only rock album produced by DICAP during the UP years, joining the many Nueva Canción albums (by Violeta Parra, Quilapayún, and Jara, among others) that dominated DICAP's catalog.[135] This led to a vague sense among music fans, especially after the 1973 coup, that the band was politicized and pro-Allende, given DICAP's conspicuous place in the cultural politics of the Left. Orrego noted that nothing could be further from the truth. Friendship, not ideology, was the key factor, with Jara and Los Blops developing close bonds after the former had encountered the latter's music in the late 1960s. In fact, Jara became a big fan of rock music (a fact not publicized by UP or DICAP) and regularly attended rock concerts at venues like the Marconi Theater in Providencia as well as weekly rock recitals at the University of Chile's theater during the Allende years.[136] Desperately seeking their first record deal, Los Blops turned to their friend for help. Jara proposed a Los Blops album to DICAP executives, who responded negatively and noted that the band's members were "petit bourgeois" and decadent, thus not anywhere near what the record label wanted to promote and project. After all, powerful forces on the Left linked rock music to "bourgeois" sociability, culture, politics, and economy during the late 1960s and early 1970s. Tension mounted between Jara and DICAP. The situation was resolved when Jara essentially threatened to leave DICAP if Los Blops were not given an album deal. The label relented, and *Blops* became the fourth album on DICAP's 1970 list.[137] The Los Blops–Jara relationship was almost certainly in play, too, when the Allende government sponsored a short Los Blops tour of working-class communities, which struck Orrego and his bandmates as odd in light of leftist accusations that the band was "imperialist" and that their instruments stood as empirical proof.[138] Gatti explained, "They [leftist leaders and media] called us imperialists because we played electric guitars. We lived between two infernos [the Left and the Right], always. What made us look out of place was that we had a consistent outlook but we were not committed to a party." He added, "Those were tough times. One felt a strong sense of oppression toward anything that was different or what lay outside that formal canon, above all in a country like Chile, which is a tremendously formal country."[139]

Meanwhile, suspicions that Los Blops members were Marxists were further stoked by their cooperation with Jara on his 1971 album *El derecho de vivir en paz* (The Right to Live in Peace), which includes the unabashedly revolutionary songs "El derecho to de vivir en paz," "Plegaria a un labrador" (Prayer to a Laborer), "A Cuba" (To Cuba), and "B.R.P.," the acronym for the Brigada Ramona Parra (Ramona Parra Brigade), a branch of the Jota.

Again, however, their friendship and mutual respect for art, not a shared political ideology, was the adhesive. What is more, Orrego explained that a careful look at Los Blops's lyrics reveals the true nature of the band's outlook. Take "Los Momentos," which was inspired by Covacevich's *New Love.* The song is about alienation, but not the sort of alienation usually discussed by Marxists. It includes the lyrics: "Your silhouette goes walking with a sad and sleeping soul / The dawn is no longer new for your large eyes and for your face / The sky and its stars have become muted, distant, and dead for your unconnected mind."[140] "Los Momentos" and the rest of Los Blops's music collectively constituted an existentialist gesture, with the search for a sort of enlightenment and freedom rising above materialist and political concerns. Feeling trapped by their parents and the older generation, Los Blops's art was about "change, an awakening, opening yourself to other realities," Orrego said.[141] Indeed, the band, while often sounding as if in line with the utopianism of leftist discourse circa 1970, was inspired by esoteric thought, especially that of the Arica School, founded by the Bolivian thinker Oscar Ichazo in Arica, Chile (discussed in chapter 6).[142]

After the success of their debut album, Los Blops went on to record two more LPs during the Allende years—*Del volar de las palomas* (Of the Flight of Doves), produced by their friend Ángel Parra and released in 1971 by the Penã de los Parra label, and *Locomotora* (Locomotive, taped in 1973 at RCA's studios in Buenos Aires and released in 1974—both of which exhibited the band's transition to experimentalism, improvisation, instrumentals, and, in general, to progressive rock, which, like jazz, set aside carefully conceived and packaged music.[143] (Their live performances, especially after the band was booed mercilessly by a conservative crowd at the 1972 International Festival of Song in Viña del Mar, became displays of spontaneous creativity, incorporating more electric guitar and a sense of abandonment to the artistic moment.) *Del volar de las palomas* (also known as *Blops II*) includes the track "Manchufela," which honors the band's residence, the "Manchufela Community"—a *peña*-like site for living, making music, and, in general, being countercultural with the intent of "changing the paradigm," as Orrego put it. The large former convent, located in Santiago's municipality of La Reina, became a magnet for musicians and artists who sought communal living and freedoms of thought and practice, with Los Blops largely footing the bill as the most financially successful Manchufela residents. As the periodical *Onda* described in 1971, one walked into Manchufela and noticed many long mustaches on its male residents, a lamp emblazoned with the peace symbol, and images of the

Beatles on the walls. There were rooms for rehearsal, the making of artisan crafts, and a kitchen. It was a lively space, with Manchufela dwellers taking turns buying vegetables and meat, but, hinting at the locale's bourgeois elements, the leftist *Onda* noted that there were no real communal rooms—just an assortment of small rooms with particular uses—and that hired "help" arrived every morning to clean the kitchen.[144]

Manchufela became well known in and outside musical and countercultural circles, with, for example, the trendy *Paula* calling the residence "a strange musical community," a phrase that likely brought smiles and feelings of pride and accomplishment to its residents. Los Blops told *Paula*'s writer, Isabel Allende, that the band was more serious and artistic than what counterculture usually demanded (e.g., simply copying foreign beat and rock music) and that it didn't share the "marihuanero" vibe of hippies and "pseudo-hippies."[145] Some thirty-five years later, Orrego recalled feeling disappointed toward "superficial" hippies whose counterculture was based only on the consumption of marijuana or rock (though Los Blops enjoyed both, as did Los Jaivas), without self-reflection and commitment toward the betterment of the spiritual self. In this way, he explained, Los Blops were more in line with the more "real" counterculture of the United States, which spoke of social justice, social transformation, and a return to nature.[146] The last point is of particular applicability, given that Orrego, as noted above, went on to become one of Chile's leading ecologists and environmentalists by the 1990s.

It was (and remains) difficult to precisely identify the music of Los Blops. Over time, the band evolved from folk-rock beginnings in the late 1960s to a progressive-rock sound by 1973. Los Jaivas likewise was an enigmatic group, stirring a rich stew of folk, rock, and some progressive-rock ingredients. Far less ambiguous was Aguaturbia, which mixed swirling psychedelic rock and heavier, pounding acid rock, resulting in a deep and reverberating sound—much like that of San Francisco's Jefferson Airplane. Indeed, Aguaturbia's vocalist, Denise (the *nom de rock* of Climene María Solís Puleghini, born in São Paulo but raised in Chile), brought to criollo rock a powerful and resonating voice quite similar to those of Grace Slick and Janis Joplin. Denise met Juan Carlos Corales, a former Nueva Ola guitarist and member of the abovementioned Los Jockers, in 1968. In that year, they formed Aguaturbia (Turbid Waters) by adding bassist Ricardo Briones, a strong admirer of Hendrix and Cream bassist Jack Bruce, and drummer Willy Cavada, who was influenced by such forces as Steppenwolf, Hendrix, and Cream. By 1969, when Denise and Corales married (she was seventeen),

Aguaturbia was recording its first album, *Aguaturbia*, which appeared in 1970 under the Chilean label Arena (founded by famed Nueva Ola producer Camilo Fernández) and the U.S.-based label RCA. The album made quite a mark—even before anyone had listened to it. On the cover, the group appeared nude in a photo that apparently escaped the attention of censors and scandalized many when it was reproduced on the front page of the Santiago newspaper *La Segunda.* "Chile's first underground group," the caption reads, "looked to break the mold by imitating John Lennon and Yoko Ono," in reference to the famous cover of Lennon and Ono's 1968 album *Unfinished Music No. 1: Two Virgins,* where the two appear nude.[147]

Unabashedly and unmistakably, Aguaturbia wanted to replicate U.S. psychedelic rock and counterculture on both sonic and visual planes. Denise, who was one of the extremely few lead female rockers in Latin America at the time, ratted out her hair and often sported large glasses and short shorts, while Corales and the others donned colorful, striped pants and grew facial hair. "It was required," she reflected. "It was an opera."[148] Key, too, is that the band wrote and performed most of its compositions in English—a trend that had appeared in early Nueva Ola and beat but had largely fallen out of favor as the rock music scene matured during the late 1960s. Those compositions often focused on matters distant from the existential explorations of Los Blops, for instance. The track "EVOL" ("LOVE" spelled backward), from the group's second album, *Aguaturbia Vol. II* (1970) is a case in point:

Love is the way
to be alive
Everybody making love
Everybody making love
Everybody making love
Adam and Eve made love
Adam and Eve made love
Adam and Eve made love
Cleopatra made love
Cleopatra made love
and the gods made love
and the gods made love
Everybody making love
Love
Love
Love[149]

The nearly nine-minute track includes a guitar solo by Corales, many changes in pace and mood, and imparts the characteristically psychedelic traits of unconventional vocalizations (Denise pitching her voice high and seemingly howling to open the song), extended instrumentals, and a certain disjointedness.

Aguaturbia's earliest public performances in Santiago, which began in 1969, took place in such sites as the bohemian hangout Casa de la Luna Azul, the Museum of Fine Arts, and St. George's College, an elite private high school known for its upper-class hippismo. The band soon graduated to more impressive venues, including the First Encounter of Vanguard Music (alongside High Bass [Los Jaivas] and Los Blops) in January 1970 and the capital's Caupolicán Theater, where renowned Welsh folk singer Mary Hopkins was in attendance.[150] Then, as 1970 came to a close, Aguaturbia left for the United States, finally settling in New York City, where the band lived, performed live, and recorded for the next two years—and where Denise and Corales welcomed their first child, Indira.[151]

Aguaturbia's music and aesthetic fell well within the contours of criollo rock but were stylistically different than those of Los Blops, Los Jaivas, and other groups. This speaks to rock's diversity and malleability in the late 1960s and early 1970s, which was essentially mirrored by the heterogeneity and elasticity of counterculture. Before turning to a robust discussion of counterculture—the subject we have been contextualizing and basically skirting thus far in this book—we must return briefly to October 1970 and a dusty, hilly property in a corner of the municipality of Las Condes. Then and there, a rock festival (the "Chilean Woodstock," as many have referred to it), which boasted performances by the leading groups of the era, including Los Jaivas and Los Blops, became a conspicuous intervention in intergenerational relations amid a deepening youth question. It was a watershed moment in the history of youth and culture, underscoring the presence of counterculture in the public sphere and making it far more apparent in the everyday concerns of families, political groups, the nation, and the state.

That Gig at Los Dominicos

As rock festivals go, the "Woodstock" at Los Dominicos—a much remembered and momentous three days that awakened many to criollo counterculture—basically sucked, or so Juan Pablo Orrego and other festival performers recalled. In early spring 1970, Los Jaivas, Los Blops, Aguatur-

Rodrigo Murillo, bassist for Lágrima Seca, jams with his band and Los Ripios at Piedra Roja (1970). Courtesy of Paul Lowry.

bia, and other groups signed on to play the "youth song festival" upon receiving invitations—which could be better described as pleas—from festival organizers. A winding grapevine of friends connected Jorge Gómez and his assistants to the rock-music scene and its most prominent artists, providing the kind of personal links strong enough to convince performers that showing up at the "Half-Moon Festival"-turned–"Piedra Rajada"-turned–"Piedra Roja" would be worth their while. The festival's headliners and supporting bands were already familiar to young people who frequented rock concerts at venues like the Marconi or Caupolicán theaters, in addition to high schools, cultural centers, and other sites, but performers like Los Jaivas, Los Blops, and Aguaturbia, who were joined by their rock peers Lágrima Seca, Los Ripios, and Los Trapos, had not yet become the sensations they later would be. Piedra Roja provided all of those groups an opportunity for unfettered fun, creativity, and some cultural marketing.

After hours of waiting for the bands to arrive, and amid the crowd entertaining itself with guitars, bongos, and songs, the festival's organizers were pleased to finally see invited performers take the rickety stage on the afternoon of Sunday, October 11. There had been some challenges, but things had fallen (enough) into place by the afternoon for Piedra Roja to become a rock festival, or at least something that resembled one. As Sunday night unfolded, performers had to deal with an array of complications. Los Blops managed to play nearly a complete set essentially in the dark, with only a lightbulb glowing onto the stage, and with the challenge of having too little juice flowing to their instruments and amplifiers, as our opening chapter described. Carlos Lowry, a co-organizer of the festival who often hung out at Manchufela with Gatti and the others, recalled that the difficulty involved in seeing and hearing Los Blops that night added to the scene's improvised and mysterious atmosphere.[152] But issues beyond these ultimately derailed the group's performance and left some negative impressions. With no barrier erected between the stage and the crowd, not to mention the complete absence of security personnel, problems in the audience wound up being problems for the bands. Orrego and Gatti recalled that one audience member had apparently imbibed too much of an intoxicating substance—likely alcohol or marijuana—during Los Blops's set, so the band stopped to attend to the unconscious young man.[153] Defending Los Blops as countercultural but not superficially so, Orrego lamented that at Piedra Roja festivalgoers got wasted on a cocktail of Romilar (a common cough syrup) and red wine, young men were sexually aggressive to the point of committing crimes, and, in general, mayhem was afoot. As a result, Los Blops were disillusioned, to say the least. Orrego recalled, "It [the festival] was a disaster. It was poorly organized."[154]

Fortunately for the crowd, Los Jaivas were among the few performers to perform full sets. Bassist Mario Mutis explained that participating in Gómez's festival proved consequential in the quintet's evolution and for their collective public persona, notwithstanding the event's bothersome attributes. Their journey away from the mainstream—where High Bass emerged and did pretty well—brought with it much creative freedom and growth, but also prompted many to question their cultural legitimacy and morality. At the festival, however, Mutis and his bandmates were in their comfort zone, and they did not disappoint."[155] Los Jaivas's gig at Piedra Roja electrified the crowd and the group's look on stage screamed counterculture, capturing the festival's impetus and meaning. "They were just amazing, you know? Especially Eduardo [Parra]—he just had an amazing look to him. For years they were just the epitome of a Chilean hippie," Lowry explained.[156] The band's conspicuous role at Piedra Roja and its distinction in criollo rock culture were not lost on director Raúl Ruiz, who turned to Los Jaivas to record the soundtrack for his 1973 film *Palomita Blanca,* a coming-of-age story set around the time of Allende's victory in late 1970. The film's first scenes are of (a recreated) Piedra Roja, and Los Jaivas's members appear on stage in what was Ruíz's rendering of Enrique Lafourcade's like-titled 1971 novel. (We will return to Lafourcade's *Palomita Blanca* in chapter 8.)

By the time Piedra Roja happened, Aguaturbia was well known on Santiago's rock scene—more so than most every band at the festival. They were enjoying success after the release of *Aguaturbia,* and the band (and *La Segunda*) had shocked the country thanks to the Lennon and Ono–inspired photo on the debut album's cover. To have Aguaturbia at Piedra Roja was a coup—something that would draw young people, for sure. Things unraveled, however. Upon arriving at Luis Rosselot's tract of land, the band's manager found the entire setup in Los Dominicos, especially the stage and its iffy power supply, to be cheap and amateurish—and it was. Organizers had little money and had never before put on such an event. Furthermore, Aguaturbia soon realized that a performance schedule did not exist; performers came, played, and went in no particular order and without guidance. The band did not know when they would go on stage; they were confused and milling about as a result. "I don't think anyone had a clue about what was going to happen as far as music was concerned," Gary Fritz recalled.[157] Aguaturbia's manager suggested that the band leave; they concurred and thus missed out on performing at the country's most memorable rock event of the era.[158] Despite Aguaturbia's lament, one can argue that such disorganization was an indispensable contribution to Piedra Roja's countercultural vibe. Indeed, how countercultural and "hippie" could a festival of that sort be if it boasted a sleek, professional look and ran like clockwork? Moreover, the festival's undisciplined essence was exactly what many young people wanted. For Mario Soza of Los Ripios, playing the festival was a way young people like him could rebel against "dictatorial parents"—to get away from what was stale, regimented, normative, and prescriptive in mainstream society.[159]

The festival's rock vibe meant that absent from the list of invitees were more well-known and mainstream performers on the country's music scene, such as the Bobby Darren-like crooner José Alfredo "Pollo" Fuentes, whose songs were very popular at the time, or the highly visible artists of Nueva Canción. Generally speaking, the festival was as much a counterpoint to all other pop music and "popular" music as it was a showcase for rock bands inspired by such performers as Led Zeppelin, Cream, Bob Dylan, the Doors, and the Rolling Stones. Interestingly, rock and Nueva Canción shared something in common in 1970: both were fighting for listeners on a music scene dominated by "Pollo" Fuentes and foreign performers. Nueva Canción, for instance, was never popular enough to have much of a presence on radio stations and fared poorly in terms of album sales.[160] Moreover, in a study the Mattelarts conducted in 1968, Fuentes ranked higher than any "protest music" act among urban and rural workers who were polled, while Frank Sinatra, the Beatles, and French-Armenian singer Charles Aznavour proved highly popular among university students and white-collar workers.[161] By 1970, not much had changed, at least according to "Top 10" rankings published in the industry periodical *El Musiquero*. A sampling of editions from the months around Piedra Roja indicates that while Nueva Canción and rock were enjoying more commercial success than they had two years earlier, both still lagged behind performers like "Pollo" Fuentes, Tom Jones, and some Nueva Ola acts, such as Los Ramblers and their Uruguayan peers, Los Iracundos.[162]

It can be said that for criollo rock, the festival marked the best of times and the worst of times. It showcased the yields of a creative boom that was drawing in many young people as followers and fans, and it also marked the beginning of intense public scrutiny and a deluge of insults and accusations from almost every corner of the public sphere, as a later chapter explains. The festival also threw the youth question into sharp relief, and the counterculture became a subject of focused conversation and wrath among the major political constituencies of the era. Also, there is no denying that although bands that performed complained of incidents and problems— including the questionable behavior of some festivalgoers—Piedra Roja remains fixed in a special, nostalgic place in the memories of those who played the gig.

Sex, drugs, and rock came together in far more places than Piedra Roja. Such convergences happened in private homes, in cars, and in other spaces where many young people could explore certain sensations, sensibilities, and dialogue that, separately or together, can be characterized as countercultural. To many young Chileans, criollo counterculture was a way of life. Others sampled it from time to time. For many, it was something to avoid and condemn. Though only a minority of the overall youth population, countercultural young people made marks in their families, in their schools, in public, in culture, and in the discourses of varying social, political, and cultural actors of the era. In our approach to the complexities of the subjects and period at hand, Piedra Roja served as our starting point, and discussions of the youth question, sex, drugs, and music have operated as contextual categories as well as analytical points of access into consequential happenings and attitudes in society. Essentially, we have been sketching out the milieu in which countercultural ideas and practices emerged and to which they contributed. Thus, the remaining chapters examine counterculture in a more direct way, with primary attention given to hippismo and Siloism, both expressive and integral components of criollo counterculture, and to the reactions that emerged in response to such heterodoxy.

. . . .

Sex, drugs, and rock culture converged in a dramatic and unconcealed fashion at Eve, Vitacura's discotheque, in early 1972. In the wealthy eastern suburb of Greater Santiago, young people gathered to see a "tribe" of Chileans and Argentines called Uno (One) present a spectacle inspired by acts in the rock opera *Hair*, which had exploded onto New York's Broadway in 1968. Much to the dismay of a writer for the current-events magazine *Novedades*, the lively recital included many youths high on marijuana and engaged in various forms of sexual interaction, including homoerotic ones, all while performing for (and with) an engrossed crowd that included a good many young women in miniskirts. The audience "danced frenetically" to blaring rock, the witness described, while "lights flashed and changed colors [in psychedelic fashion] to make one go crazy." Soon, six couples gathered under a large bed sheet and proceeded to give the impression of participating in, to put things academically, certain manifestations of vigorous corporeal intimacy. The event then apparently climaxed as the dozen young people, perhaps needing to come up for some air, suddenly cast off the sheet, allowing the captivated (and stoned) audience to gaze upon their nudity.[1] The evening's display struck the *Novedades* observer as highly sexualized, morally vapid, and simply over the top. A correspondent for the Jota's *Ramona* also was in attendance. She described the event as typically bourgeois in its prurience and capitalist underpinnings, the latter evidenced by an admission price of 500 *escudos*—an amount that would buy a sizable quantity of groceries for the typical family. The troupe, she added, "set up shop in none other than the center of the consumerist society that the people [*el pueblo*] are attempting to destroy."[2]

To many Chileans, what the press described went far in summing up a torrent of libertine behavior by young people that posed a daunting danger to the country. For its celebrants and critics alike, the happening at Eve crystalized modes and means of cultural heterodoxy in Chile and elsewhere during the 1960s and early 1970s. It is unlikely what took place within the discotheque's walls gave rise to total disbelief among most readers thumbing through *Novedades* or *Ramona*. After all, by that time the transnational youth question was as apparent as ever and criollo counterculture had burst onto the scene in the form of Piedra Roja. The dance floor at Eve, though, represented yet another space of countercultural sociability, among the many that had been popping up in the capital since the late 1960s. Building on our discussion of the hippista happenings and sensibilities that made Piedra Roja what it was, this and the subsequent two chapters more closely examine both hippismo and Siloism as countercultural variants whose heterodox modes and means of "revolution" and "liberation" posited and exposed a generational fissure just as the country's body politic was fracturing amid class conflict, political animosities, and Cold War tensions. As Pink Lizard of Piedra Roja fame put it, counterculture "was an awakening for youths in extremely tense political times."[3] While hippismo claimed headlines in the press and Piedra Roja provoked Chileans, in one way or another, at the beginning of the eventful 1970s, Siloism emerged as a distinct combination of esoteric, revolutionary thought and practice that differed from hippismo in important and conspicuous ways but nevertheless was countercultural. Unlike hippismo, Siloism was rooted in doctrine and discipline, but Silo's early followers were countercultural in that they offered young people a fundamentally heterodox epistemology and sociocultural schema that eschewed institutions, politics, and essentially the entirety of society, as it existed. Indeed, two notions tethered the most serious practitioners of hippismo and Siloism: focus and energy lay in the transformation of the self—an individual's transformative experiences—and such transformation was concomitant with practices that flouted social, cultural, and political norms and demonstrated anti-establishment and antisystemic dispositions.

Counterculture was about varying means of liberating the self—but by whom, from what, and to what end? Many young Chileans who sought to realize ephemeral or lasting states of freedom and sovereignty did so by means of the trappings of Providencia, free(r) love, rock music, smoking marijuana, Piedra Roja, Manchufela, and the like. That is to say, practicing cultural heterodoxy—in private or in public, piecemeal or holistically—was both an avenue and an expression of an emancipatory impulse fueled by alienation, problems with parents or at school, boredom, or simple curiosity. It also was a powerful marker of identity, whether adopted by young people themselves or branded onto them by disappointed and disgusted family members, journalists, and political constituencies. In light of counterculture's variegation and slipperiness, an academic study such as this faces the challenge of defining something that was hard for many to grasp *then*, not just now. Yet, there are shared temporal, generational, behavioral, and conceptual attributes that may help us define some of counterculture's supple parameters and better understand its heterogeneity and short-lived but revealing role in the social, cultural, and political history of Chile during the late sixties and early seventies.

As with the youth question to which it was coupled, criollo counterculture's emergence and growth obviously did not transpire in a vacuum. The youth question and its ties to emergent discourses on sex and gender, greater focus on drug use, and the development of rock music all were linked to the rise of counterculture both internationally and in Chile. One manifest area of media and social interest was countercultural rebelliousness in the United States and Europe, and even a cursory appraisal of the era's periodicals reveals varying shades of expressivity vis-à-vis countercultural affairs abroad. As subsequent chapters describe, news, commentary, and conversation about foreign counterculture fed a common conception that many critics shared: that hippismo and Siloism alike were of foreign manufacture and therefore not truly and authentically criollo. However, we should not fall into the analytical trap of assuming that criollo counterculture was merely foreign counterculture being practiced locally. Rather, we should borrow and broadly apply to criollo counterculture Alejo Carpentier's notion that music produced in a certain place but played in a different spatial and cultural context becomes the music of that different context due to cultural nuances and a distinct audience—what he called the "local air."[4] Thus, it serves to first turn to manifestations and imprints of foreign hippismo that held significance for young Chileans and in the cultural marketplace in general. Without question, hippismo was an import, but how that import was understood and how it played out in Chile tells us much about the social, cultural, and political dynamics of the era.

Snapshots from Abroad

Conspicuous in Chile by the end of the 1960s were internationally recognized cultural-material hallmarks of counterculture—in particular, those of U.S. origin, evident in San Francisco's Haight-Ashbury district, Berkeley, Woodstock, Paris, Mexico City, and the like—that were displayed, consumed, and talked about, especially by (but not at all limited to) young Chileans with the economic means to (re)produce vernacular counterculture. Music, films, the recounted experiences of young travelers returning from abroad, and the very same periodicals that openly lamented and condemned the criollo counterculture were but some of the many conduits of information through which young people of varying economic means came to understand and appreciate counterculture enough to mimic it. There is no doubt that the criollo counterculture was an offshoot of countercultural movements that arose in the developed countries of the West or that it drew heavily from such phenomena as the 1969 Woodstock festival in upstate New York and the rebellious events in Paris in 1968. Gary Fritz, one of Piedra Roja's co-organizers, observed, "What was happening up in North America and parts of Europe was having a big influence on some sectors of the youth [in Chile], so there were plenty of people with long hair, and [hippie] clothes, and listening to [rock] music and reading about it."[5] Another former hippie noted, "Hippismo was very much influenced by the United States; there weren't a lot of hippie thinkers in Latin America."[6] As we have seen in this book, matters of sex, drugs, and rock 'n' roll—in association with the youth question—were sites in which one may spot the potentialities of countercultural impulses, and all had transnational dimensions. Piedra Roja, the film *New Love*, the discotheque Eve, a production of *Hair*, and locales like Manchufela were but a few of the many means through which those potentialities became practice.

In the weeks just prior to Piedra Roja, the three-hour documentary film *Woodstock: Three Days of Music*, directed by Michael Wadleigh and coedited by Martin Scorsese, was showing at cinemas in Greater Santiago. Its influence on young people like Jorge Gómez and Fritz was powerful, leading to the hatching of the October 1970 festival in Los Dominicos. Also appearing in the capital was the 1969 film *Busco mi destino* (I Search for My Destiny, a.k.a. *Easy Rider*), starring Peter Fonda and Dennis Hopper. As the long-haired and motorcycle-riding protagonists Wyatt and Billy, Fonda and Hopper make their way to Mardi Gras in New Orleans, meeting some interesting people, including hippies, along the way.[7] "It [the Woodstock film] had a huge impact, that and *Easy Rider*. I was totally, I mean, that was what I wanted to be," recollected the former hippie Carlos Lowry, an American who grew up in Chile, learned English second, and was part of a circle of friends and acquaintances that included Piedra Roja organizers.[8] Not everyone was so enthused, to say the least.

Just three days after the Piedra Roja festival ended with well-publicized thievery and brawling in mid-October 1970, the conservative *El Mercurio* published an article on rock festivals in the United States and Europe in its weekly entertainment-related insert, "Topsi." Titled "La guerra del beat"

(The Beat War), it centers on a characteristic evidently shared by the major beat and rock festivals of that era: violence. Referring to outbreaks of hostilities at Woodstock; the beat and rock music festival on Britain's Isle of Wight in 1968, which drew an estimated 600,000 young people; and at similar festivals in France and Holland, the article asserts that the "hippie credo" of "peace, love, and music" was more of an idea than a practice; indeed, "it is only partially upheld" during large counterculture-related events. In short, "hippie" music festivals, as the author describes them, almost invariably cast off "peace" and replace it with "war," hence the article's title. "It [the violence] can happen at other festivals as well," the writer concluded.[9] A more evenhanded approach appeared in a May 1970 issue of *Ritmo*. While bemoaning darker aspects of Woodstock, the piece nevertheless struck a balance when quoting the festival's medical director. "I still don't know if I was dreaming or if I was awake," said physician William Abruzzi. "I had never seen something so strange, so much exotic clothing or such collective craziness. But in reality, I don't know who's crazier, them or us. I felt happy that I could save so many precious lives [mostly in drug-related emergencies], and I don't think I have ever seen such amiable, cooperative, and peace-loving people."[10]

The Woodstock phenomenon—the idea, the event, the people, the meaning, the film, and the consequences—was the topic of various articles in Chilean periodicals before and after Piedra Roja took shape on the outskirts of Las Condes. The timely visit of Woodstock icon Country Joe McDonald, who arrived (sans the Fish) in Santiago on the eve of Piedra Roja, amplified the attention being given to the Woodstock film—and very likely to Jorge Gómez's festival. The highly respected and widely read current-events magazine *Ercilla*, with ties to the Christian Democrats, devoted two full tabloid-size pages to Country Joe, then twenty-eight years old, who did not look like a stereotypical hippie but nevertheless was recognized as a key contributor to the countercultural milieu. "His popularity is grounded in a movement and in the attitude of young *norteamericanos* toward their lives and society," *Ercilla* contributor Juan Ehrmann wrote, noting that Country Joe's music echoed the frustrations of a generation experiencing the realities of war in Indochina. The article included a chronology beginning with the singer-actor's earliest politicization in high school to his military service to his musical exploits in San Francisco and beyond. The interview was wide-ranging, with references to beatniks, the eventful 1968 Democratic National Convention in Chicago, folk music, and drugs. Speaking on the latter, Country Joe observed, "There are two things influencing [young people in the United States]: the consumption of drugs and the repressive attitudes of the authorities, which have not allowed rock festivals to happen on many occasions." He also emphasized, "[The authorities] are wasting their time with marijuana; it is a secondary affair. If the government really wanted to stop the sale of heroin or other hard drugs I'm sure that it could." More broadly speaking, Country Joe asserted that a generational revolution was at hand:

> [The spirit of] Woodstock lives on. Peace and love as well. But other things are going on. There's a social revolution happening. The authorities fear rock. [The revolution] represents a new form of consciousness: antiwar, anti-imperialist, and anarchist. Its philosophy is "do what you want unless it hurts someone else." [The older generation] doesn't like that. It's something too big; it threatens their position. It's a good philosophy so long as they are allowed to live it. If not, we see tensions and confrontations. At Woodstock, the police were intelligent and behaved themselves. In other cases they didn't behave and the result was violence. Others fear that young people are taking drugs, that they are living their sexuality. They fear that young people will make mistakes. But the [countercultural] scene grows despite it all. . . . The days of "movements" are over. Now, it's all about waking and developing your spiritual consciousness. It is another way of establishing a new system.[11]

Although Country Joe, who led the Woodstock audience in a famous "F-U-C-K" chant, counted himself among those engaged in a revolutionary struggle against "the authorities," he, like many other countercultural individuals, could not escape contradiction. As the singer explained, "What am I going to do? I have a manager and an accountant. I have a tour manager, two agents, and two publicists. All these people have assistants and secretaries. I am an industry! I felt ridiculous at the start, with all that machinery. I'm now accustomed to the unavoidable. Luckily, they [his employees] are friends of this environment."[12] All told, *Ercilla*'s readers were presented with a surprisingly sympathetic treatment of the counterculture in the United States and of Country Joe, who comes across in the story as conscientious, politically informed, and well mannered despite his evidently hippie tendencies.

Ercilla's apparent lack of outright enmity toward the counterculture, at least in its article on Country Joe, did not last—and Piedra Roja had everything to do with it. Less than a month after printing the wide-ranging interview, *Ercilla*, in November 1970, published a less-than-compassionate interpretation of the counterculture in an article on the "Hippie Crusade" in Europe. Focusing mostly on French hippies and hippies of other nationalities in France after the 1968 student uprisings in Paris, the *Ercilla* article includes various statements by André Bercoff, noted author and journalist, which had been published previously in the French magazine *L'Express*. Bercoff explained that rebellious young people, in modern countries like France, were on the verge of creating the social realities of the twenty-first century, for better or for worse: "By way of their hopes, their naiveté, and their shouts, the hippies have begun to draw up, in front of the stupefied eyes of the men of the Old World [the older generation], a universe that no one could imagine a decade ago: the outline—still not yet totally defined—of society in the twenty-first century." *Ercilla*'s writer then intervenes: "To build on [Bercoff's] reflections, one must say—from the Latin American and Chilean perspectives—that this explanation is the key to understand why the vast majority of our local hippies are simply swindlers. In the USA and Europe the old social structures have been too entrenched. When they could not be destroyed through revolution, what's left was the mystical [the hippie 'revolution']. Among us [in Latin America and Chile], on the other hand, the revolutionary option—violent or peaceful—remains possible."[13] The criollo counterculture was, in essence, out of context; the historical moment for hippismo had not yet arrived to the developing world where more orthodox forms of revolutionary change were still feasible. Although *Ercilla* was not known for being a Marxist periodical or a conspicuous UP supporter, the writer's conclusion is interesting for its timing: the opening weeks of UP's road to socialism.

The issue of lawlessness, accentuated in "La guerra del beat," was a repeating theme in the international and Chilean press as it related to youth, counterculture, and hippismo. Add to this the notion that countercultural young people were prone to violence, and one begins to understand how people like Charles Manson came to be, or such was the suggestion of an article published in the rightist news magazine *Vea* in February 1970.[14] The article's text—translated into Spanish from a United Press International wire report—is a straightforward chronology and description of the Manson "family's" highly publicized murders of actress Sharon Tate and others in August 1969 and the legal proceedings that had followed. The authorship of the headline, "A New Hippie Massacre," is unknown, but the message is certainly to the point, as is the caption just below a photo of the odious psychopath: "Charles Manson smiles upon the scenes of the crimes committed by those he directs. While all of the United States attends to the Satan's trial, his hippie hordes murdered again."[15]

Later that year, *El Mercurio* published an editorial about the Manson family's request for the court to call John Lennon to the stand, presumably to testify on the alleged influence of his music on what amounted to radical hippismo. The conservative newspaper explained that even though Lennon was no Manson, Lennon and the Beatles nevertheless were responsible for many of counterculture's excesses, thus underscoring the power of music as an agent of change. "The Beatles certainly have constituted a symbol for young people in England [and] initiated a global movement of rebellion and protest that was soon transferred to many latitudes," it argued.[16] Moreover, two weeks after Piedra Roja, the Communist *El Siglo* also suggested that in the United States hippismo and criminality were inseparable. The newspaper published two articles on the search for young people who allegedly murdered a notable physician, his wife, and their two young children before burning down the family's mansion in Santa Cruz, California. The articles describe the local police's search for three "hippie types" who were said to be occultists and radical environmentalists infuriated by the wealthy family's "materialism." A letter left at the murder scene read: "Materialism must die or humanity will."[17]

Country Joe's visit to Chile underscored the fact that foreign-minted music was a vital component in criollo counterculture's coalescence. As we saw in chapter 3, the UP government applied a 94 percent tariff on imported records, thus protecting the domestic music industry. This was positive for the Nueva Canción movement and the Jota's DICAP label, for sure, but also for homegrown rockers who were recording with foreign-owned labels, such as RCA-Chile, until a wave of nationalizations by the UP government. As a result, foreign albums were very hard to come by in Santiago stores, and youths who got hold of some were "the coolest people in town," noted Fritz, the Piedra Roja co-organizer.[18] One avenue for "importing" foreign albums, especially rock records (and periodicals like *Rolling Stone*) from the United States and Europe, were the peregrinations of both Chilean and American families back and forth between countries. Trips to Argentina or visits from trans-Andean friends and family also provided an opportunity to acquire records. These channels were obviously restricted to folks who could afford the trips, and thus the wealthier countercultural teens of the period, such as those attending The Grange School (a British-run prep school in the municipality of La Reina that catered to foreigners and the capital's elite), were the first to enjoy such products. Moreover, U.S. missionaries living in Chile—including the Methodist missionary families with Piedra Roja links—were important conduits, given their frequent trips home. All of this had the effect of engendering competition between youths over who could get the newest and best albums before anyone else. That music would then be diffused through borrowing, parties, and chitchat. As Lowry recounted, "So you would find out who had these records; you'd go to their house to listen to them. I remember the first time I heard Cream and those bands . . . a classmate of mine's brother had gotten records and we went over to his house to listen to them. I mean, you know, I remember some Hendrix and stuff like that [available for purchase in Chile] but we pretty much had to get it from the States."[19] Moreover, rockers of the era would make cultural pilgrimages to the United States and Europe for inspiration, albums, and equipment. Eduardo Gatti, who, like Julio Villalobos and Juan Pablo Orrego, spent a significant amount of time abroad, was a huge Cream fan and collected foreign records, and Los Blops covered Cream songs, along with those of the Doors and others, early in the group's career. They also drew much early inspiration from the Beatles, who also were important in the development of rock and counterculture in Chile.[20] For instance, John Lennon's impact is evidenced by, among other things, the provocative image on the cover of Aguaturbia's debut album in 1970.

Films like *Woodstock* and *Easy Rider*, the experiences and purchases of travelers, the presence of young foreigners, media reports, and other related conduits of information and material culture linked rock music to sex and drugs, together constituting elementary components of a transnational counterculture that inspired vernacular expressions. As previous chapters suggested, Chileans were largely aware of foreign circumstances and debates regarding sex, gender, and illegal drugs, and these issues often appeared couched in counterculture's international proliferation. For instance, a 1971 series of articles, titled "¿Cómo es la juventud americana?" (What Are Young Americans Like?), in the music magazine *Ritmo* focused on the economic prosperity of young people in the United States who "never have to fear hunger" and love their automobiles. Hippies are the subject of the final installment, which draws attention to their drug use, what amounts to a primitive hippie tribalism, and a wedding in which hippies used the music of the Rolling Stones (instead of a traditional wedding march) and quoted in their nuptials Simon de Beauvoir, the revolutionary feminist and author of *The Second Sex* (1949), who questioned monogamy, among many other normative practices.[21]

Drug problems, meanwhile, were commonly associated with outsiders, and news of drug-related trends and factors abroad found resonance in national media. LSD, for example, was a problem not of Chile but was becoming one for Chileans, and some political constituencies went as far as to identify American families living in the country as traffickers of LSD. What is more, updates in the country's press on the exploits of Charles Manson—often cast as a hippie and a product of drug use—did not help matters for foreigners suspected of disseminating drugs and propelling an imported drug culture. In the case of marijuana, it was obvious the problem was serious abroad, and it was becoming a significant question in Chile at the end of the 1960s (see chapter 3). The story of a seventeen-year-old American hippie, known simply as Alicia, was one of many that hammered this home to Chilean readers as a sign of "an infernal stairway downward" facing young people in the United States. The young woman reportedly died as a result of using hard drugs, including LSD, after beginning with a curiosity toward marijuana.[22]

There was much more to counterculture, abroad and at home, than the sociocultural modalities that we have pinpointed thus far, and there certainly was more to it than what one gathers from representations of those modalities in film or periodicals. Counterculture did entertain and reinforce some basic ideas and philosophical elements, though not in a uniform fashion across its spectrum and not for everyone who practiced its varying forms to one degree or another. That said, a good number of young Chileans simply parroted foreign counterculture, which is unsurprising because it originated in places historically, geographically, and conceptually distant. Counterculture in the United States, for instance, arose from a decades-long process that involved such circumstances as the civil rights movement, the free speech movement, and fallout from the Vietnam War. Yet there is a wealth of evidence, from the music of Los Jaivas to Siloism, that many youths also took counterculture seriously and developed personal and collective ways of molding and expressing it for the sake of the genuine transformation of self and society—in ways beyond what imitation could entail—as they crafted a criollo permutation of the phenomenon.

Like the youth question, counterculture had local expressions in other Latin American countries, and Chileans were not short on news and images from those reaches. One such place lay just across the Andes. Argentina was home to a considerable counterculture, and Chilean youth were often in touch, especially in the music scene. Youths and adults browsing through *Paula* in March 1972 came across a long feature story on a hippie community tucked away in the Andes in the Argentine southwest. It details the daily lives of its fifty hippies (thirty-five men and fifteen women) who smoke marijuana and take LSD, make love openly, play music, and leave their doors open to any passersby. The community began when a cadre of twelve, who had made some money performing renditions of *Hair* in Buenos Aires, took to "nature" and purchased some government land. Others then joined, all to "be free" and live without rigid expectations and standards. One young woman explained, "Each of us knows what to do [to support the community]. We don't tell a person to do this and a person to do that. We get up in the morning and do what we want. If we want to cut wood, we cut wood. If we want to cook, we cook." The virtue of such a life, a young man said, is "the freedom to choose" and "enrich ourselves spiritually and culturally."[23] Such spiritual and cultural growth had taken the community's core group of *Hair* performers across the border to Chile some two months before the *Paula* story appeared; theirs was the very "tribe" of hippies that put on the immodest spectacle based on the Broadway production at the discotheque Eve in the municipality of Vitacura.

Thus far we have touched on a junction involving foreign developments and a Chilean context in which many young people were seeking a different world. Like the associated youth question, the criollo counterculture is where the lives of many young Chileans intersected with certain generational and transnational tastes and happenings. Indeed, there would not have been a considerable vernacular counterculture if not for personal decisions—minor as well as major ones, each contingent on distinctive possibilities, means, and intentions—that young people made every day. Perhaps the best way to conduct our more robust discussion of counterculture is to take a virtual journey through its most pronounced spaces. Criollo counterculture happened somewhere, and in many more places than Piedra Roja; hippismo, itself diverse, was a most obvious expression of its development.

A Short Hitchhike Through Hippismo

Politics and culture were played out in the streets in the late 1960s and early 1970s. Greater Santiago's principal avenues, neighborhoods, plazas, parks, and other spaces were settings for the shouts of protestors, the creativity of zealous muralists, provocative graffiti, and placards of all kinds that reflected the paramount conflicts of the day.[24] But also populating those environs were signs of countercultural experimentations, which were often baffling to observers, and utterly "revolutionary" in a heterodox sense, given the predominant conception of the term in Chile and Latin America. While the former scenes were projections of class conflict and the wrangling of political parties, the latter's manifestations hinged on a generational identity and often cast matters both public and private in generational terms; they lay outside the normative framework of public expression and exterior to predominant understandings of what is to be expressed. One could say, then, that while Piedra Roja took place in the hills of Las Condes, its fundamental qualities found quotidian expression in the streets, parks, and other sites in Allende's Chile.

In the Santiago metropolitan area, a great many hippies like Jorge Gómez were affluent Chileans with time on their hands, and they spent much of it—and their money—in "Provi" (to use the era's hippista lexicon). The municipality, bordered by Las Condes on its eastern edge and downtown Santiago to the west, was the cradle of the barrio alto counterculture, and seeing a hippie or a Siloist on Providencia Avenue was common by the end of the 1960s. On the sidewalks of Providencia's principal boulevard, and mostly between Pedro de Valdivia and Tobalaba avenues, countercultural young people mingled, smoked, chatted, and, more generally speaking, shared elements of an emergent and divergent lifestyle. With top-notch boutiques and restaurants around them, youths frequented businesses like Coppelia, which served sandwiches, ice cream, and coffee. Providencia's most popular and widely identified site of hippismo's boldness and banalities, Coppelia was packed on Saturdays, with crowds spilling out onto the sidewalk of the avenue. Youths stood nearly shoulder to shoulder, with many expressing their hippismo outwardly through hairstyles and dress, including miniskirts and bell-bottoms. In particular, hippies who frequented Coppelia "thought about things differently than the rest [of Chile's youth]," Gómez reflected.[25] The café's locus in counterculture is complicated by the fact that many youths came to see Coppelia's crowd as more superficial than others, since a main purpose of sitting for a coffee was to be seen and show off fashions rather than to have a heady experience. For this reason, former hippies like Carlos Lowry, who was deep into the criollo rock scene, considered things like the creative grittiness and meaning behind the music of a group like Los Blops to be much more deep and compelling than what Coppelia offered.[26]

Any quick look at the crowd at Coppelia showed that Provi provided all the necessary amenities, such as quality blue jeans, hot pants (for young women "without inhibitions," as one advertisement described), miniskirts, and high boots for the teen or twentysomething who wished to be consonant with the hippie vibe.[27] Next to Coppelia stood Palta, a store that sold

A woman wearing hot pants and go-go boots draws attention in Santiago in 1971. It is unknown whether the child is hers, but the juxtaposition of edgy style and an apparent motherliness bewildered the onlookers, or so expressions on some faces suggest. Courtesy of the Colección Museo Histórico Nacional (Santiago).

the latest fashions for young people, but the very heart of Provi counterculture consumption lay across Providencia Avenue and down the block: El Drugstore, a mall, of sorts, catering to young *santiaguinos* who sought colorful shirts, short skirts, and jeans. With a name that apparently had nothing to do with drugs but instead reflected the building's great variety of products (like in a drugstore), El Drugstore boasted walls that were painted with swirled colors—in psychedelic fashion—and half of the galleria was (and still is) a floor below street level; such was the subterranean material nourishment of a sprouting counterculture. Nearby, moreover, was the Carnaby Street record store, named after the London shopping district, where youths could find Chilean recordings of Los Blops and Los Jaivas, and possibly some quite expensive imports. Café Kali, just across the avenue from El Drugstore, sold sandwiches and hot dogs, and sandwiches also were all the rage at the Café Kika, further down the avenue near Tobalaba.

At or near Coppelia and El Drugstore (colloquially referred to as El Drógate Store—"The Drug Yourself Store"—and the Galería Jai[28]), the casual observer would witness countercultural youths conversing about most anything. Among them might be a few Siloists, identifiable by their austere hairstyles and black attire that often included turtlenecks. In the vicinity, passersby might have noticed walls emblazoned with Siloist graffiti: a triangle-inside-a-circle motif or perhaps the phrase "Silo is coming!" It was not uncommon to see youths distributing pamphlets (outlining Siloist goals, perhaps) or handbills advertising a rock concert or a festival, such as Pink Lizard's flyer for Piedra Roja. Others paused at newsstands to buy some cigarettes or gum and to check out the latest covers of magazines like *Ritmo* and *Paula*. Overall, locales like Coppelia and El Drugstore and other hangouts along Providencia Avenue constituted a conspicuous and key hub of the country's counterculture.

Criollo rock music, an important part of the countercultural scene, got its start in Provi, for the most part; and the Marconi Theater, just off the main avenue, was an important site in the music's development, which was also aided by birthday parties and events at high-end high schools. The Marconi (now the Nescafé Theater for the Arts) opened in 1949 and was a movie house that aired Hollywood films primarily. Rock music, however, found its way onto the stage during the Allende years, drawing spectators from all classes and some figures from outside the countercultural vibe, especially Nueva Canción icon Víctor Jara, a rock aficionado and close friend of Los Blops members. By 1970, the theater was playing host to such bands as Los Blops, Los Jaivas, and Aguaturbia on Sundays at noon, which struck performers as oddly ironic. Sundays, obviously, were Mass days, while a new religiosity was developing inside spaces like the Marconi. As Mario Mutis of Los Jaivas reflected, it was "a crazy thing because to do a rock concert or vanguard music at noon on a Sunday was like going to church, more or less." The theater, meanwhile, was not equipped for the power loads demanded by electric instruments and their amplification, and the stage's backdrop often amounted to a few hanging bed sheets. In other words, like the progressive rock of Los Jaivas and Los Blops during the Allende years, and similar to Gómez's festival and counterculture in general, the Sunday spectacles at the Marconi were born of improvisation and sheer will. Consequently, the venue holds a special place in the memories of those who walked onto its stage. Mutis identified the Marconi Theater as a symbol of what rock was forging despite the very negative reactions to such "hippista" conduct during the era: "The doors were quite shut [in

1969 and early 1970]," he recalled. "Little by little, some doors were beginning to open until this movement exploded. And from there we finally
arrived to the moment of the first festival held in this country, which was
the Piedra Roja festival."[29]

Discotheques, like the aforementioned Eve in Vitacura, brought recorded
rock, especially that of foreign bands, to young people in Santiago and other
places. Most such spots were open late on Friday and Saturday nights, primarily catering to the Provi crowd. In the summer, the scene would migrate
to the coast. One hangout was the disco Topsi-Topsi, where youths
danced, as one observer remarked, without any unifying rhythm and with
a notable dose of "self-seduction" to the music of Joe Cocker, the Doors,
Creedence Clearwater Revival, and others. Mentioned in the 1972 book *Viaje por la juventud* (Travels Among Young People) by leftist journalists
Lucho Abarca and Juan Forch, the happenings and sensibilities at the pricey
disco, located in the high-end beach town of Reñaca, a few kilometers north
of Viña del Mar, exposed one of the youth question's essential causes and
characteristics: bourgeois decadence. Their account of Topsi-Topsi tells of
a young female hippie with silken hair, light-colored eyes, an Apache-style
headband, and tight pants resembling "a second skin." Such young women
socialized with young men who looked countercultural—including one who
had donned a "vertically striped pullover over a horizontally striped shirt,"
and another who flaunted a sweatshirt emblazoned with the words "University of Texas."[30] As Abarca and Forch deduce, "[These young people] are
sincere and do not hide anything. The vast majority of the bourgeois youth
who go to 'Topsi-Topsi' go to live the Great Adventure. For a few hours they
manage to break away from the boredom of an existence that is idle, grey,
and without horizons." Intent on investigating what lay before them, the
authors struck up a conversation with one young woman: "Have you thought
that this [form of entertainment] is too exclusive—that other young people
couldn't come here even if they wished to?" they asked. She replied, "Of
course! And that's the way it should be." One of the authors responded:
"Hold on. It's just that another [type of] youth also exists. For example,
what's your opinion about young people who study, work, and help others
all at the same time? Ones who embrace an ideal and are committed to the
people?" The young woman is said to have answered, "Well, those guys are
happy in their own way. It's good that they are trying to get out of poverty.
To me these questions don't mean a thing."[31] Indeed, poverty and related
issues meant a great deal to many young people who, aside from dedicating themselves to schoolwork and holding jobs, were politically mobilized

and marching in the streets in defense of social justice and the "road to socialism," the authors emphasized. That is an issue to which this book shall return.

Notwithstanding the glib remarks of a likely "Provi hippie" spending vacation time at the Reñaca discotheque, rock music—whether performed live or enjoyed via albums or the radio—had the intrinsic ability to cross class lines as part and parcel of a countercultural impulse that exploded socioeconomic and conceptual boundaries and showed evidence of potentially eclipsing class-rooted antagonisms in a country where such divisions were otherwise rigid, contested, and defended. Piedra Roja taught the public as much. A revolutionary formula that did not center on class, but rather on generational markers of identity and culture, was—to say the least—a heterodox gesture in Chile in the late sixties and early seventies. It suggested to youths that the dominant discourses of the era did not adequately capture or address the reality of their lives, which instead rested on the authority of parents who, Right or Left or something else, were autocratic. That formula emerged in the thick of trying circumstances framed by much more than the prevailing political climate. As Los Blops guitarist and vocalist Eduardo Gatti made clear, young people like himself, who felt oppressed by the older generation, were not indulging in some sort of affectation; there was abundant proof of such maltreatment. Gatti noted, for example, that when Los Blops played gigs around Santiago, the Carabineros would pay visits—"to fuck with us"—even though the band's performances, save the one at Piedra Roja, were uneventful in terms of audience behavior. "We had a lot of faith in what we were doing. It wasn't easy," he said.[32] Standing amid the crowd and dust at Piedra Roja, an unidentified young man declared, "We [young people] don't have a place in this society. We have no recourse but to isolate ourselves in order to live our own reality, our own philosophy." He then demanded, "You [the older generation], go live in your world and leave us alone to live in ours."[33]

Reflecting this capacity for cross-class linkage, a "popular" countercultural constituency that included hippies and a few young people who embraced Siloism was quite conspicuous by 1970. Hippies of lesser social standing, while sometimes making the pilgrimage to Provi or to the Marconi Theater, congregated mostly in the old downtown area—at the wooded Parque Forestal, known as a hive of marijuana consumption when Salvador Allende assumed the presidency. Piedra Roja's organizers had aimed to unite the Provi and downtown crowds at a "youth song festival" in the hills of Las Condes in October 1970, as our opening chapter illustrated. Gómez put it this way: "Parque Forestal was full of intellectuals, of people from the lower middle class, of people struggling [working class], of painters, of other artists, and people with real, deep roots in what it was to be Chilean and with a bit of resentment toward those who would get together at Coppelia. [They would think] 'What do they have, aside from money, that we don't have?'"[34] Most of the park's young people were from municipalities like Estación Central and Quinta Normal, in the eastern reaches of the metropolitan area.

The park was a sight to behold in 1970. Tents and hippies dotted the landscape, sexual relations and marijuana use were commonplace, and the sounds of acoustic guitars and bongos joined the chirps of birds in the ether. One would only need to add some well-to-do hippie types, a few bands, and iffy concert infrastructure to conjure a festival. Parque Forestal was a very attractive environment for hippies like Jaime Román, who journeyed across Greater Santiago and into the hills of Las Condes to attend and revel in Piedra Roja. There were few spaces in the capital, from the wealthiest to the poorest neighborhood, where Román felt he could "just be" without judgments hurled around and upon him—not necessarily originating from his family, but from his society in general. Admitting that he began his foray into counterculture by trying to imitate (on a restricted budget) hippies from Providencia, he soon found personal meaning in counterculture. "I was attracted to the liberation of it, to be able to smoke a joint, for people to not care that you had long hair," Román explained. "That's what I remember liking best about hippismo: the liberty."[35] He also discovered, as previously noted, that "morenos" like him and "blonds" from the upper classes shared more than either group previously thought. Rock music, some canoodling, and a few pitos at Piedra Roja transcended, if only for a time, class boundaries and hostility that had been taught to them by an older generation that countercultural youths generally found oppressive. While hippismo could sometimes mute or suspend the power of class in a classist society, it nevertheless could not truly shed it. Providencia hippies and Parque Forestal hippies were different and had distinct and separate hangouts, but counterculture was a conduit through which they could (and did) communicate across the barricades of class.

In the Parque Forestal area, working-class hippies shared space with bohemian-inspired writers, painters, and iconoclasts from across the socioeconomic spectrum, living in and near the Bellavista neighborhood, which remains the capital's principal *barrio bohemio* today.[36] Such intellectual, beatnik, and countercultural types enjoyed congregating in the Barrio Lastarria, which today surrounds the Plaza Mulato Gil de Castro (constructed in the early 1980s)—on José Victorino Lastarria Street, a short walk from the Parque Forestal, Bellavista, and the Pontifical Catholic University. There, it was common to see poets, including young, cutting-edge writers. One was Tito Valenzuela, who was part of a larger circle of writers who influenced Eduardo Parra (no relation to the Violeta Parra family), himself a poet and writer in addition to his success as a founding member of Los Jaivas. The visit to Chile in 1960 of U.S. beat poet Allen Ginsberg (along with Lawrence Ferlinghetti) was influential for such young Chilean writers—and for Ginsberg. He had been invited by avant-garde poet Gonzalo Rojas to an international gathering of authors at the University of Concepción, where Ginsberg became friends and resided with poet Nicanor Parra (Violeta's brother), whose body of work included the highly lauded *Poemas y antipoemas* (1954). Nicanor Parra captivated the U.S. writer. Ginsberg also spent time with Pablo Neruda (winner of the Nobel Prize in Literature in 1971) and Pablo de Rokha, who Ginsberg described as "old Chilean literateurs [sic] and veterans of ancient literary latinamerican [sic] wars."[37] Moreover, Ferlinghetti, who operated City Lights Bookstore in San Francisco, arranged the translation of Parra's *Poemas and antipoemas*, appearing in English as *Antipoems* in 1960, published by City Lights.

The most renowned lair of bohemian counterculture in the capital was the Casa de la Luna Azul (House of the Blue Moon) on Villavicencio Street, just steps from Parque Forestal and near the Museum of Fine Arts. A beatnik-inspired countercultural scene emerged at the Casa, with cutting-edge art exhibits, readings, and discussions. The site, which functioned mostly as a gallery, hosted showings of some of Chile's most important artists early in their careers, including Gonzalo Cienfuegos, Mario Murúa, and Hugo Marín. Meanwhile, a vanguard theater group also found an appreciative audience in "discontented bourgeois" young people who made the Casa a locus of their sociability. Enrique Noisvander, a mime who worked with famed writer Enrique Lihn (the closest to being a Chilean beat poet), also was a fixture at the Casa de la Luna Azul, putting on productions like "Educación Seximental," which included male nudity, on a patio stage called Petropol in the back of the building. (A leaky roof eventually motivated the group to move elsewhere.[38]) Notably, one of Noisvander's students in the mid-1950s was Víctor Jara, who went on to become one of the country's most important and, upon his murder by the military in September 1973, most remembered musicians. Moreover, the Casa also became known for being a space that allowed the experimental use of LSD—the substance that, as noted in a previous chapter, was circulating in the country and made for some political intrigue.[39] At the Casa, then, artistic and intellectual pursuits, in addition to drug use, contributed to the locale's persona and reputation as a countercultural hangout.

The intellectualism seen at the Casa de la Luna Azul suggested there were certain philosophical notions that some believed counterculture entailed (or should involve). As was the case with rock and other aspects of counterculture, Chileans looked abroad for models and inspiration. Hippismo "lacked theorization in Chile," but there was plenty going around to sample, said Oscar Ortiz, a former hippie who became a historian and professor. Groups began to form in 1969 and 1970 to play music, read American beat poetry, and grapple with varying existentialist concerns. Ortiz recalls discussing Hermann Hesse's Eastern philosophy and spiritualism; Herbert Marcuse (especially after the Parisian events of 1968), who wrote in the 1960s on alienation, the repressiveness of capitalism and communism, and sexual freedom; Wilhelm Reich's *Function of the Orgasm* (1927), which posited that the emotional experience of sexual release was deeply important to the spiritual self; and the writings of the Marquis de Sade, which particularly piqued the interest of anarchists. Also of relevance were works on the peaceful civil disobedience of Henry David Thoreau, Mohandas Gandhi, and Martin Luther King Jr.[40]

Young people often bought books across the border in Argentina, in frontier cities like Mendoza, where such publications sold for much less than Chilean products, especially before the advent of the Quimantú publishing house. In one instance circa 1972, Ortiz paid the equivalent of $35 (U.S.), which was an enormous sum at the time, for an imported book—by either Marcuse or G. I. Gurdjieff, he recalled. High tariffs, like those assessed on foreign-made albums, pushed prices to such altitudes while the state-owned Quimantú essentially controlled the domestic marketplace under the Allende government. The works of many "heterodox" thinkers, including Freudian Marxists like Marcuse and Eric Fromm, were conspicuously absent from Quimantú's lists. Ortiz quipped, "Quimantú produced and produced and produced. But what did it produce? The *History of the Russian Revolution* by Trotsky, in three volumes. Control was quite subtle."[41] Also perused in countercultural circles were the works of the aforementioned Gurdjieff and P. D. Ouspensky, as well as readings on Taoism, Sufism, and anarchism.[42] That being said, it should be emphasized here that one did not need formal philosophical grounding or some sort of clear epistemological framework to be countercultural. The Siloists did offer those elements, as we shall later see, but they were among the most doctrinaire of criollo counterculture's contributors. With or without parental problems and alienated or not, the practitioners of hippismo—from the affluent young woman who secretly smoked pitos and listened to Los Blops to the young man who grew his hair and pitched a tent in Parque Forestal—were nevertheless partaking in a large and vague universe of signs, symbols, and sensibilities that were specific to a generation and an era.

While the Casa de la Luna Azul was a happening hub of the capital's *barrio bohemio*, in a manner of speaking there were similar spaces scattered throughout the metropolitan region by 1970: the *comunidades hippie*, or hippie communities, some more "intellectual" than others but most all with some philosophical foundation. As noted in the previous chapter, the rock group Los Blops lived in a community called Manchufela, where, appropriately, they penned the song "Manchufela" for their 1971 album *Del volar de las palomas* (Of the Flight of Doves) as well as numerous other songs, such as "Que lindas son las mañanas" (How Beautiful the Mornings Are) and "Pintando azul el mar" (Painting the Ocean Blue), devoted to the beautiful mysteries of nature. Los Jaivas, who, like Los Blops, were headliners at Piedra Roja, also chose to live in a countercultural community in Argentina after Allende's overthrow. The public got to know a bit about such communities through the media.

The magazine *Ritmo de la Juventud*, known for its dutiful reports on the domestic and international entertainment industry, published an article in 1972 titled "*Macondo . . . un mundo aparte en Santiago,*" where "people act, live, and think differently" and "live in the moment," or so the subheading reads.[43] "Macondo," the name adopted by the hippie comunidad in question, refers to Gabriel García Márquez's fictional town Macondo, which appears as a place as well as a sensibility in *One Hundred Years of Solitude*. At the time of their interview with *Ritmo* writer María Yolanda González, the Macondo hippies were on the verge of relocating from the capital to Laguna Verde, near Valparaíso, a place where, in the words of one hippie, "police won't bother us by looking for things that don't exist; we can't explain why they bother us."[44] The article opens with the author's broad reflections on the community, the size of which its hippies could not discern because "in all reality," as one hippie explained, "we don't pay attention to how many are here." González reported seeing hippies of all sorts: "intelligent hippies, stupid hippies" and "clean hippies and hippies whose deodorant abandoned them by mid-afternoon." She continues, "Seven years ago it would have been crazy to think that a group of young people (even though I saw a 'hippiesaurus') that would marginalize themselves from society to live in whatever way they want, without laws, without anything concrete, only thinking about the present, would establish itself in Santiago. Today, it is a reality and that reality is called the Macondo community."[45]

At Macondo, located in an unspecified place on the edge of Santiago, the writer came across Chileans, Argentines, and Brazilians living communally, and among them was an unmarried pregnant hippie named María del Carmen, a Chilean. When questioned about raising a child out of wedlock, María del Carmen responded with a smile, "[The baby] will stay with me until she no longer needs me; [the baby] will then have her own life."[46] Members of the community, including María del Carmen's partner, a Brazilian named Erick, went on to delineate aspects of mainstream society that they detested. María del Carmen noted, "I don't understand wars, the kilos of TNT that the scientists have put aside for each one of us, nor the trips to the moon. Why spend so much money when it's only about a struggle for power? This is a world of contradictions and a world that doesn't know how to do things." And on the subject of contradictions, the mother-to-be mentioned that she was aware of one of her own: "I am a materialist!" María del Carmen declared in reference to her necklaces. "Yes, I'm a materialist and I like to have what is mine but I am not in league with society." But while Macondo hippies like María del Carmen seemingly were aware of the broader relevance and problematics of their hippismo, González went on to mention seventeen-year-old Raúl Bellone, who reportedly ran away from home at age twelve. "He talks a lot about peace, of love, but in ways ungrounded," González opines. "He basically is a proto-hippie."[47] *Ritmo's* discussion of the Macondo hippie community essentially portrays hippies not only as fairly hedonistic (in the sense that they live for themselves, not for society, and that they live in the moment) but also as young people who were wasting their lives. But González also conveyed some of the more concrete reasons why hippies were hippies, evinced by María del Carmen's complaints about contemporary society.[48] Depending on the viewpoint of the reader, the utterances of María del Carmen and other Macondo hippies either reinforced existing stereotypes about the counterculture or made hippies less enigmatic in a society experiencing a cultural upheaval.

Hippismo was a diverse phenomenon, running the gamut from "Provi" types to bohemians and from "community" dwellers to working-class youths of Parque Forestal, all of whom were sharing many of the same sensibilities, tastes, and modes of agency that were undeniably and unabashedly countercultural. But signs of counterculture appeared outside the capital as well, including on the beaches of the central coast, which in summer essentially became extensions of *santiaguino* sociability, countercultural or otherwise. Beaches were sites of youthful expression, where young people might take off their clothes in acts of rebellion. Central-coast beaches saw youths of varying economic means engaging in everything from skinny-dipping to peddling and smoking marijuana; years later, Channel 13—a Church-affiliated television station—used the same sands to film a good portion of its 2004 soap opera, *Hippie*. Viña del Mar's Caleta Abarca beach and beaches at nearby Reñaca, Horcón, and Quintero were well-known hangouts. Countercultural youths nestled in their Peugeots or Austin Minis could make the drive from Santiago in no more than two hours—which could allow for a clandestine day-trip during school hours, even perhaps including a stop for some marijuana, grown in agricultural communities like Los Andes and San Felipe, both near the capital.[49] Bus and train transport were options for those of lesser socioeconomic means.

In the summer of 1970–71, backpacking, hitchhiking, and escaping in general from home and parents were all the rage, and the coast and some provincial towns served as prime destinations. Such youths were "on the road," per se, experiencing the liberty of space and of the body in motion. Trains became sites of marijuana use as counterculture continued its transformation, largely initiated by Piedra Roja, from being a private experience to being a public spectacle.[50] In the middle of that summer, only a few months after his festival in Los Dominicos and during a serious falling out with his parents, Gómez traveled by train to Viña del Mar to see a concert featuring Los Jaivas. "I remember it well because the train leaving from Mapocho Station [in the downtown area] made a loop around Limache, and in that area a lot of marijuana was cultivated [for manufacturing]. The train, surprisingly, went two or three kilometers per hour at one point, and hippies jumped off the train to harvest some," he reminisced. "It was really amazing."[51] Like Gómez, Lowry also took memorable train excursion to the coast: "I went to the Parque Forestal a couple of times. I hung out a lot in [the municipality of La Reina], just east of where I lived, with a group of kind of middle-class hippies up there, and in the summer hippies back then would go to Quintero," he explained. "I remember taking a train out to Quintero with them and it was just packed with kids that were Parque Forestal hippies, and getting to know some of them. I remember a girl named Marina."[52] But not all countercultural youths heading to the oceanfront fared so well. Later in 1971, a tabloid reported that some three hundred hippies, young men and women, bound for a music festival were not allowed to board a train destined for Viña del Mar and Valparaíso because they "tried to ride the train for free." These hippies, "with their typical clothes," as the leftist *Puro Chile* noted, "had already consumed enough marijuana that they could have flown on their own from wherever they had been to Viña del Mar."[53]

Complicating matters for beach-going hippies, in November 1970 police found the naked body of a murdered young man, later identified as twenty-three-year-old Pablo Cristián Gacitúa Stermann, on Viña del Mar's Caleta Abarca beach. The local police homicide investigation unit worked the case, using leads provided by the victim's brother, Andrés, who was traveling to Viña del Mar to identify the body. As the Marxist newspaper *El Siglo* put it, "Even though the identity [of the victim] is not yet definitive, the detectives had an interview with Andrés Gacitúa Stermann, apparently the brother of the murdered man, who told police that for some time Cristián had been dedicating himself to live with 'hippies' and the last thing he heard from his brother is that he was going to [nearby] Valparaíso." The victim had "frequented places where there gathered young people with hippie ways." Meanwhile, a police dragnet operation was busily rounding up hippies who "were of modest means and who worked at Caleta Abarca." Police took eight young men into custody; one was under greatest suspicion—a twenty-four-year-old Argentine "hippie" named Jorge Chinnoca who, *El Siglo* emphasized, very likely committed the crime "under the influence of marijuana."[54] Soon, however, police declared that none of the young men had anything directly to do with the murder, although they also announced that those "hippies" would remain in jail as "suspects" for an unspecified length of time.[55] As evidenced when countercultural-looking youths could be rounded up and jailed despite being cleared of wrongdoing, the very act of being a hippie on the beaches of Viña del Mar aroused suspicion. What is more, it may easily be inferred from Andrés Gacitúa's statement to police that his brother's death was linked, in some way, to the fact that Cristián had been living as a hippie and among hippies.

To say the least, there were many Chileans who cringed when gazing upon hippies hanging out on Providencia Avenue or in Parque Forestal. Accounts of hippismo in the media did not make countercultural young people many friends, either. In everyday conversation inside homes or in public discussions involving elected officials and police, scrutiny cast upon counterculture reached a fevered pitch in the wake of Piedra Roja and continued thereafter. A confluence of extraordinary events during the very month of the spectacle in Los Dominicos certainly made matters worse for young people trying to live heterodox lives in a quite "formal" society, as Gatti put it. In that milieu, a generationally based gesture that was intertwined with the youth question offered a heterodox conceptualization of revolutionary behavior and a counterhegemonic range of sensibilities and outlooks that alarmed those poised to defend shared mainstream cultural values even while they were warring among themselves in the political trenches. All of this unfolded amid momentous change in Chilean society that sharpened hopes, fears, and animosities during UP's road to socialism.

5 Contesting *Hippismo*
Bad Vibes and the Politics of Incrimination

• •

Malucha Pinto was horrified when her angry mother appeared at Piedra Roja, grabbed her by the ear, and paused to scold all those who were hanging out with "Maluchita" before removing her from the scene. "I wanted to die," Pinto said more than four decades later. The then-teenager's journey to Los Dominicos began with a lie: she said she was going to spend the night at a friend's house. Instead, she traveled with that friend and others to the outskirts of Las Condes to witness Jorge Gómez's festival, news of which was making headlines as it was unfolding. "We left with a group of friends and a tent, and we were going to stay the night there," Pinto reminisced. "There was an enormous excitement." Her mother, María Luisa Solari, a famous award-winning dancer and choreographer, discovered the deception when she called the friend's home, only to be told that the girls had gone to Piedra Roja. The jig was up, and having already heard rumors of drug use, drinking, and sex going on at the festival, Solari tracked her daughter down. Although Pinto's time at the festival was cut short, it left lasting impressions, or perhaps put better, enduring sensations for the current actress and writer. "We were happy, happy to be alive, happy to be together, happy because it was true: it was possible," she said. The "possible" was the realization of new ways of being and a world in which "liberty, solidarity, community, coming together, [and] justice existed; it existed somewhere and could be possible." The triumph of Socialist Salvador Allende in the 1970 presidential election inspired many to imagine new scenarios, even utopian ones, whether they were truly realistic or not. Hippismo, then, arose in a period of hope and possibility, and young Malucha felt it. Many young people felt it. The response of Pinto's mother is also telling, for it resembled the more general reaction in society and politics that cast Piedra Roja and the criollo counterculture as immoral and dangerous.[1]

October 1970 was quite a month for families like the Pintos, who had to reckon with Piedra Roja. It was also a remarkable month for all Chileans. The Christian Democrat-controlled Congress voted Allende, candidate of the Marxist-led UP coalition, president of the republic, as protocol demanded when he did not receive an outright majority of the popular vote; Army Commander-in-Chief General René Schneider, who had pledged to honor Allende's election in the name of the country's constitutional tradition, was shot multiple times in his staff car—the victim of a hastily organized and executed right-wing plot—and died days later; and news of Gómez's festival reached the pages of the country's major newspapers and magazines, sparking discussions around dinner tables and complicating the lives of countercultural youths.

Allende's election was a turning point in the country's social, political, and economic history, as his compatriots—friends and foes alike—waited with bated breath to see what UP's "road to socialism" would look like. Over the next three years, political affairs were replete with animosity and contempt as middle-of-the-road politics began falling away, essentially leaving Left-Right polarity as the elementary framework of the body politic until the bloody military coup of September 1973. The stakes were high on Allende's road to socialism, and countercultural youths were caught up in the tension of it all. Leveraging our previous examinations of the youth question, sexuality, drug use, and rock culture—all sites of spontaneity, sensations of the mind and body, and the contestation of mainstream expectations—this chapter looks closely at the reactions hippismo stirred in culture and politics during the UP years. For all sides, whether prominently positioned for or against UP's national project, to lash out against hippies was to defend common decency and a convenient way to stake claims to, and dispute, a wide array of social, cultural, and economic issues. Commensurate with one's ideological viewpoint, anticounterculture discourse could lend a hand in fighting capitalism, imperialism, radicalism, or the loss of religiosity. This meant that any sociopolitical group compelled to denounce and combat counterculture effectively could fight more than one battle at a time, with countercultural types collectively constituting the common— and bemoaned—denominator across the board.

Throwing Stones at Piedra Roja

The festival's problematic denouement, on top of its general implications, made matters terribly complicated for youths who were blamed by Las Condes Mayor Ramón Luco Fuenzalida for "tarnishing the prestige of Las Condes." Piedra Roja's young people had willfully violated the respected, normative, and immutable laws of proper social and cultural conduct, or so the mayor and many others essentially declared in the press. In one tirade, published in the mainstream weekly news magazine *Ercilla* (a voice of the Christian Democratic Party, PDC), Luco identified Piedra Roja as "an orgy of drugs and corruption made worse by the fact that the participants in these immoral acts were minors." Indeed, Piedra Roja was an orgy of many sorts—of consumption, of hedonism, of rebelliousness—that Luco read as egregious misconduct. Lashing out at anyone associated with the event, Luco also suggested in the press that Luis Rosselot, owner of the *fundo* that hosted the festival, should be included in any investigation by authorities.[2] It did not come to pass, which was, one can deduce, a good thing for Luco, since both had accepted the very same premise of a "youth song festival." If Rosselot were to be held legally responsible for being duped, then Luco could be held to the same standard.

Meanwhile, a Las Condes *regidor* (municipal council member) offered a description of Piedra Roja similar to the mayor's: "In the end, the only thing coming to light from this orgy," explained Carlos Gana of the Socialist Party, "is that there were groups of young people, in the minority, who did what they did out of imitation, who consumed drugs and alcohol and, with impunity, humiliated the public morality."[3] Gana also could not refrain from politicizing the issue. He promised that UP would closely monitor the behavior of youths and that such a task would be assigned to a new ministry— the Ministry of Family.[4] Such a ministry never became a reality. Also spurred into action was Luis Pareto González of the PDC, a prominent member of the Chamber of Deputies, who took his complaint to the Congress building in downtown Santiago with, according to the pro-UP *Clarín*, veins in his neck swollen by anger and his face made red by intense disgust.[5] The government-owned *La Nación*, in the final days of the presidency of the PDC's Eduardo Frei Montalva, also condemned the "criollo hippie festival"—its young men with "long hair, mutilated blue jeans, and multicolored bandanas around their necks"—for its marijuana and for demonstrating a good measure of immorality.[6]

As noted in the introduction, in the days following Piedra Roja, and reminiscent of what happened to teenage Nueva Ola starlet Nadia Milton after she posed in a bikini for *Can-Can* magazine in 1960, the Ministry of Public Education banished Gómez permanently from Liceo No. 11 and from all other secondary schools in the country.[7] Mayor Luco had filed a report with the local Carabineros, which, in concert with the outcries and efforts of Pareto, Gana, and others, got the ball of punishment rolling. Gómez was then summoned to the office of Sergio de Los Reyes, rector of Liceo No. 11, who broke the news: " 'Look, Don Jorge, I find this all terribly unfair and very lamentable because academically you have excellent grades'—and I was even a member of the Math Club. Imagine how bored I was—I was just sick of it all. And he said to me, 'I have instructions from the Ministry of Education that your ability to enroll in all educational establishments in Chile has been nullified, so to be able to finish [secondary schooling] you'll have to study abroad,'" Gómez recalled. Furthermore, the quite animated Pareto was the first to call publicly for expelling from school not only organizers like young Jorge but all "marihuaneros" of secondary-school age who attended Piedra Roja.[8] It was simply impossible to identify, for the purpose of expulsion, every suspected festival-going marihuanero in high school. As a result, widespread expulsions did not materialize, but the threat lingered like smoke in still air. The call for expulsions en masse from Liceo No. 11, in particular, rested on reports like one in *Ercilla*, which included Luco's mistaken and rather paranoid suggestion that Piedra Roja was the outcome of a carefully planned and executed conspiracy hatched in the halls of Gómez's school—by the entirety of its student body and the administration, no less. The rector of Liceo No. 11, De Los Reyes, responded in no uncertain terms: "The mayor has not said it expressly, but one gathers from his declarations that there was involvement on the part of the school in the festival. Not so. The student Jorge Gómez (and he himself admits this) organized it on his own volition. We, the teachers, believe that he did it because he was motivated by his ideals and [youthful] enthusiasm."[9] Young Jorge was telling the truth: Liceo No. 11—its student council, to be more precise—had rejected a proposed sponsorship. In the meantime, in declaring the festival was his doing and his alone, he protected Gary Fritz, Carlos Lowry, and others, as well as their families, from the onslaught that engulfed him.

By the end of the month, Gómez faced potential legal prosecution at the behest of Mayor Luco and Gana, the Socialist *regidor*. One report, published in a government-owned daily, made sure to point out that Gana was soon going to join the UP government as its new "Minister of Family" (which never came to be), thus simultaneously underscoring Gana's moral-political credentials to continue persecuting Gómez and the threat to family values that Piedra Roja and its principal organizer posed. More important to the mayor seemed to be clearing his municipal government of all suspicion of incompetence or, worse, complicity. "It is evident," Luco wrote to the local judge in Las Condes, "that the mayor's office was surprised by the festival's realization and by outcomes that could not logically have been foreseen, and it rejects it all in the most categorical manner."[10]

Hoping to help his situation by explaining his original intent to hold a "youth song festival," Gómez appeared on the University of Chile's Channel 9 Television (now called "Chilevisión") in late October. The effort went nowhere, and even led to his physical assault at the hands (and feet) of "older people," as he described them. Just outside the doors of Channel 9, Gómez was thrown to the ground and kicked in the head, stomach, and back; a passerby stopped the attack before one of the assailants could return with a car jack. Apparently, the assailants were parents angered by their daughters' escapes to attend the festival, particularly because some of their children had not yet returned home.[11] The fallout in the Gómez household was perhaps even more painful. It was "terrible," he said with sorrow. As his father was in England, Gómez's Scottish mother received the scandal's brunt. "The television channels, the radio stations, the press, everyone was at my house," Gómez said. "My mother didn't want to speak to anyone." He added, "The face [of the festival] was mine." His relationship with his parents quickly dissolved, and Gómez left home. Lonely and dejected, he soon married a young woman he had met at Piedra Roja, had a child, and then chose to escape the city whose inhabitants would routinely spit upon him (literally) in the streets for his alleged nefariousness. They chose to live in a small hippie community in the Andean foothills, on the road from Santiago to the winter resort of Farellones. The young Gómez family lived a communal life in the mountains, planting food, cutting firewood, and getting by on the most basic of means, until the military coup took place in September 1973, when life changed dramatically once more, as we shall later see.[12]

The days immediately following Piedra Roja were also quite challenging for many other hippies. Anticounterculture voices—rife with moral panic and pursuant to their moral politics—focused on drugs, sex, and, to a lesser extent, rock music as ills that threatened culture and the nation.[13] The media and public's attention to Piedra Roja pressured police to do something about hippismo, and the distinctive correlation between sex, drugs, and rock—not imagined, but rather witnessed in full display at the festival—made the already conspicuous hippies even more obvious targets for arrest and harassment. Indeed, police had a public-relations problem on their hands for what happened, or, better said, what *did not* happen, in Los Dominicos. As news of Piedra Roja's problems spread briskly by word of mouth and the media, law enforcement officials—much to the frustration of hippismo's critics—admitted they had done nothing to curtail the spectacle or even to maintain a close eye on the festival's grounds until Carabineros finally closed down the event on Monday. Police later explained that Piedra Roja had transpired on private property, thus limiting their enforcement capability, and that the municipal government of Las Condes had in fact given Gómez official permission, which would not have been conferred without the landowner's approval. One official of the Carabineros, moreover, had flatly stated to the leftist *Clarín* before the festival's end, "In any case, one of our vans is patrolling that sector around the clock, and there have been no incidences of any kind, outside the location [of the festival]."[14] Meanwhile, Luis Jaspard, director of investigations of the Carabineros' First Precinct in Las Condes, said he did not want to comment on the hippie phenomenon and law enforcement's inaction vis-à-vis Piedra Roja. He then did so nevertheless: "I see that these sorts of things [such as Piedra Roja] often take place in European countries and police do not intervene."[15] Another Carabinero concluded, remarkably, "It would be stupid to contain a social revolution with gunshots."[16]

While the sidewalks, stores, and hangouts like Coppelia along Providencia Avenue were quite conspicuous locales for barrio alto counterculture, the most densely populated space where hippies congregated was Parque Forestal. This zone for working-class and bohemian countercultural youths, with its tents, undisguised enjoyment of marijuana, and overall vibe, proved to be a convenient site for authorities—Carabineros, the capital's Anti-Vice Brigade (Brigada Contra el Vicio) and the Brigade for the Repression of Stupefying Substances and Games of Chance (Brigada de Represión de Estupefacientes y Juegos de Azar)—to exercise some policing muscle amid the initial postfestival public outcry. Sandwiched between major avenues, the park was perfectly suited for policing: not only could authorities find plenty of hippies, but passersby in cars could see officials in action, acting ostensibly in defense of decency and the family, thus providing the state a public-relations boost. Within two days of the festival's end, Carabineros had arrested eighty young male and female Parque Forestal hippies—identified as such in light of their dismal "corporeal hygiene," as one report put it—on charges of smoking and selling marijuana.[17] Those arrested were loaded onto waiting buses and taken to local police stations. Carabineros gave the press free rein to interview the young people, likely because officials thought that so-called marihuaneros would incriminate themselves. Indeed, some did, acknowledging that they smoked marijuana and that it meant something consequential to them. "We [hippies] don't support this environment of hypocrisy and underhanded scandal that our parents put upon us at home," a young man said. Only a handful—three

Chileans, an Argentine, and a U.S. citizen who ranged in age from eighteen to twenty-two—were formally charged and made to appear before the special investigating judge (*ministro en visita*) assigned to the cases: Hernán Cereceda Bravo, the antimarijuana crusader discussed in chapter 3.[18]

Six weeks after the first large roundup in Parque Forestal, undercover officers dressed as hippies conducted an operation in the same area that apprehended some three hundred marihuaneros of both sexes; forty eventually faced charges for disorderly conduct and possession of illegal narcotics. An official from the Brigada de Represión de Estupefacientes classified three types of hippies arrested in the raid: "professional hippies" (those who "really identify with the movement"); "hippie candidates" (those who "imitate hippie vulgarity);" and "hippie salespeople" (purveyors of illegal drugs, especially marijuana).[19] Charlie Alvarado, a musician and Parque Forestal hippie who recalled sleeping under stairwells and in abandoned buildings in the vicinity of Lastarria Street, was caught up in one of the marihuanero sweeps. Alvarado found himself in the local jail, along with enough hippies to fill ten cells, he said. "The first thing they [police] wanted to do was to cut our hair," Alvarado recounted. "And we mutinied. We all mutinied—they weren't going to cut our hair." Guards soon showed up, beat the youths with log batons, and proceeded to cut the prisoners' hair. Alvarado and his companions were released the next day.[20]

Provi hippies were largely spared from the crackdown in the weeks following Piedra Roja, which had been hatched and organized by youths from Providencia and adjacent municipalities of the barrio alto. The relative ease of rounding up lower-class hippies allegedly seen smoking or selling marijuana in Parque Forestal, where marihuaneros gathered in large numbers, served the immediate need of law enforcement authorities hoping to get out from under intense pressure put upon them by politicians and the media to punish "immoral" conduct. What is more, there was no outcry from the Left about the socioeconomic one-sidedness of the marijuana-related roundups, possibly because its representatives wanted to avoid accusations of defending counterculture. But the pro-UP press minced no words when identifying fault in the spread of counterculture's vices to working-class youths. Shortly after Piedra Roja, *Puro Chile* noted, "In Chile, all of this started in the summer of 1968–69. That period marks the beginning of widespread marijuana use among adolescents from families with abundant economic resources. But soon it expanded to people with lower incomes and budgets."[21]

As policing transitioned from a hands-off policy that prevailed during the festival to a more aggressive posture in subsequent days and weeks, government officials were busy doing what government officials do in such circumstances: talking a lot and demanding investigations. The aforementioned Pareto, the Christian Democrat deputy, took his complaints against hippismo and the festival directly to the Congress building within twenty-four hours of Piedra Roja's conclusion. Impelled by Pareto's disgust and that of many other officials, the Chamber of Deputies, in the final days of the Frei administration, voted on Tuesday, October 13, to investigate the use of narcotics among young Chileans "in light of what happened last week [in Las Condes]." The Chamber called for cooperation between Interior Minister Patricio Rojas and Public Health Minister Ramón Valdivieso in coming to grips with what went on at Piedra Roja and why. Deputies concluded that "the spectacle put on by the criollo hippies at Los Dominicos constitutes a grave threat not only for the sector of our youth who participated [in the festival] but also for the future of the country, and it is necessary to take energetic measures to keep 'festivals' like that from happening."[22] The inquiry was imperative because events in Los Dominicos amounted to "a national scandal," in the words of Deputy Roberto Muñoz Barra of the pro-Allende Radical Party.[23] Muñoz chaired the Chamber's education commission, and thus was central in any government discussion, given the participation of many students at Piedra Roja. Clearly perturbed, he focused on the prevalence of marijuana at the festival as a sign of other major problems. Expressing sentiments percolating through mainstream society and politics, Muñoz declared, "Smokers of marijuana arrive at sexual promiscuity, including prostitution and homosexuality, like we see in the case of Los Dominicos."[24] The government's *La Nación*, moreover, announced a police investigation having to do with "the consumption of drugs, erotic excesses, robberies, and the disappearances of minors at that orgy of long hair." Before the month was out, Pareto called on the Ministry of Finance to "intensify its oversight of customs against drug contraband," the Ministry of Health to be more vigilant in matters of pharmaceutical sales, the Ministry of Education to pay more attention to teaching about drugs in high schools and in the public universities, and for the Ministry of the Interior to cut the hair of any young man apprehended for drug-related offenses.[25]

On October 19, the Ministry of Education issued a special decree constituting a commission to "study the problem of drug use" and especially marijuana, which was "a grave problem that affects students."[26] The commission met on at least two occasions over the next two months, including a December 19 meeting with newly appointed UP Interior Minister José Tohá González, a Socialist, in charge of internal security.[27] Little became of the commissions under Frei and Allende. It is difficult to discern just what the commissions could have effectively added—aside from extra hype and posturing—to the conversation about what was going on, given the prevalence of important studies and mounting media reports on marijuana and similar topics (see chapter 3). There was plenty of information in the public sphere about drug use and why it was increasing. But, again, the government had to do something to demonstrate its disgust with the happenings at Piedra Roja and to advertise the importance of marihuanero roundups in Parque Forestal and elsewhere. Calling for commissions and investigations also benefited officials because such efforts suggested they had little or no previous knowledge as to the extent to which counterculture had infected the country. This suggestion of innocent ignorance served to absolve them of any preceding inaction or incompetence. Regardless, Allende made the UP government's position quite clear. In January 1971, with the roundups of marihuaneros in Parque Forestal and elsewhere still being discussed, the president called for "a rapid and effective solution" for problems "as serious as the consumption of marijuana," which he included on a list of such social ailments as mental retardation, psychosis, and "antisocial" behavior. It is worth noting that Allende delivered those words before an audience at a mental health convention.[28]

Compounding matters for hippies in late 1970 was the reason at the root of Gómez's assault outside Channel 9: the reported disappearances of young women from the festival grounds, which fed the fear that they were victims of sexual violence and kidnapping at the hands of lascivious hippies. The Communist Party's *El Siglo* was among the first newspapers to ring the alarm regarding Piedra Roja and countercultural prurience. Soon after the festival ended, it emphasized, with the connotation of disgust, that a "majority of the young girls who arrived [to the festival] did so with contraceptive pills in their purses and bags," underscoring the not-so-subtle notion that the festival was about getting high and having sex to the music of Los Jaivas and Los Blops.[29] The leftist *Clarín* was equally critical, publishing a photo of two Piedra Roja revelers engaged in a tight embrace. The caption prognosticated the outcome: "This couple is caressing in front of the whole world. Others who were more inclined did other little things with results that we'll see nine months from now." Moreover, many girls and young women, *Clarín* explained, unfortunately "lost their virginity" at Piedra Roja—a claim not disputed by witnesses interviewed more than three decades later.[30] The Left-leaning current-events magazine *Vea* also chimed in, describing Piedra Roja as a sexual orgy. It noted that a particular young woman was so "enthused by the music and weed" that she disrobed "in front of everyone." The writer apparently came across "many couples making love without worrying about being seen." Parents, *Vea* concluded, should be "alerted" to the blatantly scurrilous and indiscrete behavior of their wayward children.[31] What is more, the press did not shy from deploying a bit of mockery when seizing on the festival's sexual occurrences. Three days after Piedra Roja, the pro-UP *Clarín* declared in a large headline: "They Have Not Returned Home! Eight 'Hippie' Girls Still Haven't Put Their Clothes Back On!" The subhead read, "They were part of the marijuana festival."[32]

Were there young people having sex at the festival? There indeed were, and such things exemplified the openness and liberation that took hold in Los Dominicos.[33] Denise of Aguaturbia recalled sex like that practiced at Piedra Roja had spiritual and idealistic dimensions: "The ideal that we all shared was the same. It was about love. It was about love, but a love that was pure. Not like today, where love is sex."[34] Moreover, Gómez noted, "Many palomas by Saturday morning took off their tops and went topless. Nobody looked at it strangely. And there were lots of young kids—two or three years old—walking around totally naked, in bare feet."[35] Within a week of the festival's conclusion, the number of missing young women had risen to nine, and to fourteen by month's end. They ranged in age from twelve to nineteen, and their worried parents filed reports at local police stations.[36] Media covering the disappearances (now in a much more solemn manner) placed such concerns in the context of hippismo's unruliness and hedonism. The pro-UP *Vea* described the happenings on Luis Rosselot's land quite succinctly: it was a "festival of drugs and sex."[37]

In that context, Aguaturbia's Denise chuckled when recalling her contribution to the festival's air of sexual freedom: "I remember that many girls would come up to me. I was a curiosity. . . . I wore a necklace made from boxes, which were pretty little things, like little holograms, that held contraceptives, which had just arrived in Chile. And I used that necklace [at Piedra Roja], so it was quite attractive."[38] In the end, one assumes that the missing young women either returned to their homes or their parents learned of their whereabouts because news about them disappeared from the press. But the issue, and many others, indelibly influenced and reinforced how the public, the media, and the state viewed hippies and young people like Gómez. Hippies at Piedra Roja denied any responsibility for disappearances and also rejected the notion that sex and sexual aggression at the festival was a problem. *El Mercurio* noted, "The hippies [the festival's organizers] claimed innocence saying that 'we can't stand the climate of hypocrisy and scandal of the sort we find in our homes and with our parents.'"[39] Furthermore, a young man identified by *Clarín* as one of the festival's organizers insisted that instead of depending on hearsay and weak suppositions, the media should provide concrete evidence of alleged sexual crimes.[40] The media failed to meet that demand over the subsequent weeks and months. However, decades later, Pink Lizard recalled that he and two other co-organizers saw one young woman being chased by a man holding a knife, only to see them kissing and caressing a few moments later.[41] He was unsure as to whether it was dramatic expression or genuine violence. Generally speaking, Pink Lizard, Fritz, and Gómez agreed that things went south on Monday. "We had all kinds of problems. Buses arrived with prostitutes. I don't know. The whole feeling had been lost. I was completely frustrated. None of that was my idea," said Gómez of the festival's final hours.[42]

While drug use and sexual promiscuity were foremost themes in post-festival denunciations—and in the memories of Piedra Roja revelers—rock music escaped neither critical notice nor fond remembrances. According to *Vea*, "Various bands of ultramodern music attempted to create an atmosphere that was fitting for the event."[43] The term "fitting" says much; the event, as media reports, testimonials, and hearsay depicted it, was an orgy of drugs and sex, and thus the festival's performers and music dovetailed nicely with vices on full display in Los Dominicos. The newspaper *La Tercera*, an independent daily that opposed Allende and supported the 1973 coup, likewise drew conclusions about artistic merit before the festival was over. One headline read: "Hippie Festival in Los Dominicos: An Abundance of Long Hair and Bizarre Music." The "beat and soul" music ("beat" and "soul" were interchangeable with "rock" in the media) at hand was "in the style presented at Woodstock" and, according to one young spectator, "people [in Chile] know what that's all about." The newspaper went further, singling out one of the headlining acts, arguing that Los Jaivas were "dedicated to the exploitation and corruption of minors."[44] Meanwhile, the leading Nueva Canción group, Quilapayún, made something perfectly clear: they had not been scheduled to perform at the happening in Los Dominicos and they "were not down with the festival" in any way. While preparing for their tour of communist Hungary, the group emphatically declared they would have turned down any invitation, they had nothing to do with the "hippie movement," and that they repudiated the conduct of organizers for using Quilapayún's name to promote the festival.[45] Scuttlebutt had circulated that Quilapayún was going to show up on Luis Rosselot's land, although it was not mentioned in the flyer devised by Pink Lizard and distributed by Gary Fritz and others. Instead, it was the government-owned *La Nación* that had propelled the rumor by listing Quilapayún among the festival's performers. For Quilapayún's members, the fact that the band's name had appeared alongside "High Bass" (Los Jaivas) and "Aguaturbia" was insulting, especially in light of the article's headline: "Marijuana and Soul Music at the Criollo Hippie Festival."[46] Quilapayún's Eduardo Carrasco declared, "Instead of fighting for change and making a better society, [hippies] smoke marijuana and drug themselves."[47]

Instrumentalizing Hippismo

Although some elements of the youth question were under heightened public scrutiny, mainstream news about criollo counterculture was scant before 1968. This does not mean hippies were absent from Santiago's streets. Events that unfolded in Providencia in the spring of 1967—the momentous year of the university-reform movement—say much about the emerging presence of criollo counterculture and the happenings to come. Weekend rumbles involving Provi's Coppelia-El Drugstore crowd and cadets from the Military School in Las Condes are the stuff of legend—long-remembered instances of early conflicts between hippismo and its detractors, with little to no generational sympathies shared between them. Gómez recalled that Coppelia hippies would call the cadets *empanadas* (traditional savory pies) because, like the cadets, *empanadas* would appear at noon on weekends. In one instance, a hippie playfully grabbed the hat of a cadet and lightly patted the young soldier's face with an open hand. Mario Soza of the rock band Los Ripios recalled that the cadet went back to the school to organize a group of peers to mount a response. They returned the next weekend. "We got scared when we saw the military buses arrive full of cadets," he explained. "They disembarked with their swords in the air to strike us. To put it in vulgar terms, we ran our asses off."[48] Carlos Varela, now a shopkeeper, was a cadet at the time, and he recalled that some four hundred cadets showed up. "It was an historic fight," he said in an interview. The next day, the school commandant summoned the cadets to assemble in the school's yard; they feared a reprimand was coming. Instead, they were congratulated for defending the school's honor.[49] Other fights between cadets and the Coppelia crowd popped up from time to time—essentially becoming a rite of passage for the former—but epic battles happened rarely.[50] As for Varela, he left the military before the decade's end, eventually finding himself at Piedra Roja in October 1970. "The human quality experienced at the festival has not been seen again. Ever again. Of all the festivals in which I participated, in Chile and other places, that festival is the only one that gave me . . . that made me vibrate and at one moment made me become emotional with what we experienced," he expressed.[51] He was a changed young man.

Until 1970, news in Chile about countercultural young people and happenings largely focused on foreign manifestations, ranging from news about Woodstock to the latest exploits of John Lennon. However, Álvaro Covacevich's *New Love* had shown audiences in 1968 that criollo counterculture was on the rise well before Piedra Roja. The weekly magazine *Paula* was one widely read periodical that showed interest in criollo and foreign counterculture early on, just as it had been an early leader in reporting on women's movements and sexual liberation. In 1968, a regular *Paula* contributor told readers of her recent run-ins with some hippie-looking compatriots; she injected a good measure of humor into what can only be construed as a vigorous objection to hippie modalities. Isabel Allende, who went on to become an accomplished novelist, paused to reflect on the attributes of hippies and "pseudo-hippies," whom she collectively called "impertinent." She explains, "I happened to see in the streets a few ladies well along in size and in years [*damas entradas en carnes y en años*] with boots and miniskirts, as well as some bank employees with pink shirts and flowery pants. These pseudo-hippies look ridiculous, and one has to understand that to remain in style it is indispensable to mind the details." In keeping with *Paula*'s commitment to fashion and with tongue firmly in cheek, Allende goes on to list some characteristics of specific styles she calls "Masculine Hippie" and "Feminine Hippie":

MASCULINE HIPPIE

1. Let your lank moustache and dirty hair grow. Try to have dandruff.
2. Do not brush your teeth. At most, suck on anise tablets.
3. Stain your pants with oil and hands with ink.
4. Put a flower on your ear and take off your socks.
5. Do not answer when spoken to, spit on rugs, and push women around.

6. Have a flowered shirt and don't do military service.
7. Adopt the habit of losing money you borrowed. It's not necessary to return it.

FEMININE HIPPIE

1. Have long hair and use a sailor's beret.
2. Paint your eyes and get tattoos on your knees.
3. Wear robes and a mini-skirt or go bare-footed and with a tie.
4. Become a Buddhist and eat sweet lollypops.
5. Don't get on *micros* [urban buses]. Hitchhike.
6. Admire Martin Luther King, your uncle Alejandro, and Ho Chi Minh.
7. Hang a sign on your back that says 'Make Love, Not War.'
8. Buy some homeopathic pills and say they are LSD.[52]

To Isabel Allende, a relative of Salvador Allende, male hippies apparently violate some basic precepts of manliness by wearing flowers (either on the ear or printed on a shirt) and not engaging in military service, and, as a result, are open to ridicule. Meanwhile, women who might flaunt signs of sexual liberation—represented by the literal "signs on their backs" that signal a preference for making love over making war—likewise cross a boundary of proper and reasonable conduct. Moreover, a bit of art accompanies these jocular but trenchant observations: a photo of Isabel Allende peering down, through reading glasses and with a serious expression (akin to that of a scientist looking through a microscope), at a group of cartoonish hippies clutching flowers, strumming guitars, and looking rather bohemian and unkempt.

Also in 1968, the Communist *El Siglo* paused to reflect on transnational counterculture, chiding male hippies for their flowery shirts and for "detesting soap." Throwing doubt on "this form of hippie rebellion" in a world in which people "cannot throw flowers to stop armies or police charging toward them," the newspaper claimed that the only people reaping the benefits of hippismo were textile barons, owners of department stores, music executives, and others invested in aspects of "hippie style."[53] Likewise in 1968, the conservative press declared that hippies everywhere stood steadfastly "against economy, discipline, logic, education, and intellect." And instead of working with others to improve society, hippies "find refuge from reality by way of fanciful detours" and demonstrate a trait that *El Mercurio* editorial writer Luis Vargas Saavedra found repulsive: passivism. While real social and political struggles gripped nations, hippies turned to "Buddhism, yoga manuals, pornography, and nineteenth-century art nouveau."[54] On the whole, *El Siglo* and other notable left-wing publications would go on to join conservative voices in much more robust and caustic condemnation of hippismo.

Hippismo and counterculture in general were unfortunate and worrisome imitations of movements and sensibilities born elsewhere in the world, the Left figured. "What really bothers us," wrote one columnist in the Communist *El Siglo* in October 1970, soon after Piedra Roja, "is the imported and imitative nature [of hippismo]. Young people [at the festival] acted as if they lived in North America and that they were victims of a consumerist society rather than being in an underdeveloped society that only now is conquering its destiny." The writer then explained, "The majority [at Piedra Roja] were under the illusion that they were at Woodstock; scenes from the film were mimicked as much as possible. Those dressed as hippies arrived ready to use their repertoire of words in a precarious English. Spanish was barely spoken." Indeed, as the Marxist press argued, hippismo was "Made in the USA" and Piedra Roja "was not a manifestation of youthful vitality but, rather, was a sign of a colonial mentality."[55] Meanwhile, Marxists concluded that youthful energy wasted on hippismo should be redirected toward the *proceso* (the revolutionary process). Just as Allende explained in his inaugural speech, the Communist *El Siglo* called upon young people to "funnel their feelings of rebelliousness and their patriotism toward not smoking marijuana or imitating Woodstock. Instead, those energies should be focused on constructive work that's needed, like never before, now that in Chile the people have taken power for the first time in our history."[56] But the bourgeoisie and the bourgeois mentality stood in the way. From the Left's perspective, the defenders of bourgeois values were those who had allowed a transnational capitalist system and culture industry to infect the nation's youth with maladies like hippismo. Yet, the Right expressed similar concern with such openness and vulnerability, essentially bemoaning an ongoing loss of Chile's national character—the result of cosmopolitanism and transnational culture—that had led to such problems as counterculture and Piedra Roja.[57] They did so, however, without overly criticizing the United States, in keeping with the Right's pro-U.S. outlook and Cold War positioning, which was embodied in the rhetoric and activity of the elite's National Party.

As might be expected, Marxists brought class struggle and attacks on the "bourgeois" characteristics of hippismo to their rhetorical fusillade. Children of the bourgeoisie and petty bourgeoisie, including those who engage in hippista pursuits, are "indifferent toward our national problems, they show an absolute lack of dedication toward the destiny of the people and, in all reality, are accomplices of reactionary politics," one *El Siglo* contributor said. He added, "It is true that these young people really haven't rebelled against anything. They only show conformism in light of their class's loss of values."[58] The Left's evaluation of hippismo and counterculture became a critique of bourgeois morality (or the lack thereof) and "reactionary" politics, which naturally led to a direct frontal assault on capitalism. Ten days after Piedra Roja, yet another *El Siglo* columnist, this one fresh from a trip to the Soviet bloc, observed, "Such social deviance does not happen in socialist countries. And I didn't see hippies in the Soviet Union. Nor did I see vagrants or other varieties of idleness—enemies of society. In socialist countries young people identify themselves with ideals of the common good."[59]

There were two obvious "material" indications, among others, that the events in Piedra Roja were very much associated with the moral bankruptcy and imperialist implications of capitalism, or so the Left explained. One was the presence of the Andina Coca-Coca Bottling Company on festival grounds, which reflected and reinforced not only bourgeois consumption patterns but also the economic and cultural reach of a U.S.-based corporation.[60] The Socialist *Las Noticias de Última Hora* decried, "Hippie bands, which performed thanks to the sponsorship of Coca-Cola, got bored while performing their original songs, so they laid down and smoked joints like everyone else."[61] The Communist *El Siglo* went so far as to argue that Andina's role at Los Dominicos merited the attention of the Congress, but nothing became of that idea.[62] Interestingly, the leftist press never realized just how many "bourgeois" young North Americans had been involved in helping Gómez realize his vision of a criollo Woodstock. Pink Lizard and Gary Fritz, a student at the prestigious Nido de Aguilas School, took on the task of publicizing the event, and other American-born youths, including Carlos Lowry and his brother, Paul—both students at the affluent British-run The Grange School—and another Lowry family member were also critical in making Piedra Roja come to pass. The Left's second "material" indication was the fact that Gómez's "youth song festival" transpired on private property, which led to the police's reluctance to intervene during the fateful weekend in Las Condes.[63]

El Siglo emphasized the fact that Piedra Roja happened on private property, which, it argued, hampered intervention even though some mothers asked the Carabineros to get their daughters out of there.[64] Marxists seized the moment to make the case that Rosselot's status as a private landowner negated the greater social and cultural good, which essentially would have entailed police crushing the festival; private property was as much a cultural and moral menace as it was a source of socioeconomic abuse and alienation. For Marxists, then, to fight hippismo was to fight capitalism, and to fight capitalism was to identify, vilify, and combat its structural elements and cultural manifestations. Indeed, hippies rested their identities on capitalist patterns of consumption as much as anything else. Alienation, angst, parental authority, transnational trends and circumstances, and other factors fed criollo counterculture, but a key component of hippismo was its format of outward expressivity. If we agree there was a hippie "look," then hippies shared priorities and understandings regarding material consumption in the capitalist marketplace, thus promoting a species of fetishism. What is more, hippies expressed the imperative of individuality (liberation, freedom, etc.), which prioritized the self over the social totality and social good, thus reflecting the self-centeredness at the heart of capitalism.

Marxists explained that such traits were in full view along Providencia Avenue and other streets of the municipality. To contest Provi's cultural characteristics—hippismo, in this case—was a form of class struggle against the barrio alto and what it represented in Chilean society. In 1971, the pro-UP *Ahora* asked, "Providencia: ¿tontódromo o fascistódromo?" (Providencia: Arena of Dummies or Fascists?). The municipality is a "showcase of things foreign [goods, lavish consumerism, and so forth] anchored right in the center of Santiago's barrio alto," a contributor to the magazine explained. There, near El Drugstore and Coppelia, the correspondent and a photographer came across "a young man whom at first we mistook for a girl and gave us the finger," as well as other youths with the evidently telltale signs of capitalism and what *El Siglo* had earlier called a "colonial mentality": T-shirts "emblazoned with 'Love' or 'Yale University'" as well as "ripped blue jeans."[65] The writer declared, "They are kids who are tied to the establishment, to what they easily have been given." Their form of "rebellion" is a sign that many of Providencia's young people were only concerned about themselves instead of "the society in which they are entangled."[66] What is more, there was no better proof of the aloofness of Provi's young people—hippies included—than a statement made by one unidentified young man who was hanging out on Providencia Avenue. "In Providencia all are against the [Allende] government," he noted. "I need to protect where I'm from." He added, "It's evident that this government wants to take away our things, things that we've earned." The article's author then argues, "The Popular Government is seriously damaging the interests of the Chilean bourgeoisie and, therefore, the young people with whom we spoke take on a class consciousness and assume a militant role. But nothing is truly clear to them, since the foreign values they entertain are quite strong." Indeed, the correspondent explains that young people in Providencia, hippies or not, "lack any clear political and ideological conceptions" amid Chile's political struggles, and despite their supposed rebelliousness, their defense of a characteristically "bourgeois" lifestyle "protects the interests of the oligarchy." The article concludes by answering the question it posed: Provi's hippies are probably just stupid, and by being so they abet the fascists.[67] *Ahora*'s treatment of Providencia and its young people is interesting on more than one level. It unreservedly recognizes Provi as a lair of the bourgeoisie and its foreign "ways," including hippismo, and indicates that the Allende government was busily trying to put an end to both (but not without strong resistance). Furthermore, not only were hippies and their milieu impediments to UP's social revolution, but hippista young men lacked proper manliness. Mistaking a young man for a woman effectively feminized the male hippie, stripping him of legitimacy—social, cultural, or political, or so it appears. It will become evident that manliness was an important attribute of the "real" and youthful revolutionary in Allende's Chile, and male hippies were notably bereft of it, Marxists suggested.

While publications such as *Ahora* are good indicators of what orthodox Marxists were thinking, the Left was a diverse assemblage of radical thought and practice. The MIR (Movement of the Revolutionary Left), founded in Santiago but with a leadership dominated by radical students from the University of Concepción (in the country's center-south), offered a Castroist, combative, armed, and radical option to UP's incrementalism. While it mostly commented on Siloism when criticizing counterculture (for reasons that will be explained in the next chapter), it also tackled the problem of hippismo in a way that both criticized capitalism and the traditional cultural values and outlooks of Allende's Left, including that of the Socialist and Communist parties. Hippismo, one mirista wrote in mid-1971, questioned cultural and social values and was creating new ones, and capitalism, so flexible and adaptive, had generated a "hippie industry" featuring clothes and such. (El Drugstore, Palta, and other Provi locales presumably were among the representatives of such "industrialism.") That power must be combated by a "Chilean vanguard" with its own intense and dynamic project of cultural change. The UP Left, while complaining ardently about hippismo, nevertheless carried an "attitude that is the same as that of the bourgeoisie," the writer argues. This manifests itself as a focus on policing and degrading young people seeking an alternate reality, in addition to objectifying women in a discourse focusing on their family roles as mothers. The way forward, the author concludes, is clear: "In Chile, where there has not been a social revolution but instead a process of change rooted in bourgeois legality, the tendency for the durability of institutions and values of a reactionary fashion is very strong, and those can only be counteracted if they truly become the objects of attention and become central concerns in the operation of the most revolutionary sectors."[68] At the same time, however, the miristas, whose males often sported beards (like Cuban guerrillas) and longer hair, wore black, and fostered a strongly masculine and sober look, replaced some norms with others.

As historian Florencia Mallon describes, "Mirista leaders effectively countered both upper-class and leftist morality as forms of social control. In so doing, they promoted a heroic, resistant, and romantic subjectivity that was especially attractive to the younger generation of all classes." Yet, by denying a discourse of "traditional" family values, the MIR "had the tendency to overlook the powerful attractiveness of family imagery not only to the male workers and peasants who had never had the resources to actually support their families in an 'honorable' way but also to the working-class and peasant women who yearned for economic security and familial stability and were not represented within the mirista romance." For the MIR, to link the orthodox Left and Allende's coalition to conservative cultural outlooks was more than rhetorical: it was a realistic statement about the presence of such elements in the driver's seat of Allende's road to socialism. Within that orthodox Left, there were conversations and debates that addressed the complicated issues of family values, gender roles, what was culturally "revolutionary," and so forth. Yet, reflecting broadly on the traditional Left, Mallon states, "The working-class family was considered the basic and most effective unit of class struggle, and both men and women were encouraged to carry out their prescribed roles within it."[69]

One thing leftists could agree on was that the Right was a dangerous stalwart of convention in a rapidly changing society and world. A mere two days before Piedra Roja opened in Las Condes, the pro-UP tabloid *Clarín* printed a bold headline: "La Derecha Tiene Muy Aburrida a Juventud" (The Right Has Young People Very Bored). Allende, at the time, had garnered a plurality of the electorate in the September 1970 election, and UP was waiting for the Congress to vote Allende into office, as protocol dictated.

The Right, Marxists complained, had launched hit-and-run assaults on the headquarters of the FECh (Student Federation of the University of Chile) and similar places, with the FNPL (Fatherland and Liberty Nationalist Front) having a hand in such deeds, in the months after the election. The Popular Unity Youth Command (Comando Juvenil Unidad Popular), an association that included the PCCh's Jota and its equivalents in the Socialist and Radical parties, among others, pledged to defend Allende in the face of "fascist" attacks. "In all of such actions we find the hand of North American imperialism," *Clarín* explained. "Popular Unity's young people advise and notify the fascists of today and tomorrow that Chilean youths will not allow the legitimate triumph [of UP] to be snatched away." The publication concluded, "We call on the young people of our Fatherland to remain permanently mobilized in the defense of the peoples' victory."[70] Such sentiments were typical of the pro-UP media and soon were intertwined with a searing critique of hippismo and the counterculture. The cultural politics of anti-hippismo saturated *allendista* discourse, as the UP called on Chileans young and old to rally behind the road to socialism and defeat imperialism, capitalism, and immorality—all of which, they emphasized, were evident in hippismo and counterculture.

Notwithstanding the question of whether or not the Right had made young people bored, the Right certainly was not bored. On October 3, 1972, the Coppelia café in midtown Providencia went up in flames. That most popular and widely recognized hangout for hippies during the Frei and Allende years had fallen victim to young "fascist hordes" of the FNPL, which was bent on destroying the businesses and properties of people "with progressive ideas," the Marxist press declared. Coppelia's owner, though known to be somewhat of a UP sympathizer, was not a militant in any political party, but the FNLP had placed Coppelia on its "black list" as part of what *allendistas* called the Right's "psychological bombardment" of the public. Marxists argued that the elite's National Party (PN) and a group of young nationalists within it called the Rolando Matus Command (Comando Rolando Matus), named after a small property owner who protested agrarian reform and later was found murdered, conspired with the FNPL to torch Coppelia. And behind the intolerable action of those groups stood the right-wing Santiago newspaper *Tribuna*—"an embarrassment of our national press in which one only finds the work of writers in the service of imperialism and the oligarchy," leftists argued.[71] *Tribuna* had, in fact, published a list on August 22 (republished daily for the ensuing three days) that identified Santiago businesses, including Coppelia, which had not

An elderly woman holds a placard advertising the right-wing newspaper *Tribuna* at an anti-Allende rally (1972). It reads: "Know What's Firm by Reading *Tribuna*." Courtesy of the Colección Museo Histórico Nacional (Santiago).

shut their doors during an anti-UP national strike of small businesses on August 21—a strike that prompted the Allende government to declare a state of emergency in the capital. *Tribuna* identified 123 businesses in the Santiago metropolitan area, including thirty-five in the barrio alto (the municipalities of Providencia, Las Condes, and Vitacura), which, interestingly, was an anti-Allende stronghold. Restaurants, bakeries, grocery stores, cafes, soda fountains, bookstores, and clothing stores of varying types constituted the bulk of the businesses in question.[72]

If the strike demonstrated "a lack of respect and an insult to all Chileans" it also "inspired the majority of our citizens who believe in authentic democracy," Marxists emphasized.[73] In the words of *Tribuna*, however, the strike was "an energetic protest against the government's economic policies that are leading this country into bankruptcy."[74] Meanwhile, Marxists did not construe the destruction of Coppelia as an anti-hippista statement—a cultural act. Instead, they interpreted the event as an assault on progressive political values and the *proceso*, regardless of the fact that Coppelia's owner was not a political zealot. Moreover, given that Coppelia was in the heart of the barrio alto and was a space in which "adolescents of the bourgeoisie licked ice cream while wearing eye-catching clothes," the Communist *El Siglo* found itself in the thorny position of having to defend "bourgeois" private property—popular with hippies, no less—from a "horrendous manifestation of Nazism reincarnated in the form of Patria y Libertad." As an editorial by *El Siglo*'s Santiago del Campo explained, "Hitler ordered the boycott and later the destruction of all businesses that belonged to Jews. It was a prelude to the most infamous crime in history. . . . Today, these underdeveloped fascists [the FNLP] transform the Left into the source of their phobias. And now it's not just the Communists who risk their businesses and their necks; so, too, does anyone who professes progressive ideas."[75]

There is no direct evidence establishing that anticounterculture sentiment drove hooligans to attack Coppelia. Yet, it is clear that FNPL members had little patience for hippie modalities and counterculture, and thus disrupting a renowned setting of hippista sociability came with an added bonus. In addition, while there were some discernable (but not catastrophic) generational fissures within the Left, the most visible organization of militant right-wing youths unwaveringly furthered and reinforced the ideological framework and vitriol of older rightists. In a 1971 article in the FNPL's periodical, cleverly called *Patria y Libertad,* the movement identified "youth problems" and pointed an accusatorial finger at a "generational confrontation" between parents and children. "What is the root-cause of that conflict?" the tabloid-magazine asked. "We believe that it is a religious crisis shaking the world." It then identifies hippismo and Marxism essentially as secular-religious movements—with their own belief systems and practices that were godless and morally bankrupt—with the paradigmatic hallmarks of "materialism in their doctrines." Hippismo was materialist in the sense that a delimiting aspect of it was the consumption of certain forms of material culture—marijuana, clothes of a certain variety, and so forth. Marxism, meanwhile, professed a historical interpretation rooted in the material reality of social being, grounded fundamentally in the concept of dialectical materialism. This compelled the *Patria y Libertad* contributor to proclaim, "[The] Front invites youth to complete the sacred task of saving Chile from a communist dictatorship and, at the same time, it incites young people to conquer the challenge of building a just, prosperous, free, and sovereign Fatherland. And young people are responding magnificently."[76]

Juan Pablo Orrego of Los Blops got to know—in a sense—some young men he construed to be FNPL members. Sporting long hair and other hippie identifiers, Orrego was accustomed to being called a "fag" (*maricón*) in public by the defenders of varying political fronts. That was harassment, yes, but fell well short of his more harrowing experiences: Orrego was assaulted twice during the Allende years—not for being a *rockero* but for having long hair, he explained. In one instance in 1971, he was on his bicycle pedaling up Principe de Gales Avenue in La Reina, a working- and middle-class municipality adjacent to Las Condes, when he suddenly was struck from behind. After falling, he looked up to see four to five male assailants, dressed in suits and with short haircuts in the FNPL style. Orrego got on his feet and grabbed a rock; a worried look descended upon the men's faces, and they scurried to their car parked up the street. They left in a hurry. Orrego then looked behind him and saw that more than a dozen construction workers from a nearby building project were walking up to the scene. "There they were—workers defending the hippie," Orrego quipped. He reasoned, however, that the workers' aggressive posture toward his nicely attired attackers was less about assisting him and more about wanting to rumble with men who, "because of their appearance, their attitudes, were the enemy." In other words, class warfare was afoot.[77]

It would be incorrect to assume that such violence against hippies only emanated from the Right. Members of the Jota's BRP (Ramona Parra Brigade), renowned for their revolutionary muralism, went about Santiago with bamboo canes and chains in hand and hurled rocks to harass enemies on the streets and on university campuses. Declaring itself "against decadent hippismo," the brigade made targets of countercultural young people but mostly battled against organized and armed foes—the FNPL, especially.[78] Perhaps one of the most telling examples of BRP aggression toward hippismo reportedly happened in October 1971 in the working-class shantytown of San Joaquín (now in the municipality of San Joaquín), near Rebeca Matte Street. On the 12th (perhaps coincidentally, a year to the day after Piedra Roja), some 150 working-class young people, many of them hippies, met on some vacant lots to play music and dance—a "festival," they called it. The youths had responded to a flyer that circulated in the barrio that called upon young people to simply "bring an instrument and yourself."[79]

Participants and witnesses later reported to what surely was a very interested *El Mercurio* that the BRP had descended brutally upon the revelers with canes and chains. The *brigadistas* then scolded revelers essentially for not sharing the UP vibe and, by virtue of not committing to the *proceso*, for betraying their social class and its collective interests. One victim of the incident was Carlos Salvo Villagrán, who was beaten by BRP members for having "long hair and for wearing unusual clothes." Friends took Salvo to a nearby house, only to face harassment by police who seemed uninterested in helping. Instead, upon searching the home in which Salvo lay beaten and bleeding, police produced a package of marijuana, accusing Salvo's helpers of a crime.[80] This episode, in which defenders of the working class assaulted members of the working class, underscored the prospect of working-class youths dropping out of the heated political struggles happening around them. This alarmed a Left that in its marches chanted, "*¡El pueblo unido, jamás será vencido!*" (The people, united, will never be defeated!), which also is the title of a Quilapayún song; leftists expected more of young proletarians than the hippismo some were practicing in places like Parque Forestal. Allende remarked in December 1970, "Youths could not be spectators in this great economic and social transformation of Chile, youths must be and are a most important part of this era in the nation's life. We need, we demand, and ask for the creative energy of youth. Its revolutionary loyalty will be placed fully at the service of Chile and its people."[81] If the "hippie" situation worsened among working-class youths, it threatened to weaken Marxist discourse on class and potentially young people's place in the *proceso*. The Right did not want young people to be spectators, either, and they reasoned, hippies were living in a countercultural world that was superficial at best and farcical at worst.

Just days after Piedra Roja, the pro-PN *El Mercurio* chastised the Woodstock documentary (that had inspired Jorge Gómez and his associates to organize a criollo iteration), "developed societies," and lax Chilean border and airport authorities for harming the younger generation. U.S. popular culture, mediated through the Woodstock film, "seems to have been behind the decision among some Chilean adolescents to put on a similar event," an editorial complained. "It is evident that our youth, just like those around the world, act without inhibition. . . . They skirt their educational responsibilities, they show pride in the way they treat their parents, and they adopt habits like smoking marijuana." Conservatives called for immediate action on the part of the state: "The immigration authorities need to demonstrate seriousness in identifying undesirables who continually bring with them germs that will dissolve the character of a generation of young people we must protect."[82] The newspaper later described Chilean hippies as "improvised" and sarcastically lamented that "authentic hippies" from outside the country were surely unimpressed by their "criollo emulators," or "hippie imposters."[83]

The way hippies looked was particularly intolerable to the Right. One *El Mercurio* editorial, published a year after Piedra Roja, explained, "Before, young people dreamed of dressing well, and when they donned an outfit they felt like they were the center of attention. They cared that the crease on their pants was impeccable." It then affirmed, "Today, that's not the case." Worse, the editorial argued, was how easy it had become to mistake a man for a woman in light of the inclination among many young men to grow their hair. Such phenotypic ambiguity, by virtue of violating normative conceptions of gender and sexuality, was simply repugnant, *El Mercurio* strongly suggested.[84] Likewise, the conservative press later pinpointed the "criollo taste for imitating the negative things that come from the outside."[85] This was colerismo at its most brash. As the newspaper explained, "They [hippies] believe that smoking marijuana and the passionate cultivation of laziness is a way of protesting the system; but there, in the smoke of marijuana, begins and ends the rebellion. That is to say, it is a fraudulent form of rebellion that is maintained by their parents' money."[86]

Another aspect of how the conservative press treated hippismo and Piedra Roja was its (correct) assertion that young people from all social classes were present on Rosselot's land during the fateful weekend in October 1970—something that the Left was quite slow to admit, hoping to avert a discursive pitfall. *El Mercurio* contended, "It would be incorrect to assume the participants of that orgy of marijuana and sexual excess . . . were young people from one identifiable class." The periodical concluded, "All of this speaks to the effects of a type of moral denationalization [*desnacionalización*], of a crisis of family values and young peoples' loss of the sense of themselves, due to certain circles of youths who fortunately only represent a minority seeking publicity" and that without a doubt, "tolerance [of hippismo] is a grave error."[87] The Right, then, obviously found it useful to embrace "the family" as a key conceptual category in their conflict against UP, but the Left, too, had a history of such mainstream outlooks when it came to family, gender, sexuality, and the like; protecting the nuclear family entailed denying youths the waywardness of such things as counterculture and capitalism. In essence, the Left's normative conceptions of revolution and the family were merged, just as conservatism's "family values" rhetoric dovetailed with its charge that leftist revolutionary politics led to anomie.

Building on the "family values" argument, *El Mercurio* expressed sympathy for parents in a September 1971 editorial in light of the "difficulties that stand before youths." It referred to a meeting of the local Federation of Parents and Guardians, which was held under the auspices of the municipal government of Providencia. Among the problems addressed were how to "defend children from pornography," how to keep juveniles "busy in healthy and useful ways," and the need to protect the community's "basic moral values." Although *El Mercurio* assumed a practical stance when observing that it was unnecessary "to profess Puritanism to energetically censure moral libertinism," it nevertheless traced many of the moral problems that most everyone associated with hippismo to the Allende government and its media apparatus (the state-owned Quimantú publishing house, presumably), though specific manifestations of state-sponsored vice, other than vague references to pornography, were left unmentioned. *El Mercurio* asserted, "Unfortunately, the cultivation of immorality is taking place through the means of communication that belong to the government. . . . In this way, the authorities not only have failed to deal with such abuses and protect proper manners but also have permitted printed material owned by the public to join campaigns of indecency." It continued, "Moral upbringing, sports and cultural activities, and the patriotic work of social assistance are among the initiatives that parents suggest will fill the minds and imaginations of young people with values that channel their enthusiasm toward an upstanding and generous sensibility."[88] A month later and in the same vein, the right-wing *Tribuna* argued that the governing coalition used "state funds to destroy families and cultural values" and "foment hatred among Chileans" by subsidizing a youth theater group called Saltamontes (grasshoppers) to which miristas, young Communists, and many foreign young people belonged. Designed as a theater group sworn to represent and defend the interests of the working class, Saltamontes was, according to *Tribuna* contributor Jaime Valdés, yet another government-funded group of young "delinquents" with "nefarious objectives."[89] To the Right, then, from the ideas and policies of the UP government sprang youth-related activities that damaged culture, morality, family, and the proper upbringing of youths. Just as the FNPL had argued in the pages of *Patria y Libertad* when discussing a Marxist "religion," *El Mercurio* and *Tribuna* claimed that immorality was at the very core of Allende's administration.

In their unrelenting criticism of the Allende government, conservatives also focused on Marxism's materialist epistemology, and they began associating it with hippista consumerism. Indeed, Marxism's detractors often branded hippismo in particular as undeniably materialistic, lacking a *properly* spiritual dimension, notwithstanding the FNPL's proclamation that hippismo and communism constituted religions, with "religion" suggesting a following with an inherent devotion—in a word, faith. Although some hippies may have believed that their lifestyle approximated that of medieval mendicants—wandering, barefoot, poor—the exact opposite was the case, according to conservatives. Indeed, hippies gave into orgies of materialism and consumption that included "eroticism and drugs." The typical hippie, moreover, spent more money on marijuana "than Churchill did on cigars." What is more, a 1971 conservative editorial titled "Sociedad de no consumo" (Non-Consumption Society) showered accolades on American-born Thorstein Veblen's *The Theory of the Leisure Class* (1899), which criticizes consumerism in modern society. Veblen coined the term "conspicuous consumption," something that was associated with transnational counterculture in no small way, as Saturdays in Provi made abundantly clear.[90] Meanwhile, Marxists offered an interpretation of counterculture that centered on the materialism and consumerism of capitalism, all under the dark shadow of U.S. imperialism.

While the Left and Right had their says about counterculture and each other in the wake of Piedra Roja, the centrist Christian Democrats often struck a more delicate and thoughtful note. Between Piedra Roja and Allende's rise to power, the government-operated (and pro-PDC) *La Nación* pointed an "accusing finger" not at the hippies but, rather, at "themselves"—a generation of parents and statesmen who should seriously try to understand hippismo instead of fabricating one caricature after another. As one editorial declared, when dealing with hippies—contributors to a truly "mass phenomenon"—it made little sense to "use a pair of scissors to cut their hair, to say nothing of the fascist suggestion to bathe them and put them to work." Instead, the statist periodical explained that to address hippismo one must first understand the problem of "idle youth," which, among other things, explains the presence of many working-class young people in hippista circles. The capitalist system (or "subcapitalist" system, as *La Nación* put it) in underdeveloped nations like Chile makes for unemployment and free time, which, in turn, provide the ideal environment for the development of a hippista phenomenon that is the embodiment of lethargy. Consequently, "Chilean hippismo is indeed a copy [of foreign models] but it is a copy perfectly adapted to the Chilean reality."[91] The prevailing discourse of President Frei's administration in the era of the Alliance for Progress centered on critiques of capitalism and Marxism amidst the PDC's "Revolution in Liberty" and the embrace of a "third way." The insinuation above, then, is that ameliorating the most obvious negative results of capitalism (by way of a state-capitalist project), in addition to understanding and counteracting hippismo in proactive and positive ways, could energize the country's young people constructively, just as the Frei-led PDC had rallied the tens of thousands of youths who took part in the March of the Young Fatherland (Marcha de la Patria Joven) in 1964.

As noted above, the statist press dismissed simplistic calls for cutting the manes of hippies or forcibly bathing them en masse—ideas promoted by militants on the Left and Right. Instead, the government's mouthpiece drew attention to the transnational youth question and moral and cultural faults of the older generation. Quoting Socialist educator Eduardo Taibo, director of a school for gifted children, *La Nación* repeated the point that hippismo was an imported phenomenon, but suggested it could have been quite limited in Chile if not for the disintegration of families and the lack of contrasting models of behavior, including sexual behavior, in the country's "rigid" schools. Taibo went on to cast blame on mothers "liberated" by feminism, who, in the context of family disintegration, preferred to date and have sexual adventures (what the article referred to as "male preroga-tives," ordinarily) rather than be "mothers" to their children. Essentially, Taibo argued that young people could see the cultural and moral degrada-tion of their parents, and this caused grief, loneliness, and alienation among the former, with many then turning to hippismo as a species of narcotic to dull their pain. "One of the more immediate measures would have to be the de-alienation of youths by way of the means of communication, that those be healthy and positive, that they provide a new type of information," Taibo explained. "We want Chilean values and, I would say, Latin American na-tionalism [in the face of imported hippismo]."[92]

There were some basic points of confluence in discussion and debate about hippismo and criollo counterculture from 1970 through the Allende years. Opposing forces defended some of the same mainstream concep-tions of moral behavior—including refraining from "liberated" sex—that helped buttress broader arguments about class, economy, imperialism, the family, gender, and religion. Like those positioned on the right and in the center, Marxist political and cultural actors pulled few punches in their con-demnations of hippismo. As this and the subsequent two chapters show, these forces and the state applied various forms of pressure—from policing to peer—on purportedly wayward youths who valued their waywardness. For UP, its genuine (but internally debated) commitment to democracy and pluralism meant that its response to counterculture, while alienating and ex-asperating for many young people, was a world away from what so-called antisocials faced in the mid-1960s during the most renowned socialist revolution in Latin America. Cuba's controversial Military Units to Aid Production (Unidades Militares de Ayuda a la Producción, UMAP) were forced-labor camps where nonconformist youths—delinquents, hippies, homosexuals, political prisoners, practitioners of various religions, and other alleged apostates—were subjected to miserable conditions and harsh treatment for having flouted the Castro government's normative view of revolution: it was to be disciplined, manly, and policed. Founded in 1965, the UMAP camps came under internal and international scrutiny, and, upon admitting their heavy handedness, Castro began closing them in 1967.[93] Culturally heterodox Chileans did not encounter repression until after the September 1973 coup, in the face of another brand of discipline, manliness, and policing.

The Siloist movement, with a delineated doctrine, a nonhippie aesthetic, and some ideas that were not in line with typically hippista sensibilities, was also the focus of significant attention during the Allende years. Followers of the Argentine thinker known as Silo, such young people were alleged to be transgressors, perverts, and outlaws, just as hippies were. Indeed, voices in the public sphere often conflated Siloism and hippismo, not pausing to figure out that they were different in terms of theory and praxis. Yet, Siloism and hippismo both focused on avenues of personal transformation and liberation, offering alternative values that not only undermined mainstream culture but also rebuffed institutions of power and authority managed by *los viejos* (the old folks), including the nuclear family and the government.

· ·

In 1970, María Ester Lezaeta, having just graduated from high school, was attending career-training courses at ManPower Inc. in Santiago with the hope of landing a secretarial position. Although she was from an upper-class family, Lezaeta did not want to share in that existence and also was eager to find something more spiritual, meaningful, and impactful in her life. For a while, she thought she had found it: hippismo. "What I liked about the hippie vibe," Lezaeta recalled, "was its search, its search for something else." That "something else" was a new way of being, but for Lezaeta hippismo did not provide what she sought; it lacked the capacity to truly change her and the world around her. "I'd get together with people with hair down to here," she said, pointing to her shoulders, "and we'd smoke some joints and we'd talk about peace and love and all that." Bored and uninspired, Lezaeta felt the need for a deeper spiritualism. She had skipped the university en-trance examination, much to the chagrin of her parents, and sought a new path of self-discovery and growth. After Lezaeta married in 1971, her husband had a chance encounter in Providencia—a polestar of criollo counterculture—with a Siloist, which changed the lives of the couple: "Many of us who entered [Siloism] in those days came from there, from the hippie thing, from hippismo, from the drugs, from that whole story, and here [in Siloism] we encountered something totally ascetic." She added, "I didn't think I could find what I was looking for in hippismo because the hippie movement [as opposed to Siloism] didn't have any type of ideology."[1]

In the nuclei of hippismo and Siloism, and conspicuous in stories like those of Lezaeta and many others, lies the notion of self-discovery and liberation—a trek toward the "something else"—and Lezaeta's account par-ticularly points to the fluidity and compound substance of counterculture, made up of sensibilities ranging from the most informal to the doctrinaire. Siloism speaks to that diversity. The movement emerged at the end of the 1960s as a potent countercultural alternative to modern society as well as to hippismo, connecting with Eastern philosophy, anarchism, Western Marxism, and other threads of thought to create a complex philosophical framework. Embodied in the group Poder Joven (Young Power), the Siloists were not melenudos (men with melenas or flowing manes), nor were they marihuaneros (potheads). They did not advocate promiscuity. They did not wear bright flowery shirts or huge earrings with peace symbols. Rather, their aestheticism and asceticism reflected a sober demeanor—which was still soundly countercultural—that focused on a new consciousness, generational conflict, and "total revolution," all of which some, like Lezaeta, found attractive, others deemed a bit creepy, and still others declared patently dangerous. Those who criticized and condemned counterculture paid rather little attention to the contrasts between hippismo and Siloism, therefore betraying a certain self-induced ignorance regarding important aspects of cultural change happening around them. This lack of attention created and promoted in the public sphere a simplistic and blurry construction of the countercultural "other."

The formation and development of Poder Joven, whose membership numbered in the low hundreds but seemed larger to many critics, and the ensuing reactions of anti-Siloists, especially those of the orthodox Left, further point to the seriousness of intergenerational dissonance that emerged alongside, and in relation to, class struggle. These events also accentuate the possibilities and limitations faced by heterodox revolutionary movements under Salvador Allende's UP government. Despite an avowed commitment to "socialism," Siloists found no allies in UP, nor did they seek any. The Marxist-led government, which identified itself as the realization, if not the pinnacle, of Chilean democracy, effectively branded the unarmed and apolitical Siloists as enemies to the state, culture, and morality. This chapter examines what Siloism and Poder Joven were, what they stood for, what they did, and what they meant in the context of tremendous social discord, acute political strife, and the radicalization of a great many young people. Siloists, simply put, rejected existing authorities and nearly all aspects of contemporary society. They did so under difficult conditions and at some risk, as they were confronted by the policing powers of both media and the state during Chile's road to socialism. While leaders of the Left decried Poder Joven's alleged fascism, the Right warned of Siloism's "socialist" revolutionary objectives. Most everyone branded Siloists as cultural outcasts, social deviants, drug addicts, perverts, pedophiles, and kidnappers, and Silo's associates were investigated and jailed during the Allende years. Amid these conditions, Siloists went about developing and defending a movement that began in earnest with Silo's first major public declaration in May 1969.

An Andean Homily

Silo's "sermon on the mount," as some later called it, took place high up in the Andes near Mendoza, Argentina, at midday on May 4, 1969. Days earlier, Mendoza's municipal officials, in accordance with the national government's restriction of civil liberties, had denied a public meeting space within the city's limits to Silo, the pseudonym used by the Mendoza native Mario Luis Rodríguez Cobos, whose first pronouncement would have taken place as early as 1966 if not for his country's repressive environment. Under the military government of Juan Carlos Onganía, police in 1969 had ransacked the homes of Silo's early acolytes in Mendoza.[2] Seeking a space in which to assemble, the Siloists formed an impromptu convoy and traveled a meandering road into the towering mountains, with inquisitive police never far behind, until they eventually gathered on a rise named Punta de Vacas. There, surrounded by rocks, dust, and shrubs, Silo and his enthusiasts engendered a youth movement whose repercussions would soon be felt strongly across the border in Chile, where profound political, social, cultural, and economic change lay on the horizon. That day at Punta de Vacas, with police observing from a short distance away, dozens of young people listened as Silo shared his thoughts on such things as pleasure, desire, suffering, and the violence of "philistine morality." What they witnessed was the seminal oration that defined and inspired a species of counterculture, esoteric and original to the Southern Cone.

The presence at Punta de Vacas of Chileans, who comprised more than half the crowd of about one thousand, stemmed largely from Silo's visit to Chile the previous January. During his stay, when local officials in Aconcagua Province (near the capital) forced him from a rural "place of meditation," Silo found refuge on the country's central coast—a hotbed of hippismo. There, Silo continued to develop the philosophy he later shared in the Andean oration, drawing followers along the way.[3] Chile offered an opening but also posed some major challenges for the movement. "[Chile] was very polarized, and being so polarized they didn't see other things [beyond their own ideas]," Silo recalled in a 2005 interview."[4] Silo's followers in Santiago and environs nurtured their nascent movement and formed Poder Joven, which brought together self-described revolutionaries in their mid-to-late teens and twenties and from all of Chile's urban classes—a budding generation in a turbulent yet pluralistic and democratic polity. Rooted in their collective aspiration to achieve a higher state of being through self-transformation, guided meditation, and "self-work," Siloists tested the official boundaries and meanings of such concepts as liberation, revolution, and socialism in their response to Silo's call for "The Healing of Suffering"—the title of his Punta de Vacas address.[5]

Less than twenty minutes long, "The Healing of Suffering" began with a simple declaration: "If you have come to hear a man because you think he will communicate wisdom, you are on the wrong path, because real wisdom is not conveyed by way of books or speeches; real wisdom is in the depth of your consciousness, just as real love is in the depth of your heart." Silo then spelled out his understanding of suffering, noting that besides the physical dimension of suffering (from hunger or a wound), there exists a "suffering strictly of your mind" that "is always rooted in the violence that exists in your own consciousness." He explained that one suffers "because you fear losing what you have, or because you lack, or because you fear in general. These, then, are the great enemies of humankind: fear of sickness, fear of poverty, fear of death, fear of loneliness. All of these sufferings are in your mind." Silo connected suffering and its source—a violence within the mind—to the destructive power of human desire. "The more violent a person is," he warned, "the more crude, the more base are that person's desires." Such "inner violence," nourished by desire, naturally leads to violence in the "outside" world, as humans driven by desire (for goods, social status, political power) inflict violence on others. Physical violence is an obvious extension of desire's command, Silo argued, as is "economic violence," which "is the violence through which you exploit others." Economic violence occurs "when you steal from another person, when you are no longer a brother or sister to others, and when you become a bird of prey who feeds upon other people."[6] Poder Joven's conception of economic violence, developed by Silo at Punta de Vacas, later framed the movement's peculiar socialism, which focused on the psychological bases for economic and social justice rather than a (Marxist) materialist interpretation of social being.

Silo's attention to suffering and desire took him beyond a critique of economic conditions to denounce racism and religious intolerance, as well as condemn what he called "philistine morality," which he saw as symptoms of brutish desire: "You wish to impose your way of life upon another person; you wish to impose your vocation on another person. But who has told you that you are an example to be followed? Who has told you that you can impose your way of life because it pleases you? What makes your way of life a model, and what makes it a pattern that you have the right to impose on others? This, then, is another form of violence." He went on to warn his audience, "There is no politics that can solve this mad urge for violence. There is no political party or movement on the planet that can end the violence." Silo then suggested that young people should be wary of any group or institution promising to rectify grievous worldly conditions through traditional means: political reform or revolution, the restructuring of economies, the creation of welfare states, and so forth. Without a transformative process within the self, which nullifies an individual's desire and brings about true joy and love that will "elevate your spirit" and "elevate your body," authentic change in all areas of human experience—true and expansive liberation—simply cannot happen.[7] Such self-transformation would be the result of meditation guided by the teachings and coaching of those whose minds are free.

Unpacking the substance of "The Healing of Suffering" is something that Siloists did and continue to do, as they applied and still apply the pronouncement's words to changing conditions in their lives and in society. There are some obvious echoes of Eastern philosophy in Silo's short "sermon," which are worth noting preliminarily. Buddhist notions about the sources and remedies of desire are present, as is Taoist philosophy best summarized in the proverb, "Manifest plainness, embrace simplicity, reduce selfishness, have few desires." The other guiding sensibility is that humankind, not a god, is responsible for suffering; there exists no metaphysical force exercising its whims or will on humans. In Eastern thought, there is no God-Satan, Good-Evil dichotomy as seen in the West, and thus humankind also has the ability to overcome the kinds of desire and suffering Silo described at Punta de Vacas.[8] This speech gave listeners a taste of a more complex philosophical framework that continued to be developed during the Allende years through the published works of Poder Joven, most of which appeared in 1971 and 1972, and through Silo's written and public pronouncements.

Silo was not yet widely known by name in Chile when he delivered "The Healing of Suffering." He lived a seemingly mainstream life in Mendoza, which he called home until his death in 2010. The product of a middle-class family, Rodríguez attended a Marist (Society of Mary) high school, where he first became aware of social problems in light of the order's emphasis on peace and justice. He briefly studied law in his hometown before buying a motorcycle and embarking on a four-month trek across Argentina in the late 1950s. He later traveled to Colombia and Chile. "The thing I most remember about Chile was the suffering of its people. Free people, people with mental agility," he noted in a published interview. This period of his life reads like Che Guevara's *The Motorcycle Diaries*. Like Che, whose Marxism

Silo shunned, Silo was in his twenties when he made the journey, learning about the lives of others and perhaps a great deal more about his own. Also, this was the era of Jack Kerouac's *On the Road* (first published Spanish in 1959 as *En el camino* by Editorial Losada in Buenos Aires), a Beat Generation classic, which sought to undermine mainstream culture and conformity. Silo returned to Argentina, where he studied political science and became interested in sociology. He later journeyed again to Chile in early 1969 at age thirty-one. As late as 1971, he was selling such products as olive paste (for sandwiches) and brake fluid to make ends meet.[9] By then, Silo was known, as was Poder Joven, in Greater Santiago and elsewhere in Chile, and problems were mounting for the Siloists.

Generating "Young Power"

In a 1971 interview with the leftist youth magazine *Ramona*, Silo accused *los cerdos* (the pigs—people in positions of authority, especially police and government officials) of labeling his Punta de Vacas address a "sermon on the mount" in order to give it an unwarranted and unwanted messianic overtone. "The important thing was to talk to the young people," Silo said. "Then the pigs got scared. It's logical. Because the *Cordobazo* happened twenty days later. We could smell it coming, you know."[10] Referring to the student and worker uprising that shook Córdoba, Argentina, in late May 1969, Silo described a larger upheaval in the making, led by a new and innovative generation of young people victimized by prevailing institutions and destructive ideas—pursued and reinforced by an autocratic older generation—that defined their inner and outer worlds.[11] In essence, Silo drew on the *Cordobazo* to exemplify the growing militancy of youths who, he said, desired a transformation in their lives that went beyond the economic and the political. Indeed, in the *Ramona* interview, Silo prognosticated a "new revolution against everything that is." Young people, he explained, "don't participate in anything, and they are the only ones capable of making a real revolution."[12] Put broadly, Siloism asserted that in order to achieve the transformative possibilities and promise of such a revolution, one had to begin by elaborating a liberating psychology, derived from a process of self-discovery and understanding that would produce a more humane cosmology. Inner change, if realized, would then be expressed in the outer world as pacifism, freedom, justice, happiness, and a particular species of socialism made real and fostered by the younger generation.

The *Ramona* correspondent who traveled to Mendoza, Mario Gómez López, was a journalist best known for articles in the leftist newspaper *Puro Chile*. Not a Communist himself, Gómez was a UP supporter and helped found *Ramona*, published by the Jota (Communist Youth), for which he submitted articles from time to time during the Allende years. *El Siglo*, a voice of the PCCh (Communist Party), was too dogmatic for his tastes, he explained, so he never published a drop of ink in it. *Ramona*, a youth magazine, sent Gómez to Mendoza to get to the bottom of a "Silo thing" that was gaining more and more attention in Santiago in 1971, in the midst of the already widely shared concern over hippismo in the wake of Piedra Roja. While Gómez followed Silo around Mendoza as the thinker sold brake fluid, the two discussed politics, philosophy, and most everything else, leading Gómez to conclude that Rodríguez was easy to interview, open, and cordial. While walking around town, Silo even asked Gómez to be a witness at his upcoming wedding to Ana Luisa Cremaschi, a performer in the Chilean National Ballet. The journalist agreed, later describing the ceremony as "very bourgeois."[13] What resulted from Gómez's visit, overall, was a *Ramona* piece that gave Silo space in which to talk about his movement's ideas and refute claims that had been surfacing. This put Gómez at odds with his peers at *Puro Chile*, which was highly critical of Silo and Poder Joven, accusing the countercultural youths of being agents for the Right.[14]

In 1970, a tumultuous year in Chile to say the least, Siloists were meeting in groups to meditate and challenge what they considered mental barriers and explore openings, always engaging with the latest thoughts in Poder Joven's publications and those coming from Mendoza. Silo would arrive in Santiago from time to time. Meanwhile, Silo-related graffiti was showing up on walls around the capital, young people were talking with or about members of the movement, and books like *Manual del Poder Joven*, among the first published works of Chilean Siloism, were in the making. Siloist graffiti—"Long Live Poder Joven!" "Read the Manual of Poder Joven!" "Total Revolution!"—were becoming conspicuous along Providencia Avenue and elsewhere, and Poder Joven members often stood out in crowds, especially the movement's young men, who preferred the austerity and measure of seriousness that black clothes and short hair projected. Hippismo's explosion onto the scene toward the end of 1970 deepened public scrutiny and opinion regarding youth groups outside the mainstream, which, in Chile, was a wide swath of thought and practice, ranging from the revolutionary Left to the reactionary Right. Not until 1971 did Poder Joven begin publishing books based on its formulations of Siloist thought, rooted ultimately in "The Healing of Suffering."

The ideas that Silo expressed at Punta de Vacas, and that Siloists subsequently built upon, expose a complex synthesis influenced appreciably by Buddhist principles, libertarian–anarchist ideas, including those of Pierre-Joseph Proudhon, as well as the thought of Herbert Marcuse, Wilhelm Reich, Erich Fromm, and G. I. Gurdjieff, among others. Silo's formulations, such as his views on the validity of political parties, continued to evolve until his 2010 death at age seventy-two, but they remained wedded to the principles of the Punta de Vacas address and the movement's early publications. Siloism's later manifestations are not of prime interest here, given our periodization. Examining what Siloism was between 1970 and 1973—during the Allende years leading up to the coup—provides insight into the movement's countercultural impulse and its complicated relationships with hippismo and the MIR (Movement of the Revolutionary Left), in addition to imparting some clues as to why the public and the state acted aggressively to censure Poder Joven.

For the Siloists, Chile during the Allende years was a more permissive place than Silo's home country, which was emerging from the Onganía dictatorship only to fall further into civil strife, with two more military dictators leading the country before the Peronists regained power in 1973. However, what began as an "opening" for Poder Joven, as Silo saw it, shrank as polarization took hold in Chilean politics and society. "Here [in Chile] there was much more liberty, even for our things, to move about—with limits, because [political groups and leaders] would deform what we would say. So here, [Poder Joven's members] organized. That's a big difference [compared to Argentina]."[15] Moreover, Chilean culture was still shot through with a conservative streak, including normative views on sexuality and the family that were deep, powerful, and shared across the political spectrum. Thus, regardless of Chile's pluralistic tradition and the revolutionary political environment of the early 1970s, Silo's followers soon found out just how much their understandings of such things as liberation, revolution, and socialism troubled Allende partisans and others. Indeed, that Poder Joven preached liberation in the broadest sense, as well as generational struggle, in effect challenged UP's road to socialism. Siloists opposed the government's materialist project for the nation and, although they were self-proclaimed socialists, denied the relevance of Marxism's most basic component: class struggle. The Siloist movement also rejected party politics, labor unionism, and any other structures of the ruling generation, including matters most sacred to the Right: religion and capitalism.

Guided by Silo's teachings set forth at Punta de Vacas and in early Siloist literature but not commanded or micromanaged by the charismatic Mendoza native, Poder Joven's members used Silo's general philosophical system to interpret Chile's social, cultural, economic, and political present, thereby applying Siloist thought to interpret a particular national context. What developed in Chile, then, was an idiosyncratic Siloist literature that differed in practical ways, by virtue of space, time, and circumstance, from other variants of Siloism that arose in and outside Latin America during the 1970s and 1980s. Thus, Poder Joven's works centered not only on Silo's teachings but also on the individuals, groups, ideas, and things around which a Chilean national debate swirled.

During the first year of Allende's government, a small circle of Chilean Siloists developed what they called the "school of internal liberation" based on a series of books written between 1971 and 1973 by one "H. Van Doren," a figure who appeared out of thin air. Van Doren never put pencil to paper. Van Doren never appeared in public (or in private, for that matter). In fact, Van Doren never existed. The UP-era press often identified Bruno Von Ehrenberg, a leading voice of Poder Joven and an enigmatic fellow, as the "real" H. Van Doren, which only added to the mysteriousness of early Siloism, at least in the eyes of many. However, it was Silo, with some assistance from a handful of followers in Santiago (Von Ehrenberg among them), who wrote under the pseudonym and produced Poder Joven's foundational works, including *Manual del Poder Joven, Silo y la liberación* (Silo and Liberation) and *Exordio del Poder Joven* (The Beginning of Poder Joven) each first published in 1971, and *Meditación Trascendental* (Transcendental Meditation), published in 1973, all by a new and Siloist-funded publisher in Santiago aptly named Transmutation.[16] These publications described Siloist thought to friend and foe, grounding ideas in the Chilean context while also identifying global trends and broader human conditions. Their genealogy begins with "The Healing of Suffering," which was the Siloists' functional equivalent to the *Communist Manifesto*, from which much of Marxism sprang.

Manual del Poder Joven probably was the most read of Transmutation's releases.[17] The book is its title: a manual or guidebook, and, more specifically, it is a primer for what Poder Joven and H. Van Doren called "total revolution"—a vague, attractive, and lofty concept, to say the least, that rested on commitments to humanistic concerns and nonviolence.[18] The premise is as straightforward as it is titanic: the destruction of all forms of coercion, including imperialism, private property, and bourgeois (that is, "philistine") morality. It would not come to pass via the rifle but rather through realizing Silo's message of psychological liberation, which ultimately hinged on the spiritual energy and revolutionary potential of young people. The book begins with a thinly veiled condemnation of the Left's traditional party apparatuses (UP, essentially) for choosing to reform but preserve bourgeois society rather than to undertake a bona fide (total) revolution. This, however, was not an endorsement of more radical leftists who embraced the idea of armed insurrection. The problem, Van Doren explains, is that any sort of modern "revolutionary" impulse, reformist or radical, led by a vanguard or a party or a class, is inherently coercive and entails layers of physical and psychological violence. In countries where armed leftists carried out revolutions, the resulting regimes were led by "closed elites without deep roots in the masses," Van Doren maintains, obviously jabbing at Guevarist and Marxist-Leninist models of revolution and revolutionaries. Here, Van Doren suggests that fronts such as the 26th of July Movement in Cuba and the MIR were driven by, and necessarily led to, the manifest elitism (vanguardism) of an "enlightened" minority, despite their discourses of popular liberation. Such groups held both Lenin's view that a new consciousness must be *brought to* the working class and the Guevarist commitment to armed struggle (guerrilla warfare). Yet, Van Doren finds connectivity between Siloism and the concept of the "new man," developed by Guevara in *Socialism and Man in Cuba* (1965).[19] Siloists essentially spoke of a "new man," applicable to both genders, as the coherent and liberated psychology of the individual living in a coherent society liberated of authority. (We shall return to this point). In the end, any revolutionary change that does not prioritize the transformation of the self, or so Van Doren indicates, is cosmetic, materialistic, and coercive, whereas Poder Joven offers a more holistic revolutionary model that integrates the psychological and material worlds and captures the "creative capacity of youth."[20] Youthful individuals whose minds are free, the book implies, are Siloism's revolutionary subject—not a class or party.

At the very heart of Siloism and "The Healing of Suffering" is the imperative of transforming the self, leading to meaningful and just worldly outcomes, Van Doren argues. This philosophy, *Manual del Poder Joven* contends, tackles the "formulations of the past generations" and the "entire view of the world that has existed until now," adding, again, that social change piloted by Marxist revolutionary movements had only re-created "the same mental structures of the old world."[21] Transforming the self meant journeying into, and coming to terms with, one's own consciousness and psychological formation, ultimately focusing on the question of desire, which, as the Punta de Vacas pronouncement explained, fed "a violence within the mind" and thus caused and propelled suffering in the individual and in the world. The epiphenomena of desire included violence in all forms, from one's self-destructiveness to the most banal expressions of coercion (hierarchy, parental authority, cultural conventions, and the like) to war. Only through the development of a new consciousness by individuals could outward change—social, cultural, political, and economic—unfold. In other words, a new reality would arise from a peaceful yet revolutionary and generational upwelling of a new consciousness propelled by individual young people—energetic, alienated, and searching for Lezaeta's "something else"—who shed the compulsion of desire, the fundamental theme at Punta de Vacas. This would be accomplished through a "hermeneutics of the self" and self-actualization.[22] As Silo noted in 2005, "We wanted, above all, a society that was autogestionary [based on self-direction]."[23]

Central to *Manual del Poder Joven*'s description of self-transformation's social potential is the concept of *socialismo libertario* (libertarian socialism), a term with anarchist roots. When applied, libertarian socialism would cultivate a socialist society where "production is the material correlation of solidarity" and is "not authoritarian, not bureaucratic, not partisan." This form of socialism, heavily influenced by Proudhonian anarchism and French utopianism of the nineteenth century, differs from existing socialisms in that it promotes solidarity without coercion of any kind. Van Doren explains, "To desire freedom is not to desire a socialist world in which the authoritarianism of the previous era is replaced by another."[24] Through this, Van Doren conveys Poder Joven's expansive concept of authoritarianism, which goes beyond political systems or states to include generational and parental authority. The new generation understands this authoritarianism and also recognizes the possibility of ending it. As Van Doren puts it, the emergent generation lives a historical moment in which forging momentous change is realistic, yet it confronts nihilism and disenchantment fostered by the those of the previous generations—the "individualists, the conformists, and the rest of the cynics [who] deny all possible value in life and justify everything from opportunism to treason" and "negate the historical moment" in which young people "desire changes in social structures and changes in their own mental structures."[25] (Our "youth question" once again comes into view.) In short, previous generations created all the repressive structures and constructs inside and outside the contemporary human being; those mechanisms govern (control) an individual's psychology and the society in which he or she operates, all fixed to and reproducing the "violence" described by Silo at Punta de Vacas.

Youth empowerment and intergenerational conflict—the "generational dialectic," echoing José Ortega y Gasset and Karl Mannheim's generationalism of the 1920s—were common transnational themes and discourses during the period under consideration here. Counterculture was part of the mix. Siloism fundamentally was countercultural, rather than subcultural, because, among other things, it questioned all convention and was grounded in the individual agency of the heterodox young person. Much of the countercultural gesture projected collectivity—as seen in the Macondo or Manchufela communities discussed earlier in this book—but such arrangements rested on the sovereignty of individuals "doing their own thing" as they flouted the pressures and expectations thrust upon them by elders and mainstream society in general. While culturally heterodox youths in Providencia, Parque Forestal, and the *barrio bohemio* shared a broader countercultural milieu with Siloists, a great deal separated Siloists from hippies (and avant-garde bohemians, as well). In my 2005 interview with Silo, he bluntly observed, "[Hippismo] didn't work at all."[26] He explained, "We accepted the hippies who would come, but later they wouldn't work out. They wouldn't work out because they were inconsistent. They would go one direction then would go another." He recalled a group of hippie artists who identified themselves as "self-actualized," which, Silo noted, "sounded very good to us." One became popular and began making good money, getting his pieces displayed in top galleries. He left the group and dropped his hippie friends. "They could never work in groups," Silo said. Hippies essentially were flighty and only focused on themselves, he argued, which might strike one as hypocritical on Silo's part, given that his movement focused on individual liberation. Yet, there were collective elements in Siloist thought, as we shall see, that placed individual agency in a broader framework and context.[27] Such individualism, lacking real transformative depth, if embraced as an end in and of itself (as hippies basically did, Silo indicated), would ultimately create narcissism and anomie—not an enlightened, convivial, and libertarian-socialist society, or so Silo and Siloist thought suggests. In other words, Manchufela would not last because untransformed individuals would ultimately succumb to desire, and thus self-interest and suffering.

Manual del Poder Joven rejects drug use and is critical of sexual promiscuity (which can be construed as a form of narcissism) within the hippie community. Van Doren asserts that hippismo does not radically reject bourgeois society but rather helps debilitate true forms of opposition; the social and cultural ills that are marijuana use and free love, for example, create false consciousness—thus a bogus "liberation"—that is a tragic substitute for a genuine transformation of the self and the inherent social promise of such a transformation. Hippies essentially fail to sincerely and deeply engage in a hermeneutics of the self, that is, a deeply inward interpretation of the self, although hippies may have thought they were doing just that. Siloist focus on the self also smacks of narcissism, but Siloists identified the inward turn as an imperative for outward social transformation—for the good of everyone, all the time. In other words, turning inward was not the problem; it was a social and human imperative. The problem centered on method, consciousness, and purpose. Without inward transformations that blunted desire and suffering, a new consciousness could not arise, and therefore a new society could not arise. This is a particularly important point because it separates the "awakened" and the "sleeping." The hippie subject is asleep and dreaming, living something not real. Marijuana, then, did not promote the creation of a new, lasting, and authentic consciousness, only a passing and false one, Siloists argued. It clouded and confused the mind. Sexual liberation, meanwhile, was a complicated matter, and the way many hippies viewed it differed significantly from how the Siloists understood it. *Manual del Poder Joven* considers sexual freedom that is not geared toward fundamental psychological change as a practice that merely funnels the energy of a repressed psychology toward one act: a physical moment that alters the mind by easing only sexual repression, temporarily and falsely. As Van Doren points out, the liberated exploration of sexuality, if not appreciated as *one* part of total liberation, becomes empty and, by extension, is the source of "all the pornography" associated with it.[28] Siloist Pía Figueroa Edwards, who joined the movement at age sixteen in 1969, observed, "What we did and we continue doing is to take great care of sexuality. We saw it and we continue to see it as a source of much energy, of a tremendous potentiality, and if it's oriented well you can develop, with great clarity, not just your creativity but also your feelings and a good life. Therefore, we, without having any conservatism in us, always try to have a suitable situation to have good sexual elaboration, and that situation is that of a couple, a couple that could dissolve if it didn't work out. But while in it, you develop its functionality, a care for sex, and you go on trying to explore your sexuality in a way to develop yourself as much as possible."[29] At the same time, this posture did not signal Poder Joven's rejection of sexual freedom, which *Manual del Poder Joven* and other Siloist literature endorses for men and women equally.

As noted above, Siloists likened false consciousness to sleep and dreaming. The notion of sleep, which is an undercurrent in *Manual del Poder Joven*, frames *Silo y la liberación*, a collection of Silo's statements from late 1969 and 1970 (with added commentary from Van Doren) that further elucidates Siloism's school of internal liberation. Silo often harnessed the power of the parable when explaining his philosophical points, which did not help him escape the "messiah" label. A parable Silo first shared in Valparaíso in 1969 underscored Poder Joven's concerns about "sleep" and its perniciousness:

> There once was a powerful man who owned a large number of sheep. In order to prevent their escape, he erected a fence. Yet, some sheep broke through the prison walls and managed to escape. To keep that from happening, the powerful man brought in dogs to keep watch night and day.
>
> Despite this, some sheep were able to flee, and others were killed by their guardians, who ruined the sheep's meat and fleece with ferocious teeth. Enthused by this, the guardians returned to the pen and continued the slaughter.
>
> The powerful man saw that fencing was too fragile and dogs were dangerous guardians.
>
> He then called for a magician, who put all of the sheep to sleep, making them dream they were free. When they awoke, they continued to believe they were free, remained there voluntarily, and no longer left their place.
>
> As a result, the powerful man took down the fence and removed the dogs, and he took whatever sheep he needed for food and hides.[30]

Silo then explains, "The sheep is the spirit of the human being. The powerful man wants control. The fence, the dogs, the magician assist the oppressor. To fence in a spirit is to separate it from the world. To surround it by overseers is to keep it docile by force or by violence, driving fear into it. Finally, putting it to sleep is to degrade the spirit through persuasion and beautiful falsehoods."[31] In short, the sheep parable is to be applied to existing power relations in any society that negate liberation and the lived life, that is, a self-actualized and "awakened" life. Critical here, moreover, is that *Silo y la liberación* and Poder Joven's conceptions of sleep and awakening expose a problem in Siloist thought: if a person (like Silo) awakens spontaneously and then helps wake others from their sleep, then the revolutionary subject seems to be the exceptional person who wakes up the others. Is, then, Poder Joven's revolutionary subject the young individual who realizes the lived life, or is it the special individual who awakens spontaneously and shows others the way to complete consciousness? What does this connote regarding hierarchy? *Silo y la liberación* couples the sheep parable with Van Doren's explanation of the obvious conundrum: some people—like Silo—wake from their sleepwalking and realize they were sleeping without being taught how to wake. Such an individual (or select group) essentially constitutes a revolutionary vanguard, although "Van Doren" would scoff at the notion. This hints at a hierarchical tendency in early Siloist thought by suggesting Silo is *the* revolutionary subject—a one-man vanguard, in a manner of speaking. Far from admitting that Siloism displayed any hint of hierarchy, which would conflict with the bulk of the movement's critical statements on structures of power and control, Van Doren simply observes, "Some men possess an understanding of superior states [of being]," although such spontaneous enlightenment is, admittedly, "hard to explain."[32] Reverence for Silo was potent.

Without doubt, Chile's governing Marxists would have interpreted Silo's sheep parable in *Silo y la liberación* as a slur against their road to socialism—and correctly so, especially in light of Siloism's critique of UP and all Marxists in *Manual del Poder Joven*. Indeed, there is much in Siloist thought that UP partisans found to be antirevolutionary, antisocial, immoral, and simply a form of subversive psychobabble. Likewise, if one accepts the lesson of Silo's sheep parable, adopts Poder Joven's concepts of liberation, total revolution, and libertarian socialism, and endorses Siloism's discourse of generational struggle, UP becomes a coercive deception. It becomes a ruling elite (of an authoritarian generation) characterized by hierarchical structures (parties, unions, and so forth), a materialist philosophy, and incomplete, if not insidious, conceptions of liberation, revolution, and socialism. This line of reasoning, moreover, concludes that Chile's road to socialism was not predicated on the liberation of the self but rather was dependent on false consciousness; Allende was, in essence, yet another magician whose power relied on the collective sleep of others, especially that of the younger generation, by convincing people they were being liberated by a genuine revolution. By not engaging in the transformation of the self, empowered Marxists could not achieve their personal healing of suffering and therefore would fail to eradicate desire, according to Siloist logic. The net result would be the impossibility of ending economic violence (the goal of Poder

Joven's *socialismo libertario*) or any other form of violence described by Silo at Punta de Vacas.

Another of Van Doren's books, *Exordio del Poder Joven*, which appeared at the end of 1971, defiantly recaptures much of what is developed in "The Healing of Suffering," *Manual del Poder Joven*, and *Silo y la liberación*. It begins with a bold declaration: "Behold the hurricane of young rebellion that began to form at the beginning of history." That storm is strengthening at a particular moment in time, the book explains, which establishes not only the timeliness of Poder Joven but also its historicity: "Poder Joven is recognized as an expression of the historical moment in which generational struggle takes up radical positions about which opponents are becoming aware. Poder Joven proclaims the great universal principle of the old being surpassed by the young and in theory and practice declares expired all tendencies that divert from the true issue, the issue of total revolution in the hands of its authentic executors, young people. Total revolution by the new generations for their redemption and that of all humankind."[33] That is powerful and attractive language, to be sure, especially in relation to the youth question and unrest in Chile and around the world. It also brings the matter of the Siloist revolutionary subject to the fore: Is the Siloist revolutionary subject a generation? Is it Poder Joven? Perhaps it is Silo? Is it all or a combination of these?

More explicit is Poder Joven's declaration of its "nine points," which, as *Exordio del Poder Joven* describes, constitute neither principles nor a plan for a future society. Instead, they express an "idea-force" to "mobilize revolutionary action" against what the group called the "calloused and reactionary generation." The movement identifies objectives of its struggle as: the elimination of private property and realization of collective property (a pillar of *socialismo libertario*); the end of all "apparatuses of power" in the hands of a social minority (the bourgeois elite) to actualize "direct power in the hands of the people"; the eradication of physical, economic, racial, and religious violence; the creation of a "collective" educational system that children enter quite early; the cultural and technical "elevation" of the people; free and spontaneous access for young people to all fields of work and knowledge; the "collective governance" of education; the escape from all taboos and mental fetishes; and the destruction of the "false psychological expectations" that promote consumer society. These may be realized via a revolution "simultaneously manifested in the social, the cultural, and the psychic."[34] These points are heavily weighted toward external, or worldly, outcomes rather than internal liberation. However, the former remains wedded to the latter but are pursued simultaneously. This departs from what Silo suggests in "The Healing of Suffering," which, in the Buddhist tradition, focuses on the transformation of the self as a predicate for worldly change.

Exordio del Poder Joven also is pertinent for its condemnation of socialism practiced in Chile and elsewhere, anchoring such criticism in a broader discussion of "vertical societies." As Van Doren notes, guilds and syndicates (apparently without hierarchies, or so the author assumes) controlled by a central authority—a state or an umbrella union—were victims of hierarchy, which is entrenched and "does not produce change." This again exposes the movement's anarchist elements. Poder Joven then defends its call for a horizontal society based on "real [social] links with multiple connections" that are not subject to "uniformity" but rather create "real power" and form "a synthesis that we recognize as a Movement."[35] This bottom-up organizational model for social change, which meshed with Siloism's inside-to-outside, individual-to-social approach to transformation, effectively questioned not only the vanguardism of Marxist-Leninism but also the party and union structures of UP and the hierarchies of all institutions, models, and systems of the older generation.

In concert with "The Healing of Suffering," the three Poder Joven publications examined thus far—*Manual del Poder Joven*, *Silo y la liberación*, and *Exordio del Poder Joven* capture early Siloism's general philosophical framework and ground that architecture largely in the context of UP's road to socialism. Yet, not readily apparent in those works is how an individual might work "internally," through the school of internal liberation, toward a new enlightenment, and thus contribute to totally revolutionizing the world around her or him. For this, Siloism offered methods and barometers, some written down and others not, and members guided each other in one-on-one situations or in small groups. The transformation of everything ultimately rested on the transmuted individual, and certain readings and experienced members guided what Siloists refer to simply as "personal work" (*trabajos personales*).

That personal work of early Siloism is something that critics and other observers did not understand, simply did not want to understand, or understood but rejected, Silo claimed. When reflecting on UP activists, he explained in 2005, "There was no way, from the standpoint of the UP, to respond to our point of view. There was no way. . . . I remember attending a conference [in Santiago] in an important theater of the era, with the whole world filling the theater, and they prohibited us from giving talks. And who prohibited us from giving talks? The UP. Incredible." He added, while scoffing at UP's discourse of pluralism, "I don't think it was that [Poder Joven] wasn't understood. I think they weren't even interested in understanding the phenomenon. It was outside [UP's] realm."[36] The event to which Silo referred was a series of presentations he planned in Santiago in October 1972. He had already given the same four talks in Buenos Aires in August, and Chilean Siloists were anxious to hear the Mendoza native engage the series' subject: Transcendental Meditation. The lectures delivered in Buenos Aires appeared as the book *Meditación Trascendental* in 1973, with a prologue by H. Van Doren that provides some background:

> The four lectures on transcendental meditation were given by Silo in Buenos Aires on August 16, 17, 18, and 19 in 1972. In Santiago, Chile, only the first two were given on October 12 and 13 in that same year. The other two were suspended following the inconvenient happening to recount. The meetings: they were held in the 'La Reforma' room, part of the University of Chile, at the time controlled by the Communist Party. After the second conference, a member of the Central Committee demanded a list of six hundred people 'who would be made responsible' if depredations occur. Soon there were enough signatories, given that the locale had been rented by a group that had met all requirements satisfactorily and, in the end, the room had been used without any problems so far. This case is no different than another, back in 1969, when in Punta de Vacas armed gendarmerie demanded documentation of all those attending the historic speech. At that time, the measure was prompted by the fascist Right that was in power. Now, by a reformist bureaucracy. Impartially considered, the two cases can be reduced to the same authoritarian and stupid attitude.[37]

Someone obviously did not like the topics broached on the first two days, and, broadly speaking, much had happened involving Siloists in Santiago by 1972, as we shall see. The complete series of lectures focused on the meditative components of the school of internal liberation, establishing the basic goals and skeleton for one's turn inward. The guidelines are complicated and perhaps esoteric.

Silo's four presentations captured in *Meditación Trascendental* covered interrelated themes. The first placed meditation in historical context, with attention paid to propensities toward superstition and day-to-day "internal and external" fetishization. The second distinguished between "simple or everyday meditation" and Transcendental Meditation, the latter serving to overcome "the perceptions, images, representations, and tendencies of the structure of consciousness," unlike the former, which remains confined to them. It included the first six steps of the twelve-step process in the transformation of the self and understanding the relationship between one's consciousness and the world, including "learning to see" (discovering one's structure of consciousness) and "seeing consciousness in the senses," that is, comprehending that perceptions are organized through the structure of consciousness. This second conference also rested on complicated psychological notions, including *"ensueños"* (daydreams or reveries)—a term to describe the mind's transient imaginings in response to external stimuli (say, a smell) and internal stimuli (a hunger pang, for instance). The mind compensates by picturing, as if in a dream state, the smell's origin and the sandwich that would satisfy the grumbling stomach. These "daydreams" derail mental focus precisely because they are ephemeral, only to be succeeded by different stimuli in a continual bombardment of the psyche. The third talk, pertaining to the second six steps, included discussion of the power exerted by external structures on consciousness and the consciousness-world relationship. The fourth summed up and synthesized the first three, emphasizing the notion that a "transcendental reality" is both the product of the mind and of things in the world.[38]

The process of self-discovery and transformation relied on the help of others, usually gathered into small groups. Silo explained, "We would do it [Siloist meditative practice] in a type of sequence of meditative steps in which we would include what we would come to call 'guided experiences.' Guided experiences were a species of story that, while being told, people meditate over it, and they discover their own difficulties they have in the face of the story being posed. And so in the face of a story, people go on meditating and they describe the resistances they have, the clashes that they have [with the story]. That is one method." A story, for instance, would provoke imagery (*ensueños*, essentially) that Siloists would confront and work through, in a meditative state and with help, by applying the multistep process of coming to terms with their own consciousness and its relationship with the world. Everyone involved would then discuss the experience, sharing their thoughts and discoveries. This process, at its heart, was about self-understanding, but as that self-understanding was pursued in groups, some observers came to see the practice as a sort of cultish reprogramming. The ultimate goal of such a process is to mitigate desire, which forms the basis of suffering. In the end, however, ending desire is unlikely, Silo re-flected, with a caveat. "I believe that we can advance but we can't throw [desire] all away. It's not that someone can simply eliminate desire but if someone can overcome desire," he observed. "That is one of our key points: one can be better."[39]

"Being better" meant becoming more attuned to oneself and to the sur-rounding world, which required that minds and bodies be tested and taxed. Thus, the Siloists would go on retreats into the countryside and high up into the Andes, where they would live and meditate under challenging con-ditions. Couples were separated so as not to distract from personal work—all were there to be individuals, not defined in reference to anyone or any thing. Physical activities, such as digging holes and moving rocks, were meant to help an individual focus his or her mind under difficult circum-stances, including exhaustion.[40] The resulting inner clarity and fortitude could then act in and upon society (and against the older generation in charge) via a generational dialectic, just as society acted upon the individ-ual. This was an attractive message in the late 1960s and 1970s, when spiri-tual awakening in the West coalesced in the form of numerous esoteric movements, such as New Age, and when many young people were search-ing for something else as the youth question became readily apparent.

Wanting to realize *socialismo libertario*, "be better," and attain total rev-olution internally and externally, those who formed the core membership of Poder Joven came from the middle and upper classes of Santiago and, to a much lesser extent, from other cities. They reflected the alienation and disenchantment that gripped many young people in those classes, and some, like Lezaeta, had dabbled in hippismo before joining the Siloist cause. Others gravitated to Poder Joven from political movements. Young people came and went, and a key requisite for participation, former Poder Joven mem-bers recalled, was the will to act upon one's own psychology and thus pro-duce worldly outcomes. "I always believed that life is about doing something big with it," Figueroa remarked, noting that Poder Joven would only rebuff youths who were violent, in whatever form, and were not seriously pursuing the Siloist path for the healing of suffering. "No violence meant no violence toward oneself or violence toward another," she said. This was key, Figueroa continued, and, in the spirit of Mohandas Gandhi and Martin Luther King Jr., reflected a transnational impulse toward peaceful yet revolutionary change. She explained, "If a system is violent in its conception, in its spiri-tualism, in parent-child relations, in its gender relations, it is completely violent. For us, to question violence and to aspire to a way of life without violence, we have to look at the roots of violence in all its forms."[41] Julián Burgos, also a Poder Joven member, noted, "For us, we gave the [peace symbol] meaning. For us, it was fundamental to think, feel, and act in the same direction" and without prejudice toward marginalized people.[42] Hippies, homosexuals, all were welcome, and women and men enjoyed equality within the movement, Siloists declared. "I believe that the movement always had total liberty in those aspects," Silo asserted in our 2005 interview.[43] This sentiment echoed Silo's invitation in a 1971 interview; while explaining that he was neither gay nor a hippie nor a drug addict nor a Marxist nor a Catholic, Silo said, "Let them come! Let them come to us! We accept the whole world, everyone."[44]

Sexuality and sexual liberation were subjects on which Poder Joven did not dwell, but they nevertheless were components of total revolution. Silo and Von Ehrenberg, the most conspicuous figures in the movement, were in their thirties in 1970, but many young participants were coming of age, physically speaking, when they joined. For them, sexuality was on their radars, and members like Figueroa found great value in the movement's approach. "You have to remember that in those years we, people who were Siloists, had just emerged out of our childhoods. In '68 I was fifteen, and I was a virgin when I started to get interested in Siloism, and there [at fifteen] begins our ideological development. I began to participate in [the Siloist circle] and I started to participate in a movement, and I had never participated in a movement. And certainly my body also started to develop. And there came the moment in which I had my first sexual relations," she described. "Basically, we have treated sex with love. We have not used sex loosely. . . . We have been very libertarian but very careful." Figueroa added that although they did not accept "free love" as it was being pursued and practiced during the era, by no means did Poder Joven accept what she called the "conservative" viewpoints of the Right and Left regarding birth control pills, abortion, and divorce, for instance.[45] Yet, there were a good number of Siloists (and even Silo himself) who saw in Allende's election, in particular, an opportunity for change, though not along the lines being sought by UP. Although Siloists soon realized that their heterodox ways of thinking and being would not be met with tolerance, much less acceptance, they remained steadfast. "We did have a lucid vision, that everything else was a lie, and that everything else didn't have any moral weight," Poder Joven member María Eliana Astaburuaga affirmed.[46]

Synthesis and Sensibility

Poder Joven's "lucid vision," framed by Silo, did not simply appear out of the ether. At its core was a creative synthesis born of a dialogue involving Eastern and Western thought that was mediated by and through a particular individual and his group of followers in a certain historical context. What developed was a doctrine (not dogma, Siloists maintained), the very existence of which distinguished it from hippismo, which, while exhibiting certain patterns of thought and behavior, lacked that Siloism's level of coherence. Our discussion of Silo's synthesis will largely focus on Buddhism, anarchism, and Marxism, although Siloist thought reveals many more angles to pursue. Whether directly present in Siloist formulations or wafting in the air that Silo and Siloists were breathing when thinking and writing, such influences speak to Siloism's complexity. Eastern thought, especially Buddhism but also Taoism and Sufism, was gaining ground in the West after World War II and came to influence the Beat Generation in the United States, among other movements. However, Buddhist thought was not at all widely known or understood in Chile in the late 1960s and early 1970s. Needless to say, it clashed with mainstream understandings of spiritualism and psychology in a strongly Catholic society.

Buddhist underpinnings are evident in "The Healing of Suffering," as previously noted, and Silo himself, at the very beginning of the oration, established the same principal premise that Buddha did: he was no savior. Instead, Siloists saw Silo—and Silo saw himself—as a pedagogical presence in Poder Joven's development, and we see this role clearly in the group's publications during the Allende years. The Siloist focus on the self as the site, process, and outcome of awakening does not rely on the intervention of a supreme being—some sort of miracle or otherworldly gesture, let us say— but rather on the transfer of psychological tools (not outcomes) from Silo to his followers. The self is in control, or is trying to gain control, of consciousness. Buddha explained, "By oneself, indeed, is evil done; by oneself is one defiled; by oneself is evil left undone; by oneself, indeed, is one purified. Purity and impurity depend on oneself—no one purifies another."[47] Such internal change has outward results, Buddhists held, thus linking the transformative self to social change. As Buddhist scholar Walpola Rahula puts it, "Buddhism arose in India as a spiritual force against social injustices, against degrading superstitious rites, ceremonies and sacrifices; it denounced the tyranny of the caste system and advocated the equality of all men; it emancipated woman and gave her complete spiritual freedom."[48] The notion of liberating the self by ending one's personal suffering dovetailed with anarchism's general aim, on a social scale, to do the same thing. Thus, anarchism provided Siloists with a social goal to layer upon a personal one.

Influenced by such thinkers as Proudhon, the Russian anarchist Mikhail Bakunin, and the Italian immigrant to Argentina Errico Malatesta, Argentine and Chilean anarchism, in turn, informed Siloism appreciably. Facilitated by immigration from Italy and Spain, a strong anarchist tradition emerged in Argentina toward the end of the nineteenth century, and libertarian ideas spread to Chile by way of printed sources and Chileans' contact with Argentine workers and intellectuals.[49] Anarchism found significant support within the Chilean labor movement between the turn of the century and the time of the Bolshevik Revolution, after which Marxism grew to overshadow it in working-class circles.[50] Upon tiring of strict hierarchy within the Left, a few former MIR members and some radical Socialists joined with a handful of anarchosyndicalists to form the Libertarian Federation (Federación Libertaria) in 1972. It was small and ineffectual, but it lashed out at the Allende government as "Marxist-Leninist," thus the purveyor of "a false socialism," and that opposition reflected the anarchist-Marxist divide over hierarchy, the mechanisms for revolutionary change, and the problem of totalitarianism.[51] (Meanwhile, the Marxist-Leninist MIR attacked Allende for being a Stalinist reformist.) What is more, there existed a sizable circle of anarchists associated with Juan Rivano, a professor of philosophy at the University of Chile. Rivano had fled the MIR for its tendency to be heavy on political action and light on theory, while eighty to ninety young people who subsequently were part of the "Rivano Group," which published the journal *En el límite* (At the Limit), ended up in the MIR.[52] There is no evidence of any direct Siloist-Federation or Siloist-Rivano ties, but it is clear that anarchist thought was contributing to the radicalization of young people during the late sixties and early seventies.

Generally speaking, anarchism—in rejecting politics, capitalism, and hierarchies of all kinds, and in taking a thoroughly egalitarian stance with regard to gender equity, women's sexual oppression, and women's mobilization for revolutionary goals—deeply influenced the Siloists' particular form of revolution.[53] Silo found the works of Proudhon particularly attractive, and one clearly recognizes the Frenchman's sway in Poder Joven's publications. Private property, for instance, was theft, and all government was repressive. "To be GOVERNED is to be watched, inspected, spied upon, directed, law-driven, numbered, regulated, enrolled, indoctrinated, preached at, controlled, checked, estimated, valued, censured, commanded;

all by creatures who have neither the right nor the wisdom nor the virtue to do so," Proudhon declared.[54] But Proudhon's effect went beyond the anarchist's views on property and power. Proudhon developed a nonviolent anarchist philosophy (anarchopacifism) influenced by his socialist-utopian compatriots, especially Charles Fourier, and, in turn, Proudhon influenced Bakunin, Leo Tolstoy, and others. Chilean anarchism had a history of shying away from violent confrontations, although its champions participated in rallies and other sorts of public action. This changed during the dictatorship, when anarchists took up arms against the regime.

During the UP years, anarchism had some influence on two organizations that did condone armed struggle: the MIR and the Organized Vanguard of the People (Vanguardia Organizada del Pueblo, VOP). Internal conflict among miristas pit top figures Bautista Van Schouwen and Luciano Cruz against leader Miguel Enríquez. Van Schouwen and Cruz criticized Enríquez for pursuing "verticalism," that is, a revolutionary formula that was strictly hierarchical. Anarchism was more discernable among members of the MIR subgroup, the Movement of Revolutionary Shantytown Dwellers (Movimiento de Pobladores Revolucionarios), which was much more committed to autogestion than was the MIR.[55] Essentially, for Enríquez, there was no wavering from Marxist-Leninism and the Guevarist mentality. (As we shall later see, there was more than an intellectual link between Juan Bautista Van Schouwen and Siloism). Reflecting on the period, Silo explained that many miristas were not far from Siloist thought, but the question of violence clearly separated the MIR and Siloists. Less influenced by anarchism than the MIR, the VOP, which assassinated former Frei Interior Minister Edmundo Pérez Zujovic in September 1971, was absolutely committed to violence, he added.[56] What is more, given that Proudhon and Bakunin, unlike Lenin, could see a revolution happening peacefully, pacifistic thought provided as least a small point of commonality between Siloism and Allende's position on revolutionary change.

Although Poder Joven was quite critical of Marxism in general, Western Marxism—and that of the Frankfurt School in particular—had a place in the development of Siloist thought. What we might call "orthodox" Marxism—an umbrella designation under which fall the "older" Marx (of the *Communist Manifesto, Capital,* and so forth), Stalinism, and Marxist-Leninism's commitments to historical materialism, the dictatorship of the proletariat, vanguardism, and so forth—was not at all attractive to Siloists who instead focused on the "psychosocial." The Siloists could sympathize, to an extent, with the Frankfurt School's Freudian Marxism, for its interest in the psychosocial, the psychological repression of the self, and alienation. Moreover, the revival by Erich Fromm and others of the "young" Marx, a Marx concerned much more with the self and humanism, found some applicability in Siloist thought.[57]

The topic of discussion in Chile by the late 1960s, with many of the intellectual's works in Spanish translation by then, Herbert Marcuse was regularly quoted and paraphrased (without citation, usually) in Poder Joven's most notable literature, and his work appeared on reading lists supplied to prospective members.[58] After he took up residence in New York in the late 1930s, Marcuse directly grappled with Freud, psychoanalysis, and (more to the point) the interrelatedness of self and society, as he (along with fellow members of the Frankfurt School and the Institute for Social Research) pondered the psychological barriers to real social change, combining Marxist deductions with Freudian insight, in his criticism of industrial societies.[59] As we have seen, Silo's "The Healing of Suffering" addressed the self–society relationship by positing that social change would take place only in relation to a psychological transformation within the individual. Indeed, the Punta de Vacas speech suggested that new pleasures of and for the mind and body—a more authentic state of joy and love—would arise from psychological metamorphosis. This echoed, to some extent, Marcuse's 1938 defense of hedonistic philosophies and their focus on happiness, but Marcuse and Poder Joven did not limit their philosophical frameworks to a certain hyperindividualism in view of a concern with social totality and the generality of social theory.[60]

Other elements in Marcusean thought, especially views on liberation and economy, informed Poder Joven. In the Freudian *Eros and Civilization* (1955), Marcuse faults the bourgeois ideology of love, which, among other things, represses freedom and pleasure and, as a result, limits the psychological potential for freedom.[61] His *One-Dimensional Man* (1964) addresses the tremendous power of economic structures, which he sees as preventing the expression of freedom, choice, and self-determination. Liberty is illusory, Marcuse argues, for those embedded in the existing capitalist system (directed by the U.S. and Western Europe) or in the Communist reality of the USSR; in either context, existence is conditioned completely by various psychological and institutional mechanisms of standardization and restraint. (Marcuse, of course, was critical of "real existing" socialism, not the idea of creating a socialist society.) In other words, Marcuse contends that existing capitalist and communist systems and states fail humanity by negating true equality and liberation. This notion anticipated Siloism's rejection of real-existing socialism as well as bourgeois capitalist democracy.[62] Moreover, Marcuse in the 1960s looked to marginal groups (students in particular) for leadership in creating and deploying new and truly liberating revolutionary formulae that would destroy what he saw as the "oppressive totalization that was contemporary society," as one scholar described.[63] Silo and the Siloists, for all intents and purposes, developed one such innovative revolutionary formula.

The UP intelligentsia disliked Marcuse, to put mildly. His "psychosociology," one Chilean critic argued, "has influenced hippies and 'beatniks' and other youth movements." That accurate assessment did not bode well for Marcuse in Chile. Indeed, many questioned if Marcuse's interest in such matters as youthful rebellion as an agent of change (thus downplaying class conflict), sexual repression, and the self—all things important to Siloists— qualified him as Marxist at all. "If Marcuse, as he affirms, has studied Marx, he evidently does not have a deep comprehension of it," wrote Carlos Maldonado, a Communist and figure in the Chilean Institute for Marxist Studies in 1970.[64] Noted Marxist Sergio Vuskovic flatly argued, "[Marcuse] is not a Marxist."[65] These statements appeared in a volume of essays with a provocative title: *¿Lenin o Marcuse?* (1970). Readers were to make a choice, and, needless to say, the book wants them to side with the former. Maldonado also links Marcuse to the "extreme Left" (the MIR, essentially) by noting the German's criticism of the Soviet Union, a state that UP leftists like Maldonado and Vuskovic found much more palatable (if not downright laudable). The MIR instead held the Cuban Revolution in the highest of esteem, and Marcuse saw the Soviet Union as a stifling force in the global struggle against capitalism. Moreover, the book castigates Marcuse's support for youthful spontaneism. Maldonado calls out Marcuse's "pseudoscientific theories" for being an "exaltation of youth, of instincts, an apology for spontaneity as well as violence and sex, just like any 'Western' filmed in Hollywood."[66] Vuskovic adds, "The exaltation of the instinctive and the person without consciousness translates into a defense of spontaneity as a method of action." He simply sees Marcuse as antitheoretical and prone to anarchism, which UP derided as undisciplined and excessively libertine.[67]

Marcuse's *Soviet Marxism: A Critical Analysis* (1958) also was unpopular among fans of Soviet Communism in and outside Chile, in part because they were peeved that the material upon which it was based came from Marcuse's research for the U.S. Office of Strategic Services (the precursor of the CIA) during World War II. In addition, when fleeing Germany in the

1930s, Marcuse and the Frankfurt School crowd went to the United States, thus exposing some sort of ideological truth, or so more orthodox Marxists argued. Furthermore, one of Marcuse's early works was his 1932 review of Marx's *Economic and Philosophical Manuscripts of 1844*. The manuscripts had just been published for the first time, revealing a "young" Marx interested in the human experience, alienation, and "human nature and its essential powers" rather than the scientific socialism present in his later works.[68] Erich Fromm took up this theme.

Like his Frankfurt School associate, Fromm rejected the repression of both industrial capitalism and bureaucratic communism. In particular, Fromm's contemplation of the self and destructive tendencies in his *The Fear of Freedom* (1942) found resonance among Siloists deeply concerned with the question of violence and psychology.[69] As Fromm argues, "The more the drive towards life is thwarted, the stronger the drive towards destruction; the more life is realized, less is the strength of destructiveness. *Destructiveness is the outcome of unlived life.*"[70] The Punta de Vacas address, as the reader will recall, implored individuals and a generation to realize a "drive towards life," thereby depriving society of an impulse toward violence, an obvious form of destructiveness. Insightful, too, is what amounted to Fromm's psychologically informed libertarian socialism, which transcended economic relations to embrace a "humanist" spirit that broke down the barriers between individual and society and valued the human condition and human freedom. This humanism, like Marcuse's attention to human nature, focused on the earlier works of Marx, with special attention to the *Economic and Philosophical Manuscripts of 1844*, which did not appear in Spanish until the 1960s.[71] "Socialist humanism" or "Marxist humanism," as it came to be known, is much more interested in alienation and matters of the self than on the economic structures of interest to the "older" Marx and his champions. Hegelian notions of freedom and self-awareness, which also informed the development of psychoanalysis (and thus fostered the link between Freud and Frankfurt School Hegelians like Marcuse and Fromm), were present in the young Marx, much to the chagrin of the older Marx's aficionados.

In the early 1960s, Fromm's reintroduction and vigorous defense of the young Marx in *Marx's Concept of Man*, which accompanied an English translation of the *Economic and Philosophical Manuscripts of 1844*, marked an important juncture in the history of Marxism in the West. Many intellectuals who, like Marcuse and Fromm, were horrified by Stalinism and the totalitarianism of the Soviet Union, searched for new Marxist options in the

1950s and 1960s, and many of them embraced socialist humanism. To Fromm, Marxism is humanism, thereby underscoring moral, ethical, and spiritual dimensions. Fromm went so far as to group Marx's attention to the human spirit with the "Messianic hope" of the Old Testament and the spiritual leadership of Tao Tzu (the founder of Taoism) and Buddha.[72] One might see why Siloists would find this attractive. Not unexpectedly, mainstream (or Old Left*ish*) Marxists in Chile and elsewhere found the early Marx and his fans hard to swallow. A leading critic was the Frenchman Louis Althusser, a French Communist who turned his back on the Parisian student movement in 1968. A significant influence on Chilean Marxists, Althusser, known for his defense of "structural Marxism," often expressed a visceral dislike of socialist humanism. As Tony Judt argues, Althusser instead offered a "subjectless theory of everything" in which economic, political, ideological, and theoretical structures reign supreme over human volition, agency, and essence.[73] In other words, consciousness comes to you from the outside, not from within; it was imperative among structural Marxists, then, to bring theory "within reach of the masses," as sociologist and political scientist Tomás Moulian described.[74]

Chile's Marxists, and Socialists in particular, adopted a specific reading of Althusser largely attributable to the influence of the pro-UP Chilean Marta Harnecker, who studied with Althusser in France. She posited that revolutionary consciousness and agency (in a word, subjectivity) would come to the working class through teaching and academic institutions. This was, in effect, a take on Marxist-Leninism (with a "Soviet tendency") that many leftists found attractive.[75] Communists, though largely in agreement with Harnecker on major ideological questions, were not enamored by her motivation to strip Marxism of its "bureaucratic parlance in the style of the commissars," as historian Joaquín Fermandois observed.[76] During the Allende years, furthermore, Harnecker, in collaboration with Gabriela Uribe, elaborated the *Cuadernos de educación popular* (Popular Education Schoolbooks) for use in public schools for urban and rural workers. The state-owned Quimantú published more than 250,000 copies. According to Harnecker, "It principally was an educational effort to provide workers with a knowledge of Marxist-Leninism in such a clear and reasoned way that the memorization and mechanical repetition of knowledge gained would be unnecessary." She further explained, "In the thought of Louis Althusser was a flow of instruments for studying Marxism, to avoid dogmatism, to understand the deep thought of Marx and Lenin, but he wrote in a hermetic way, very difficult to read. And I wanted to divulge it."[77] This Althusser-

Harnecker-Socialism connection helps us better understand the sour reception that Marcuse received in Chile, and thus provides more clues as to why UP interests shared contempt for Siloist thought.

In Siloism, one also discerns notions expressed decades earlier by Wilhelm Reich, whose translated works also circulated among Poder Joven's members and were widely read by the bohemian-intellectual crowd.[78] Reich's writings discuss sexual instincts, sexual repression, and destructive tendencies, arguing that sexual liberation was central to the realization of a liberated self and the mitigation of outward aggression and violence.[79] He believed that most all repression was grounded in sexual repression, and Reich thus advocated psychological liberation based almost exclusively on sexual freedom and the transformative capacity of the orgasm. Marcuse's *Eros and Civilization*, it should be noted, criticizes Reich for offering a strikingly reductive interpretation of what constitutes liberation. Marcuse makes it clear that sexual liberation could not be an end in and of itself but rather should be a component of a much more amplified liberating psychology.[80] Poder Joven took Marcuse's position on the matter but accepted Reich's basic argument about the transformative potential of sexuality, as well as his general approach to the interrelatedness of the self, destructive tendencies, and liberation.

External to prevailing variants of Marxism and evident in Siloist thought were G. I. Gurdjieff's esoteric and proto-New Age teachings.[81] Crafted mostly during the 1920s and 1930s, Gurdjieff's body of work, much like that of his neophyte, P. D. Ouspensky, relates to the identification and facilitation of true consciousness, and his conceptions of authenticity and humanity influenced Silo's and Siloist views on psychology and society.[82] With special interest in astrology, phenomenology, and pre-Christian history, the Armenian-born writer contemplated a more "real" state of being that would allow humans to experience the ideal union of body and mind—physical sensation, sentiment, and reason—as well as truly comprehend their individual places in the cosmos. Gurdjieff believed that most humans sleepwalk through life, clinging to an illusion of individualism and a false consciousness created largely by forces—people, institutions, ideas, and so forth—outside the self. The act of waking, in turn, comes only through the exhaustive examination of the self and the development of a full awareness of what may be called the body-mind, or a total understanding of "I am." Simply put, what Gurdjieffians call "The Way" rests on the transformation of the self, with the result being a genuinely lived life, to borrow from Fromm.[83] The Siloists of Poder Joven imagined positive and progressive social and material outcomes from such a self-transformative process, as the Punta de Vacas speech shows. The most glaring application of Gurdjieff was in the case of Silo's sheep-and-magician parable reproduced in *Silo y la liberación*. The parable addresses false consciousness and awakening precisely along Gurdjieffian lines. Moreover, the Gurdjieffian "body-mind"—a denial of the Platonic, Aristotelian, and Cartesian dualistic separation of the mind and body—is discernable throughout most all of Siloism's early works.

Gurdjieff also was an inspiration in the development of another esoteric movement with a Chilean connection: the Arica School. Established by the Bolivian Oscar Ichazo, the school took its name from the northern Chilean city where Ichazo taught his first cadre, a group of more than fifty Americans, in 1970.[84] The Arica School, like Siloism, was about consciousness, but Arica's route to attaining a higher and clarified state of being differentiated it from Silo's teachings. Ichazo encouraged the use of drugs, for instance, to aid in the process of enlightenment. Like Siloism, the Ichazo School strove for the creation of a new and unified global society. Ichazo never became as well-known (and thus reviled) in Chile as Silo, but his teachings drew many Chileans, including Los Blops. "And all of the members of Los Blops—all of us—were members of the Ichazo group. And it's very important if you listen to the lyrics. It soaked into us, evidently; it cut through our daily lives—our everyday lives. We lived, in reality, as a function of Arica and music," recalled bassist Juan Pablo Orrego.[85] Los Blops became familiar with Ichazo's teachings as early as 1968, when the Bolivian lectured at the Institute of Applied Psychology, a private institution in Santiago. The Arica School left Chile, on Ichazo's own volition, for New York City in 1971, thus perhaps saving it from what befell Poder Joven.

One concept that transects the ideas of Buddha, Marcuse, Fromm, Reich, and Gurdjieff—and that became Poder Joven's ideological keystone—is the realization of the "lived life," which proved a very attractive concept to Siloists in light of its totality, revolutionary potential, subjectivity, and vagueness (and thus applicability). While there were Marxists in Chile who acknowledged the individual in revolutionary processes, they mostly subsumed that individual within a larger revolutionary vanguard and/or structuralist framework. From that perspective, the transformation of the self, in essence, was to take place from the outside in, enacted and conditioned by forces that cloud the mind and produce false consciousness, Siloists held. The "lived life," moreover, informed the hermeneutics and transformation of the self as well as the Siloist subject's relation to and interaction with all inhabitants, environments, and material conditions of the outside world. In Allende's Chile, this was all dangerous stuff with alarming ramifications, evidently.

Policing "Silo"

Policing takes multiple forms. It may entail a wide variety of acts of observation, manipulation, control, and repression mustered by and through state and nonstate actors.[86] In terms of the policing powers of the state, which became quite conspicuous to hippies and Siloists alike, the Allende years were complicated from an institutional standpoint. While UP controlled the Ministry of the Interior, which included the Investigations Police (Policía de Investigaciones, PDI, the Chilean equivalent to the FBI), it did not command the courts, especially the Supreme Court, which proved to be a thorn in Allende's side. Courts had (and have) investigative powers and were largely in the hands of UP's opposition—a fact that hindered the road to socialism in no small way, further frustrating Allende's radical-Left critics and giving some solace to the opposition. In terms of policing counterculture, this distinction does not really mean much. That is to say, UP was fully behind the close policing of hippies and groups like Poder Joven, and thus it agreed with friends and foes as to the necessity for suppressing couterculture.

The policing of Siloism began before Poder Joven came to be. Indeed, Silo's reputation preceded him—and his address at Punta de Vacas as well. His time on the Chilean coast in early 1969, in addition to his early pronouncements in Mendoza, earned Silo and his followers a degree of attention from curious observers. Also, supporters had spread the word in Mendoza and Chile on the eve of what a Santiago newspaper sarcastically called the appearance of a "New Christ the Redeemer." More than four hundred Chileans were going to be making the trek to Punta de Vacas, according to the conservative *La Tercera*. (It was a fairly accurate guess.) Nothing in the article addresses what Silo would say at Punta de Vacas, but it certainly indicted that there was a messianic element at play.[87] The first report of what transpired on May 4 appeared in Mendoza's daily, *Los Andes*. Like the *La Tercera* piece, *Los Andes* was quick to jump on the Mendoza native's alleged messianism, calling the crowd "adherents to the church of Silo," setting that tone in the first paragraph of an extensive article. After the speech ended, the correspondent approached Silo, likely wondering if the *maestro* (teacher or master), as followers called him, would offer some words.

When asked if he intended to create a church, Silo reportedly responded, "My adherents are thinking about a church, but that doesn't appear right to me. It [his teaching] is about individual study. An organization would, in this case, have a new violence."[88] Meanwhile, the Santiago press told of two Chileans who traveled to see Silo with hopes of being cured of serious ailments—a "healing of suffering." "However, miracles didn't happen at the encounter," the writer noted.[89] Once again, a supposed messianism was at hand. What is more, *El Mercurio* joined in by noting that Siloists had mentioned the relevance of Genesis 49:10 ("The scepter will not depart from Judah, nor the ruler's staff from between his feet, until he to whom it belongs shall come and the obedience of the nations shall be his.") when identifying the "teacher," who had addressed the crowd in an "evangelical" tone.[90]

According to *La Tercera*, Silo phoned its newsroom on May 7, likely peeved by the coverage he was receiving from the Santiago press. The "teacher," as the newspaper began referring to him, agreed to meet at the newspaper's headquarters. Alas, he failed to show. "He didn't keep his promise," correspondent and poet Orlando Cabrera Leyva explained. "In these times during which everyone distrusts everyone, Silo, the philosopher, the saint, the misanthrope or whatever he is, must have had a human confrontation with reality."[91] Cabrera clearly thought Silo, ultimately, was not willing or capable to face scrutiny. Silo, however, could take solace in the statements of young people like "Sergio Miguel." The Chilean, who had been in the audience at Punta de Vacas, told *La Tercera*, "Silo is not crazy." He explained, "That guy is neither crazy nor a politician nor someone taking advantage of the masses who follow him." Silo, he said, wishes to banish, once and for all, violence in politics, economy, and culture.[92]

UP's key constituents grew concerned by, among other things, Siloism's discourse of generational struggle and its call for absolute liberation of the mind, body, and spirit, which clashed with key precepts of the nation's Marxist leadership and those of other important social interests. While Siloists held that individual liberation would feed collective liberation, most Marxists believed the opposite. More politically conservative Chileans, meanwhile, also criticized Siloism in the strongest of terms, and the subsequent military regime took Poder Joven quite seriously—likely due to the negative press about the Siloists during the Allende years. Although it never numbered more than one hundred core members and another one or two hundred fellow travelers, Poder Joven apparently seemed much larger than it really was, a fact that we can attribute to media reports, police investigations, and the assiduous propaganda efforts of Siloists themselves, whose graffiti and symbol (a triangle inside a circle, imbued with a variety of meanings by and among Siloists) were as ubiquitous as they were recognizable.[93]

Poder Joven's run-ins with the state during Chile's road to socialism were few but significant. They also were extremely well publicized, particularly in periodicals supportive of UP, as well as in conservative newspapers, including Santiago's largest daily, *El Mercurio*, published by the conservative Edwards family. After leading relatively unfettered lives during UP's first year in power, Siloists increasingly found themselves under intense public scrutiny, as sociopolitically dissimilar sectors identified reasons to persecute the movement. It is not a coincidence that policing of Siloism intensified at the very time that marijuana sweeps were occurring in places like Parque Forestal, all in the months following the Piedra Roja festival. Any space for unfettered counterculture was narrowing quickly in the public sphere. Indeed, the forcefulness of the anti-Silo barrage caught Poder Joven members by surprise, especially following the arrests of Siloists (including Von Ehrenberg) in the spring of 1971. The Siloists in question were accused of luring young women to orgies of sex and marijuana—the topics of widespread discussion in the public sphere since Piedra Roja. This episode lends significant insight into the pervasive negative interpretation of Siloism during the Allende years and serves as another point of access into some often-overlooked cultural conflicts of the era.

On September 30, in the more affluent neighborhoods of the capital, the police's Anti-Vice Brigade apprehended six Siloists later identified by the media as Poder Joven's "divine teacher" and other top figures.[94] Taken into custody were three men, Von Ehrenberg, thirty-three; brothers Carlos Eugenio Palma Ariztía, twenty-five, and Andrés Palma Ariztía, twenty-two; and three women, Pía Figueroa Edwards, eighteen, María Eliana Astaburuaga, nineteen, and Constanza Raquel Díaz de Valdés, twenty. Five soon appeared in Santiago's Sixth Criminal Court, with Díaz de Valdés escaping further inquiry. At least fourteen parents of young women had filed police reports and sought criminal prosecution for kidnapping; Poder Joven, they claimed, had encouraged their children to leave their Santiago homes, and in some cases to abandon formal education, so as to "follow the pseudo-spiritual movement directed by an Argentine with the pseudonym 'Silo,'" as *El Mercurio* put it.[95] One of the fathers involved, Gonzalo Figueroa Yáñez, reported that his older daughter, the arrested Pía Figueroa Edwards, had successfully encouraged his sixteen-year-old, Dominga, to leave home and join Poder Joven. (It was an allegation that leftists likely found delicious because Figueroa was a member of the Edwards family—owners of the conservative *El Mercurio* and other media.) Another parent, Víctor Arce, father of nineteen-year-old nursing student and Siloist María Angélica Arce, echoed the sentiments of other parents quoted in the press. He explained to reporters in early October, "It's horrible. There are hundreds of homes destroyed by the situation." Víctor Arce made clear that María Angelica "is a human who lives but does not reason. . . . I don't know where she is. All I can say is that she's not the daughter I knew. She's an automaton, and if she returned she'd do so physically but her soul would not be the same."[96] Such accounts prompted the state-owned *La Nación* to bluntly state, "Silo is no joke."[97] Figueroa recalled the frustration she felt in jail and under such intense social and media scrutiny: "In all of October 1971 there was not a single interview with us. There is no basis for what they said."[98]

The Supreme Court, after receiving petitions from lawyers representing the concerned parents, advised a lower court to name a special prosecutor to examine Poder Joven, a "movement of perverts" that "infiltrated the country's student youth," the communist daily *El Siglo* told its readers.[99] By October 5, however, the parents had decided to withdraw all official complaints and not pursue criminal or civil charges. Almost immediately, the jailed Siloists were "liberated" because the parents in question preferred to "avoid scandal," thus leaving no testimony for authorities to collect or use.[100] Their release did not occur before the jailed Siloists managed to cobble together the bones of what would become "Van Doren's" aforementioned *Exordio del Poder Joven*—their own version of Antonio Gramsci's *Prison Notebooks*, per se. The book's confrontational tone speaks to the frustration gripping the jailed Siloists who were subjected to the power of media and a state they regarded as authoritarian, violent, and philistine.

El Mercurio, El Siglo, and other publications suggested the parents did not wish their children's experiences to be made matters of public record. At the time, the disappeared young women returned, one by one, to their homes and, more importantly, denied they had been kidnapped.[101] The state's investigation continued, however, under the direction of a court-appointed *ministro en visita*, just as reports of Poder Joven groups outside Santiago, including ones in the coastal resort city of Viña del Mar and the southern city of Concepción, surfaced in the press. Siloist groups also were reported in the smaller cities of Chillán, Talca, Los Angeles, and Talcahuano in the country's center-south, as well as the southern city of Valdivia.[102] In Concepción, at the very time the five Poder Joven members were facing prosecution in Santiago, the media blamed Siloists for the disappearance of a fifteen-year-old working-class boy, Ciro Olmeño Salazar, who had joined the "sect." Like those in the capital, the Concepción Siloists were accused of being "a movement of perverts" with "hippie activities," sexual aberrations, and sadism—and Olmeño most certainly was in danger. The boy appeared within twenty-four hours of the initial report, and the details of his disappearance were far less prurient than the press had likely hoped—but nevertheless entertaining. It would seem that Olmeño had stolen a small bus, gone on a joyride around Concepción, and then wrecked. Injured, he feared a return home, so he went to the house of a female schoolmate, who took the boy in.[103]

Back in Santiago, some young Chileans—many of them teenage girls, the media reported—demanded that Von Ehrenberg and the Siloists be left alone. The newspaper *Clarín*, a voice of UP, noted that some of the "kidnapped" girls, including Dominga Figueroa Edwards and Magdalena Vergara Vicuña, defended the "priests" of Poder Joven, which *Clarín* described as an organization "bolstered by elements of the extreme Right . . . in order to provoke social unrest while Popular Unity undertakes measures to strengthen the Chilean family by way of socialist government."[104] What's more, *Clarín* went so far as to identify Von Ehrenberg as a Nazi and as a dictator within the supposedly fascist Siloist movement.[105] Not helping Siloism's defenders were the alleged experiences shared publicly by some Poder Joven recruits. The pro-UP media reported that newbies were forced to take part in group sex and engage in meditative practices with the help of strong drugs.[106] At roughly the same time, the Right accused Siloists of using hallucinogens and for engaging in "homosexual sadism"—"naked," even—and described Silo as "a homosexual and false prophet."[107] Poder Joven also was suspected of Satanism, based on "sinister" and "strange rites," such as uttering guttural cries and chanting in Hindi when burying one of their own, Eugenio Puga Pinto, twenty, at Santiago's General Cemetery in late October 1971.[108]

As the investigation unfolded, parents not involved in the official complaints at the Sixth Criminal Court also took their stories to the press, and pro-Allende periodicals delved deeper into what *El Siglo* called, on its editorial page, a "sinister organization of foreign origin that began in the middle and upper social sectors but now has been transferred to others."[109]

The father of Carmencita Espinoza Acosta, fifteen, a student at Santiago's Liceo Ignacio Carrera, accused the "degenerate disciples of Silo" of the September 30 "kidnapping" of his daughter, who for some time had been coming home from school with "strange magazines" and had become "reclusive and uncommunicative with her parents."[110] The very same day her father's words appeared in print, Carmencita returned home and spoke to the press. She said that while she had been interested in Poder Joven, she found its members "odd" and boring, and chose to discontinue her association with them.[111] In fact, Carmencita explained, her disappearance had nothing to do with Poder Joven; she had run away from home after a dispute with her parents, finding refuge for a week at a relative's house.[112] The parents of Susana "Chanita" Gómez Olivares, fifteen, from Santiago's working-class barrio of Conchalí, reported their daughter's disappearance as news spread of Poder Joven's legal entanglements. Chanita's distraught mother declared, "If my Chanita doesn't return during the course of this week, I promise that I will kill myself."[113]

Statements like that of Chanita's mother were emotional and compelling, but Siloists explained years later—just as they had argued at the time—that Poder Joven did not kidnap anyone.[114] In the end, the charges brought against the Siloists went nowhere, largely due, as noted above, to the gradual appearance of the "kidnapped" young women and their parents' desire to keep their children's deeds private. Interesting and telling here is that parents who publicly denounced Siloism, both in the press and in the halls of the Sixth Criminal Court in October 1971, were overwhelmingly fathers of young daughters. In fact, no parent of any young man associated with Poder Joven lodged an official complaint during this episode. Siloism, it seems, endangered young women much more than young men, and its endorsement of sexual liberation *for women and men* as a component of complete liberation, as seen in *Manual del Poder Joven* and elsewhere, apparently posed a particular danger to young women, whose sexuality was to be restrained and overseen. The results of not doing so were obvious, the Edwards-owned *La Segunda* demonstrated. As the arrests and travails of Siloists were being reported, the newspaper published a photo of four pregnant young women, with the caption: "What exercise will Silo teach us today?"[115] Fathers involved in the events of September and October basically described their daughters as innocent little girls who had been corrupted, either directly or indirectly, by two perverted and lascivious men, Von Ehrenberg and Silo, even though Silo was not in Chile at the time. Yet, neither Carmencita Espinoza Acosta, nor Dominga Figueroa Edwards, nor Magdalena Vergara Vicuña, nor any of the other young girls interviewed by the media spoke of Siloist coercion, although this obviously does not mean it never happened.

UP's media response to Poder Joven's ideas concerning sex and sexuality also merits attention, given that it illustrates how conspicuous elements of the governing coalition (its diversity notwithstanding) approached the issues of women's liberation and feminism. What sincerely bothered UP sectors, it seems, was Poder Joven's position that sexual liberation—and total revolution, for that matter—*was not gendered*, just as libertarian socialism was not tied exclusively to the working class and a revolutionary vanguard. Quite simply, Siloists envisioned a sexual liberation for all—men and women—who pursued self-transformation and the healing of suffering, all while "treating sex with love," to refer to Figueroa's aforementioned assessment. Indeed, the Siloist notion of self-transformation makes no allusion to any gendered (or class-conditioned) psychology, and the totalizing humanism of Siloism—which questions all socially, culturally, and politically constructed categories and divisions among humans—necessarily explodes the traditional gender roles endorsed by some leading Chileans, Marxists and otherwise. As noted earlier in this book, UP was slow to address the concerns of women—even working-class ones—and trailed both Christian Democrats and conservatives in this regard. Such was the case despite the fact that some leftists, and younger ones in particular, were more attuned to the international women's movement.

Poder Joven's very real encounters with the intentionally intimidating authority of a generation and its national state, as Siloists understood it, did not end when the parents' official complaints were dropped. On October 11, less than two weeks after being arrested by the Anti-Vice Brigade, Von Ehrenberg was briefly detained once more, this time by the Brigade for the Repression of Stupefying Substances, a police unit charged with carrying out the state's highly publicized crusade against marijuana post Piedra Roja. According to *Clarín*, police took the opportunity to snap mug shots of Von Ehrenberg when he and the other freed Siloists returned to the station to gather their personal belongings. A police spokesman said the narcotics squad took the photos "just in case something happens in the future."[116] Months later, in March 1972, the Sixth Criminal Court and a new special investigating judge reopened the case against Poder Joven. While the move did not lead to any arrests or formal charges, it did produce yet another negative treatment of Siloism in the press.[117] After March 1972, eighteen months passed before Siloists experienced another significant and direct confrontation with police. Overall, Siloism's enemies found in the media a rather effective and efficient way of defining and attacking what *El Mercurio* called "an immoral sect."[118]

Amid the events surrounding the arrests of Von Ehrenberg and associates, Poder Joven found itself in crossfire. From the Left there emerged a discourse that condemned Siloism for having an elite social pedigree, for attempting to corrupt the working class, and for taking part in a right-wing (and therefore upper-class) conspiracy against UP.[119] Meanwhile, *El Mercurio* and other conservative interests suggested Poder Joven was a manifestation of Marxism's corrupt, collectivist, and overly liberating tendencies. Ironically, both the Right and the Left (which typically disagreed sharply on most everything) opposed Poder Joven because it supposedly endangered the nuclear family: conservatives saw the family as the anchor of traditional culture, while leftists considered it a fundamental unit of the Chilean road to socialism.

When assessing Poder Joven, the Communist newspaper *El Siglo* argued, "Behind Silo are sinister intentions. It's not only about exporting [from Argentina] hippie rites of imitating demented criminals like Charles Manson. Silo wants to destroy our young people, to separate them from any valid concern, to distance them from their promise to the people [*el pueblo*]. The movement was born in the wealthy neighborhoods [el barrio alto], and its ideologue is a fascist with psychiatric deformities. What's dangerous is that Silo's sermon has spread. It has penetrated the high schools in the working-class neighborhoods [*los barrios populares,* such as Conchalí]."[120] This passage conveys the concerns of many Marxists regarding Poder Joven's reach into sanctified spaces—schools and working-class neighborhoods—as well as the UP media's failure to discern hippismo (in this case, embodied by a depraved and dangerous "hippie") from Siloism. The term "hippie," used as an insult in *El Siglo*, suggested a general lack of respect for others and institutions, sexual promiscuity, drug use, a certain condition of vagrancy, and even the possibility of senseless violence. In the matter of drugs, for instance, the leftist press went so far as to accuse Siloists of manufacturing and distributing LSD.[121] Broadly speaking, Marxist media regularly conflated Siloism and hippismo, despite the condemnation of hippies in *Manual del Poder Joven*, which eschews drug use (deemed a contributor to false consciousness, among other things) and sexual liberation simply for the sake of sexual liberation. *El Siglo* concluded that, despite the best efforts of police and astute parents to eradicate Siloism, "it would be best if young people organized to disarm [Poder Joven's] fallacies."[122]

"Clearly. Absolutely we were hippies. Absolutely we were," Silo said sarcastically in our interview. He explained that Poder Joven's critics, like those in the UP press, adopted a certain method when dealing with Siloist ideas: "Don't understand what we're saying, deform what we're saying, but don't really know what we're saying." In other words, denial and purposeful ignorance formed the basis of reaction to Siloism, rather than an attempt to grasp it before rejecting it on its merits. Thus, the Siloists became hippies, in the eyes of the ignorant or those who consciously wanted to mislead the public. That is why Transmutation, the publisher, came to be, "so that [the movement's ideas] would be known," he said. "Whether they were from the Left or the Right, they would recognize us, and they didn't sympathize with the idea that we could express our point of view, no."[123] Sometimes Poder Joven's members were accused of hippismo; other times they were considered part of a reactionary (if not downright fascist) conspiracy. In October 1971, the Marxist magazine *Ahora* called Poder Joven a reactionary movement, citing its rejection (in *Manual del Poder Joven*, specifically) of Marxist political parties, orthodox revolutionary politics, and UP's brand of socialism. The anonymous *Ahora* writer added, "These aging youths [Silo and Von Ehrenberg were in their thirties] consider themselves the chosen ones to direct the destiny of the world because 'Silo is happiness.' "[124] Equally critical is an article that appeared in *Onda* just two weeks before the arrests of Von Ehrenberg and company. It accused Silo of being an agent of a New York-based occult network—once more underscoring Poder Joven's imperialist credentials—and added that in the United States "the invention of new cults is a business that seems rather lucrative." Poder Joven, the article contends, views all "forms of organization to be rotten in and of themselves."[125]

Aside from general condemnations of Poder Joven, the leftist media zeroed in on Von Ehrenberg with particular zeal, given that his very name supposedly betrayed certain important facts. As *Onda* reported, before becoming known (albeit incorrectly) as Van Doren and as the spiritual leader of Chilean Siloism, Von Ehrenberg—a political-science graduate from the University of Chile who lived on a small hacienda in the Andean foothills outside Santiago—had been a member of the Chilean Nazi Party.[126] The article does not point to any ideological shift from fascism to Siloism on Von Ehrenberg's part, which reflects the Left's view that Poder Joven and "fascists" of the barrio alto were of like mind to begin with. The Quimantú-published *Mayoría*, moreover, explained that it likely was not coincidental that Siloist graffiti appeared right next to that of the FNPL, a fascistic crew known for its violence against leftists, hippies, and others. "They even use the same paint," the magazine noted.[127] *Novedades*, a widely read magazine that was outside UP's media circle, backed the Silo-fascism theory. Von Ehrenberg's wife, Ana María Parot, recalled in an interview that her husband's college friends told her that he "was a strange man and had fascist inclinations." But he changed, she added.[128] Von Ehrenberg, by other accounts, was indeed strange. Missing an arm and with a background draped in mystery, Von Ehrenberg even concerned Silo. Although his relations with Von Ehrenberg began well, the two clashed at times. Silo noted, for example, that Von Ehrenberg did not like any openness to hippies as potential Poder Joven recruits, and Silo disliked Von Ehrenberg's statements that painted the orator of Punta de Vacas as some sort of messianic figure—something that the public used against Poder Joven. "It wasn't clear how he operated," Silo added.[129]

Spurred by leftist discourse on Poder Joven and the call to young people to organize a defense against Siloism, the Jota's BRP (Brigada Ramona Parra) pledged to corral Siloism in Santiago's working-class neighborhoods.[130] Beginning as early as 1970, Siloists recall, Poder Joven members were harassed, threatened, and chased from public streets by the BRP.[131] In the wake of the 1971 arrests of Von Ehrenberg, Figueroa Edwards, Astaburuaga, the Palma Ariztía brothers, and Díaz de Valdés, one unidentified *brigadista*, angered by Poder Joven's discourse of generational struggle, told the leftist periodical *Ahora*,

> We are like all the young people. That's exactly why we oppose those who want to separate us from our essential duties. We want to be responsible to the process [the road to socialism] that our country is living through, responsible to the people and their struggles. Silo's agents try to conquer unpoliticized sectors [i.e., young people] in order to corrupt disoriented youths who have problems at home and for whom life is a labyrinth from which they momentarily cannot escape. Silo is a carrier of fascist political contraband. . . . We believe that age based on calendars does not matter. It's pure fascism for youths to confront their seniors [*los viejos*].[132]

Ernesto Ottone, a Jota leader and future adviser to President Ricardo Lagos, added, "The fundamental thing at this moment is to build socialism. Silo is opposed to this. We want to show that building socialism is the most youthful of all tasks."[133] Class struggle and generational struggle simply could not coexist, young Marxists and *brigadistas* argued; authentic young revolutionaries, they declared, should recall how Ho Chi Minh led the Vietnamese Revolution with a "flag held high" until his death at age 79.[134]

These statements, though articulated by only one sector of the Chilean Left, nevertheless captured UP's prevailing opinion concerning Poder Joven's discourse of generational struggle and Siloism's definitions of liberation, revolution, and socialism: they made no historical sense and had little, if anything, to do with the practicality and material reality of social being. In real terms, the Siloists (and hippies, for that matter) threatened the recruitment efforts of groups like the Jota among working-class youngsters, and any perceptive Marxist leader would have been aware of the possibility that young leftists might very well be tempted to dabble in Siloism, hippismo, or both. After all, one need not reject class struggle to read "The Healing of Suffering" or become interested in the serious exploration of sexuality. Leading figures like Ottone could speak for their organizations but could not ensure uniformity of thought and practice among the rank and file.

Not only did governing leftists scorn Siloism's denial of class struggle, they also suggested that combating Poder Joven was, in fact, itself an act of class struggle. As noted earlier, the Marxist press was well aware of Poder Joven's origin in the barrio alto and expressed concern about its spread to popular neighborhoods. El Siglo reported in mid-October 1971 that residents of the San Joaquín settlement in the capital's working-class municipality of San Miguel were troubled by the presence of suspicious youths. The newspaper described the expulsion of "Siloists and potheads" from San Joaquín at the hands of "workers, students, and residents" who resisted an "effort by the sinister sect of Silo to infiltrate the popular sectors."[135] Those outsiders were Poder Joven agents (many with blond hair and Argentine accents) who cruised the streets of San Joaquín in new cars and had established "good relations with some of the young people," explained the magazine Ahora. High on marijuana and with extra to go around, Ahora said, these Siloists asked working-class youths to "abandon everything" and join Silo (presumably to pursue sexual escapades), thereby threatening the Chilean family.[136]

While denunciations of Poder Joven circulated in the leftist press, conservative interests also addressed the movement's alleged threat to culture and society. Telling examples of the conservative standpoint appeared regularly in El Mercurio in October 1971. The capital's leading daily, for instance, interviewed a prominent and outspoken anti-Allende priest, Father Raúl Hasbún, who declared Poder Joven to be a movement "without destiny," because it lacked core morals. He thus urged youths to "love your father and your mother."[137] In the same issue, *El Mercurio* basically identified Poder Joven as a cult when describing the group's alleged initiation rituals: "They undergo all types of torture, including electric shock, forced physical exertion, and brainwashing, and to end the day's training they confess in front of the entire group their thoughts and weaknesses. In addition, they experience inhumane punishment, sadism, and masochism. Corruption is the result. They burn money and destroy their watches in order to affirm their absolute independence."[138] *El Mercurio* went on to conclude that Poder Joven's "principles fly in the face of all moral, religious, and social norms."[139] The rightist current-events magazine *Qué Pasa* also participated in the onslaught, accusing Silo of being "in the business of abomination." In addition to reporting exaggerated Poder Joven membership figures (somewhere between 1,500 and 6,000), the periodical asserted, "'Silo' has become a frightening name for many families. Until recently, [the name] only seemed like a stupidity."[140]

Although Poder Joven rarely responded in the press to the myriad accusations put upon it, the events of September and October 1971 spurred Von Ehrenberg to grant an interview to *El Mercurio*. The otherwise reclusive Siloist denied vehemently that Poder Joven even remotely approximated the type of group depicted in the press and described by the parents of "kidnapped" children. Von Ehrenberg began by denying that Siloism was authoritarian and hierarchical, thus responding to the media's use of "leader" "director," "chief," or "boss" when identifying him or other conspicuous figures in the movement. Appearing before the reporter with María Eliana Astaburuaga at his side, Von Ehrenberg went on to dismiss accusations that the movement had endangered the Chilean family and had encouraged young people to leave their homes. Such rhetoric, he argued, was the product of a coalition of the Catholic Church, right-wing oligarchs, and "the infantile Left." He proceeded to restate that Poder Joven eschewed drug use, understood as a characteristically hippie pursuit in the public sphere, but remained supportive of sexual liberation, which "has value for whomever wishes to practice it." Astaburuaga added, "It's not true that we use drugs. From the sexual point of view, to each his [or her] own."[141] Above all, Von Ehrenberg explained, while Poder Joven was, in fact, a socialist revolutionary movement, it was pacifist, antiguerrilla, and unarmed, and had nothing to do with the violent political extremism of either the radical Left or radical Right.

Von Ehrenberg also took the opportunity to reaffirm Poder Joven's opposition to UP. Unfortunately, he said, Chile's road to socialism was merely reformist, noting, "[T]he only revolution that I recognize is socialist [and the] the only person who can accomplish it is Silo."[142] Here once more, the problem of the Siloist revolutionary subject surfaces. At Punta de Vacas and in the pages of *Ramona*, Silo refuted the notion that he was a chosen one or gifted seer—a messianic figure leading disciples; he was not *the* revolutionary subject in and of Siloism's total revolution. Yet, when Von Ehrenberg declared that only Silo could bring about socialist revolution, he basically denied the revolutionary subjectivity of anyone but Silo, making Poder Joven and Siloism seem to be more about Silo's guidance and less about self-transformation, the healing of suffering, ending economic violence, and so forth. It therefore makes sense—whether or not they were right—that many parents, political leaders, and newspapers involved in the uproar of September and October 1971 described Poder Joven as a cult; they saw it as being led by a messianic figure whose esoteric and shadowy groupies enticed and reprogrammed young people.

When reflecting on the policing the Siloists experienced during the Allende years, Julián Burgos, citing the examples of Mohandas Gandhi and Martin Luther King Jr., observed, "Every struggle for liberation has been that way." Burgos was not equating what happened to Gandhi and King to what befell his Siloist friends and colleagues in late September and October 1971, but rather was plugging Poder Joven into a longer history of "liberation" movements that have encountered great resistance. Siloists were "dangerous to the family, to the state, to the Church. . . . We were doing something interesting and new that attracted young people," Burgos added.[143] Nothing that Siloists experienced under UP would match what happened to some of Poder Joven's members when that government fell, as the Epilogue describes.

The Concepción Connection: Siloism and the MIR

El Mercurio and other rightist publications made a sport out of bashing hippies and Siloists. Just as the Left recklessly conflated hippismo and Siloism, the Right attacked Poder Joven by identifying Silo as an Argentine hippie and, more cleverly and subtly, by pasting reports related to the September 1971 arrests of Von Ehrenberg and associates conspicuously near hippismo-related stories on the government's effort to control "intoxicating substances" and reports on recent marijuana busts.[144] By no means did the Right go about its attacks on Siloism in an uncalculated way, and glaring examples of such manipulation can be seen in rightist accusations that

Poder Joven was collaborating with the MIR. The Santiago newspaper *La Prensa*, for instance, reported in October 1971—during the "kidnapping" brouhaha—that between Siloism and *mirismo* existed "suspicious coincidences" that "were not products of journalistic imagination." Rather, the suspicion was based on "a series of happenings" that should be investigated by a *ministro en visita*. The evidentiary base included the fact that Von Ehrenberg was originally from the city of Concepción, from whence the bulk of the MIR also came; that Von Ehrenberg had been a member of the Marxist-Rebel Revolutionary Vanguard (Vanguardia Revolucionaria Marxista-Rebelde), a precursor of the MIR at the University of Concepción; that miristas had participated in a Siloist gathering in Buenos Aires in November 1969; and that MIR and Siloist ideas about revolution and change seem to be associated. "All of these deeds tend toward one sole objective: to look for new values among youths," the daily *La Prensa* observed.[145] The conservative *Tribuna* also gave its two cents, declaring that "MIR" and "Silo" were two names but were "one filth."[146] It also claimed that Silo and the MIR were in cahoots to woo "idealistic youths." Together, the groups were "a cancer to be extirpated."[147] The root of the matter was their shared Marxism, the newspaper contended, hinting that Siloist radicals may have been involved in the assassinations of both General René Schneider in October 1970 and Pérez Zujovic in September 1971.[148] The former was killed in a failed kidnapping plot led by a right-wing general, and the latter was murdered by the VOP.

One of the main points of interest in accusations of MIR-Silo ties involved the well-known Van Schouwen family. It was often reported that one of Poder Joven's leading figures in Concepción, Jorge Van Schouwen, was in fact the brother of a MIR leader, Bautista Van Schouwen, thus alluding to a genetic and ideological relationship between the two groups—a family resemblance, per se.[149] It was also not a coincidence that the Von Schouwen connection was most publicized by the Right amid the moral panic (and moral politics) involving the alleged kidnapping of the young women, which resulted in the arrests of a handful of Siloists in October 1971. As further evidence of Poder Joven's alleged radical Marxism, the newspaper claimed on another occasion that a Siloist had identified himself unabashedly as "an authentic socialist revolutionary."[150] No press outlet made reference to the fact that the MIR, in its periodical *Punto Final*, had made a point of attacking Siloism on occasion.[151] Figueroa, a Siloist who had been jailed in October 1971, did not see anything remarkable in the Van Schouwen connection; it was a sign of the times. "It was just as contradictory for the Van Schouwen family, or my family, or for the families of the people of the shantytowns who also joined the movement. Because there emerged on the historical scene a new generation, and in reality not just our families, but all families, like those who had a hippie child or a Marxist child, all of the families were shocked by our generation, and I'd also say in the world as a whole because, like in Ortega y Gasset, there appeared a new generation that moved the social scene," Figueroa reflected.[152]

The relationship between the MIR and Siloism ran deeper than the Von Schouwen connection; charges of intellectual links were not entirely off base but still greatly exaggerated. The MIR was a Guevarist movement that sprang onto the scene as a splinter group of the Socialist Party (PS) in the mid-1960s. By 1967 it was in the hands of a group of young student rebels from the University of Concepción, and it rose to challenge the UP's democratic and legalistic road to socialism by promoting the immediate seizure of the means of production. MIR ideas reflected a blend of Marxist-Leninism, *guevarismo*, the Guevarist image of the heroic guerrilla, and Marcusean youthful spontaneism that some others, such as the Socialist Youth (JS), also found attractive. The MIR's rallying of rural workers, peasants, and urban squatters to engage in *tomas* (property takeovers), in defiance of Allende's call for a legal and incremental road to socialism, speaks to the group's spontaneism.[153] Some miristas denied Marcusean influence, however. In 1971, the MIR periodical *Punto Final* noted that Marcuse attempted to justify "the hippie movement," which was a "symptom of the decadence of consumerist societies."[154] The Siloists essentially shared the MIR's appreciation of Marcusean youthful spontaneity (via Poder Joven's call for young people to defy any forms of authority that exert force in their lives); a methodological commitment to "revolutionary" vanguardism (but not *mirismo*'s Marxist-Leninist ideology); more "liberated" views on gender, sex, and sexuality; and a general disdain for leftist "reformism." What is more, the miristas and Siloists also connected in the matter of the individual's transmutation, to an extent, which appeared in MIR discourse under the rubric of the Guevarist "new man." There is another point to consider as well. The PCCh's aforementioned attacks on Siloism may be construed as veiled criticism of the vanguardism and spontaneism of the PS's radical wing, the JS, and the MIR. After all, Poder Joven, given its often-cloudy message regarding subjectivity and agency, could be seen as an adventurist "socialist" vanguard not in tune with the Chilean "reality." Meanwhile, the MIR's criticism of Siloism was an opportunity for the group to show a moderate face, culturally and ideologically, and distinguish its vanguardism from that of the Siloists.[155] Thus, multiple tendencies of the Left could find criticism of Siloism (and counterculture in general) useful, not only out of genuine concern and shared cultural outlooks, but also as an instrument in a larger ideological debate.

While Siloists could not disagree with Guevara's hope for "a new human being who will represent neither nineteenth-century ideas nor those of our decadent and morbid century," they departed from Guevara's notion that the new man would *come from* social revolution. After all, Guevara described the need to "create" that new human being by way of the revolutionary process.[156] *Manual del Poder Joven*, however, establishes that the transformation of the self must *propel* "total revolution." It argues, "The new man will not come after social change but at the same time, if there exists a practice of internal change, guided by the libertarian ideal of total revolution."[157] Moreover, miristas and Siloists agreed that personal transformation, whatever its timing or essence, was imperative for men and women alike, pointing to a shared humanism.[158] Broadly speaking, the factors above were indicators of New Left movements in the region; they shared what Greg Grandin, in his definition of New Leftism, called the "will to act."[159] But the connections between the MIR and Poder Joven did not go much further than that, other than the interchange of some members and the Von Schouwen familial link. Nevertheless, Siloism arguably meets the threshold for constituting a New Left movement.

Among the most pressing points of departure was the Siloist rejection of all materialist ideologies, whether (nonlibertarian) socialist or capitalist. Silo put it simply: "We said it was impossible: human relations based on material things. It's impossible."[160] This helps explain the defection of some sympathetic miristas to Poder Joven, but the question of method was a more critical factor. Luis Fernando Lira was one mirista who left the group to join Siloism due to the MIR's endorsement of armed struggle: "The problem was that after a while the moment arrived in which I had to make decisions. When I saw myself with a gun in my hand, then everything became complicated. The gun was to use, not to defend myself, or whatever. That made me rethink everything."[161] The pacifist Siloists rejected the MIR's increasing calls for revolutionary violence during the Allende years, as well as its idea of revolution (one of and for the working class). In 1971, such differences led Silo to call MIR members *"pendejos"* (punks) in a reaffirmation of Siloism's rejection of violence as a tool for change.[162] To Siloists, only the healing of suffering, the transformation of the self, and the end of psychological violence, as Silo termed it at Punta de Vacas, would truly address grievous social and economic problems and foster an autogestionary (thus not imposed) *socialismo libertario*. "I felt that the Poder Joven movement was more revolutionary than the MIR because it revolutionized the minds of people," Lira declared.

Siloism was countercultural in its approach to the self, society, and the transformation of both. It ran afoul of mainstream understandings of power and authority, liberation, and revolution, as evidenced by the attacks it faced from the Left and the Right. Poder Joven was not a "subculture" in that it essentially rejected most everything underpinning modern society and culture. Few things could have been more "counter" to Chilean culture than Siloism, and this helps us account for the uproar it caused. But there was more at hand. The main political constituencies of the era used Poder Joven in their campaigns against each other, with the Left insisting that Siloism was a fascist bourgeois plot and the Right claiming that Poder Joven was a Marxist cancer, like the MIR. Siloists were caught in the middle. When recalling being labeled a fascist, a smiling Silo responded, "They [Marxists] said that about everyone." But, he added, at least the Left had the intellectual capacity to understand Poder Joven. It only chose not to do so. The Right, however, was a lost cause. "It seems to me that you don't have to expect the Right to have clear ideas about these matters," he said.[163]

This author has been asked, "Well, what did Siloists *do*?" Accounts of Transcendental Meditation, graffiti, and hole-digging do not suffice as answers. The question is of the sort historians must always keep in mind, but it nevertheless succumbs to normative conceptions of what thoughtful young people did or should have been doing during the 1960s and 1970s. Hippies have not provoked the same question, for the things they "did" are widely considered the types of deeds that hippies tended to do. The difference is that Siloists had a doctrine in a country of clearly defined doctrines that were expressed politically and culturally, not to mention economically. That Siloists (and hippies, for that matter) did not engage in party politics or marches in the streets might, unfortunately, convince the onlooker that Poder Joven did not "do" much at all. Responses to the rise and presence of Poder Joven, however disproportionate they were, indicate otherwise. The Siloism controversy exposed many cultural issues, intergenerational struggles, and intragenerational conflicts that have not been adequately studied in Chile in light of the power of class and party politics as categories of analysis and identity. In sum, then, what the Siloists "did" was often lost on their contemporaries, either purposefully through some sort of self-imposed ignorance, or because Siloism simply was a tough nut to crack. The very question "Well, what did Siloists *do*?" gives us some insight into (still existing) normative conceptions of youth and youthful agency during the late sixties and early seventies. It is to that subject we now turn.

7 Good Young Chileans

. . . .

The documentary film *Descomedidos y chascones* (The Excessive and Shaggy Ones) was supposed to screen in September 1973—on the 11th, some say. That did not come to pass. The UP government fell that day, and President Salvador Allende took his own life in the presidential palace after the Socialist's final words were broadcast on the radio. The documentary, filmed between September 1971 and December 1972—right in the middle of Allende's presidency—captures the reactions of young men and women of all classes, from Las Condes high schoolers to university students to factory workers, as they watched two clips: one of the Progressive Rock festival held in Viña del Mar in 1971 (second only to Piedra Roja in criollo counterculture lore, as festivals go), the other of high school and university students—young women and men roused by Allende's call to action—engaged in the Popular Unity (UP) government's *Trabajos Voluntarios* (Voluntary Work) program. The clips could not have been more contrastive, with the former showing many hundreds of outwardly carefree hippies throwing their bodies around frenetically to the sounds of rock music, and the latter exhibiting young people digging into rocky soil to build irrigation canals in the countryside, sharing water from large jugs, and smiling while the sun beats down upon them.

Directed by Carlos Flores and hatched in the halls of the University of Chile's film department, the piece gets at what young people were thinking about themselves and each other during a momentous era. At a deeper level, *Descomedidos y chascones* is about normativity and negations: who to be and not be. After gazing upon clips of the Viña festival, at which Los Jaivas and Los Blops (among others) performed, one leftist working-class university student declares, "I believe we, people who work, are the ones who have to get together and talk about what is happening, why such things happen, and see who really represents the young people, Chilean young people. I think those who best represent Chilean young people are the young coal miners, the young students that ultimately worry about bettering themselves, and those who really represent the Chilean youth are those who are working and participating in the task of production." Another quips sarcastically, "It's very difficult to find a hippie coalminer." On the flip side, a bohemian hippie in his twenties, after seeing film of generational peers digging ditches, flatly states that he was uninterested in traditional work. That young man, with long wavy hair and a moustache, was Tito Valenzuela, a poet and fixture of Santiago's *barrio bohemio* who made an appearance in chapter 4. His friend adds nonchalantly, "Work isn't for me, either."[1]

The chapter at hand returns us to the youth question and politics but from an analytic angle made particularly useful by our discussions of hippismo and Siloism. It explores competing and contrasting notions of "the good young Chilean"—ideal types and tangible examples—that were key in political discourses during the UP years among both young people and their elders. We have examined criollo counterculture and criticisms hurled at it by political forces with distinct ideological positions, with those detractors negating the countercultural individual or group as a legitimate actor and blaming rival ideologies and organizations for counterculture's appearance. Such voices also imparted normative conceptions of the good young Chilean to further create "us-versus-them" dynamics, distinguishing upstanding teens and twenty somethings from both countercultural youths and young activists of opposing ideologies and organizations. But normativity also was debated within political camps, and signs of intergenerational dissonance—most notably within the Left—reflected and reinforced "generation" as an important point of identity and divergence on a discursive landscape largely framed by class and party affiliation. As Flores's documentary exposes, battles ensued over the meaning of "youth" and the place of young people in a changeful society.

Piety, "Liberty," and Belligerence

From the leadership of political parties to the right of the UP, that is, essentially from the National Party (PN) and the Christian Democratic Party (PDC), similar impressions arose of the good young Chilean, just as they wielded comparable analyses and criticism involving the criollo counterculture. The PDC leadership began moving closer to the PN shortly after Allende's inauguration and subsequent to giving critical support to the Socialist in the Congress, when choosing the next president fell to that body. This transpired after the PDC ran its own candidate, Radomiro Tomic, who came in third behind Allende and the PN-backed Jorge Alessandri Rodríguez, the former president. Tomic's harvest of votes ensured Allende's victory in a trifurcated electorate, but as UP began implementing its road to social-ism, many PDC leaders, including former President Eduardo Frei Mon-talva, an anti-Marxist, emphasized the questionable legality of reforms pursued by the Marxist government. Interestingly, Tomic, who led the PDC's left wing, did not abandon Allende, and this progressive strain within the party can be seen in the discourse of the Christian Democratic Youth (Juventud Demócrata Cristiana, JDC), as we shall see. We must not overlook, moreover, that the PDC began in the 1930s as the Falange Nacional—founded by Catholic university students, including Frei, who broke from the traditionalist Conservative Party—and only took its party name when it merged with the Christian Social Conservative Party (Par-tido Conservador Social Cristiano) in 1957. In 1964, the Right threw its sup-port behind Frei, clinching the Christian Democrat's win over Allende (in the latter's third of four tries to win the presidency). Frei went on to initi-ate significant change, including the beginnings of agrarian reform and the nationalization of nearly half of the copper industry, all under the PDC's communitarian "Revolution in Liberty" and with the support of the United States and its Alliance for Progress program.

Notwithstanding the Tomic situation, an expeditious process of bipolar-ization took hold between early 1971 and September 1973, with the PN (formed in 1966 out of the old Liberal and Conservative parties) and much of the PDC on one side, and UP and other leftist groups, including "progres-sive" Christian Democrats, on the other. For the purposes of this discussion, it serves to examine mainstream non-Marxist voices and groups in the same breath, while understanding that variances existed in terms of ideology and worldviews between PDC centrists and the Right, and even between compo-nents of the PDC. Given these circumstances, it should not surprise that "morality," linked to a Christian spirit, was an identifying characteristic of the good young Chilean from the perspective of both PDC and PN interests during the late 1960s and early 1970s.

In July 1970, numerous young people started gathering periodically at Catholic high schools in Santiago for "youth days." One such meeting hap-pened in October, a week after Piedra Roja. More than three hundred young women and men—high schoolers and some university students from the upper and middle classes—met at the Colegio De La Salle, located in what is now the Municipality of La Reina, adjacent to Las Condes. That assemblage, like ones before it, had multiple aims, subsumed under the broader goal of getting together "young people who want to concern themselves with others in the Christian spirit and under the theme: 'Try to be a young Christ.'" This particular meeting took on added meaning thanks to the festival in Los Dominicos, but its overarching themes remained the same as previous confabs. The purpose was less about adding to the press assault on the architects and revelers of Piedra Roja or criollo counterculture in general (there was a bit of that, though) and more about portraying a positive image of the good young Chilean—a moral, focused, respectful, and clean-cut person. Those attending endeavored to inspire each other to act ethically in the face of grave social problems, including marijuana, that were affecting all age groups. The event's facilitator, María Angélica Quilán, a nun and teacher at the Colegio Santa Teresa, organized the young people into groups of ten, each with a discussion leader, to tackle such topics as the political, social, and economic situation in Latin America, young people in the contemporary world, religious faith in action, and "Christ's presence today." At day's end, one young man explained that he and his peers dealt with reality "not through the fictitious means of marijuana, but through the reflections and spontaneous conversations among sectors of our youth." He added that such interaction was "a clear reflection of the fact that the Piedra Roja festival does not, in any way, represent the entirety of our youth, who ultimately are the future."[2] As the voice of the PN, *El Mercurio* raved, "One should rejoice in happenings like that at the Colegio [De] La Salle, which, in addition to representing an intrinsic value, adds a disclaimer regarding a suspected degradation of Chile's youth."[3]

Guillermo Yungue was a young man along the lines of those who pleased Sister María Angélica—and folks like Frei. Yungue was a high school student, a member of the JDC, and made headlines in late 1971 when he defeated a pro-UP candidate to win the presidency of FESES, the Federation of Santiago Secondary-School Students, which had been founded in 1948. In a letter to Yungue, Frei praised his "esteemed friend" for "great service to the country and the party." He explained, "It is profoundly encouraging that we see that a majority of youths [involved in the FESES election] love Chile, love liberty and justice, and realize that the transformations our Fatherland is living should transpire under the banner of respecting the principles and values that guarantee the dignity of the human person and his rightful liberty [and] that comprehends the importance of maintaining political pluralism, which destroys all totalitarian pretense and all sectarian eagerness." Frei then relayed a moral imperative:

> For the country to realize its potential, it needs youth with moral principles, with courage, with integrity. A youth that does not

believe that the best way to serve the country is leisureliness or shouting. The country will need men capable of work, with discipline, with knowledge. The world is of those who know. If in Chile we do not form a generation of people with scientific and technological capacities, all the shouting will fade into backwardness, in misery, in rancor and frustrations. That is why your deeds have an awakened political consciousness that should translate not only into the work of your organization and in the daily fight for your ideals, but also into taking advantage of these years of study and effort to answer to your families and your Fatherland. At a time in which we see the disintegration of so many values and how some groups have distorted the process of social advancement, . . . you are a breath of refreshing and clean air. A new society needs to be modeled, with another spirit, with another hierarchy of values. Money and power will not be its fundamentals. I'm certain that it will be inspired by a real humanism.[4]

The former president of the republic defended a sort of Christian humanism that emphasized individual freedom and dignity as well as social and material justice. Relatedly, he criticized, in a not-so-subtle way, the "shouters" in the streets who fed "disintegration"—partisans of the UP and of the extreme Right, likely—and lacked commitments to liberty, pluralism, and the respect for others. Yungue was a good young Chilean for representing and defending noble ideals. He did such a fine job at it, apparently, that Communists later cast aspersions on Yungue for his repeated berating of UP and for allegedly attempting to manipulate the FESES election of 1972, won by a UP slate.[5]

In addition to being hailed by Frei as a positive sign for vitality and virtue, Yungue's victory in 1971 was a big deal in national politics. With major university federations, including the powerful and influential Student Federation of the University Chile (FECh), in the hands of UP supporters, the FESES win was a needed and emboldening one for the PDC, and especially for the party's conservative Frei faction.[6] Yungue was tied to the Frei wing, though his peers in the JDC largely backed the progressive Tomic.[7] Of note, too, is that Yungue was not from the moneyed eastern municipalities of Greater Santiago; he attended three different high schools (one near Santiago's city center, one in the municipality of La Granja, and the other in the municipality of Conchalí), each of them working- and middle-class sectors of the capital. Accordingly, his support of the PDC

Members of the Federation of Santiago Secondary-School Students (FESES), a leading student group involved in politics, gather in 1971. Courtesy of the Colección Museo Histórico Nacional (Santiago).

could be seen as a slap in the face to UP forces, which drew heavily from those areas.[8] While Yungue spoke for the FESES (until UP's slate defeated his in late 1972), he did not speak for the JDC, which was much more radical than the party's Frei wing.

By the time of Allende's victory in late 1970 and with Tomic as their touchstone, the JDC projected a message and image not terribly unlike those of UP youth organizations. Earlier in the 1960s, however, the JDC had firmly supported Frei's antioligarchic but also anti-Marxist "Revolution in Liberty" and the party's call for "communitarian socialism."[9] When Allende took power, the JDC wanted to "finish off the *momios*, wherever they are!"— *momios* being a play on the Spanish word for mummies, used as a mocking epithet against the Right. They declared that they "do not believe in youth power" but instead "believe in the power of the workers," and rather than pursuing a reformed and more just form of capitalism, as Frei sought, they appealed for unity between urban workers, rural labor, residents of shanty-towns, and students to destroy capitalism and replace it with a new social order.[10] At the same time, the JDC called for political pluralism, making one wonder if "pluralism" included everyone but the *momios*, and also defended the organization's Christian foundation, explaining that its members were "inspired by Christian principles" and struggle for a revolution that "leads to a new, just, humane, and fraternal society." Such Christianity means "accepting certain fundamental values of Christian doctrine and applying them to political action by way of a revolutionary ideology and a humanist morality." This also entailed "work and sacrifice" and readiness to "complete the tasks conveyed by the party and to demand as much from comrades and leaders," thus imbuing a young person with "the riches of solidarity, fraternity, growth, and collaboration."[11]

Divisions between the Frei and Tomic camps had erupted in 1968, after the party leadership voted to back Frei's more conservative line. This stoked the truculent rhetoric of young Christian Democrats as a pro-Tomic faction gained the upper hand in the JDC.[12] Moreover, young party activists, deeply influenced by liberation theology and Vatican II, and upset with Frei's close relations with the United States, split from Christian Democracy in 1969 to form the MAPU (Unitary Popular Action Movement). It sided with UP and Allende, and some young Tomic supporters in the PDC bolted to embrace MAPU's brand of Christian socialism. A handful of influential MAPU members later left that body to join with some JDC figures (including JDC president Luis Badilla) in forming the Christian Left (Izquierda Cristiana, IC) in 1971.

While the Right and Christian Democrats embraced religiosity as moral fiber for the politically informed and active young person, and despite the flirtation and cooperation between the PN and PDC leaders like Frei as the Allende years unfolded, there was no shared conception as to the goals and outcomes envisioned by their youth organizations, each with thousands of members. To the right of the JDC, which reflected Tomic's closeness to UP, was the National Youth (Juventud Nacional, JN) of the PN, with a discourse that stood in sharp contrast to the JDC's, thus further complicating political affairs, generational dynamics, and conceptions of the good young Chilean. For the JN, political action was a necessary duty in the face of Allende's road to socialism, and it was unfortunate that conditions warranted such engagement. Two years before Allende's election, for instance, the PN lamented that youths were getting in over their heads in terms of national politics; perhaps they should enjoy being youngsters a little longer, without entering a political fray that was an "adult" pursuit.[13] The Marxist government, however, made it so no young person could escape party politics and "political consciousness." One JN publication called on parents in 1972 to intervene in their children's lives to stamp out Marxist ideological orientation being pressed upon their children through various means of communication and in public schools.[14]

The JN also was vocal in terms of hippismo and Siloism when describing its ideal young person. It directly confronted the happenings at Piedra Roja, reminded readers of the alleged kidnappings of young women at the hands of the "malignant" Poder Joven in 1971, and called the Siloists' *Manual del Poder Joven* a "sad publication." A statement published by the JN's Providencia branch in September 1972 explained, "These days we have been witnesses to multiple youth movements that have nothing to do with Silo, marijuana, and other things, but do have something to do with 'LIBERATION,' and I'm referring to groups of students who have demonstrated strength, fighting for their ideals and combatting those they see as wrong." That "liberation" was freedom from Marxism. The same issue tells of a gathering of many hundreds of JN members and supporters that filled a Providencia theater. There, PN elder and leader Sergio Onofre Jarpa, who also edited the right-wing periodical *Tribuna* (a big fan of Yungue's victory), lamented that the job of defeating Marxism would already be over and done with if not for Chile being "a country full of fags" who were not willing to commit to the fight against leftist revolutionaries. Who those "fags" specifically were remained unsaid, but one might assume Jarpa was referring to hippies and other nonpolitical youths who stood on the sidelines, in addition to politically committed youths, like the JDC's Allende supporters, who should know better. Andrés Allamand, president of the JN's Providencia chapter, also spoke at the event, earning praise from his peers as "a young leader ready to defend the ideals of young people at any cost."[15]

A point of pride for the JN was its Rolando Matus Command (Comando Rolando Matus, CRM), formed in 1971 and named after a young rural worker killed by revolutionaries who invaded the land of a small property owner. Known for wearing construction helmets, slacks, buttoned shirts, white armbands, and stern expressions, the CRM, which numbered in the low hundreds, was the street muscle for the PN and JN, much like the BRP—the Ramona Parra Brigade—was for the PCCh (the Communist Party) and UP.[16] It goes without saying that CRM militants promoted an image of the good young Chilean who rejected Marxist theory and praxis in the name of the nation, the family, and morality. They also projected a normative masculinity—with construction helmets on full display, for example— that provided an antithesis to apathetic or politically ill-informed youths effectively homosexualized in Jarpa's rhetoric about weak "fags." The ploy was unexceptional during the era, and political groups across the board called it into service.

Rolando Matus combatants (and PN members more broadly), according to JN propaganda that circulated in 1972, were "young people [nearly exclusively male] sound in body and spirit, ready to serve the country even at the risk of their physical integrity. They are of all ages, from sixteen to twenty-five years old, and they come from the most diverse social sectors: the university, the high school, the guild or syndicate."[17] One example of such a committed young person, as noted above, was the sixteen-year-old Allamand, president of the JN's branch in Providencia, the hotbed of criollo counterculture. In an October publication, a photo of Allamand appears next to his summons for "nationalist youths" to oppose Marxism. Amusingly, the photo shows him sporting wavy hair that nearly reached his shoulders.[18] His peers and elders in the PN never publicly accused Allamand of being a hippie at a time when long hair on a male usually was all the evidence necessary to make such an identification. What is more, Allamand obviously was not reflected in Jarpa's conception of "fag," which the PN patriarch presented without any qualifications in the abovementioned theater address. Allamand's case is one sign, among others (as we shall see), that many young men who stood against counterculture nevertheless wanted to be stylish, and thus it was quite reasonable to have longer hair; distinguishing Allamand (and his immediate peers) from hippies was the matter of a "right" sort of political commitment and sober demeanor. Allamand, it should be added, went on to have quite a career. After attending the Liceo José Victorino Lastarria and St. George's College in the eastern suburbs, he earned a law degree and entered politics. Allamand cofounded the center-right party Renovación Nacional (National Renovation) in 1987, as the country began taking steps toward democratization. He was elected to the Chamber of Deputies in the 1990s and subsequently to the Senate, where he currently serves. Allamand was minister of defense from 2011 to 2012 and unsuccessfully ran in a primary campaign for the presidency in 2012, falling to a fellow member of RN's alliance with the *pinochetista* Independent Democratic Union (Unión Demócrata Independiente).

On the right also stood fringe groups, the most notable of which was the FNPL, the fascistic Fatherland and Liberty Nationalist Front (Frente Nacionalista Patria y Libertad), which made the CRM look quite moderate, or so one might jest. A quarrelsome and intimidating organization of extreme right-wing youths, it terrorized hippies, torched the Coppelia café during the Allende years, and made a pastime out of street brawls with leftist youth groups, including the BRP. The FNPL's most spectacular deeds, however, were its participation in an attempted coup against UP in June 1973 and its assassination of Naval Captain Arturo Araya Peeters, an aide to Allende, the next month. Pledged to "defend democracy" and liberty, it deployed tyrannical means as convention, seeking out confrontation on university campuses and most everywhere else, and also with most everyone else, including countercultural youths. Juan Pablo Orrego of Los Blops, as the reader will recall, was on the receiving end of an FNPL assault; the musician's long hair was the spark. But more conflictive were the FNPL's dealings with leftist youth groups and organizations.

At its inception in September 1970 (first as the Movimiento Cívico Patria y Libertad), the organization's goal was to deny Allende the presidential sash by pressuring Congress to choose Alessandri as president. After that failed, the group worked to harass and destabilize Allende's government. Shortly after the Socialist's victory, the FNPL held one of its first pubic rallies at the Pontifical Catholic University, where many of the FNPL's members studied. Pro-Allende groups began whistling and chanting during a speech by FNPL leader Pablo Rodríguez Grez, who called for a new election "in defense of democracy." The situation rapidly devolved into a brawl between the FNPL and UP youths just outside the university's main entrance, along Santiago's principal thoroughfare, La Alameda.[19] The incident set the tone for happenings to come. By way of its own press apparatus, the periodical *Patria y Libertad*, and through the actions it took in the streets, the FNPL cast an image and message meant to intimidate political opponents. It also promoted its own conception of the good young Chilean.

In 1972, *Patria y Libertad* reported that the UP government's "political police" (the FNPL's term to identify the Policía de Investigaciones, or PDI) had arrested four FNPL members who had been painting political murals on walls along Pocuro Avenue in residential Providencia late one night. They had been among a group of thirty, but only the four were taken into custody after police reportedly approached with guns drawn. Supposedly, Allende's motorcade had passed through the area earlier that night, with the president himself taking notice of the muralists at work. Police descended a short time later at Allende's behest, the FNPL asserted. Andrés Vergara, just fourteen, was one of those arrested. Over the course of three hours, he was interrogated at a local police station, facing questions about his politics while receiving punches below the belt and other physical abuse. "They asked about my personal background and then wanted to find out details about the organization," Vergara recounted in a *Patria y Libertad* interview. "With each question they gave me a slap to the face or the head." He explained, "They also asked about how many members there were and what we talked about in our meetings." Vergara, apparently, did not crack, or simply did not know the answers. The young man, who entered the FNPL in 1971, earned his organization's praise for a "lofty spirit of sacrifice that he has shown in all his work." He demonstrated, under the duress and oppression orchestrated by "enemies of democracy," that he was "ready to keep fighting to the end for the nationalist cause." Antonio Küpfer, eighteen, was "submitted to intense interrogation and vexation very appropriate to the Marxist mentality of the [PDI's] chiefs," the FNPL declared. "They called him a fascist and seditious, and they insulted him and his family." Nevertheless, the young man "always remained in a good emotional state and says he faced the interrogation with calmness." Küpfer, like Vergara, thus showed his resolve and "is ready, more than ever, to fight for nationalist ideals." Such "nationalist ideals" outlined by the FNPL were many, not the least of which were support for a military coup to defeat Marxism ("in defense of democracy") and restoration of the rule of law undermined by Marxist revolutionaries, all of which could only be accomplished if nationalist youth took up their collective role as "one of the nation's pillars."[20]

The FNPL openly called for the military's "nationalist" intervention from the very beginning of the Allende administration, but it was not until the latter months of UP's road to socialism that mainstream voices from the PN and the PDC's conservative faction consistently did the same. The military had remained on the sidelines of Chilean politics since the early 1930s, and it was divided politically during the Allende years, much to the chagrin of rightist hawks. Interestingly, major political forces did not commonly position the soldier as a model for the good young Chilean. The military's apolitical posture, in line with the country's tradition of constitutionalism, was a concept that took some time to decay between 1970 and 1973. Even then, PN and PDC leaders (like Jarpa and Frei) believed that a revamped democratic system, bereft of Marxism, would soon follow any military coup. In other words, if the good young Chilean was ardently *political*—a dominant expectation of any good young Chilean during the Allende years—then the military's traditionally *apolitical* posture did not fit into the formula. (Under a military regime that practiced a politics of antipolitics, to steal a phrase, the good young Chilean became the embodiment of *chilenidad* [Chilean-ness] as an apolitical nationalist.[21] We shall return to this subject in the Epilogue.)

There were many organizations operating to the right of UP, but there nevertheless existed a "Right" to which the PDC became attached, in the eyes of many of its members and opponents. Generally speaking, an outsider peering at the sheer number of organizations and interests at play in the political arena could easily conclude that Chile was a chaotic mess. Not to oversimplify, but by virtue of bipolarization during the Allende years, that arena largely rested on an "us-versus-them" formulation, with Left and Right facing off. This was a widely shared notion, and it became the butt of satire in *Descomedidos y chascones*. In one scene, a tall, slender man appears, donning a suit and derby hat. The question at hand: "Are you left-handed or right-handed?" To answer, the man instructs the viewer to find a newspaper and cut out one of every letter of the alphabet. He or she must take a hat off with the left hand, place the letters in it, and slowly mix the letters with the right hand. Without peeking into the hat, he or she should reach into it and take out letters, one at a time. If the person happens to have selected letters that spell "USA, CIA, UPI, PN, PDC," then "your world is of the Right." If the letters instead create "CUT, FLN, UP, PCCh, MAPU, PS, IC," then "your world is of the Left." If, the man adds, he or she picks out "LSD"—the film then switches abruptly to footage of the Progressive Rock festival in Viña del Mar.[22]

To Be Young and (Properly) Revolutionary

Sequences in *Descomedidos y chascones* featuring hippies at the Viña del Mar festival made the moneyed classes look pretty bad, thus supporting what leftists were saying about bourgeois corruption and immorality in the late sixties and early seventies. Without giving any attention to what working-class hippies were up to at Parque Forestal or places like San Miguel, the film shows clips of well-to-do young men and women at the Viña del Mar spectacle prancing about, smoking, and looking quite stoned, juxtaposed with scenes of young Marxists taking to physical labor in support of building a new society. Hippies are "filth," one leftist university student proclaims in the film. "I didn't believe these things happened in Chile." The documentary also cuts to businesspeople walking to or from work, with briefcases, suits, ties, and the like, interspersed with flashes of dollars with U.S. President Richard Nixon's face on them. Then, an image of a topless woman appears. The connotations are not elusive: there exists a relationship between counterculture, the wealthier classes, U.S. imperialism, and degeneracy. Moreover, near the end of *Descomedidos y chascones*, images of race cars at the Las

Vizcachas track, just southeast of the capital, zoom across the screen. Well-to-do race aficionados (nearly all young males, competitors and spectators alike) are dressed rather sharply, obviously enjoying their money and leisure time on a beautiful sunny day. The film then cuts to workers who had just seen the Las Vizcachas footage. One working-class woman explains that such "bourgeois" diversions are good for the revolutionary cause. "And we, the proletarians, the lower class, the marginalized, the marginal, we organize and prepare. For what? Because in case tomorrow or the day after there's a confrontation, which is very possible that it will come [and] we will be prepared," she asserts in a forceful voice. A male companion joins in, noting that countercultural and bourgeois youths live off their parents who take wealth away from the working class. The solution, he declares, is socialism.[23]

These scenes obviously communicate socioeconomic divisions and the resulting animosity circulating among classes and political groups in Allende's Chile. They also foreground a common occurrence: the Left's branding of "bourgeois" youths as inherently feckless and shameless—a perspective associated with leftist identification of counterculture as a particularly bourgeois phenomenon, especially after Piedra Roja. On the flip side, good young Chileans, from the Left's perspective, are everywhere in Flores's documentary. They include the aforementioned interviewees, BRP members holding long bamboo canes and marching in unison, like soldiers, and many other young people participating in street demonstrations, holding aloft the image of Che Guevara.

After Guevara's death in Bolivia in 1967, his likeness became common, but not entirely ubiquitous, in leftist rallies. The heroic image of the selfless revolutionary was quite attractive, and so was the "*barbudo*" (bearded one) himself, with his piercing eyes, flowing hair, and rugged features. He added an aesthetic appeal—shot through with masculinity—to a revolutionary message in the late 1960s and early 1970s, when young people who rejected counterculture nevertheless responded to fashion trends of the day, finding Guevara's melena (long mane) modish but not bourgeois. Guevara's conception of the "new man," and "his" possible realization in revolutionary Cuba, was a particularly powerful tool and template for many young people seeking to better understand the individual's role in Marxist ideology that otherwise assigned revolutionary subjectivity to a class—or a vanguard purportedly working on its behalf. Eduardo Gatti of Los Blops recalled, "In those days, I remember, in the days of Popular Unity, it was about the coming of the 'new man.' That was a political slogan at the time. Between us [in the band] we always talked about that there would be no 'new man' unless we changed ourselves individually."[24] With the "new man" came reverence for the Cuban Revolution, whether from Chilean Marxists who considered it a model to follow precisely (the MIR and some Socialists) or those who did not support armed struggle but found value in the revolution's anti-imperialist and social-justice impulses. Moreover, the "new man" had blatantly masculine overtones. It implied revolutionary masculinity, but it also entailed both genders transcending their petty bourgeois origin and pleasures like dating or family in the name of complete dedication to the cause. This was quite evident within the MIR, according to mirista women.[25]

Communists and Socialists also emphasized revolutionary discipline and sacrifice when essentially addressing the "new woman" and the good young (female) Chilean. Yet, those conceptions remained tied to traditional, normative gender roles. The publication *Paloma*, a leftist variety magazine geared toward women in their late teens and twenties, praised women who, in addition to their duties at home, worked for the betterment of the patria. Appearing in September 1973 (on the eve of the coup), a *Paloma* article affirmed that women had mobilized for the government out of "political consciousness" and solidarity in the face of UP's enemies. It explained, "And so throughout Chile there exist thousands of women who before had small worlds, individual ones, and that now are devoted to the community and work to solve its problems." Those women, the article noted, are now "women-people," reflecting a new sense of wholeness that makes for "happy husbands" and "more profound marital relationships." Such are women who "feel useful and fulfilled" as contributors to the road to socialism. It may not be surprising that an adjacent advertisement promises pregnant women they will feel "elegant, comfortable, and young" in a boutique's latest maternity clothes.[26] The concept of the "new man" and mainstream leftist conceptions of the good young Chilean were grounded in notions of revolutionary commitment and the common good, and although generically applied to men and women, they nevertheless specified roles based on gender.

Allende, a former student leader at the University of Chile and cofounder of the PS in his mid-twenties, had much to say about the ideal young compatriot. Many statements on the matter appeared in material published by Quimantú, the state-owned enterprise that produced numerous periodicals and a great many books, most all in support of the UP government, in one way or another. Quimantú periodicals serve the historian as a representative source of UP's general considerations regarding the good young Chilean. The coalition's constituent parts also brought the subject to bear, as did the MIR, by way of speeches and published material.

On the night that Allende won a plurality of votes in the 1970 presidential election, the Socialist gave a victory speech to a huge crowd of supporters packing La Alameda in downtown Santiago. He did so from the balcony of the headquarters of the FECh, the largest and most influential university-student organization in the country. Led by the Communist Alejandro Rojas Wainer (in his mid-twenties), the FECh had provided pivotal support to UP's campaign by marching, distributing pamphlets, and rallying students and workers. Allende had been a FECh activist in his youth, and the UP candidate found great meaning in—and wished to impart significance through—the act of privileging the student organization on that historic night. Allende reiterated his coalition's pledge to use socialism to lift the working classes, urban and rural, from misery and subservience. He singled out the many who had helped propel UP to victory, laying much credit at the feet of the younger generation of leftists. "Young people of the Fatherland were the vanguard of this great battle, which was not one man's struggle, but the people's struggle," he proclaimed.[27] A few weeks later, Allende expressed similar thoughts and paused to add, "Young people have a lot to do for this country."[28] This typified the president's appeals throughout his administration, including in its last hours.

Broadcast on Radio Magallanes from the presidential palace on the morning of September 11, 1973, Allende's final address to the nation thanked and praised young people "who sang and gave [to the revolution] their joy and their fighting spirit."[29] A joyous and happy disposition in the building of socialism was a theme that Allende used often when addressing young people. In a 1971 interview, for instance, the Socialist asked youths for "enthusiasm, happiness, and revolutionary passion, for them to dance, sing, and to be fully young, that they be excellent students, workers of the vanguard, that they love their compatriots."[30] The good young Chilean is a cheerful person dedicated to revolutionary aims and willing to walk the walk in addition to talking the talk. Such were attributes of Allende's conceptualization of the Chilean with new values who, as he pinpointed in a speech to open the 1971 school year, fights "for the Fatherland, a new society, and a new man in the fruitful hive of labor [colmena fecunda del trabajo]."[31] On the whole, this vision served Allende in combatting much negativity circulating in the public sphere amid the youth question, lamentations about counterculture, and great conflict among young people in the streets.

Youths harvest onions as part of the Trabajos Voluntarios program in 1972.
Thousands of urban young people gave up their summers to engage in such work
in support of UP's road to socialism. Courtesy of the Colección Museo Histórico
Nacional (Santiago).

Trabajos Voluntarios provided opportunities for the direct application of
youthful, revolutionary energies. A centerpiece of UP's youth initiative, the
Trabajos, with roots in the Frei years, put tens of thousands of volunteers,
most of them university and high-school students, to work in infrastructure
construction and economic and cultural development. In addition to digging
the irrigation trenches that appear in Flores's documentary, volunteers mined
copper and coal, constructed and repaired houses, mended roads, taught
school, worked in factories, and led sports and artistic programs, among
other activities.[32] They also provided labor during strikes, including the
damaging strike of private trucking companies in 1972.[33] In the program's
first year under UP, participants came from more than a dozen organizations, including the FECh, the Student Federation of the State Technical
University (Federación de Estudiantes de la Universidad Técnica, FEUT), the
FESES, the Jota, the MAPU, the pro-Allende JDC, and the Youth Department of the Central Workers' Union (Central Única de Trabajadores, CUT),
a massive communist-led federation of unions that represented members from
both the working and middle classes. An early Trabajos pamphlet calls on

youths to "continue building a new Chile, with fervor and a revolutionary spirit that characterizes the young people of Chile."[34] Luis Corvalán, former general secretary of the PCCh, recalled that in mid-1971 some four hundred FEUT members volunteered to work in state-owned copper and saltpeter mines in the arid north, while another one hundred labored in state-owned factories in the capital.[35] That was after some 1,500 FEUT activists returned from summer work. Moreover, the FEUT's publication, *Brecha,* observed that under Frei, summer work was about "feeding the official hype" of PDC elders, while Allende's program "is being realized under the banner of a real collaboration between workers, rural folk, and students to create a new Chile."[36] Those workers might have, by chance, run into Víctor Jara, Quilapayún, or Ángel Parra, among the Nueva Canción performers who visited Trabajos worksites as part of what were often called "cultural caravans."[37]

Totals vary, but the UP government estimated that by 1972 some 300,000 young people had engaged in the Trabajos, and in 1973 alone, CUT youth pledged 30,000 workers.[38] The CUT's participation points to the significant involvement of youths not attending universities, although a good many young CUT members were engaged in matriculated studies. By 1972, the Trabajos planning duties had been handed to the short-lived Presidential Youth Secretariat (see chapter 2). Its leader, Francisco Díaz, made the government's depiction of a good young Chilean abundantly clear: "Our action is based in a real and concrete deed: Chilean youths have a high degree of social awareness and want to participate in the transformations happening in the country."[39] Oscar Ortiz had such social awareness. In 1971, he was an anarchist with bohemian and hippie leanings. Now a history teacher, Ortiz recalled with a smile, "It was notorious. It was something bothersome. They [young UP militants] would say, 'Comrade, join the Trabajos Voluntarios.'" He did not partake.[40] As Ortiz's reminiscence suggests, some young people felt pressured to engage directly in the prevailing sociopolitical struggle, and for the UP government the young volunteer worker was a powerful recruitment tool and discursive device. Yet, the Trabajos were far from repressive, and instead were an outlet for thousands of young people to act in ways they found meaningful and constructive.

An official mechanism for fostering good young Chileans was the public school system in a young country, demographically speaking. For our purposes, the general orientation of the Allende-era pedagogical program provides some insight into schooling's role in the multifaceted process of shaping a "new society."[41] The Marxist-Leninist and Louis Althusser neophyte

A young woman participates in Trabajos Voluntarios by helping transport lumber for UP construction projects (1972). Courtesy of the Colección Museo Histórico Nacional (Santiago).

Marta Harnecker's *Cuadernos de educación popular*, as we saw in the previous chapter, were essentially statements of principles dedicated to the intellectual and political formation of the young revolutionary subject (the Chilean "new man"). The series, published by Quimantú during the UP years, was widely used in public high schools, handling such themes as the "capitalist exploitation," "the party: vanguard of the proletariat," and "strategy and tactics." Such books were to provide the necessary knowledge from which political and cultural practices would spring. This was of particular importance given that many young people, as we have seen, were slugging it out in the political trenches. The forces of revolution very much needed to inculcate youngsters with certain ideals and outlooks that would either directly support or dovetail with those of the road to socialism. Accordingly, increasing enrollment was part of the strategy to both lift people out of poverty and also foster the UP program.

Allende could boast of significant gains in matriculations throughout the country, and he did. When the new school year began in 1971—a mere four months after Allende took office—10,000 more children entered pre-schools (an 18 percent jump), 140,000 more enrolled in primary-level schooling, and 50,000 additional students entered high schools (a 15 percent increase) than in the previous year, far outpacing general population growth. Meanwhile, the 1971 academic year saw university matriculations increase 28 percent over 1970 levels. The increase from 1969 to 1970 had been 8 percent.[42] The Ministry of Education was committed to the continued democratization and expansion of the school system to, it declared, "powerfully raise the cultural level of the people."[43] Formal education would be an important factor in making a new society and a new man, and political action and social life would also figure centrally. As Allende observed, "For us, all of society should be a school, and schools should be an integral part of that larger school that society should be." He added, "For us, education and governmental action in the scope of a new society must signal to the young person that they are the executor and the builder of the new society for which we yearn, the great dignifying task, ripping it away from oscillation and vice."[44] With such words, Allende pushed for the Escuela Nacional Unificada (National Unified School) project, a broad reform effort to deliver education to all, better connect schools and vocations, and submit private schooling to state authority.

Certainly, UP's media apparatus provided additional examples of good young Chileans, including ones who demonstrated cultural and artistic creativity. Quimantú's *Onda*, for instance, praised revolutionary student groups and neighborhood youth centers in late 1971 for putting together a public poster exhibition promoting young people's involvement in building socialism through art. It took place in a park in a working-class sector of the capital, where "in the spirit of the decisive attitude of Ernesto Guevara, [the poster makers] displayed their messages to the community." In that vein, one poster declared: "With a new culture, youth will take on a creative role," alongside renditions of students working in factories and playing sports. Another poster depicted alienation—a central theme of the youth question and, in a certain application, Marxist ideology—in the forms of modern fashion and "frivolous magazines and pornography." The good young Chilean, instead, takes in only poetry (that of Communist senator and poet Pablo Neruda, one imagines) and folklore (a nod to Nueva Canción).[45] As one infers from the specific reference to Guevara, this undertaking contributed to the making of the "new man."

The FECh's cultural work also drew attention. A "gift" from President Allende, the federation's cultural center opened in the winter of 1972 on Villavicencio Street—smack dab in the center of the *barrio bohemio*. More than two hundred students exhibited their pottery, sculptures, and other pieces at its opening.[46] Placing the new center in the *barrio bohemio* was not incidental, but rather symbolic. The move spoke to the government's recognition that the neighborhood was artsy, but more importantly indicated that bohemianism and hippismo would be challenged by the artistic project of young people committed to UP's cause. It is worth noting, too, that the article in question is titled "Our Youth Acquire Responsibilities"—responsibility being a concept that pops up quite frequently in youth-related UP discourse. Young activists often included the idea in their statements and declarations. A high schooler identified simply as Rulo captured this most clearly in an interview with *Onda* in October 1972. "It seems to me that to not participate in a [political] group implies that you're not taking up a responsibility. If you really know the social problems that we have, you can't distance yourself from them. That's why it's necessary for a young person to participate in a political party," he said.[47] Meanwhile, many youths yawned at such an assertion, including a group of well-to-do, "tuned out" teenagers, with a bit of a hippie vibe, who appear in *Descomedidos y chascones*. They grumble about how politicized Chile is and that people are too devoted to marching around in the streets, complaining about or defending this or that. Only conflict, violence, and "fanaticism" result, they agreed.[48] There were many leftist youth groups that might have qualified as purveyors of all three, for better (in some eyes) or for worse (in others).

The PS and PCCh had youth groups—the JS and the Jota, respectively, with members ranging in age from their early teens to late twenties—and also had more militant wings that engaged in some dirty work in the streets. Allende's links to those organizations were complicated. Generally speaking, Allende had a better working relationship with the Moscow-obedient PCCh and its Jota than he did with his own party's radical wing—led by Senator Carlos Altamirano Orrego—and the JS, both of which flirted with the MIR. The PCCh, which maintained a Popular Front-era commitment to a democratic path to socialism, cooperated closely with Allende's incrementalist project, and the Jota was very clear in its pro-Allende sympathies in the matter.[49] (An interesting circumstance is worth mentioning here: Altamirano's cousin was the father of Los Blops guitarist Juan Pablo Orrego, and the musician's mother was the PS leader's secretary. One might imagine interesting conversations over the extended Orrego family's dinner table.) Again, UP was an odd beast, given that it fundamentally was an Old Left in power when New-Left elements, like the MIR, were significant protagonists in Chile and elsewhere in Latin America (the 26th of July Movement in Cuba being the prime example). This largely explains why conflicts arose pitting the PCCh and Allende's wing of the PS (the older Left) on one side, and the Altamirano PS and JS crowds and the MIR (the newer Left) on the other. Personality conflicts were also involved. In all, leftist groups made for spectacular episodes that added fuel to a fire being stirred up, too, by groups like the FNPL and the CRM.

The JS formed in 1935, not long after the founding of its parent. Overshadowed by the PCCh's Jota during the late 1960s and early 1970s, the JS nevertheless was important in UP's initiatives on youth under a Socialist president.[50] Under Carlos Lorca Tobar, a former general secretary of the FECh, elected to the Chamber of Deputies in 1973, the JS headed up the Allende government's association of UP's youth organizations. For the Marxist-Leninist JS, to create a truly just country, the good young Chilean must "conduct a double battle: the battle to construct a socialist society and the battle to definitively liquidate ways of life, cultural categories, usage and modes, put upon us by the powerful societies of the capitalist universe." Meanwhile, enemies of that battle were many, and not just confined to rightist parties and organizations. It claimed, "Hippismo, the use of drugs, Poder Joven, and Siloism obey philosophies and attitudes that apparently are contrary to the system of bourgeois life, but in the final analysis, end up getting cozy with it."[51]

In the defense of socialism, and standing in stark contrast to the rightists, hippies, and Siloists, the JS also praised the revolutionary zeal of its conspicuous subgroup, the Elmo Catalán Brigade (Brigada Elmo Catalán, BEC), named after a Chilean journalist killed in 1970 while fighting for the guerilla in Bolivia. Young Socialists looked upon the BEC with pride. Early in the Allende years, their leadership put the subgroup's efforts this way: "Now, despite the difficulties and the vices that still persist, we have seen a vigorous and combative youth, with cohesiveness like we've never seen with our party and with its national leadership, with great influence in their decisions, and endowed with a high responsibility in the realization of their promises. The Brigada Elmo Catalán has done its work, with great sacrifice and valor, to imprint everywhere the names and slogans of the party."[52] The BEC essentially was the JS's gritty street presence, although the latter participated in marches, protests, and the like as well. But the BEC, numbering in the hundreds and known for painting murals in support of the UP throughout the country, could also do things that the JS did not want to do, or, at least, did not want to be seen doing. It was widely known (and praised or derided) that the brigade used physical violence as means to address political disputes.

Flores's documentary gives viewers a glimpse of the BEC's reputation. In one scene, a young man, obviously from the moneyed classes and quite cynical about politics, tells of his experience with BEC militants. While there is no way to independently verify the account, it strikes one as reasonably believable in light of the climate on the capital's streets during the Allende years. The teenager recounts one day in 1971, during local elections, when he and some friends were busy painting over the campaign murals supporting a leftist candidate in an eastern suburb of the capital. Two cars rolled up, he explained, and shots rang out. He and his friends scattered. The young man then describes how BEC members caught and beat him, leaving him injured on the street.[53] Of course, the assault could have been conducted by a number of groups, but such activists usually could be differentiated from each other by way of the armbands or other insignias they displayed proudly.

Founded in the early 1930s and with a self-reported 40,000 members by 1971, the Jota (or "J," slang for Communist Youth) functioned much like the JS, with a general membership from which a more activist wing sprang: the BRP, which took its name from a Communist young woman shot dead at age twenty during a Santiago protest in 1946.[54] Led by Gladys Marín, who was elected to the Chamber of Deputies in 1965 (at age twenty-seven), the Marxist-Leninist Jota was a highly visible agent in the UP government's cultural politics.[55] Its Discoteca del Cantar Popular label (DICAP), as the reader will recall, produced nearly all of the Allende era's Nueva Canción music, and its magazine, *Ramona*, kept young readers up to date on cultural issues. Part and parcel of a revolution that was "cool," as Marín put it shortly after Allende's inauguration, thousands of Jota members participated in the Trabajos Voluntarios and other forms of community work, constituting a key component of the Left's conceptualization of the good young Chilean who lived to "fight, work, and study."[56] Jota leaders, like other Marxists, emphasized responsibility in the making of a new society and a new man—a concept that was applicable to both genders despite being steeped in masculinity.

Young Communists and Socialists march in the streets of Santiago in support of Allende and UP in 1972. Third from the left is Gladys Marín, leader of the Communist Youth. Courtesy of the Colección Museo Histórico Nacional (Santiago).

The young leftists called for youths to cast aside "egoism" in pursuit of "new values in the conduct of the young generation," in the words of David Canales, member of the Jota's central committee, spoken shortly after Allende's inauguration.[57] Marín herself was "cool" for young revolutionaries, especially women, looking for an example of such new values as well as for a Communist Party invested in projecting a conception of the good young Chilean. She was exceptional as the only female leader of a leading revolutionary organization at a time when men dominated politics. Sporting a fashionable hairstyle and often in a skirt and heels, Marín was the epitome of the "modern" Communist woman: dedicated to the working class, respectful of the party's leadership, and a proponent of a "new man" ideal that was not necessarily just about men.[58]

Part of the Jota, the BRP was, in effect, the alter ego of the Right's Rolando Matus and Patria y Libertad crowds. Known for its colorful muralism in support of UP, the brigade also offered protection to leftist marchers and proved to be both defender and enforcer vis-à-vis rival political groups and other enemies, including countercultural young people, regardless of their social class.[59] Pointing to violence against young Communists, the PCCh backed the Jota's right to defend itself in a country in which the blood of youngsters had been spilled often, victims of the enemies of the people.[60] With most every report of Jota members being victimized came stern condemnations and warnings for the Right.[61] In November 1972, for instance, assailants that the Communist press called "reactionary delinquents" shot brigade member Juan Ibáñez, eighteen. He had been part of a group of BRP members hanging posters along principal streets south of the capital's downtown, in preparation for a rally. Without warning, bullets rained down on them. Ibáñez was the only one injured. In the words of the victim's father, the incident was "not an action of Christians or any other normal people, but rather comes from people filled with hate."[62] The Jota and BRP certainly had to be wary of possible attacks from the Right, but they also kept their guard up in regard to some other leftists. MIR-UP clashes were not uncommon, including one at the University of Concepción (the MIR epicenter three hundred miles south of Santiago) one month after Allende took office. Scuffling broke out between Socialists and Communists on one side and miristas on the other, with a MIR member suffering a fatal gunshot wound to the head. President Allende immediately made a special appeal to activists in Concepción for peace and conviviality.[63]

Leaders of the PDC, among others, accused the BRP of being an armed militia.[64] It was not, but BRP members often could be seen armed, by the naked eye and in press photographs, with long bamboo canes that served to intimidate or injure. For countercultural youths and others deemed to be living outside the bounds of good behavior by Jota militants, the BRP posed a real threat. Siloists María Eliana Astaburuaga and Pía Figueroa Edwards, both Poder Joven members who were arrested in October 1971, pointed to an instance of BRP aggression with grave consequences. While a group of Siloists were painting graffiti on walls in Providencia in late October 1971, they noticed BRP members, clutching their canes, quickly approaching. The Siloists scattered. One Poder Joven member, upon running onto the street to avoid the *brigadistas*, was struck and killed by an automobile.[65] The deceased, Eugenio Puga Pinto, twenty, was the young man buried at Santiago's General Cemetery in what was, according to the leftist press, a "Satanic" funeral (see chapter 6). The *allendista* newspaper *Puro Chile* made no mention of the BRP when reporting Puga's death—only that he died in an "automobile accident."[66] Moreover, BRP rhetoric pegged the Siloists to fascism and the FNPL, however questionable that is. Yet, that "link" meant something to the *brigadistas*, who took their responsibility se-

A member of the Communist Youth's militant Ramona Parra Brigade (center) marches with his bamboo cane in hand (1971). Courtesy of the Colección Museo Histórico Nacional (Santiago).

riously. Additionally, youths who were "tuned out," including one who comments in *Descomedidos y chascones*, were quite aware of the BRP: "There are some [in the Brigada] Ramona Parra dedicated to painting. There are others dedicated to starting melees."[67]

The BRP really did not like hippies, in addition to despising the Siloists. The line separating groups like the BRP and cultural nonconformity seemed quite stark—and, in many ways, it was. However, this does not necessarily mean that transnational trends marked by generational forces lacked influence among youths who did not share a countercultural identity. One episode in particular captures this dynamic: a debate over melenas. The fashion statement was a powerful symbol of radicalism and New Left agency, especially when Guevara sported a melena that looked rather "hippie." The very issue of long manes on young men was far more than an aesthetic question. It involved meaning and normative conceptions of gender, which were quite powerful in Chile. Critical here is that the very young people UP empowered made claims as to what radicalism could be and look like.

Growing Resistance

In a short editorial published on March 10, 1972, the *Chicago Tribune*, as it had on many occasions, opined on the subject of Allende's "road to socialism." It observed, "Ever since the Chilean congress adopted a constitutional amendment sharply restricting the power of President Salvador Allende to impose state control over private companies, the Marxist leader and his non-Marxist opposition have been moving rapidly toward a collision. The only question is what issue will lead to the showdown." But the editorial indicated, with tongue firmly in cheek, that it was "now safe to say that it won't come about over an issue that has rocked many a United States campus—the length of a young man's hair." What the *Tribune* found interesting, and indeed somewhat humorous, was a policy issued by Allende's government regulating the length of young men's hair in secondary schools. "In the northern hemisphere," the *Tribune* went on to note, "shoulder-length hair has long been a trademark of the nonconformist and radical. Straight critics of the youth subculture have tended to equate long hair with Communism or any other far left ideology. Not in Chile." What the *Tribune* deemed entertaining enough to include in its editorial content revolved around the UP government's declaration that "hippie-length" hair was a "manifestation of decadent capitalism and that youth sporting it would be barred from classes when Chile's new semester started March 6." The editorial then concluded, "None of this may settle the significance of long hair, but it certainly seems to eliminate one issue from Chilean politics."[68]

Although the *Tribune* apparently found reason for jocularity and a good measure of mockery in its treatment of the Allende government's decree, the hubbub over young men's hair actually was germane and not merely for its links to manifestations, meanings, and aesthetic profiles of capitalism and socialism during the Cold War—a consideration that, to some extent, did not escape the *Tribune*. It was relevant to generational conflict and was interrelated with normative and heterodox conceptions and projections of masculinity that were of great consequence during the long 1960s in the context of the transnational youth question and the emergence of counterculture. The melenas policy of 1972, issued by the Ministry of Education

A melenudo socializes at Piedra Roja (1970). Critics viewed long hair as a moral problem in addition to being an eyesore. Some young leftists, however, came to see it as a (proper) revolutionary gesture. Courtesy of Paul Lowry.

in early March, threw into greater relief such matters in society, with ramifications for and within the Left especially. Men's hair became a subject of some discord between UP leaders and elements of the Jota in the wake of Director of Secondary Education Jorge Espinoza Pérez's dictation, on behalf of the minister, of the government's policy regarding melenas and melenudos (young men with melenas). The question of young men's hair serves as a useful point of access into generational, cultural, and gender(ed) conflicts, contested considerations of the body within the Left, and overall reactions to criollo counterculture during the Allende years. Such tussles unfolded in the interstices of a discursive universe dominated by class, political economy, and party politics, but they nevertheless coalesced in relation to those centers of gravity.

Female or male, the body is an inherently private domain often on public display. It is a place of external signs and symbols that reflect sensibilities and predilections that are either organic to it or forced upon it. The body-as-signifier may be subtle and coy or obvious and striking.[69] Accordingly, one might consider the body an active conduit or messenger—a vehicle upon and through which normative or subversive discourses are expressed in varying local, national, and transnational contexts. If we accept these conceptualizations of the body, then we must look upon it as a tremendously important and conspicuous site of ideas, identity, and agency during the long 1960s, as certain modalities in sexuality, appearance, and consumption reflected and reinforced new ways of thinking, including countercultural ones, about society, culture, politics, and even the economy. Conversations regarding the female body, as we have seen, focused on such subjects as contraception and sexual liberation—elements of a larger, transnational debate over the meaning and control of that body. The male body, too, saw contestation. Men with long hair faced considerable scorn. As Mario Soza, drummer for the rock band Los Ripios, described, "In my [middle-class] neighborhood, they'd say, 'Here comes Mario, here comes the hippie. He's a marihuanero, stoned.' It got to the point that my parents told me to cut my hair or leave the house. And what was my response? 'I'm gone.'" Soza went to live with his band in a hippie *comunidad* in the municipality of La Reina.[70] Many ridiculed melenudos as effeminate, if not homosexual, as the testimonies of the former Parque Forestal hippie Jaime Román and Los Blops bassist Juan Pablo Orrego indicate. Oscar Ortiz, a former anarchist who grew out his hair in 1969, said his mother took it poorly because people would say, "How could your son run around with fags?"[71] Broadly speaking, the youth question and counterculture did not initiate public discussion about the body, but novel factors and permutations were put into play during the 1960s and early 1970s.

An aforementioned 1968 article by Isabel Allende in *Paula* on "feminine" and "masculine" hippies (see chapter 5) illustrates how young people's appearance was a subject of public interest and comment, especially when related to counterculture, hippismo, and gender. Young men's hair was in the mix. A few months before Isabel Allende's commentary appeared, *El Mercurio* ran an article titled, "Women Have Managed to Feminize the Clothing Style of Men." Taken from a statement made by a young male interviewee, the article's title very much cut to the chase: men were apparently looking a lot more like women, and young men's long hair had much to do with the phenomenon. One eighteen-year-old male noted that young men were "imitating" young women by wearing "flowered shirts" and having "long hair," both of which are characteristically feminine "anywhere one looks." He added, "It's absurd to have [male] idols with long hair." But some young women expressed their taste for long hair on men, noting that such a look was "youthful" and that "a man can be masculine whichever way he looks."[72]

Paula chimed in during the UP years, as it had previously, on the issue of long hair on men. One 1971 article argued that men were opting for longer hair out of vanity, knowing that women appreciated the new trend. *Paula* contributor Constanza Vergara wrote that men were "defeating old prejudices" and that those with short hair, in their "eagerness for [sexual] conquest," grew their hair simply because they could not "accept being rejected because women favored men with long hair." The article concluded that men were surrendering themselves to "female domination, at least in terms of hair style."[73] In the case of the abovementioned *El Mercurio* article, the suggestion that men were imitating women by growing long hair essentially stripped such young men of their masculinity by virtue of essentially wanting to "be" (that is, look) feminine. The *Paula* article, meanwhile, provided a different twist, and not without jokey undertones: in an environment in which women found men with long hair attractive, men wished to grow their hair in order to achieve sexual "conquests," thus succumbing to the tastes and preferences of women. In other words, men were acting like men in their decisions to grow longer hair by yielding to the tastes, aesthetic as well as sexual, of empowered women. For the most part, the former interpretation—that men with long hair, and countercultural males in general, for that matter, were effeminate and/or homosexual— was more typical of the commentary emerging across the sociopolitical spectrum.

Critics often assigned homosexuality to young men with long hair, both hippies and those with few or no other hippista characteristics. So frustrated was one young man that he wrote to the Jota's *Ramona* in 1972, complaining about commentary from the Left with respect to melenudos. The young man argued, "Certain journalists on the Left have been going to great extents to classify all of us who have long hair or tight pants or flowered shirts as homosexuals." He then noted, "I've seen images of Marx and Engels. They had long hair. According to some brilliant theories, both would have to be homosexuals." He then went on to list others with long hair, including Guevara, Ludwig van Beethoven, and Albert Einstein, while also identifying some historical figures with short hair, including Hitler. He added, "In the United States, the main progressive forces, outside of the Communist Party and the Black Panthers, are university students. Those are the ones who protest against *yanqui* intervention in Vietnam, fight for civil rights and against racial segregation. The majority of them [the young men] have hair down to their shoulders, flowery shirts, and medallions." The writer concluded, "Let's leave the issue of hair to the barbers and stylists, because if not, according to the criteria, we would also have to deduce that women with short hair are lesbians."[74] The author clearly indicated that emanating from well-positioned leftists were normative conceptions of "female," "male," and masculine-heterosexual behavior that linked melenas to homosexuality. As we have seen in previous chapters, there is ample evidence to support the assertion that UP recurrently projected normative conceptions of "woman" and "man" that were as culturally traditionalist as those emanating from more politically conservative reaches of the body politic and from the Church, though the UP notions were incorporated in a broadly "revolutionary" discourse. Notwithstanding strongly antihomosexual rhetoric and innuendo emanating from the Left, Right, and Center during Allende years, gay Chileans forged some space in the public sphere (thought not in mainstream party politics) to demand equal rights and treatment. In 1972, the first gay rights march took place in Santiago, only to be shut down by police and rebuked by the media, including the Marxist press, in insulting terms, although many homosexuals associated politically with the Left.[75]

Further frustrating (and perhaps confusing) those young Marxists with a pro-melenas perspective were articles like one published in Quimantú's *Ahora* in 1971. "The Hairy Revolution" tells of the recent visit to Chile of U.S. "Yippie" figures Jerry Rubin and Stew Albert, leading figures of the American New Left, to witness Allende's socialist project for themselves.[76] *Ahora* found much in common between Yippies and UP members, especially their potent anti-imperialism and anticapitalism. The magazine's readers may have been nodding enthusiastically with such news until, perhaps, they gazed upon a photo showing Rubin and Albert, each with ratty, long hair. If that did not discourage straight-laced Marxists, many eyebrows probably were raised by the Yippies' endorsement of smoking marijuana as a counterhegemonic gesture. Rubin told the *Ahora* correspondent, "The role that marijuana has played in the United States has been to liberate young people from bourgeois capitalist culture."[77]

On the whole, high schoolers attracted to "modern" looks saw little consistency in terms of what they could or could not wear to class. A June 1971 *Paula* article took up the interrelated issues of miniskirts and melenas—both aesthetic expressions linked to cultural change in the 1960s and early 1970s—and the manners in which schools were addressing them. At the time, no national policy existed governing such *moda*, or style. A public relations official from the Ministry of Education explained, "The Ministry has not emitted any official declaration that prohibits miniskirts or long hair on students. These are small details that schools should deal with according to their own internal regulations." Individual school rectors thus busily went about establishing their own rules. One high school in Concepción, for instance, forbade miniskirts, which previously had fallen within the school's dress code because it dealt only with acceptable colors and fabrics. Students had taken their "normal" skirts and hemmed them, so the rector required that skirts be no shorter than ten centimeters above the knees.[78] The ministry, meanwhile, did sanction young women's use of pants for the first time in 1971, to "protect health" in the winter months and to grant wishes expressed in petitions from student organizations around the country.[79] This was a way to address miniskirts without directly addressing miniskirts. Young women found pants quite stylish in that era, and thus the move abated the wearing of miniskirts by virtue of diminishing the use of all skirts. Meanwhile, at the Barros Arana Boarding School, a public school for boys in Greater Santiago's municipality of Quinta Normal, the rector, Eliodoro Cereceda, submitted melenudos in his care to involuntary haircuts, although students with "moderately long" hair were spared. Students were not amused. "I consider whether to have or not have long hair something absolutely personal," a Barros Arana student observed.[80]

It was rare for *El Mercurio* to praise a policy pursued by Allende's government. Yet, in March 1972, the conservative newspaper embraced the government's "goodbye to the hippie melenas" for secondary schools throughout the country. "Hippie attitudes and extravagance will be eliminated from secondary education," one article declared in response to Espinoza's proclamation. It then quoted the director of secondary instruction, who said the measure would help eliminate "all types of negative ways of acting that project a false image of our youth." The director went on to say, "We teachers must safeguard both the moral fiber and intellectual formation in and outside the school" and reminded all that proper appearance, rooted in the dress code that included the required use of uniforms, was fundamentally "democratic" and blurred "social difference"—a critical theme of UP's National Unified School initiative. When asked by the reporter how long is long hair, the minister simply suggested that everyone understands what qualifies as a "hippie melena."[81] The rightist *El Mercurio*, it should be noted, did not pause to explore, in greater detail, why the Allende government took the action other than in the defense of "moral fiber and intellectual formation."

The Left's political-economy critique of men's long hair—understood as a marker of bourgeois capitalism filtered through counterculture—went unaddressed by the newspaper, unsurprisingly.

Allende's Minister of Education, Alejandro Ríos Valdivia of the UP's Radical Party, included words on the new melenas policy in his annual television address to the nation on March 6. He made it abundantly clear in "measured but firm terms," according to press accounts, that "melenas undermine and give a bad impression regarding the young person's personality. That is why correctly cut hair will be required of every student." A circular produced by the ministry went further: "To be eliminated are extravagant ways of dress, the hippie attitudes of some adolescents, and the abandonment of care in regard to oneself and one's habits."[82] Adhering to the minister's remarks, one press outlet in the southern city of Concepción alerted young melenudos they should think about getting haircuts before the first bell rang to open the school year or risk being sent home in shame.[83] As one might imagine, many young people complained about the new protocol, which came with the strong suggestion that repeat offenders would face suspension and possibly expulsion.

"I consider long hair a matter of liberty," said one sixteen-year-old male quoted in the pages of the magazine *Onda*. An eighteen-year-old female student noted, "The government has the authority to do what it did, but long hair has nothing to do with performance as a student. What interests the country is that the student studies. Plus, young people should have been consulted [before the policy's announcement]." Another high school student, sixteen-year-old Francisco, explained: "I have short hair because I believe that's about discipline. I live with my father and he has taught me so. In any case, I'm not against those who have long hair."[84] The issue of discipline, broached by the young Francisco, was an important element of the debate that raged in the days after the Ministry of Education put forth its policy. Younger Marxists, in particular, questioned whether long hair necessarily meant the absence of "discipline" and "responsibility," especially as they were understood in orthodox revolutionary discourse. "So much ruckus over some extra hair," read a headline in the Jota's *Ramona*. Indeed, some young Marxists were quite willing to engage in the ruckus, and did so in often sarcastic, humorous, and telling ways. *Ramona*, which dedicated nearly an entire issue to the subject, was most sympathetic with young people who denied that men's hair length had anything to do with the moral and intellectual capacity of those who chose melenas. Its defense of melenas, couched in what can be construed as revolutionary discourse in the context of a capitalist society on the road to socialism, focused on the premise that "the length of one's hair is not a question of centimeters, but of symbolism." Reminiscent of Rubin's rejection of authority via smoking marijuana, the article explained, "It symbolizes many things. Rebellion amid the social environment. Discontent. The rejection of ways of living, of established society. The defense of a way of seeing things that older people cannot understand. Of not wanting any more to do with the outdated, arbitrary, and repressive customs of parents and grandparents. Personal affirmation. The search for new solutions to confront personal and social problems." In short, long hair could indeed be revolutionary. After all, if appearances and the outward signs of normative "morality" were at all trustworthy, the magazine noted, then why not trust the words of an "old *momio*" over an "awakened student"?[85]

Ramona, which also delved into issues of sexuality in "liberated" ways, went further. It questioned the prevailing notion that a young man with a melena was a hippie, and thus guilty of aberrant sexuality and drug use, among other things—and went so far as to dispel the belief that long hair could even become the gateway to hippismo, which, in general, *Ramona* found repugnant for the same reason the BRP had found it repugnant: its supposed decadence. As the article points out, "It's true that to be an authentic hippie—filthy and absentminded—a precious melena is indispensible. But that is not to say that the opposite is true: that to be a melenudo means doing drugs." The underlying problem, the article went on to describe, was "an overly traditionalist spirit among the authorities" that does not "take into account the opinions" and "ways of thought" of young people. Such a move, on the government's part, was "lamentable." Woven throughout the piece is the sentiment that young people, especially those inclined to the road to socialism, properly understood and accepted as young people with their own ways of thinking and appearing, could be greater weapons in the making of socialism and the new man.[86] Accompanying the article on the "ruckus" was a piece titled "Yes to Melenas and Sideburns in Socialist Countries," written by Mario Gómez López, the journalist and founder of the leftist *Puro Chile* who had interviewed Silo in Mendoza for *Ramona* in 1971. To reinforce *Ramona*'s argument that to have long hair was not necessarily correlative of being a "filthy and absentminded" hippie, Gómez chronicled his trip through Eastern Europe, where he encountered a great many men, including government officials, with melenas and robust sideburns. "Are there or are there not melenudos in Czechoslovakia?" he asked in the article. "There are—a whole bunch of them." Those melenudos were not waging "war against soap and water." Rather, they were quite tidy and believed that melenas and beards were simply a matter of style— not a matter of hippismo and all that it connoted.[87] Moreover, less than a week after Piedra Roja, the PCCh's *El Siglo* included a correspondent's reflections on a recent journey to the Soviet Union. He found no melenas, and not even a single miniskirt.[88] Key here is that *Ramona's* article on Eastern Europe decoupled melenas and hippismo and reinforced the idea that long hair could, in fact, be properly revolutionary.[89]

When young UP Marxists pondered revolution and melenas, there was a pertinent example from which they could gain some insight: the MIR. Far from being criollo hippies, miristas nevertheless were *barbudos* (bearded ones) who saw in the scruffy facial hair and longer hair of their idol, Guevara, a rather attractive masculinity and what amounted to a New Left revolutionary authenticity. Historian Florencia Mallon explains, "Taken as a whole, this multifaceted image of the dedicated young *barbudo*, who risked everything in the name of revolutionary justice and emerged untouched and empowered on the other side, was heady stuff indeed. Although it built consciously and very effectively on the success of the Cuban Revolution, and on the ever more romanticized and rumor-filled legend surrounding Guevara, the MIR's construction of revolutionary masculinity also drew on elements of Chilean gender identities and sexual styles historically embedded in popular culture and politics."[90] Mirista commitment to revolutionary struggle was never in question. In fact, Communists, Allende, his moderate wing of the PS, and a good many others deemed the MIR radical, given their rejection of a peaceful and democratic way to socialism. Former JS Central Committee member Juan Carlos Moraga recognized the miristas as the "real revolutionaries." He added, however, that the MIR's reach was limited: it was "armed propaganda" rather than a guerilla army along the lines of Cuba's 26th of July Movement.[91]

Immediately after the minister's televised speech, leaders of UP's youth organizations met to discuss the melenas policy. The result was cut-and-dried: they criticized the move and called for the policy's immediate withdrawal. Their statement focused on two bones of contention. First, the ministry had not consulted with a single student group, which was troubling in light of how close UP youth groups worked with the highest echelons of the Allende government, including the Ministry of Education, on such matters as the National Unified School and the Trabajos Voluntarios. (Meanwhile, FESES President Guillermo Yungue, a pro-Frei Christian Democrat, opined that youth groups did not need to be consulted unless big systemic issues were involved.) Second, UP youth leaders made the prima facie claim that hair length was not an indicator of academic performance.[92] In the PCCh, it quickly became apparent that complaints from the Jota were serious, leading the "older generation" to express its support of the students' perspective. "Why pay so much attention to hairs and on the head and not what is in the head?" an *El Siglo* editorial asked—within forty-eight hours of the meeting held by the UP youth leaders. The newspaper added, "We are unfair to our young people because we commit sins of conservatism and prudishness."[93]

On March 11, 1972, less than a week after the policy's appearance, Minister Ríos held a press conference. "I gave a recommendation regarding the coexistence of long hair and students, not an order," he explained. Backpedalling was underway. He left the matter to individual school rectors, just as the ministry had done the previous year vis-à-vis miniskirts and melenas. He stated, "The directors of our instructional institutions will provide instructions so that students do not arrive at school with melenas down to the shoulders." This gave male students quite a lot of wiggle room; having some nice melenas did not necessitate shoulder-touching length. Ríos, however, could not help but express his personal view: "Some students wrongly think that [melenas] show personality, an advanced spirit. This impacts one's presentation because some students, when they are hurried, do not get to wash their hair, and this gives the impression of dirtiness."[94] In the end, the policy fell away into the shadows, disappearing from the press and from publications like *Ramona*. The lasting impression, however, is illuminating. The façade of Marxist discourse, which had stressed clean-cut (that is, masculine-revolutionary) conformity, especially after Piedra Roja, was being chipped away, and young Communists and other UP youth groups were holding the chisels. Culture was changing, and some Marxist youths were internalizing some of those changes in ways that skirted convention. This is not to say that mainstream normative views on gender, sexuality, and the like—captured in conceptualizations of the good young Chilean—were being thrown out the window. Rather, cultural space was opening up, enough to allow for flexibility and unorthodox creativity, perhaps helping induce the very "joy" Allende wanted young people to experience when building socialism and forging the "new man."

The melenas episode threw normative notions of revolution into question and lay bare the issue of revolutionary subjectivity, just as changing views on sex and sexual liberation among young Marxists did. It exposed a basilar question frequently debated among Marxists over the past century: What role does individual agency play, if any, in revolutionary change? If the working class is the revolutionary subject, as many Marxists declare, do one's individualist expressions—overt or subtle—have any real bearing? Moreover, Marxist-Leninism, which greatly affected the development of Latin American New Lefts, holds that a small group of dedicated revolutionaries, through sheer will and force, could bring about immediate and drastic change, thus paving the way for all to be transformed in the making of a new society. An individual mattered insofar as he or she was participating in a vanguard movement (bigger than the individual but not a class) that conducted the revolution. To Guevara, the "new man" was created through creating socialism, and that act had to have been started by someone or some group. That role fell to a revolutionary vanguard in the process of creating social solidarity through struggle. Again, who is the revolutionary subject or agent? A class? A vanguard? An individual? (Siloism had such an inconsistency as well.) Cultural and generationally specific change during the long 1960s, which saw particularly "revolutionary" aesthetics and practices, including melenas, sexual liberation, and rock, fostered a sense of individual agency fused with, and not in contrast to, more "macro" subjectivities in Marxist ideology. In other words, for a young Communist to sport long hair was a form of *personal* revolution that dovetailed, in his mind, with the work of a revolutionary vanguard and working class, or both, without contradiction.

Interestingly, Marxist groups—even those representing young people—did not tout marijuana (openly, at least) as a form of personal expression or as a means to spark revolutionary "joy." This stood in contrast to statements made by New Left leaders in the United States on the matter; one need only recall Rubin's utterance published in the Chilean press. The "escapism" of marijuana was an alarming matter among leftists in a developing country like Chile, where a "real" social revolution was afoot. What is more, whereas, say, long hair and sex were seen as *expressions* of consciousness that could constitute revolutionary agency, marijuana artificially *altered* consciousness altogether. Smoking pitos was an outside-in process, literally, whereas other manifestations of "revolutionary" agency were inside-out affairs. In a manner of speaking, such things as melenas (grown on purpose) and sex (the projection of needs and desires) were exhalations of an individual's consciousness, not inhalations of a false one. Furthermore, in this situation, melenas and sex were not considered commodities (although the latter can be commodified), while marijuana was, thus giving it "bourgeois" overtones when capitalist consumerism and commodity fetishism were under attack from the Left.

As we have seen, there were many "good young Chileans"—living and breathing ones as well as those constructed discursively—during the UP years. They played critical roles in defining, furthering, defending, and subverting Allende's government. Political parties encouraged their young members to exercise agency but also expected them to adhere to the normative outlooks and practices of the older generation. Friction emerged. The story here, then, is not merely one of powerful elders acting from above, but of empowered young people—especially those on the Left—who carved out room in their political and cultural lives to enjoy what they wanted to enjoy. In doing so, they forced older compatriots to adapt—if only incrementally—to changes happening transnationally, many of which were the doings of counterculture. The social, political, and cultural circumstances involving young people in the late sixties and early seventies were dramatic—the stuff of novels, really. Enrique Lafourcade thought so. Indeed, many of the good young Chileans discussed in this chapter, in addition to countercultural youths most everyone claimed were not (namely, hippies and Siloists), appeared in his 1971 realist novel, *Palomita Blanca*. Its popularity was immediate and became lasting, evincing the allure of Lafourcade's characters and settings, which throw light onto youth culture and sociability at an extraordinarily tense moment in modern Chilean history: the austral spring of 1970.

· ·

The year renowned poet and Communist politician Pablo Neruda captured international headlines for winning the Nobel Prize in Literature, another Chilean writer, Enrique Lafourcade, published a short novel that went on to become a popular culture fixture and a literary staple of secondary school curricula. His ninth novel, *Palomita Blanca*, which also coincided with Marcela Paz's release of her "Papelucho" tale *Mi hermano hippie*, is an exposé that interrogates what Lafourcade deemed to be the hidden and darker side of a countercultural upwelling that engulfed many young people and threw the "youth question" into greater relief shortly before and during Allende's Marxist national project. A member of the so-called literary generation of 1950, Lafourcade's novel foregrounds teen angst and escapism, countercultural ideas and practices, class issues, and parent-child discord in a story imbued with impossible love and political intrigue. Published in June 1971, *Palomita Blanca* (Little White Dove, a title derived from the common practice among young men to refer to young women as doves) follows the tribulations of teenagers Juan Carlos—attractive, blond, upper class, searching for meaning, and somewhat of a hippie—and María, the paloma. She is a caring, distressed, and sheltered young woman from the *bajo pueblo* (lower classes) who painfully narrates Juan Carlos's psychological, existential, and behavioral descent during the austral spring of 1970. Problems associated with counterculture get the best of Juan Carlos as he loses María and his own self, falls under the influence of a shadowy group of young people—none other than the Siloists—and makes terrible choices that affect María, his family, and the country. Unlike the fate of Papelucho's once-hippie brother, Javier, redemption never comes for Juan Carlos. Far more than *Mi hermano hippie* or, for that matter, any other youth-targeted work of fiction at the time, *Palomita Blanca* takes up counterculture as a thematic core and treats such issues as sexuality and drug use with a unique measure of frankness.

Lafourcade's biases, a penchant for overstatement, and often superficial treatment of counterculture become obvious to the informed critic. Nevertheless, *Palomita Blanca* provides an insightful and critical canvassing of manifestations and precipitating factors of the youth question. It also re-flects, in both overt and subtle ways, the prevalence of the society-wide con-versation about the youth question that swirled in the public sphere, while also providing ample tales of sex, drugs, and rock that, depending on the reader, were the stuff of excitement, repulsion, or ambivalence. In this chapter, I juxtapose Lafourcade's *Palomita Blanca* with the criollo counterculture—hippismo as well as Siloism—and an environment in which youths were touting quite different lines of thought and practice. In a man-ner of speaking, Lafourcade's narrative gives further shape to mine and, hopefully, mine to his, with the purpose of providing additional indications as to the people, spaces, conceptualizations, and general vibes that gave counterculture its form during the late sixties and early seventies.

Love, Loss, and Counterculture

Looking for adventure and whatever came their way, sixteen-year-old María and her best friend, Telma, had heard the enticing news: a rock festival was taking shape somewhere in the hilly reaches of eastern Las Condes. Early reports of happenings there had appeared in the media, piquing the excite-ment of two young women who intended to experience it. After departing from their working-class neighborhood in the municipality of Recoleta (just north of downtown Santiago proper), the young women had taken three buses, only to find themselves in Providencia—still a significant distance from the festivities. Luckily, young men passing by in a blue Austin Cooper caught sight of the seemingly lost María and Telma. Also on their way to the festival, the young men were obviously from the more affluent areas of Greater Santiago, and the driver—with blond hair flowing down to his shoulders—was especially striking, María thought. Much obliged for the young men's offer to give them a ride to the music festival, María and Telma squeezed into the car, thus entering an emerging, mesmerizing, attractive, and perilous countercultural world that neither young woman had yet experienced fully and one that Lafourcade sought to capture and critique for and in a society that was beginning to come to grips with it.

Upon parking on the outskirts of Las Condes, María, Telma, and the young men begin an uphill trek to where the festival—Piedra Roja—was un-folding. Once there, María observes, "There were tons of young guys and gals and all of them wearing pants and had guitars and necklaces," while also noticing youths enjoying marijuana openly.[1] María already had taken three drags from a pito in the Austin Cooper so as to impress its "beautiful" driver, Juan Carlos, a seventeen-year-old student at St. George's College (a private, prestigious, and exclusive Catholic school, with alumni that include Eduardo Gatti of Los Blops and many figures in politics and business). The young women were soon separated from Juan Carlos and his friends in the large crowd, and María would have to wait until the following day to see Juan Carlos again. In the meantime, María describes a countercultural scene, conveying amazement and curiosity. She and Telma notice several young blond women, including one distinguished by her obvious lack of a brassiere, and light-skinned and light-haired young men, many sporting beards; most everyone is wearing hippie-like clothes and drinking Coca-Cola. María and Telma's attention soon turn to couples engaged in acts of public affection ranging from kissing to outright sex, the latter of which prompts Telma to openly mention her titillation, to María's embarrassment. Lafourcade's dialogue and description suggest that Telma had already embarked on a road to some sort of "liberation" before the festival, but Piedra Roja further sparks her sexual awakening and stokes her affinity for *la hierba* (weed). Lafourcade describes, "Telma began smoking again and all of the youths already were half stoned from marijuana."[2] As the novel opens, then, María's character is cast as innocent but not ignorant of the types of pursuits that Telma and other young people were embracing.

Although their families would worry (including María's alcoholic mother), the young women decide to stay the night—an act of rebelliousness. But with darkness comes potential danger. That night, María, a survivor of molestation and rape perpetrated by her stepfather, Beno, drifts somewhere between dreaming and being awake, sensing somewhere in her consciousness and on her body the unwanted touches of someone—a young man who goads her to kiss him and to remove her pants. It is a sexual assault that could be a ghost from the past or evidence of the depravity of the present. "I started to scream among the dreams," María describes.[3] After waking, she sees that the zipper to her jeans is broken: an alarming sight but the only unusual thing she notices. She is wearing trendy jeans so tight that, fortunately and somewhat ironically, her assailant—presumably a real one—had been unable to strip them from her as she slept while nestled in the grass at Piedra Roja. The article of clothing that a more conservative person might see as overtly sexual apparently rescued her from a more aggravated sexual assault. Moreover, María learns of the rape of "a bunch of palomas" by social deviants who also had robbed festivalgoers of their belongings.[4] Obviously, reports and accounts of rape were believable and influential enough to move Lafourcade to include descriptions of sexual violence in his treatment of Piedra Roja in *Palomita Blanca*. In the broader scheme of things, what amounted to moral panic about counterculture's role in the sexualization and sexual liberation of young people was at hand, and constituencies across the sociopolitical spectrum shared it and expressed it.

Jolted but not turned off by the festivities around her, María later reunites with Juan Carlos and the two soon speed away from Las Condes in the latter's Austin Cooper, eventually arriving at the central coast—first at the upscale beach at Reñaca and later at the fishing village of Concón, both a short distance north of Viña del Mar. On the way from Santiago, and while listening to the Beatles, Juan Carlos turns to María and asks plainly: "Do you believe in God?" María says "yes" and that she is a Catholic. Juan Carlos snaps that the "Catholic God" does not exist. "A two-thousand-year farce," he asserts. "But there is a God! A New God!" Juan Carlos then exclaims. "But Juan Carlos . . ." María mutters. "A New God for a young and pure world!" he declares. At Concón, Juan Carlos takes off his clothes, challenging María to do the same. She does, shyly, joining him in the surf. "He began to take off his clothes," María narrates. "I was terrified looking at him. He was white, very white, and when he was naked I saw that his legs had yellow little hairs, the same as those on his head, and he also had blond hair 'down there.' He was thin and beautiful like an angel." Juan Carlos then lifts his face toward the sun and, with María, kneels in the surf. "Silo! Siiiii-looooo!" he yells. María is puzzled. Juan Carlos then announces that María, like himself, is now a Siloist—or at least a fellow traveler in a movement of young people who espoused a synthesis of ideas and practices that constituted an esoteric form of counterculture. "Yes, we're pure. Nobody will be able to separate us, ever." María soon asks, "And who is this Silo, Juan Carlos?" He responds, "A church . . . a real church." He goes on to explain, "We've been naked and bathed naked to baptize the body in the sea and in the sun."[5] Lafourcade thus uses the beaches and waters of the central coast as settings as well as metaphors. Juan Carlos and María, shortly after meeting at Piedra Roja, shed their clothes and enter the cold waters of the South Pacific, suggesting a sort of baptismal rite as they begin what becomes a very troubled relationship that ends tragically. Juan Carlos sees the ocean as a cleansing agent that kindles a rebirth of the soul and spirit. The central coast is, in essence, a haven for a character seeking transformation, just as it was a getaway for countercultural young people looking for freedom circa 1970. "Now, you're a member of my church," Juan Carlos tells Anna María. "You're of Silo, like me. No one can separate us now. No one."[6]

Their trip ends at Juan Carlos's home—"a palace," as María sees it. There, in his bedroom, are posters of the Beatles, Bob Dylan, Jimi Hendrix, Joan Baez, Judy Collins, and Che Guevara. For María, Juan Carlos's world is an alien one, just as she seems a different species to him. Earlier, for instance, María had asked Juan Carlos if she is pretty. Juan Carlos said, "You're somewhat dark skinned [media negrita] but really pretty." Indeed, María is rather "popular" in most every way, from her neighborhood to the professional soccer team for which she roots: Colo Colo.[7] Though a countercultural milieu had brought them together, María never truly bridges the conceptual and cultural gap between herself and Juan Carlos—a disconnect that proves to be one of the tragedies of Palomita Blanca. Juan Carlos makes only a feeble attempt to understand her world; she desperately tries to understand his. As the novel unfolds, María sees the chasm widen as Juan Carlos descends into self-destruction and nihilism, casting off the teachings of the "New God" he had embraced and into whose "church" he had self-baptized in waters splashing upon the beach at Concón.

As María falls deeply in love with Juan Carlos—her mind drifting away from her studies—his seemingly mysterious, if not dangerous, inclinations bring with them distance and periods of silence. María goes days and, at times, weeks without word from Juan Carlos, who, as Lafourcade suggests, is delving deeper and deeper into the ostensibly shady depths of the Siloist movement as the 1970 presidential election nears. Indeed, the winds of political change are blowing in the country, whipping up intense interest and hope in poor places like Recoleta. In the home María shares with her abusive mother, brothers, and stepfather, the Allende candidacy brings with it the expectation of dramatic change if UP were to win. María notes, "My mom would say that when Allende wins, they [officials of the new government, including union leaders] would give her a house they had taken from the rich—a good house."[8] During her family's discussion, María's mind turns to Juan Carlos's home (one filled with empty spaces), hoping that a revolutionary government will spare his family from hardship. Such hope stems from her love for Juan Carlos rather than some anti-allendista sensibility. In fact, María describes herself as an Allende supporter, though the ideological depth of that support is shallow.

While her friends reflect on smoking marijuana and other countercultural pursuits, María ponders Juan Carlos's worrisome and secretive ways, missing him desperately. Suddenly, Juan Carlos, driving his father's Mercedes-Benz, appears at María's house, hurried and excited. They drive westward toward the beach town of San Antonio where, as Juan Carlos tells

María, she will meet "the eponym." That eponym is "Bruno," the Siloist leader in Chile—the high priest of Juan Carlos's "new religion." One thing remains before María's induction into the group: an initiation, a test before the membership. She naively responds that she is not terribly good at tests, having scored a zero on a recent physics exam. The initiation, she fears, could involve something embarrassing. And it does. But Juan Carlos explains that the initiation involves shedding shame and embarrassment—freeing oneself from the "stigma" of that "original sin"—and that such transformation, if shared by all, would facilitate a "return to paradise." It would bring purity.[9]

Shortly thereafter, Bruno, described by Lafourcade as a man with lustrous eyes and one arm, asks María if she is a virgin, reinforcing the necessity of purity or purification as a precondition for full acceptance of Silo's teachings and membership in the movement. Indeed, Bruno suggests there is a test—something of a sexual nature—for anyone wanting to join. María hesitates, wondering if her stepfather's violation of her body meant the loss of her virginity, of her purity. Her conversation with Bruno then ends abruptly, as Juan Carlos and other Siloists tend to some business. Her anxiety is not lessened by Juan Carlos's admission that his initiation entailed transforming something rather private into something more public, thus freeing his self from shame or anxiety. He tells María that he had masturbated in the company of other Siloists in order to deprivatize the act—to shed its aura of embarrassment. But Juan Carlos adds (and seemingly to María's surprise) that sexual openness does not necessarily entail free love. He explains that among Siloists there is no sex before love; sex without love is bereft of real meaning and transformative depth. Here, Lafourcade seems to understand the difference between Siloist and hippista approaches to sex and sexuality.

As María becomes more exposed to Siloist ways, the political cauldron is churning. Members of her family take to the streets in support of Allende, with the hope that UP indeed would furnish them with a new home—with "a living room and everything," María adds.[10] Amid the excitement, Juan Carlos invites María to a café in the eastern (and affluent) reaches of the metropolis. Sitting in a most ardently anti-Allende neighborhood, Juan Carlos asks María for whom she will vote. For no one, she answers. But he persists. "Whom do you like?" he inquires. María again hesitates, recalling the words of a friend who had warned her that Juan Carlos probably supports conservative National Party candidate Jorge Alessandri in the 1970 election in light of his socioeconomic position, regardless of his

Siloist proclivity. "I don't like anyone," she responds. Juan Carlos goes on to explain that Alessandri will win because his father, a man with strong political connections, believes as much. "And you? Who do you like?" María asks. Juan Carlos becomes animated, exclaiming that he supports no one and that no Siloist votes. All three candidates—Allende, Alessandri, and Radomiro Tomic—are impure, Juan Carlos argues. Then, to prove his loyalty to Silo and his rejection of impurity, Juan Carlos admits that his father had been a government minister twice and now is a top official in the National Party, UP's principal foe.[11]

Juan Carlos's politics are a rejection of politics, and his actions, along with those of other Siloists, frighten María. At one point, Lafourcade creates a setting in which Siloists, with Juan Carlos among them and María in tow, confront conservative Catholic students demonstrating (presumably in support of Alessandri) on a bridge over Santiago's main river. The Siloists begin throwing rocks and other items at the Catholic youths—a group led by Juan Carlos's brother, José Luis. As the melee intensifies, Juan Carlos pulls a gun from his pocket and fires several shots toward his enemies, taking María by surprise, to put it mildly. Juan Carlos then tells María that he had "expropriated" the pistol from his father and that "now, things are going to start happening." María asks Juan Carlos if he feared wounding or killing his brother; Juan Carlos utters, "I wish I had killed José Luis." María reacts with a mix of indignation and incredulity, for she had never witnessed such violence between and among affluent youths.[12] Indeed, the scene foreshadows more notorious manifestations of violence—social, political, and generational—that will engulf Juan Carlos and his country.

Under such troubling circumstances, María reflects on spending time with her love, Juan Carlos. "And other times we'd go to El Drugstore, which was like a passageway filled with very elegant stores that were underground," she recalls for the reader. In one instance, as the couple strolled through the crowded enclosure, friends of Juan Carlos began to call his paloma "*la negra*" (or black or dark woman) in reference to her *mestiza* (mixed-blooded) complexion, which differed significantly from that of the rather white, European-looking Juan Carlos and clientele at El Drugstore. María was already aware of phenotypic markers of status, for she had specifically mentioned seeing many wealthy blond boys at Piedra Roja, just as working-class festivalgoer Jaime Román recalled the complicated and evolving racial dynamics at the event in Los Dominicos (see chapter 1). Under scrutiny from tactless commentary and extremely uncomfortable, María asks Juan Carlos if they instead could stroll through a plaza—a more public, "popular," and therefore welcoming space, away from El Drugstore's stifling, intimidating, and unjust social atmosphere. The young couple would also stop at the Coppelia café and Carnaby Street, a record store named after the shopping district and surrounding neighborhood in London where the Beatles and Rolling Stones participated in an underground music scene during the early 1960s. (The novel identifies the latter's owner as Juan Carlos's sister, Consuelo, whom the young man says is a MIR member.[13] Clearly, journeys out with Juan Carlos are difficult for María, but she values the togetherness— albeit ephemeral—they bring.

All does not go well for Juan Carlos among the Siloists. When asked by María if he had seen Bruno, Juan Carlos states that Bruno had not called. But Juan Carlos makes clear that he, Bruno, and others have a trip planned— Silo had called a meeting—and María would not be informed of Juan Carlos's destination because she is not yet a member. As Juan Carlos explains, Bruno believed María was too immature to join the Siloist cause. "Silo will change Chile! Do you understand? There are plans," Juan Carlos proclaims. "Be careful," María replies. "Carefulness! Silo doesn't fail! We're going to end the filth. Understand? Bruno says Silo is ready to make revelations, Bruno says no one will be the same afterward . . . and Bruno knows what he's talking about," Juan Carlos affirms. Juan Carlos then departs, disappearing for three days before María hears another word from him. When Juan Carlos reappears, he is unshaven, looks ragged, is dressed all in black, and is scared—as if fellow Siloists had maltreated him. Something has happened, María fears, and the young man seems transformed, his idealism swept away by an event or events he will not describe. Juan Carlos soon breaks down, crying in María's arms, pushing his head into her chest, as if the weight of the world taxed his body. Recomposed, he confides in María, "Silo has gone to shit! Understand?" He adds, "To hell with it! It's over! I only have you now, get it?" A few days pass before Juan Carlos, still in distress and drowning in cynicism, tells María that he had traveled across the border to Argentina, where he spent time with Bruno and a fellow named Mario—Silo himself (Mario Luis Rodríguez Cobos), the reader soon comes to learn.[14] As María narrates, "Juan Carlos hadn't told me about what had happened with Silo and the trip. One day he told me that he went out toward Mendoza, or nearby, in Argentina, and that he had been with Bruno, whom I never liked because he was missing an arm, and from the first time I saw him my heart skipped a beat as he was going to do something bad to Juan Carlos. And he told me that he had visited Mario, and I believe he said Mario Rodríguez or something like that, and he informed me that Mario was a sly one and that everything [in the world, Silo's move-ment included] was "shit."[15] Juan Carlos again says nothing to María about why he returned in such rough shape and with intense bitterness toward Silo. It remains unclear exactly what precipitated the fallout, but Juan Carlos's anger and angst spiral out of control as he denounces everything and every-one except for María, to whom he finally expresses his love, robbing María of her breath and filling her with happiness.

Alongside everything happening in the lives of Juan Carlos and María, the political situation is swirling, with Allende's win (later confirmed by the Congress) in the election and stories and rumors of conspiracies surfacing left and right. Juan Carlos's own family is being torn apart, with a sister, Consuelo, beholden to the MIR, a brother entrenched in rightist circles (possibly as part of the FNPL), and many other family members in the military and in government. Consuelo, for instance, castigates Juan Carlos for having Siloist sympathies, calling him a "reactionary without a social conscience."[16] In this respect, Juan Carlos's family was like many elite and nonelite families of the era, mirroring the nation's political struggles as they engaged in their own. Juan Carlos, meanwhile, grows closer to María—the only person in his world, he says—and begins to shed some of his mysterious-ness before her.

Juan Carlos, gripped by anguish, confides in María that he is a virgin. The Siloists, Lafourcade writes, had been looking for a "pure" young per-son, and Bruno had instructed Juan Carlos to remain chaste so that he may get in touch with the vibes of the earth. But Juan Carlos's fundamental prob-lem with the Siloists was intellectual rather than sexual. As Juan Carlos tells María, "That is, Bruno would say one thing and Silo would say an-other . . . and I was searching for something else, a third way, harmony. Understand?"[17] The young man had not found in Siloism the clarity for which he searched, the answers to life's vexing questions, and the peace that eluded him. His disenchantment with the Siloists had created a more emo-tive and loving Juan Carlos—toward María only—but had left a vacuous hole in his being, pushing him to the brink of insanity, Lafourcade sug-gests. Juan Carlos then asks María, "Do you love me a lot?" She responds, "A lot! A lot!" He continues, "Would you do anything I ask?" María answers yes. Lafourcade then subtly indicates they made love. But Juan Carlos's mys-teriousness soon resurfaces, as he disappears once more, for nearly two weeks. When María comes across mutual acquaintances, they inform her they had seen Juan Carlos and that he was acting quite odd. "He needs a psychiatrist," one friend notes.[18] María, who is in great pain, searches for

Juan Carlos, but to no avail, and she is unaware that grave happenings are forthcoming.

Whether the result of fate or sheer luck, María catches sight of Juan Carlos outside a grocery store. She approaches him and is taken aback by his tone and apparent disgust. "Who was it?" he probes. "Who was it?" she replies with confusion. He then asks with whom had she slept before their sexual encounter. "How many?" he demands. Juan Carlos begins to cry and to pound his fists against a storefront window. "Whore!" he yells. The confrontation, though brief, continues the next day, and, again, Juan Carlos, this time smelling of marijuana and with jealousy raging, demands to know who had taken her virginity and with how many men she had shared beds. She did not tell him of Beno, the violator, who had taken what Juan Carlos had wanted and expected. Another form of pain—corporeal—befalls Juan Carlos as well, as he is assaulted by his father, who had grown enraged by his son's lifestyle and outlooks. At one point, their conversation turns to counterculture:

Father: And you're leaving again?

Juan Carlos: I have things to do.

Father: Did you know I'm just arriving? It's been nearly two days since I've seen you. What are you up to?

Juan Carlos: Things . . .

Father: They called me from St. George. When might you pay them a visit?

Juan Carlos: I was sick, Father . . . really . . . if you want, I can get you a note from the doctor.

Father: If you fail this year, you're off to the Military Academy. Did you hear me? And I'm really tired of all the comings and goings of hippies and slackers.[19]

The father goes on to equate María—"*la negra*"—with dark-skinned, working-class prostitutes who frequent the corner of the avenues Américo Vespucio and Apoquindo in Las Condes. Juan Carlos then receives blows from his father's cane, blows of such magnitude that José Luis, the rightist who detests his brother Juan Carlos, intervenes to defend his sibling from the abuse. "You will remember me, wretch," Juan Carlos yells at his father. "I'm going to do something big, old man!" Battered and bruised, his body mirroring his spirit, Juan Carlos leaves and never goes home again. Making matters worse, Juan Carlos believes Siloists are following him, intent on punishing him for straying.

Paranoid, angry, and bruised by his father's cane, Juan Carlos soon confides in María that he is still in possession of his father's revolver, with which he threatens his father's life. Juan Carlos then disappears once more, and María searches for her love in the affluent neighborhoods of the capital. After coming across some of Juan Carlos's friends at a local hangout, his upper-class acquaintances pummel María with nasty epithets, all of which pertain to her working-class origin. During the barrage, María learns from a young woman that Juan Carlos had, quite interestingly and surprisingly, attended a dinner in La Dehesa—an elite borough—replete with *momios* (rightist thugs).

Reunited with Juan Carlos soon after, María and the troubled young man go to an apartment owned by his father, presumably the site of what was an ongoing extramarital affair. There, Juan Carlos pushes María toward the bedroom, telling her that he wishes to have sex, but María is alarmed by his tone. He then begins to break down once more, declaring, "All is destroyed." He then yells, "Everything is putrid! The world is rotten!" He then lunges upon her, frantically attempting to disrobe her as his weight presses on her body. María fears for her life as he pulls the covers over her and turns off the light. "Prove that you love me," he commands. She remains silent as the alarm clock ticks and tocks. Juan Carlos then begins to calm down, and as he nears María, she senses his warmth and affection. They make love, for the second time, which makes María scream—not from pain or fear but from pleasure, Lafourcade indicates. Afterward, Juan Carlos lifts himself from the bed and begins to dress. With shocking depravity, he then strikes the reposing María. "Whore!" he screams at her. Another lash meets her skin. With blood seeping from her mouth as she bites her own tongue and lips to keep from screaming, she receives yet another strike from his belt, as he repeats "whore!" She remains silent. "You don't have anything to say? Yell! Understand? Yell, whore!" María sees a crazed expression on Juan Carlos's face. "Speak! Say something!" he demands. "I love you so much, Juan Carlos," María responds, seemingly stunning her assailant. She then asks, "Do you have the pistol? Do you have it?" Without a reply, he stares, the belt falling from his hand. "Kill me, Juan Carlos! Please! Kill me now!" María exclaims.

Emotion overcomes Juan Carlos, and he collapses, crying, into the bed—and into María's arms. He kisses her, softly, as she trembles, and he asks for her forgiveness and professes his love for her. He then brandishes the pistol and declares that he will take his own life, pressing the gun's barrel to his head. Juan Carlos, hearing María declare her undying love, backs down and again pleads for her forgiveness. "I didn't know that I loved you so much. I didn't know. It's true," he tells her. But not long after professing his love and as they exit the apartment, Juan Carlos softly utters, "María, I'm going to do something, I promise, something that will require your forgiveness." Without inquiring, María shushes him, as if she were tired by his revelations, mysteriousness, and abuse. He persists, telling her that they would spend every day together, that they would marry, and that his devotion to her would make his past devotion to Silo seem insignificant. After dropping María off at her home, as he had done many times, Juan Carlos drives off— and out of her life, as she would soon realize.[20]

Short on sleep and long on worry, and two days after Juan Carlos's mental collapse and violent outburst, María hears alarming news over the radio: a shooting. General René Schneider, Chile's top military commander who had pledged to support the constitution and thereby defended the legitimacy of Allende's government, had been gunned down on the streets of Santiago during a botched kidnapping attempt. Here, Lafourcade firmly anchors his *Palomita Blanca* in the political intrigue and crisis that gripped Chile in October 1970, when, within two weeks of the Piedra Roja festival and a mere two days before the Congress voted Allende president of the republic, Schneider fell victim to an assailant's gunshots. The general had been rushed to the Military Hospital for treatment and was in grave condition, María learns. Rumors swirl that a state of siege would be declared in the capital, and matters turn worse when news of Schneider's death reaches a nervous public. María and her godmother witness the funeral procession, as the city's General Cemetery is nearby in their municipality of Recoleta. News then turns to word of a conspiracy of *momios* to murder Schneider and that police were rounding up suspects, including "young men of good families," as María narrates. Her concern mounts, and news of the arrest of a brother of one of Juan Carlos's affluent friends sends María into a panic. The name of right-wing General Roberto Viaux Marambio soon surfaces; he is the ringleader in his colleague's assassination and, in fact, had a history of plotting against civilian government, including a failed coup against Frei (the so-called *Tacnazo* in 1969).[21]

Juan Carlos remains absent, and María begins to suspect something terrible has happened. She decides to risk embarrassment and name-calling by paying a visit to Juan Carlos's parents. No one is home—and answers evade her once more. She tries again the next day, and Juan Carlos's maid answers the door. Juan Carlos was not home, but María persists in her attempts to learn something—anything—about her love's whereabouts.

The maid, sensing María's urgency, allows her to wait in the salon until Juan Carlos's mother descends from the second floor. The mother looks old, with white hair that was not present at their first meeting. She welcomes María's presence lovingly, and María begins to cry, knowing that such a response means dreadful things. "I came to know," she utters to the mother. Juan Carlos's father then descends, treating María as he had described her to Juan Carlos earlier, when he equated her with shabby, proletarian "whores." "There is nothing to know!" he shouts. As the mother runs to her room crying, María is left in the presence of Juan Carlos's angry and un-compromising father. He blames María for what is happening and claims that she somehow twisted his son's mind, perhaps because she is a Commu-nist. "Who sent you to spy, negra? Answer!" Two automobiles arrive out-side the home before María can defend herself from the verbal assault; she welcomes the interruption. Many people emerge from the cars. The ele-gantly dressed visitors look like lawyers, with light-colored hair, and José Luis is with them. Juan Carlos's father then orders the maid to show María the door. Although shaken by the treatment, María would have endured a beating if she could have only heard news of Juan Carlos, Lafourcade suggests. She returns home, delirious and with a fever, to the cheers of "Viva Allende!" in Recoleta, where the poor relished UP's victory and expected great deeds to improve their lives.[22]

María ostensibly becomes catatonic, not "awakening" again for weeks. Telma, her trusted friend, then reveals the tragedy—proving María's worst fears—in a stack of newspapers she had saved for her beloved friend with whom she had experienced Piedra Roja. María sees photos of Juan Carlos, with his brothers, reproduced in newspaper after newspaper, ac-companied with texts declaring them *momio assassins*," among other things, and bringing word that he had been arrested. She then reads of Juan Carlos's release and learns that he had been smuggled out of Chile by friends—possibly to Venezuela. Juan Carlos, it appears, had been among Schneider's kidnappers; he had been a gunman, the leader. In fact, his father's pistol had been used to kill the commander of the armed forces, pro-ducing a national scandal. María then recalls their final hours together—in love, with Juan Carlos pledging to never separate. But Juan Carlos also had said something else, something that had not provoked much thought at the time: that he would do something which would require her forgiveness. That forgiveness never came, but sorrow flowed easily and deeply. At times she would yell out for Juan Carlos. "Do you hear me?" "I love you very much, Juan Carlos. Very much," Lafourcade concludes.[23]

Reflections on the *Palomita*

In the novel *Nocturno de Chile* (*By Night in Chile*), published in 2000, Roberto Bolaño tells the story of a Catholic priest, one Sebastián Urrutia Lacroix, a right-wing intellectual and member of Opus Dei, who, nearing the end of his life, expresses regret for having aided the military junta—by way of teaching its members about the Marxism of their enemies, no less—soon after the coup of September 1973. At one point during his collaboration with the emergent regime, Urrutia finds himself conversing with General Augusto Pinochet Ugarte, to whom the priest shows extreme deference. When chatting about the types of books he reads, Pinochet mentions he had enjoyed *Palomita Blanca*. The general then asks the Jesuit to share his opinion of Lafourcade's story. "Excellent," Urrutia uttered. "I published a review of it and thought about it a lot." Actually, Urrutia had thought poorly of the novel, yet, it seems, he had hoped to bond with Pinochet over Lafourcade's critical treatments of youth radicalism and cultural heterodoxy.[24] The gesture is a shallow one on Urrutia's part, but it conveys what Bolaño construes as a vibe underpinning Lafourcade's novel that Pinochet would fancy. *Palomita Blanca*'s place in *Nocturno de Chile* also points to the fact that Bolaño, like many other Chileans, associated *Palomita Blanca* with the serious goings-on of the early seventies.

Palomita Blanca enjoyed immediate commercial success, with eight editions released by its publisher, Zig-Zag, in 1971 alone. The novel's effects were also immediate, according to former members of Poder Joven. They noted that Lafourcade's misrepresentations, most of which were the result of the author having read newspapers and magazines in an attempt to grasp Siloism, exacerbated an already tense situation for Silo's followers.[25] In subsequent years and decades, Chileans—of all ages and varying ideological dispositions—have read Lafourcade's novel, jogging and perhaps reshaping the memories of those who lived the road to socialism, and creating impressions among those who came of age in later years. More than sixty editions have appeared since 1971, with over one million copies sold.[26] What is more, *Palomita Blanca* became a staple of high-school literature courses in the 1980s, and today appears alongside the works of Shakespeare, Gabriel García Márquez, Edgar Allan Poe, and Ray Bradbury on students' reading lists.[27]

Literary merit and historical relevance do not necessarily coincide in novels of *Palomita Blanca*'s genre, and I leave Lafourcade's literary capacity for other scholars and critics to ponder. His novel provides readers much more than a tragic story of young love and loss; it provides a way into many of the perceived and extant problems of the late sixties and early seventies in a country experiencing sociopolitical turmoil and the challenges and opportunities of cultural change. Many of the issues and concerns associated with the youth question appear in the novel in very stark ways, including youthful rebelliousness, angst, and disconnects in intergenerational communication, not to mention sex, drugs, and rock music, which collectively speak to the sociocultural environment in which hippies did what hippies did and Siloists developed and practiced their doctrine. Such matters are components and indications of *Palomita Blanca*'s most striking and resonating message regarding the younger generation: danger lurks everywhere and regardless of class, with the genuine potential of inflicting grave damage on that generation and the greater society. Whereas Paz's *Mi hermano hippie* (1971) ends with a countercultural young man's sudden change of heart, his reincorporation into family life, and his return to proper sociocultural conduct, Lafourcade's novel offers no such resolution. Instead, Lafourcade leaves the reader on edge—Juan Carlos's whereabouts and the depth of his involvement in Schneider's murder are not divulged—and weighed down by María's suffocating sorrow. Of course, audience makes a difference, as Paz sought a younger readership than did Lafourcade, whose novel is gritty and explorative in ways *Mi hermano hippie* certainly is not. But intersecting both short novels is the notion that counterculture (whether hippismo or Siloism) is dangerous—to the mind, to the body, to the family, to everyone.

Lafourcade suggests the actuality of a rather slippery slope linking the countercultural footings, expressions, and perils of a rock festival in Los Dominicos to an arresting act of violence. At the risk of stretching a metaphor, Lafourcade suggests that the youth question and cultural change—as evidenced by sexual liberation, drug use, rock music, and the like—work as gravitational forces acting upon young people traveling that slope. Conditions that ideally would constitute braking mechanisms—such as the binding power of parent-child relationships and intergenerational communication—melt away in *Palomita Blanca*, as the reader learns of the dysfunctional home lives of the affluent Juan Carlos and the working-class María and their shared world. Moreover, those home lives are politicized—María's *allendista* family and Juan Carlos's firmly conservative brother and father are outspoken, for sure—but formal politics, in the end, makes little difference in María and Juan Carlos's relationship. In Lafourcade's twist on *Romeo and Juliet* and *West Side Story*, counterculture is the salient phenomenon that brings the young lovers together and tears them apart—not politics, family, or class, although these also matter, especially in regard to how Juan Carlos's friends and his father treat "*la negra*."

María and Juan Carlos's problems begin, for the most part, in the context of his devotion to Siloism, which Lafourcade depicts as the vague, esoteric, right-wing, and seemingly corruptive thought of a shadowy group led by a mysterious Argentine guru (Silo) and his man on the ground in Chile: "Bruno" (Von Ehrenberg, obviously). Siloism offers Juan Carlos a way to understand the universe, whatever that way may be; the young man sees it as a new religion, with expectations and rites, and considers Silo its progenitor and high priest. Juan Carlos's descent into unbridled anguish, unpredictability, paranoia, and violence coincides with his disenchantment with Siloism. While Lafourcade never reveals the details of that disenchantment, aside from brief references to dissent within the Siloist camp (possibly involving the schism that brewed between Silo and Von Ehrenberg), he subsequently depicts Juan Carlos as a young man bereft of psychological and cosmological moorings; Juan Carlos drifts out of view and into a circle of sociopaths bent on belligerence and tumult at a time when Chile's sociopolitical fabric is disintegrating with haste and the "youth question" is conspicuous. What is more, his plunge also translates into brutality toward María, who, while nearly broken by the emotional and physical consequences of her violation at the hands of Beno, endures Juan Carlos's accusations of her supposed sexual promiscuity without divulging her agonizing story about Beno's terrible transgression.

The body appears as a locus of renewal, authority, violence, and liberation. The Pacific Ocean, for instance, splashes upon Juan Carlos's body in what ostensibly is an act of revitalization. Juan Carlos and María explore each other's forms, while María hides her own scars—those inflicted by sexual violence at the hands of Beno and even her beloved Juan Carlos. Moreover, the power of generational authority wielded by Juan Carlos's father leaves his son bruised and emotionally scarred, while Juan Carlos's fits of spasmodic rage are brought to bear on María and, as Lafourcade strongly implies, upon General Schneider. In relation to music, meanwhile, *Palomita Blanca* harnesses criollo rock and a festival that accentuated it. There, at Piedra Roja, young people from varying socioeconomic layers openly share their sexuality and find something compelling about marijuana's effects on the body and mind. The crowd also includes many young men, including Juan Carlos, who see in long hair a measure of rebelliousness. Overall, then, experiences and signifiers of the body, in addition to impressions acted upon it and the mind, are central to the workings and study of counterculture, for counterculture not only reconceptualized the relationship of self and society but also reworked the very stuff that constitutes the self—the body as well as what Martin Heidegger called *Dasein*, or the "being-there" of consciousness.[28]

Another interesting aspect of *Palomita Blanca* is Lafourcade's even-handedness when illustrating and interpreting the political situation; both the Left and Right are butts of the author's disparagement.[29] As noted previously, María mentions her mother's belief that Allende would give the family a home seized from the rich by UP. Here Lafourcade hints at what he sees as simplistic promises made by Allende to reinforce the Left's support among the wishful masses. (That specific form of redistribution was not on Allende's to-do list.) Meanwhile, Lafourcade paints rightists—with Siloist connections, supposedly—as pistol-packing troglodytes, gripped by fear and driven to desperation in their mission to derail a democratic and pluralistic government. In fact, the Right had suggested that Siloists might have taken part in the killing of General Schneider in October 1970, but not as part of a right-wing conspiracy. The rightist newspaper *Tribuna* alleged in October 1971—a few months after *Palomita Blanca* appeared and in an attempt to deflect culpability—that Siloists had indeed committed the crime. It seems reasonable to think that Lafourcade's fictionalized account of Schneider's death had something to do with *Tribuna*'s ploy.[30] In the novel, Schneider is the victim of a Siloist but is not Siloism's only victim. Juan Carlos, too, is one. The young man becomes lost in hatred, coming to rest in the hands of manipulative *momios* who prey on Juan Carlos's personal crisis to advance the will of their class.

Lafourcade is not charitable in his depiction of Siloism, to put it mildly, and the novel quite purely reflects the tone of derogatory newspaper and magazine reports in 1971 on Poder Joven. To Lafourcade, the Siloist movement encapsulates much of what ails young people, to say nothing of overtones that suggest danger, strange rituals, and patently esoteric thought. In short, the Siloists avail themselves of the opportunities to recruit fellow young people while they and older generations experience the youth question. In *Palomita Blanca*, the Siloists are shady and mysterious, with only a minimal public face but with the potential of mobilizing a great many young people under the tutelage of Silo and his lieutenant in Santiago: "Bruno." While grounding *Palomita Blanca* and his treatment of Siloism in real people and current (now historical) events, including the Piedra Roja festival and Schneider's assassination (both in October 1970), Lafourcade does what the

Chilean media and public officials were doing: he glosses over a complicated Siloist philosophy that stressed pacifism, coherence of the mind and body, transcendentalism, and social, economic, political, and cultural transformation. Lafourcade's novel, in addition to animated press reports, went far in shaping Chilean public opinion regarding Siloism and counterculture in general. The novel first appeared in June 1971, months before the October scandal involving the alleged kidnappings of young women by the Siloists. One can only image how Lafourcade would have used those events as fodder.

This study, like *Palomita Blanca*, began with the characters at Piedra Roja. The counterculture that captured Lafourcade and Chile's attentions took root in the middle of far-reaching social and cultural change, to say nothing of political and economic transformations that were observed, lauded, and criticized around the globe. Counterculture was both an impetus and an effect of change, which included, among other things, reconceptualizing the self-society relationship, innovative ways of imagining and acting upon the body and mind, and pioneering forms of cultural production, reproduction, and practice. The countercultural milieu was a dynamic, swirling, and amorphous space—psychedelic, per se—that youths collectively created by undertaking even the most banal forms of sociocultural heterodoxy. Generated by the patent and the latent, the milieu was new sociocultural terrain to which characters like Jorge Gómez, Pink Lizard, Denise, and Bruno Von Ehrenberg—and Lafourcade's Juan Carlos and María, in a manner of speaking—contributed and in which they circulated.

As we have seen, counterculture was provoking discourse and debate by 1970 as mainstream actors increasingly became aware of its existence and of specific events involving hippies and Siloists. Many struggled to understand and come to terms with these phenomena. Others simply rebuffed them outright. Indeed, *Palomita Blanca*'s Juan Carlos is enigmatic in many ways, obvious in others. The reader never truly grasps the young man's thought processes or fundamentally comprehends what he needs, what he wants, or what he seeks, existentially or practically. Even if Juan Carlos's problems—or the ideas and manifestations of counterculture, for that matter—seemed knowable, they were deceptively so. Meanwhile, it proved challenging, if not impossible, for countercultural youths to escape the scrutiny of the press, the state, and civil society. Such circumstances were quite evident following Piedra Roja, which shoved an emergent counterculture to the fore. It focused and propelled anticounterculture sensibilities and gave them a sharper edge with which to slice into young people, including the intrepid young Jorge Gómez, whose music festival was, without a doubt, a defining moment. It also marked a turning point in terms of counterculture's public reception, transforming an irritant prior to October 1970 into an outright danger couched in a discourse of moral panic. Hippies and Siloists alike faced mounting public scorn and pressure as counterculture laid bare intergenerational discord, the body politic polarized, and class antagonism intensified, all of which Lafourcade captures. But as the months and years passed, cultural change proved powerful enough so that young people who might otherwise condemn countercultural young people found some elements attractive. This speaks to the relevance of generation and cultural change in a society where class and party dominated discourse and practices during the long 1960s.

Based on the novel and directed by prominent filmmaker Raúl Ruiz, the cinematic adaptation of *Palomita Blanca* was set to premier in late September 1973.[31] Yet, like Carlos Flores's *Descomedidos y chascones*, Ruiz's film would not appear on the big screen until after Chile's return to democracy in 1990. With a soundtrack by Los Jaivas, and starring newcomers Beatriz Lapido as María and Rodrigo Ureta as Juan Carlos, the film effectively portrays the country as it was: divided. Weeks before production started in the (austral) autumn of 1973, Ruiz explained to Quimantú's magazine, *Onda*, "It's not just a simple love story. I wouldn't be interested in filming that. I want to present, as a theme, two different environments. And in this I'm a realist: *Palomita Blanca* is the story of two worlds, that of the rich and that of the poor."[32] It is, for sure, but it also is a story of youth, counterculture, and politics on the road to socialism. Like Allende's national project, Ruiz's film was derailed by a military coup, shortly after which soldiers stormed and ransacked Chile Films, the state-owned production company. *Palomita Blanca*, still unfinished, was thought lost. Rediscovered in storage after the country's return to democracy, the film was re-edited by Ruiz, who had lived in exile, and debuted at the Viña del Mar International Film Festival in 1992. It earned much acclaim for its unconventional cinematography and editing, among other attributes.[33] The military coup of September 11, 1973, which toppled Allende's UP government, threw Flores's documentary on youth and Ruiz's adaptation of Lafourcade's novel into a shared state of suspended animation. Time stood still. That did not happen to the country. As the films collected dust, Chile changed dramatically in most every way when Pinochet and his collaborators ended the road to socialism and realized a new order, leaving more than 3,000 dead and imprisoning and torturing tens of thousands in the process.

Epilogue

In the period framed by the "Chilean road to socialism," a countercultural young person ran the risk of being chased and roughed up by the Ramona Parra Brigade or perhaps pummeled by the foot soldiers of the Fatherland and Liberty Nationalist Front. In some instances, accusations of kidnapping or marijuana possession landed countercultural youths in jail, and many others were ridiculed publicly, spat upon by passersby, and berated at home. *Palomita Blanca* did not help matters for hippies and Siloists, to be sure. Without downplaying such circumstances and happenings or the importance they had in the changing lives of young people who embraced heterodox ways of being, things got very much worse for a great many youths on and after September 11, 1973—the day of the military coup. To grasp this, one need only gaze upon the monument to the dead and disappeared on the grounds of Santiago's General Cemetery. Dedicated in 1994, it is an enormous marble wall inscribed with the names and ages of the military regime's identified victims, including some discussed in this book: Miguel Enríquez of the MIR; Bautista Van Schouwen, the mirista and brother of Siloist Jorge Van Schouwen; Nueva Canción icon and Los Blops fan Víctor Jara; and Carlos Lorca Tobar, former leader of the JS (Socialist Youth) and member of the Chamber of Deputies. When perusing the names, it becomes strikingly apparent just how many people under age thirty were killed. These young people were active in political parties, youth groups, unions, neighborhood associations, and other organizations across the Left.[1] The military regime's repression ran deep and spread widely. It crossed class and generational lines, and it struck far more people than those whose names appear on the monument's face. Hippies and Siloists were among those caught up in the maelstrom—simply because they were hippies and Siloists.

Jorge Gómez, of Piedra Roja fame (or infamy), was living east of Santiago, up in the Andean foothills, when the coup happened. The one-time subject of public scrutiny and ire had married, welcomed a child, and resided in what amounted to a hut in a hippie *comunidad*. Gómez and his first wife, whom he had met at his much-derided October 1970 festival in Los Dominicos, were growing their own food and living life their own way. On

September 13, 1973, Gómez and a friend, who together knew little of what had been taking place in the cities, were detained by a military patrol. "I was walking around in a tunic, with blond hair down to my waist, and they arrested me and said to me, 'You're a terrorist. You dedicated yourselves to making bombs,'" Gómez recalled. "They took away my ID card, my driver's license, and my PIFA, which was an ID that said I was a member of the Armed Forces [an old ID from his Naval School days], everything." The officer in charge accused Gómez of possessing false documentation and ordered that the hippie and his friend be held in an empty swimming pool. It happened to be on the grounds of the Casa El Cañaveral, a residence used by President Allende (owned by his private secretary, Miria Contreras), not far from where the Gómezes were living.

Four soldiers guarded him, weapons at the ready. Gomez recollected words the officer shared with his soldiers: "'At the first sign of anything, fire at them. No screwing around.'" The patrol then contacted the nearest Carabineros (in what is now the municipality of Lo Barnechea) to provide prisoner transport—to the National Stadium, where thousands of detainees were taken in the weeks following Allende's fall. An arriving Carabinero recognized Gómez, with whom he had been acquainted for some time. "'Hey, he's Jorge Gómez. I know him. He's a hippie. He lives up here. He has a young kid,'" the Carabinero blurted to the military office in command. Gomez recalled the officer's rebuttal: "'Don't you at all realize that we're in a state of war? These assholes are dangerous, so take them.'" Gómez and his friend were loaded onto a truck; it departed for the stadium. A few kilometers from Casa El Cañaveral, the truck came to stop. The rear door opened. Gómez's Carabinero acquaintance told the two prisoners to exit the truck—and walk away. "'Here we're screwed,'" Gómez thought to himself, expecting to be shot in the back. "I said to them, 'I prefer to go to the National Stadium,'" Gómez remembered. The Carabinero then explained, "'Look, Jorge, man, we've known each other for years, and you know what? Everything is going to shit, and in the stadium they are really killing people. Run back to your wife, tell all of your friends to cut their hair and don't come down [from the mountains] for a month.'" Gómez complied, in earnest, thus avoiding the realistic possibility that he would have been tortured and killed.[2] Thousands of detainees were confined and processed in Santiago's National Stadium, the country's largest outdoor sporting venue, in the months following the coup. Hundreds died there.

Others who appear in this book did not escape the treatment that Gómez had feared. Oscar Ortiz, a bohemian-intellectual hippie in those days, had experienced intolerance and shades of what he plainly identifies as repression during the Allende years; his anarchistic inclinations earned him few friends among mainstream leftists. "We already were clandestine by the time of the *golpe* [coup]," Ortiz remarked, cracking a smile. But, he said, his life changed dramatically on October 6, 1973, when he was arrested for involvement in a human rights group in association with his close friend, the noted Clotario Blest of the CUT or Central Workers' Union. The Human Rights Defense Committee (Comité de Defensa de Derechos Humanos, CODEH) was founded in 1970, toward the end of the Eduardo Frei administration, to defend workers who faced violence for demanding better wages and working conditions. When the coup occurred, the organization focused on the human rights violations of the military regime. Still a high school student when he was arrested, Ortiz finished an entire year of study in jail. He later became a historian of Chilean culture and radicalism, including anarchism.[3]

In March 1974, thirty-eight Poder Joven members were in prison. Among the detainees were Bruno Von Ehrenberg and another prominent Poder Joven member, Luis Fernando Lira. All but five of the thirty-eight were released within a few months, and many went into exile. Von Ehrenberg, Lira, and three other Siloist coreligionists experienced extended oppression—for more than a year—and were deemed sinister enough by military authorities to earn a transfer, under heavy guard, to the Pisagua Prison Camp, a notorious and long-lived detainment facility in the country's arid north.[4] There, the supposedly nefarious Siloists remained for nearly a year, in small cells, experiencing the deprivation and cruelty of a right-wing regime that (correctly) did not believe UP media reports of Poder Joven's rightist loyalties and "fascism." In February, the Inter-American Commission on Human Rights of the Organization of American States (OAS), made aware of the arrests by Amnesty International, created a case file: "*Case 1799*, February 21, 1974, reporting the arbitrary arrest of thirty-eight (38) members of the so-called Siloist religious sect in Chile. The events occurred on December 23, 1973, and on January 16, 1974. According to the report, the persons arrested (men and women) would be tried by a military court in March 1974." In a February 25 cablegram, the commission asked the regime to provide information as to the prisoners' whereabouts and legal statuses. The government responded on March 14:

1. The Siloist movement has, since its appearance, constituted a serious and continuing threat to public morality, public order, and

good conduct, and its leading members had caused public scandals and notorious trials in the ordinary courts of Justice for traffic and use of drugs, corruption of minors, etc.

2. That it could hardly be classified as a religious group and that its political character was fully documented and demonstrated by Chilean journalists (in particular by the investigation of Jaime Valdés [a writer for the right-wing newspaper *Tribuna*] made in early 1973), which established links between Siloists and the Chilean Marxist authorities and organizations.

3. That press campaigns against Siloists had occurred periodically since 1970, sponsored by defenders of the integrity of the family and Christian morality.

4. That, in the use of his legal powers, the officer in charge of the state of siege of the Province of Santiago ordered the arrest of the ten Siloists mentioned in the request for information of the Commission.

5. That Messrs. Leonardo Espinosa, Bruno Von Ehremberg [sic], and Nils Eric Knepfer Joansen were detained in the Santiago Prison and that a competent military court had Jurisdiction over the cases and would try them.

6. That Messrs. Fernando Lira, and Luis Felipe Carvallo were detained in the Chilean [National] Stadium and were not subject to military courts.

7. That Misses María Asunción Cuevas, Marta Bunster, Inés Essen Winkler, Isabel Luna, and Ana María Lavín were detained in the Women's Prison in Santiago but not tried by military courts.

8. That all the persons arrested were receiving just treatment and that it was absolutely false that they were deprived of an adequate defense since the Code of Military Justice provides appropriate measures for guaranteeing it, and the persons affected could appoint attorneys they trusted, and, if they did not do so, attorneys appointed ex officio by the court trying the case would assume that responsibility.

9. That the Government of Chile is not violating nor will it ever violate human rights and will remain faithful to the principles of justice and equity that make it possible and compulsory to investigate and prosecute the criminal activities of antisocial elements that are aimed at physically and/or morally annihilating members of the community, all of which, naturally, by means of pre-established procedures and with the intervention of competent courts in

accordance with the legal and constitutional provisions in force, and that the Government of Chile felt obliged to take energetic action, although strictly in accordance with law, in order to prevent the deceitful actions of groups or individuals that violate the fundamental rights of the human person such as his health and dignity, but it will be for the courts to determine whether they are really guilty and deserve punishment, or whether they are innocent and deserve to be acquitted.

10. That the terms of the report were unacceptable and the Government of Chile rejected them categorically, basing itself on the arguments set forth above and supported by the traditional Chilean policy of respect for human rights.[5]

In July 1974, the military government reported that many of the Siloists noted in the original February 25 inquiry, including Lira, had been freed. However, less than a month later, the regime informed the human rights commission that Lira was in fact at Pisagua, "in accordance with the powers which, under the Law of the State of Siege, the Political Constitution confers on the Executive Branch."[6] A Chilean official explained to the commission,

Furthermore, I am in a position to inform you that the Supreme Court of Justice [anti-Allende during the UP years and retained by the military government] denied by a decision handed down yesterday an appeal of amparo [closely related to habeas corpus in the United States] filed in favor of Lira, stating that bearing in mind the grounds of the resolution appealed and the fact that the transfer and deprivation of liberty of the person involved had been ordered by the administrative authority in the exercise of special powers and under the State of Siege in which the country at present is, the appealed decision is confirmed. The appeal of amparo had been denied earlier by the Appeals Court.[7]

This was the same Supreme Court that had been a principal player in the short-lived investigation of the handful of Siloists arrested in October 1971 on charges of kidnapping and, more to the point, for happening to be members of Poder Joven.

The travails of Von Ehrenberg, Lira, and their peers began shortly after the coup, when they received a summons to report to the offices of the PDI (Investigations Police). "We presented ourselves; they didn't have to look for us," Lira described. The Siloists had earlier declared to authorities that they constituted a religion, not a political movement, and thus hoped to avoid persecution. Politically active youths were being killed or arrested; the MIR, the Jota, the JS, and other revolutionary groups were being decimated. The group of five showed up at PDI offices in Santiago; they were promptly arrested and detained for a week. Upon release, they felt like the worst was behind them. However, a week later, another summons came. They again went to the PDI, this time with their girlfriends and, in the case of Von Ehrenberg, his wife. "There, they took us all prisoner," Lira indicated. "We [the males] never got out, and our partners were there for three months [one month at the PDI building and two months at a women's prison]." Lira and associates were in the PDI jail for a month, and then were sent to the Estadio Chile (Chile Stadium, an indoor sports facility). It was a horrific place of detention, torture, and death, where Víctor Jara had been murdered not long before the Siloists arrived. It was the first time the Siloists were in close contact "with the realities that were happening," Lira explained, adding that they had seen nothing egregious take place while in PDI custody.

There they were, guarded by Carabineros and soldiers inside Estadio Chile—a handful of bewildered Siloists sitting alongside members of the MIR, the Jota, and other revolutionary groups, as well as reverends from Protestant churches, soldiers who had deserted, and run-of-the-mill delinquents. Many of the detainees had the physical and emotional wounds of torture. Lira recalled that among the political prisoners in the stadium, the Siloists got along best with the miristas. "A more rebellious thing united us," he noted. The Communists, the Socialists, and others "integrated" into Allende's project, Lira observed, had gone about during the UP years saying that good things were happening, that things were good and would get better. The MIR and the Siloists had never agreed with those UP voices, and thus bonded under frightening circumstances in the stadium. As discussed in chapter 6, Lira had been a mirista before joining Poder Joven. He said it was ironic that he, a pacifist, ended up sharing terrifying moments with members of the very group he abandoned because it had embraced armed struggle. Lira and the others were at the stadium for two months. More harrowing experiences were yet to come.

"Many times I thought I would die," Lira recalled. He and his Siloist friends, along with numerous political prisoners, were flown by a military transport plane northward to Antofagasta, then taken by truck to Iquique, and then, finally, to Pisagua. The Siloists spent nearly a year there, each in his own cell, in isolation, except when they had to relieve themselves. They were the only ones at Pisagua in solitary confinement, Lira said, which spoke to just how little the captors, who understood Marxists, knew about Siloism. "It was an incomprehensible thing," he said, shaking his head. "People fear what they don't understand." Lira and the others were beaten often and subjected to psychological torture by soldiers, "some more savage than others." And just when guards would start to realize that the Siloists were not dangerous, a duty rotation would take place. A new crop of guards would arrive. More beatings, more torture. Lira explained, "I saw things that left me crazy. I tell you, if I had not had the tools of Siloism in jail I don't really know how I would have emerged from it." Meditation and "personal work" saw him through, he assured.

Lira also remains grateful for the pressure put upon the military regime by Amnesty International and the OAS, which, he believes, triggered his release in late 1974. The nightmare was not yet over, however. A week after his exit from Pisagua, Lira again was summoned by the PDI. This time, he did not go. With the help of a Lutheran minister in Santiago, Lira gathered enough funds to escape to Spain. There, with Poder Joven books in hand, he helped spread the Siloist message, not returning to Chile until 1989.[8] As for Von Ehrenberg, authorities released him in November 1974 along with nearly one hundred other detainees, including Manuel Cabieses, editor of the MIR's *Punto Final*. It is an interesting coincidence that the fates of Von Ehrenberg and Cabieses, whose newspaper attacked Poder Joven, became intertwined. Allowed to leave Chile, Von Ehrenberg settled in London, where he remained committed to disseminating the books written during the UP period by "H. Van Doren." Estranged from Silo for many years, the enigmatic Von Ehrenberg died in 2013.

The repression that hippies, Siloists, and other heterodox young people faced was carried out by a military and national police who had witnessed the media's anticounterculture onslaught in the wake of Piedra Roja. In fact, as seen above, the regime made specific reference to the media in one of its replies to an OAS human rights committee query regarding the Siloists. Constructions and representations of "the hippie" and "the Siloist" in the public sphere were such that the military and police did not know with whom they were really dealing. "There was a defamatory campaign against us [Siloists]," Lira described. "People, if they met us, would put us at arm's length—to observe us from a distance to see who we were. They didn't know how to treat us. I believe all of that contributed. The military government already had an image [of Siloism]."[9] As a result, pacifists were sent to Pisagua. Gómez was "dangerous"—standing there, in a tunic, with long hair, under guard in an empty swimming pool—and was possibly a bomb maker, to boot. It all seems absurd. Yet, for years, hippies (and Siloists) had been characterized publicly as delinquents, drug addicts, perverts, kidnappers, threats to morality, either purveyors of right-wing imperialism or left-wing libertinism, and well on their way to being criollo versions of Charles Manson. Those things took a toll.

Some in uniform, however, understood heterodox ways of life, for they had participated in aspects of counterculture's growth and practices. A former Parque Forestal hippie of working-class stock, Jaime Román loved his hippismo. He had a fetching melena, smoked pitos, listened to criollo and imported rock, and had been at Piedra Roja, where he bonded, in generational terms, with others around him, even with the wealthiest coléricos, if only for a short time. On October 10, 1973, just weeks after the coup, he was drafted into the army. For a hippie who had enjoyed the festival in Los Dominicos, which began *three years to the day* before he was called to military service, life as a soldier was a tremendous shock. "Imagine that! Me, in the service," he remarked. Of course, the army shaved Román's head, but that was the least troubling aspect of being a conscript during the early years of the dictatorship. Román witnessed many "very unpleasant things," about which he wished not to elaborate. "I was a different person after my service," he explained. "I was no longer the kid who went to Piedra Roja. I had the same body, the same face, but there was a change of mentality."[10]

The regime sought to remake youth, just as it remade Román in some ways. It endeavored to create good young Chileans who would perpetuate and conform to a set of values that focused on capitalist development and nationalism.[11] The activism of previous years was wiped away; the once-vibrant student federations, along with political parties and organizations, no longer existed. A politics of antipolitics reigned, and youths were expected to replace political energies with a commitment to Pinochet's project for the patria.[12] Pinochet understood the importance of young people in his *proceso*, and thus in October 1973 established the military regime's National Secretariat for Youth (Secretaría Nacional de la Juventud, SNJ). In their study on the dictatorship's first decade, Verónica Valdivia, Rolando Álvarez, and Julio Pinto describe the SNJ as a multifaceted mechanism with which the dictatorship strove "to funnel the inquietudes of [youth]" into the work of "national reconstruction." While many youth organizations remained illegal in the years following the coup, some, like the FEUC (Federation of Students of the Catholic University), were rebooted to serve the regime's interests. Meanwhile, an apolitical-political idealism, enveloped in nationalism, framed the work of the SNJ's principal departments: Culture (in charge of media and various artistic pursuits); Sports (to oversee competitions); Youth Wellness (training, job placement, scholarships, and the like); Special Programs (community and summer work, among other things); and Women (which coordinated activities and provided training in such areas as sewing and hairdressing in order to "produce extra income in the family").[13]

To celebrate the first anniversary of the SNJ's founding, Pinochet made clear just how different the truly good young Chilean would be from the many conceptions of him or her that had been championed previously. To move forward, he argued, young people essentially had to go back: "The same people who despised our historical tradition arrived, in its extreme expression, at wanting to remake the Chilean, as if the spirit of a nation is something fabricated in an ideological laboratory. Therefore, we reject as absurd and unnatural the awkward attempt to create a 'new man' with whom Marxism-Leninism seeks to disguise its contradictions and falsehoods."[14] Junta member and Commander of the Air Force Gustavo Leigh called on all young compatriots to "love Chile" and support a "regimen that is profoundly nationalist." He then declared, "Never again will foreign ideologues and fighters replace the role of the founders of our nationality. Never more will bad foreign influences make it so we Chileans look at each other with hate and rancor."[15] The careful use of the word "bad" allowed for "good" foreign influences—international capital circuits, multinational corporations, neoliberalism, globalization, and so forth—to flourish in Chile for many years to come.

For Chilean Siloists, the dictatorship meant repression but spurred the movement's growth and dissemination outside the country. Poder Joven members had already been taking Silo's teachings abroad during the UP era, and some escaped the violence of the coup by virtue of being outside the country when it happened.[16] Pía Figueroa Edwards, who was among the Poder Joven members arrested in September 1971, was not in Chile when the coup took place—a stroke of good fortune, she surmises. Along with a group of fellow Siloists, Figueroa had traveled to spread Siloist thought to such faraway places as the Philippines amid a worldwide upsurge in interest in esoteric philosophy during the 1970s. Absent for much of the dictatorship, she returned to Chile and contributed to the formation in 1984 of a Siloist political initiative that became the Humanist Party (Partido Humanista, PH), which played a role (albeit minor) in Chile's democratic transition after the plebiscite of 1989.[17] The PH was the first political party to begin operating during the latter years of the Pinochet regime—a fact attributable to the Humanists' courage and, likely, to the military government's realization that a comparatively small group of nonviolent, middle-aged "hippies" posed little threat. Internationally, meanwhile, Siloism took on other names, including "The Community" and "The Movement," and by the 1990s had led to Humanist political movements and parties in more than one hundred countries. The PH's formation in Chile demonstrated just how far Siloism had evolved since the early 1970s. The dictatorship had everything to do with it, Figueroa and Silo noted.[18] Politics and parties—hierarchies and all—were more preferable than the bayonets of bureaucratic authoritarianism and were better than the military regime's antipolitics, although Siloists today remain committed to self-transformation's centrality in the making of a more just world. Thus, it became acceptable among the Siloists to be a middle-aged political leader, since the paradigm shifted and time moves on.

Whether directly involved in parties or not, Siloist humanists in Chile and elsewhere have maintained many of Poder Joven's core concepts—nonviolence, the healing of suffering, and the transformation of the self, primarily—and have engaged the political issues of new contexts by championing abortion rights, the legalization of divorce, the rights of homosexuals, and environmentalism.[19] In 2004, on the thirty-fourth anniversary of "The Healing of Suffering," Silo and his followers again met at Punta de Vacas. "Total revolution" had not materialized. Humanity remained engulfed in desire and the suffering of minds and bodies. But hope remained. "We have failed . . . but we keep pressing on! We have failed but keep pressing on with our project of humanizing the world. We have failed and we will continue to fail, not just once but a thousand times again, because we ride on the wings of a bird called 'Intent' that soars above frustration, weakness, and pettiness," Silo declared. "Because this is not the end of History, nor the end of ideas, nor the end of mankind; neither is it the definitive triumph of wickedness and manipulation. And for this reason we can always continue on in our attempt to change things and to change ourselves."[20]

Jorge Gómez would agree. He kept moving forward after his life changed dramatically in October 1970 with Piedra Roja. It took more than a decade after his across-the-board expulsion from Liceo No. 11 for Gómez to finish his secondary education. By the time he graduated from an adult night school in Greater Santiago's municipality of Conchalí, he had seven children and lacked the time or resources to pursue a university degree. After working a number of jobs, including stints as a pub owner in the picturesque southern town of Pucón and as a flight attendant, Gómez became involved in his country's burgeoning wine industry, entering the wine-export business during the 1990s. He was, for a time, the leading seller of Chilean wine in China before taking on other white-collar jobs. When reflecting upon the apparently neoliberal and unhippie lifestyle that marked much of his work (typified by business deals, power lunches, cellular telephones, and the like), the grandfather declared in a 2003 interview, "Perhaps aesthetically and in terms of appearance there are modifications, but what is hippie still remains [in me]. When I lived in a hippie community it gave me no shame to take off my clothes, and today I perfectly can go to a Club Med and be naked in front of others because I still find it really enjoyable and healthy."[21] A few years later, Gómez noted, "To be a hippie I don't have to be running around in red pants and a yellow shirt with flowers on it. It's a way of life, how one educates his children, about the communication you have with your partner [and] to enjoy the simple things." As for his family, Gómez added, "They are proud of me."[22]

It seems apropos to end this study where it began: the hilly terrain of eastern Las Condes. There, an enormous boulder distinguished the grounds where hippismo exploded onto the sociocultural scene in October 1970 in the form of Goméz's festival. Upon that boulder hippies sat, and beside it they took refuge from the sun. Around it, they reveled in the music of Los Jaivas, Los Blops, Los Ripios, and others, shared pitos, and made love and friends on Luis Rosselot's land. As it happens, the enormous rock, called the *piedra rajada*, or cracked rock, had given the festival one of its original names (Festival Piedra Rajada) before the media morphed it into "Piedra Roja." Over the years, the boulder became a reminder—an artifact, really—of a previous era with a much different vibe. In 2008, dynamite blew the rock to pieces, to clear land for a housing development. The *piedra rajada* stood near where El Alba Road, along which many festivalgoers trekked to the festival from the closest bus stop, today crosses the aptly named Piedra Roja Road. Former hippies lamented the titanic boulder's loss but found some solace in knowing that landscapers used its rubble in the area's only ecological preserve. The *piedra rajada* is gone, and so is hippismo, as it existed at the dawning of the Age of Aquarius. The military regime repressed it, yes, but times also changed. New countercultural currents—punk, Goth, and others—emerged over the years in its wake. The Chilean Siloists remain, but changed in consequential ways, as evidenced by their engagement in party politics. But then again, hippismo and Poder Joven were all about change.

Notes

Introduction

1. Jorge Gómez Ainslie, telephone interview by author, October 2007.

2. On the UP years, see Joaquín Fermandois, *La revolución inconclusa: La izquierda chilena y el gobierno de la Unidad Popular* (Santiago: Centro de Estudios Públicos, 2013); Pedro Milos, ed., *Chile 1971: El primer año de gobierno de la Unidad Popular* (Santiago: Ediciones Universidad Alberto Hurtado, 2013); Pedro Milos, ed., *Chile 1972:. Desde "El Arrayán" hasta el "paro de octubre"* (Santiago: Ediciones Universidad Alberto Hurtado, 2013); Pedro Milos, ed., *Chile 1973: Los meses previos al golpe de Estado* (Santiago: Ediciones Universidad Alberto Hurtado, 2013); Arturo Valenzuela, *The Breakdown of Democratic Regimes: Chile* (Baltimore: Johns Hopkins University Press, 1978); Luis Corvalán, *El gobierno de Salvador Allende* (Santiago: LOM Ediciones, 2003); Paul E. Sigmund, *The Overthrow of Allende and the Politics of Chile, 1964-1976* (Pittsburgh, PA: University of Pittsburgh Press, 1977); and Tomás Moulian, *Conversación interrumpida con Allende* (Santiago: LOM Ediciones, 1998).

3. In 1970, 26 percent of a total population of roughly nine million fell between the ages of fifteen and twenty-nine, with another 39 percent under age fifteen. Chile was a "young" country getting a bit younger every year. Markos J. Mamalakis, *Historical Statistics of Chile* (Westport, CT: Greenwood, 1980), 2:69–72. Electoral reform in 1970 also granted suffrage to illiterates. Patricio Navia, "Participación electoral en Chile, 1988–2001," *Revista de Ciencia Política* 24, no. 1 (2004): 87.

4. Ricardo Pozas Horcasitas, "El quiebre del siglo: los años sesenta," *Revista Mexicana de Sociología* 63, no. 2 (August–June, 2001): 171.

5. Ibid., 169–91.

6. David Farber, ed., introduction to *The Sixties: From Memory to History* (Chapel Hill: University of North Carolina Press, 1994), 2.

7. "Las elecciones y los deberes del movimiento estudiantil," *Claridad* (Santiago), June 29, 1970; Fabio Moraga Valle, "Ser joven pero no ser revolucionario: La juventud y el movimiento estudiantil durante la Unidad Popular," in *Frágiles suturas: Chile a treinta años del gobierno de Salvador Allende*, ed. Francisco Zapata, (Mexico City: El Colegio de México, 2006), 402–3.

8. Eric Zolov, "Expanding our Conceptual Horizons: The Shift from an Old to a New Left in Latin America," *A Contracorriente* 5, no. 2 (Winter 2008): 50–51. Zolov makes this argument in regard to Latin American countercultures in general during the "long 1960s" (1959–1973).

9. Silo (Mario Luis Rodríguez Cobos), interview by author, Tunquén, Chile, June 2005.

10. As Zolov notes, the term "grassroots Left" might be useful in place of "New Left." Zolov, "Expanding our Conceptual Horizons," 50. Also see Van Gosse, *Rethinking the New Left: An Interpretative History* (New York: Palgrave Macmillan, 2005); Van Gosse, "A Movement of Movements: The Definition and Periodization of the New Left," in *A Companion to Post-1945 America*, ed. Jean-Christophe Agnew and Roy Rosenzweig (London: Blackwell, 2002); Jeffrey Gould, "Solidarity under Siege: The Latin American Left, 1968," *American Historical Review* 114, no. 2 (April 2009): 348–75; and Greg Grandin, *The Last Colonial Massacre: Latin America in the Cold War* (Chicago: University of Chicago Press, 2004).

11. On the Old Left/New Left relationship, see Vania Markarian, "Sobre viejas y nuevas izquierdas. Los Jóvenes comunistas uruguayos y el movimiento estudiantil de 1968," *Secuencia* 81 (September.–December 2011): 161–86; Alfonso Salgado, " 'A Small Revolution': Family, Sex, and the Communist Youth of Chile during the Allende Years (1970–1973)," *Twentieth Century Communism* 8 (Spring 2015): 64; and Zolov, "Expanding our Conceptual Horizons."

12. Salvador Allende, *The Salvador Allende Reader*, ed. James D. Cockroft (Melbourne: Ocean Press, 2000), 264, 38, 214. Also see César Albornoz, "La cultura en la Unidad Popular: Porque esta vez no se trata de cambiar un presidente," in *Cuando hicimos historia:. La experiencia de la Unidad Popular*, ed. Julio Pinto Vallejos, (Santiago: LOM Ediciones, 2005), 147–76; Martín Bowen Silva, "El proyecto sociocultural de la izquierda chilena durante la Unidad Popular. Crítica, verdad e inmunología política," *Nuevo Mundo-Mundos Nuevos* 8 (2008), http://nuevomundo .revues.org/13732. Enrique Lihn offers a nuanced approach, using Marcuse to understand the repression of artistic expression under capitalism. Consult Lihn, "Política y cultura en una etapa de transición al socialismo," in *La cultura en la vía chilena al socialismo*, ed. Lihn (Santiago: Editorial Universitaria, 1971), 15–72.

13. Allende, a physician and Mason from the middle class, and other top UP leaders (both from the PCCh and the PS) were bourgeois in origin, as were many Marxist revolutionaries in Europe and the Americas. In Chile, as Paul E. Sigmund observes, Allende's " 'bourgeois' taste in dress, drink, and the enjoyment of the good life made him less threatening to the middle and upper classes than a more proletarian candidate—although there was never any doubt of his commitment to the poor and the oppressed." Sigmund, *Overthrow of Allende*, 24.

14. Salgado, " 'Small Revolution,' " 62–88.

15. On mass media and cultural power, see Herbert Schiller, *Mass Communications and American Empire* (New York: A. M. Kelley, 1969). James Naremore and Patrick Brantlinger define "mass culture" as the combination of the "culture of the masses" and "culture mass-produced by industrial techniques." "Introduction: Six Artistic Cultures," in *Modernity and Mass Culture*, ed. James Naremore and Patrick Brantlinger (Bloomington: Indiana University Press, 1991), 1–2. Also consult Andreas Huyssen, *After the Great Divide: Modernism, Mass Culture, Postmodernism* (Bloom-

ington: Indiana University Press, 1986), and Armand Matterlart, Mabel Piccini, and Michèle Mattelart, *Los medios de comunicación de masas: La ideología de la prensa liberal* (Buenos Aires: El Cid Editor, 1976).

16. Zolov defines "Global Sixties" as "a new conceptual approach to understanding local change within a transnational framework, one constituted by multiple crosscurrents of geopolitical, ideological, cultural, and economic forces. Such forces produced a simultaneity of 'like' responses across disparate geographical contexts, suggesting interlocking causes. For Latin Americanists, the historiographical transformation under way is reflected in a new approach whose interpretations move beyond viewing Latin America in the 'long sixties' through the lens of imperialism and anti-imperialist struggle—a narrative overwhelmingly shaped by a presumption of U.S. hegemony—and toward a more complex understanding of Latin America as an incubator *for* and a progenitor *of* the imagery, actors, ideas, and soundscapes that constituted a 'Global Sixties.'" Eric Zolov, "Introduction: Latin America in the Global Sixties," special issue, *The Americas* 70, no. 3, (January 2014): 354.

17. Ibid., 349, 355–59.

18. See Eric Zolov, *Refried Elvis: The Rise of the Mexican Counterculture* (Berkeley: University of California Press, 1999) and "Showcasing the 'Land of Tomorrow': Mexico and the 1968 Olympics," *The Americas* 61, no. 2 (October 2004): 159–88; Jaime Pensado, *Rebel Mexico: Student Unrest and Authoritarian Political Culture During the Long 1960s* (Stanford, CA: Stanford University Press, 2013); Jaime Pensado, "'To Assault with the Truth': The Revitalization of Conservative Militancy in Mexico During the Global Sixties," *The Americas* 70, no. 3 (January 2014): 489–521; Elaine Carey, *Plaza of Sacrifices: Gender, Power, and Terror in 1968 Mexico* (Albuquerque: University of New Mexico Press, 2005); Victoria Langland, *Speaking of Flowers: Student Movements and the Making and Remembering of 1968 in Military Brazil* (Durham, NC: Duke University Press, 2013); Christopher Dunn, *Contracultura: Alternative Arts and Social Transformation in Authoritarian Brazil* (Chapel Hill: University of North Carolina Press, 2016); Christopher Dunn, *Tropicália and the Emergence of a Brazilian Counterculture* (Chapel Hill: University of North Carolina Press, 2001); Valeria Manzano, *The Age of Youth in Argentina: Culture, Politics, and Sexuality from Perón to Videla* (Chapel Hill: University of North Carolina Press, 2014); Vania Markarian, *Uruguay, 1968: Student Activism from Global Counterculture to Molotov Cocktails* (Berkeley: University of California Press, 2016); Francisco Barbosa, "July 23, 1959: Student Protest and State Violence as Myth and Memory in León, Nicaragua," *Hispanic American Historical Review* 85, no. 2 (May 2005): 187–221; Benjamin A. Cowan, *Securing Sex: Morality and Repression in the Making of Cold War Brazil* (Chapel Hill: University of North Carolina Press, 2016); Ricardo Pozas Horcasitas, "El quiebre del siglo: Los años sesenta," *Revista Mexicana de Sociología* 63, no. 2 (April–June, 2001): 169–91; Herbert Braun, "Protests of Engagement: Dignity, False Love, and Self-Love in Mexico during 1968," *Comparative Studies in Society and History* 39, no. 3 (July 1997): 511–49; Maria Ribeiro do Valle,

1968: O diálogo é a violência: Movimento estudantil e ditadura militar no Brasil (São Paulo: Editora de Unicamp, 1999); and João Roberto Martins Filho, *Movimento estudantil e ditadura militar, 1964–1968* (São Paulo: Papirus, 1987).

19. Manzano, Age of Youth, 5–6, 186–190; and Vania Markarian, "To the Beat of 'The Walrus': Uruguayan Communists and Youth Culture in the Global Sixties," *The Americas* 70, no. 3 (January 2014): 363–92. Also see Zolov, "Introduction: Latin America in the Global Sixties," and Dunn, Contracultura, 8–13.

20. See Patrick Barr-Melej, *Reforming Chile: Cultural Politics, Nationalism, and the Rise of the Middle Class* (Chapel Hill: University of North Carolina Press, 2001); and Stefan Rinke, *Cultura de masas: Reforma y nacionalismo en Chile, 1910–1931* (Santiago: DIBAM, 2002).

21. See Víctor Muñoz Tamayo, *Generaciones, juventud universitaria e izquierdas políticas en Chile y México* (Santiago: LOM Ediciones, 2012); Manuel Antonio Garretón, *Universidades chilenas: Historia, reforma e intervención* (Santiago: Editores Sur, 1987); Manuel Antonio Garretón, "Universidad y política en los procesos de transformación en Chile, 1967–1973," *Pensamiento Universitario* 14, no. 14 (October 2011): 71–90; Luis Cifuentes Seves, ed., *La reforma universitaria en Chile, 1968–1973* (Santiago: Editorial Universidad de Santiago, 1997); Sergio Salinas Cañas, *En tres letras: Historia y contexto del Movimiento de Izquierda Revolucionaria* (Santiago: RIL Editores, 2013); Cherie Zalaquett, *Chilenas en armas: Testimonio e historia de mujeres militares y guerrilleras subversivas* (Santiago: Catalonia, 2009); Eugenia Palieraki, *¡La revolución ya viene!: El MIR chileno en los años sesenta* (Santiago: LOM Ediciones, 2014); Marian Schlotterbeck, "Everyday Revolutions: Grassroots Movements, the Revolutionary Left (MIR), and the Making of Socialism in Concepción, Chile, 1964–1973," (PhD diss., Yale University, 2013); Cristina Moyano Barahona, *MAPU, o la seducción del poder y la juventud* (Santiago: Ediciones Universidad Alberto Hurtado, 2009); and Cristina Moyano Barahona, *El MAPU durante la dictadura* (Santiago: Ediciones Universidad Alberto Hurtado, 2010). Also consult Sergio Martínez, *Entre Lenin y Lennon: La militancia juvenil en los años 60* (Santiago: Mosquito Comunicaciones, 1996); and Gabriel Salazar Vergara, *Historia contemporánea de Chile*, vol. 5, *Niñez y juventud* (Santiago: LOM Ediciones, 1999).

22. The published studies that go farthest are Yanko González and Carles Feixa, eds., *La construcción histórica de la juventud de América Latina: Bohemios, rockanroleros y revolucionarios* (Santiago: Editorial Cuarto Propio, 2013); and Felipe del Solar and Andrés Pérez, *Anarquistas: Presencia libertaria en Chile* (Santiago: RIL Editores, 2008). Mentions appear in Rolando Álvarez Vallejos, *Arriba los pobres del mundo: Cultura e identidad política del Partido Comunista de Chile entre Democracia y dictadura, 1965–1990* (Santiago: LOM Ediciones, 2004); Julio Pinto Vallejos, ed., *Cuando hicimos historia: La experiencia de la Unidad Popular* (Santiago: LOM Ediciones, 2005); and some works on rock music, including David Ponce, *Prueba de sonido: Primeras historias del rock en Chile, 1956–1984* (Santiago: Ediciones B, 2008); and Fabio Salas Zúñiga, *La primavera terrestre: Cartografías del rock chileno y la Nueva Canción chilena* (Santiago: Cuarto Propio, 2003). Antonio Díaz Oliva's book

on Piedra Roja is a collection of press clippings and photos with little narrative. See Díaz, *Piedra Roja. El mito del Woodstock chileno* (Santiago: RIL Editores, 2010).

23. *El Mercurio* (Santiago), October 12, 1970.

24. Ludwig Wittgenstein, quoted in Hans Sluga, "Family Resemblance," in *Deepening Our Understanding of Wittgenstein*, ed. Michael Kober, (Amsterdam: Editions Rodopi BV, 2006), 1.

25. Sheila E. Anderson, *The Quotable Musician: From Bach to Tupac* (New York: Allworth Press, 2009), 137.

26. J. Milton Yinger, "Contraculture and Subculture," *American Sociological Review* 25, no. 5 (October 1960): 629.

27. Theodore Roszak, *The Making of Counter Culture: Reflections on the Technocratic Society and Its Youthful Opposition* (Garden City, NY: Doubleday, 1969), xii.

28. Pierre Bourdieu, *Sociology in Question* (London: Sage Publications, 1993) 94–95.

29. David Buckingham and Mary Jane Kehily, introduction to *Youth Cultures in the Age of Global Media*, ed. David Buckingham, Sara Bragg, and Mary Jane Kehily (London: Palgrave Macmillan, 2014), 5–7.

30. Talcott Parsons, *Essays in Sociological Theory* (New York: Free Press, 1954), 93.

31. Karen R. Foster, *Generation, Discourse, and Social Change* (New York: Routledge, 2013), 15–18.

32. See José Ortega y Gasset, *El tema de nuestro tiempo* (Madrid: Calpe, 1923).

33. Karl Mannheim, "The Sociological Problem of Generations," in *Essays on the Sociology of Knowledge*, ed. Paul Kesckemeti (New York: Routledge, 2000), 5:319–20. Also consult Brent J. Steele and Jonathan M. Cuff, eds., *Theory and Application of the "Generation" in International Relations and Politics* (London: Palgrave Macmillan, 2012).

34. Robert Wohl, *The Generation of 1914* (Cambridge: Harvard University Press, 1979), 5, 73–84, 122–59; Semi Purhonen, "Generations on Paper: Bourdieu and the Critique of 'Generationalism,'" *Social Science Information* 55, no. 1 (2016): 94–114. The noted Chilean journalist and essayist Domingo Melfi displays the pull of generationalism in interwar Chile in his *Indecisión y desengaño de la juventud: Proceso de las generaciones jóvenes de Chile* (Santiago: Editorial Nascimento, 1935).

35. Peter Winn's *Weavers of Revolution: The Yarur Workers and the Chilean Road to Socialism* (Oxford: Oxford University Press, 1986) exemplifies such nuance, using "generation" to understand how workers came to view change in the Yarur textile factory.

36. Alison Huber, "Mainstream as Metaphor: Imagining Dominant Culture," in *Redefining Mainstream Popular Music*, ed. Sarah Baker, Andy Bennett, and Jodie Taylor, (New York: Routledge, 2013), 5. Consult Sarah Thornton, *Club Cultures: Music, Media, and Subcultural Capital* (Cambridge, MA: Polity, 1995).

37. Examples include Ileana Rodríguez, ed., *The Latin American Subaltern Studies Reader* (Durham, NC: Duke University Press, 2001); Ranajit Guha, ed., *A Subaltern Studies Reader, 1985–1996* (Minneapolis: University of Minnesota Press, 1997); and

Florencia Mallon, *Peasant and Nation: The Making of Postcolonial Mexico and Peru* (Berkeley: University of California Press, 1995).

38. Mallon, *Peasant and Nation*, 6–7.

39. Huber, "Mainstream as Metaphor," 11.

40. Youth Studies scholar James Côté uses the term in a more expansive way: "The youth question at its most basic level involves how to understand the material and subjective conditions associated with the 'youth period'—that portion of the life course between what is defined as childhood and adulthood in a given society." Côté, *Youth Studies: Fundamental Issues and Debates* (London: Palgrave Macmillan, 2014), 9.

Chapter One

1. Some say the Piedra Roja festival drew forty thousand people and perhaps upwards of fifty thousand. However, estimates of three to five thousand are more realistic in light of oral-history interviews. Gary Fritz, interview by author, Charleston, IL, June 2007; Carlos Lowry, telephone interview by author, October 2007; Jaime Román, interview by author, Santiago, June 2003; Jorge Gómez Ainslie, telephone interview by author, October 2007. Shortly after the festival, *Vea* put attendance at "more than five thousand." Anonymous, "El festival de droga y sexo," *Vea*, October 16, 1970. As with the 1969 Woodstock festival in upstate New York, Piedra Roja remains steeped in nostalgia, which may very well account for inflated attendance figures. The legend of Piedra Roja intensified dramatically when the *teleserie* or *telenovela* (soap opera) *Hippie* debuted on the Catholic University's Channel 13 in the autumn of 2004. It was an unmitigated ratings flop, plagued by script problems and a directorial shakeup. *La Segunda*, March 12, 2004.

2. Pink Lizard, telephone interview by author, June 2007.

3. Gómez Ainslie, author interview.

4. Ibid.

5. Ibid.

6. *Las Últimas Noticias* (Santiago), September 7, 2003; Gómez Ainslie, author interview.

7. *Clarín* (Santiago), September 26, 1970; *El Mercurio* (Santiago), October 5, 1970; Fritz, author interview. Gómez Ainslie, author interview. On the Woodstock documentary, see Dale Bell, ed., *Woodstock: An Inside Look at the Movie that Shook the World and Defined a Generation* (Studio City, CA: Michael Wiese Film Productions, 1999). Readings on Woodstock include Abbie Hoffman, *Woodstock Nation* (New York: Random Vintage, 1969) and James Perone, *Woodstock: An Encyclopedia of the Music and Arts Fair* (Westport, CT: Greenwood, 2005).

8. *Clarín*, October 4, 1970. *¿Qué Hacer?* followed Saul Landau's 1969 film, *Fidel*.

9. Gómez Ainslie, author interview; interviews with Andrés Lewin and Roberto Cherit in *Piedra Roja*, documentary film, produced by Ann Fritz and Gary Fritz, directed by Gary Fritz (2011), DVD.

10. Interview with Eduardo Gatti in *Piedra Roja*.

11. Lowry, author interview; Gómez Ainslie, author interview; *Las Últimas Noticias*, September 7, 2003; interview with Jorge Gómez Ainslie in *Piedra Roja*.

12. Fritz, author interview.

13. Ibid.

14. Gómez Ainslie, author interview; interview with Carlos Lowry in *Piedra Roja*.

15. *El Mercurio*, October 25, 1970.

16. Gómez Ainslie, author interview; *La Época* (Santiago), June 12, 1994.

17. *El Mercurio*, October 15, 1970. Luco served as mayor of Las Condes from 1970 to 1972.

18. *La Nación* (Santiago), October 16, 1970.

19. Gómez Ainslie, author interview; Fritz, author interview; *La Época*, June 12, 1994.

20. Fritz, author interview; Gómez Ainslie, author interview; Lowry, author interview.

21. Gómez Ainslie, author interview; Lowry, author interview; Fritz, author interview; interview with Gómez Ainslie in *Piedra Roja*.

22. Román, author interview; Fritz, author interview; Gómez Ainslie, author interview. The magazine *Vea* estimated those in attendance ranged in age from twelve to twenty-five. Anonymous, "El festival," 6.

23. Gómez Ainslie, author interview; *Las Últimas Noticias*, September 7, 2003.

24. Román, author interview.

25. Ibid.

26. Audio recording of Piedra Roja, private archive of Gary Fritz, Charleston, IL.

27. Fritz, author interview; recording of Piedra Roja, Fritz archive.

28. Lowry, author interview.

29. Fritz, author interview.

30. Interview with Gómez Ainslie in *Piedra Roja*; Gómez Ainslie, author interview; Fritz, author interview; Lowry, author interview.

31. Antonio Díaz Oliva, *Piedra Roja: El mito del Woodstock chileno* (Santiago: RIL Editores, 2010), 106.

32. Fritz, author interview.

33. Anonymous, *Ercilla*, October 1970, 20–27: 14. The conservative *El Mercurio* described the suspects as young people "dressed like hippies" and out to cause trouble. *El Mercurio*, October 13, 1970.

34. Román, author interview; Patricio Reyes, interview by author, Santiago, August 2004.

35. One estimate of the total loss of equipment and other infrastructure stood at approximately ten thousand *escudos*, or a little more than US$750. *El Mercurio*, October 13, 1970.

36. *El Mercurio*, October 12, 1970.

37. Pink Lizard, author interview.

38. Recording of Piedra Roja, Fritz archive.

39. *El Mercurio*, October 12, 1970.

40. Reyes, author interview.

41. *El Mercurio*, October 14, 1970.

42. Ibid., October 13, 1970.

43. *El Sur* (Concepción), October 15, 1970. The periodical also covered Piedra Roja-related news closely, expressing the same general concerns as their *santiaguino* peers. See *El Sur*, October 14–20, 1970.

44. Ibid., October 16, 1970.

Chapter Two

1. Salvador Allende, "Inaugural Address in the National Stadium," in *Salvador Allende Reader: Chile's Voice of Democracy*, ed. James D. Cockcroft (North Melbourne: Ocean Press, 2000).

2. See Mark Kurlansky, *1968: The Year that Rocked the World* (New York: Ballantine, 2004).

3. Carlos Fuentes, *Los 68: París-Praga-México* (Mexico City: Debate-Random House Mondadori, 2005), 11.

4. Kurlansky, *1968*, xix.

5. Paul Berman, *A Tale of Two Utopias: The Political Journey of the Generation of 1968* (New York: W. W. Norton, 1996), 7–18.

6. See Fuentes, *Los 68*; Seymour Martin Lipset, ed., *Students in Revolt* (Boston: Houghton Mifflin, 1969); and George Katsiaficas, *The Imagination of the New Left: A Global Analysis of 1968* (Boston: South End Press, 1987).

7. Consult, for example, *El Mercurio* (Santiago), March 3, 15–17, 21, and 24; April 13–14; June 1–12 and 25; July 7; October 8; and December 9, 1968. The Yugoslav case was of particular interest to the conservative *El Mercurio*, which chastised the Soviet bloc and the Tito government for repressing students in Belgrade. Students had barricaded themselves in university buildings as they sought university reform, economic change, social justice, and a voice in national policy. Tito grudgingly agreed to the students' terms, but little reform materialized in the long run. *El Mercurio*, meanwhile, found the situation in Yugoslavia quite delicious: "The Yugoslav student rebellion has emerged spectacularly at a time when Soviet propagandists have tried to discredit the United States and Western Europe for racial turbulence and youth unrest." But criticism of students in the United States was not necessarily misplaced, or so the newspaper argued when assessing the Yugoslav situation. Citing widespread and alarming "belligerence," evidenced by the assassination of Robert Kennedy and student riots, an *El Mercurio* contributor writing from Detroit expressed, "If university students who are educating themselves and already have been educated aren't capable of controlling themselves and being examples to others, what can we ask of everyone else?" Ibid., June 18, 1968.

8. See Eric Zolov, *Refried Elvis: The Rise of the Mexican Counterculture* (Berkeley: University of California Press, 1999), especially chapter 6. Also consult Illán

Semo ed., *La transición interrumpida: México 1968–1988* (Mexico City: Editorial Patria, 1993); Carlos Fuentes, *Los 68*; and Herbert Braun, "Protests of Engagement: Dignity, False Love, and Self-Love in Mexico during 1968," *Comparative Studies in Society and History* 39, no. 9 (1997): 511–49. The 1971 Avándaro music festival, which drew up to 200,000, added to the wave of counterhegemonic agency, showcasing a Mexican "rock gesture," as Zolov puts it, and questioned the very foundations of normative cultural practice under the PRI.

9. See the July, August, September, and October 1968, editions of *El Mercurio*, *La Nación* (Santiago), and *El Siglo* (Santiago).

10. *Punto Final* (Santiago), April 13, 1971.

11. Consult Victoria Langland, *Speaking of Flowers: Student Movements and the Making and Remembering of 1968 in Military Brazil* (Durham, NC: Duke University Press, 2013).

12. For events in Brazil, see, for example, *El Mercurio*, April 3–5, June 22, and October 23, 1968. Also see Victoria Langland, "Il est Interdit d'Interdire: The Transnational Experience of 1968 in Brazil," *Estudios Interdisciplinarios de América Latina y el Caribe* 17, no. 1 (January–June, 2006): 61–81. For Argentina, see *El Mercurio*, June 16, 1968; for the Dominican Republic, *El Mercurio* January 15, 1968; and for Uruguay, *El Mercurio*, June 23 and August 10–12, 1968.

13. See Manuel Antonio Garretón, *Universidades chilenas: Historia, reforma e intervención* (Santiago: Editores Sur, 1987); Garretón, "Universidad y política en los procesos de transformación en Chile, 1967–1973," *Pensamiento Universitario* 14, no. 14 (October 2011): 71–90; and Luis Cifuentes Seves, *La reforma universitaria en Chile, 1968–1973* (Santiago: Editorial Universidad de Santiago, 1997).

14. *El Mercurio*, October 10, 1968. Students also obstructed automobile traffic, threw stones, and reportedly attacked Carabineros. *El Mercurio*, October 5, 1968.

15. Katsiaficas, *The Imagination of the New Left*, 41.

16. *El Mercurio*, October 5, 1968. Valdés became President of the Senate upon Chile's return to democracy in 1990.

17. Ibid., October 11, 1968. For a more sympathetic treatment of the protests, see the communist *El Siglo*, October 5–10, 1968.

18. *El Mercurio*, October 5, 1968.

19. Ibid., August 2, 1968, and *La Nación*, August 1–2, 1968. Also see Anonymous, "Los violentos sucesos del Fundo San Miguel," *Vea*, August 1968. The strike was the first of its kind under a new law governing campesino unionization and collective action. Campesinos also unsuccessfully attempted to seize the property, resulting in the arrest of dozens. The PS spearheaded the Law of Rural Unionization (Ley de Sindicación Campesina) of 1967, which the Frei government endorsed in the context of the U.S. Alliance for Progress. On the law and a subsequent peasant strike, see Cristián Pérez, "Guerrilla rural en Chile: La batalla del Fundo San Miguel (1968)," *Estudios Públicos* 78 (2000): 181–208. *El Mercurio* identified the happenings at the Institute as part of a larger "national terrorism plan" hatched by "extremist elements in the country in consultation with foreign agents." Evidence included the alleged

discovery of a "Czechoslovakian machine gun with a Bolivian insignia," *El Mercurio*, August 3, 1968.

20. *El Siglo*, July 31–August 3, 1968.

21. *El Mercurio*, December 7, 1968.

22. Ibid., June 5, 1968.

23. Ibid., June 16, 1968.

24. Paz derived her protagonist's name from that of her husband, Pepe Lucho. She died in Santiago in 1985 at age 83.

25. Marcela Paz, *Mi hermano hippie* (Santiago: Editorial Universitaria, 1975), 7.

26. Ibid., 9. Paz uses "smoke" on more than one occasion when describing circumstances having to do with Javier, perhaps alluding to marijuana as a defining element of the young man's hippismo. Yet, marijuana and drug use do not appear in the book—quite possibly a display of tact in light of the series' preteen readership.

27. Ibid., 11.

28. Ibid., 126–27.

29. María Yolanda González, "¿Existe la guerra de las generaciones?" *Ritmo de la Juventud*, November 1970, 22–24. *Ritmo* published with 503 editions between 1965 and 1975.

30. María Yolanda González, "La juventud: ¿Mentira prefabricada o la generación de la verdad?" *Ritmo de la Juventud*, September 1971, 63–65.

31. *El Mercurio*, October 18, 1970.

32. Ibid., October 31, 1971.

33. Ibid., March 25–26, 1968.

34. See Héctor Concha Oviedo, "La Iglesia Joven y la toma de la catedral de Santiago: 11 de agosto 1968," *Revista de Historia* (Universidad de Concepción) 7, no. 7 (1997): 137–48; Oscar Ortiz, interview by author, Santiago, June 2003. A subsequent association of Marxist priests called Christians for Socialism—founded in April 1971 by eighty clergymen—supported Allende's call to end discrimination against poor families who could not afford the high tuition of private schooling. The group later cooperated closely with the Christian Left (Izquierda Cristiana, or IC), established by renegades from the Christian Democratic Party and the Unitary Popular Action Movement (Movimiento de Acción Popular Unitaria, or MAPU).

35. James R. Whelan, *Out of the Ashes: Life, Death, and Transfiguration of Democracy in Chile* (Washington, DC: Regnery Gateway, 1989), 717–18.

36. Quoted in Whelan, *Out of the Ashes*, 719.

37. *El Mercurio*, August 14, 1968.

38. Ibid., August 12–13, 1968. Silva became archbishop in 1961 and cardinal the next year. He later was an outspoken critic of the Pinochet regime. See Mario Aguilar, *Cardenal Raúl Silva Henríquez: Presencia en la vida de Chile, 1907–1999* (Santiago: Ediciones Copygraph, 2004), and Miguel Alvarado Borgoño, *Cultura y universidad en el pensamiento del Cardenal Raúl Silva Henríquez: Un ensayo de interpretación* (Santiago: Universidad Católica Blas Cañas, Dirección de Investigación y Extensión, 1997).

39. *Punto Final* (Santiago), March 2, 1971. Also see the October 13, 1970, edition.

40. Whelan, *Out of the Ashes*, 720–21.

41. Shortly after the occupation, IJ published a manifesto that linked the Church, "the people," class struggle, and the dire need for greater educational opportunity. Iglesia Joven, "Iglesia joven: Hacia una definición" (Santiago: n.p., 1968), 1–16.

42. Máximo Pacheco, "La responsabilidad de ser joven," *Revista de Educación* 19 (August 1969): 53–55. Between 1964 and 1968, enrollment in public and private secondary schools skyrocketed, increasing from 139,195 to 229,339 (or nearly 61 percent). The ranks of primary- and secondary-school teachers swelled from 36,825 in 1964 to 51,015 in 1969 (72 percent). "Cuadros estadísticos," *Revista de Educación* 19 (August 1969): 21.

43. Castillo, Gabriel, José Nagel, and Andrés Domínguez, "La juventud y la violencia: Informe al Ministro de Educación Máximo Pacheco," *Revista de Educación* 19 (August 1969): 3–7, 9, 24–28.

44. Juan Gómez Millas, "¿Responden las relaciones entre la enseñanza media y superior a las necesidades del futuro y a las aspiraciones de la juventud?" *Revista de Educación* 27 (June 1970): 4–6.

45. Gómez, "Educar para el futuro," *Revista de Educación* 18 (July 1969): 5–6.

46. Patricio Rojas Saavedra, *Juventud y compromiso: Intento de armonización generacional* (Santiago: Ediciones del Departamento de Cultura y Publicaciones, Ministerio de Educación, 1970), 1–2, 7, 16–17. Educators and administrators outside the state, including those involved in Catholic schooling, also expressed concerns during the Frei years. See "Nuestra Juventud," *Revista de Pedagogía* 20, no. 142 (June 1969): 97, and "La juventud en la sociedad contemporánea: Informe sobre la juventud presentado en la 15a Conferencia General de la realizada entre el 15 de octubre y el 20 de noviembre de 1968," *Revista de Pedagogía*, 20, no. 142 (June 1969): 100–2, 105.

47. Marcel Garcés, "La juventud en la hora de Chile," *Ramona*, July 1972), 24–25. Also see *La Nación*, May 2, 1971, cited in Lessie Jo Frazier, *Salt in the Sand: Memory, Violence, and the Nation-State in Chile, 1890 to the Present* (Durham: Duke University Press, 2007), 135–36.

48. Anonymous, "Y para los jóvenes: ¿Qué?" *Onda*, December 1971, 15–16.

49. Anonymous, "Misiones y tareas de la juventud," speech by Salvador Allende, December 21, 1970, Santiago, Chile. Reproduced in Salvador Allende, *Tareas de la juventud*, No. 2, Archivo Salvador Allende (Puebla, Mexico: Universidad Autónoma de Puebla, 1998), 13.

50. Anonymous, "Y para los jóvenes: ¿Qué?" *Onda*, December 1971, 16.

51. *El Siglo*, October 22, 1970.

52. Ibid. Also see "La generación desconocida," *Ahora*, April 1971, 25–27, and *El Siglo*, December 27, 1970.

53. A professor at the Catholic University in Santiago who fled to France after the 1973 military coup, Armand Mattelart is widely known for co-authoring, along with Ariel Dorfman, *How to Read Donald Duck: Imperialist Ideology in the Disney Comic*, first published in Santiago in 1972.

54. The Mattelarts divided each social stratum into subgroups—all in equal numbers. For example, white-collar workers, each with at least a high-school diploma, were divided by gender, by professional pursuits, and by whether they were public or private-sector employees. Blue-collar respondents included factory workers, domestic servants, small-business employees, and artisans.

55. Armand Mattelart and Michèle Mattelart, *Juventud chilena: Rebeldía y conformismo* (Santiago: Editorial Universitaria, 1970), 226–27.

56. See Yanko González, "Genesis of Youth Cultures in Chile: *Coléricos* and *Carlotos* (1955–1964)," *Young* 20, no. 4 (2012): 377–97.

57. Mattelart and Mattelart, *Juventud chilena*, 111–17.

58. Antonio de Pérdigo, *Los jóvenes coléricos: Panorama, causas, remedios*, 2nd ed. (Santiago: Ediciones Paulinas, 1966), 8–13, 17–19, 46–55.

59. Darío Menanteau-Horta, "Aspiraciones y logros vocacionales de la juventud en Chile, 1969–1972," Research Report (University of Minnesota Department of Sociology, 1973), 1, 28–30.

60. Eugenio Velasco Letelier, *Algunas reflexiones sobre la juventud actual* (Santiago: Editorial Andrés Bello, 1971), 6.

61. Velasco, *Algunas reflexiones sobre la juventud actual*, 6–7.

62. Ibid., 7–9, 22.

Chapter Three

1. *El Siglo* (Santiago), August 26, 1968.

2. See Fernando Véliz, "Cine chileno e industria: El desafío que falta," *Signo y Pensamiento* 25:48 (January–June 2006): 149–69. Chile also produced noted filmmaker Alejandro Jodorowsky, known for his offbeat and creative audacity with certain countercultural underpinnings. On Jodorowsky, see Ben Cubb, *Anarchy and Alchemy: The Films of Alejandro Jodorowsky* (London: Creation, 2007).

3. The film's very title—*New Love*—is just that: "New Love," titled in English, suggesting both the criollo counterculture's foreign underpinnings and the advance of novel expressions of affection among young people.

4. *New Love*, directed by Álvaro Covacevich (Santiago, Chile: Sud Americana Films, 1968).

5. *El Siglo*, August 26, 1968.

6. *El Siglo*, March 23, 1967, and October 2, 1968. See the discussions of Covacevich in Verónica Cortínez and Manfred Engelbert, *Evolución en libertad: El cine chileno de fines de los sesenta*, 2 vols. (Santiago: Cuarto Propio, 2014).

7. *La Unión* (Valparaíso), October 12, 1968.

8. Anonymous, "La virginidad," *Paula*, April 1970, "Documento Official" supplement, 1.

9. María Ester Lezaeta, interview by author, Santiago, May 2006.

10. Historical literature on gender and sexuality in twentieth-century Chile includes Margaret Power, *Right-Wing Women in Chile: Feminine Power and the*

Struggle Against Allende, 1964–1973 (University Park, PA: Penn State University Press, 2002); Jadwiga E. Pieper-Mooney, *The Politics of Motherhood: Maternity and Women's Rights in Twentieth-Century Chile* (Pittsburgh, PA: University of Pittsburgh Press, 2009); Heidi Tinsman, *Partners in Conflict: The Politics of Gender, Sexuality, and Labor in the Chilean agrarian reform, 1950–1973* (Durham, NC: Duke University Press, 2002); María Angélica Illanes, *Nuestra historia violeta. Feminismo social y vidas de mujeres en el siglo XX: Una revolución permanente* (Santiago: LOM Ediciones, 2012); Thomas Miller Klubock, *Contested Communities: Class, Gender, and Politics in Chile's El Teniente Copper Mine, 1904–1951* (Durham, NC: Duke University Press, 1998); Lisa Baldez, *Why Women Protest: Women's Movements in Chile* (Cambridge: Cambridge University Press, 2002); and Karin Alejandra Rosemblatt, *Gendered Compromises: Political Cultures and the State in Chile, 1920–1950* (Chapel Hill: University of North Carolina Press, 2000).

11. Power, *Right-Wing Women in Chile*; Pieper-Mooney, *Politics of Motherhood*.

12. Malú Sierra, "Nuevos derechos para la mujer," *Paula*, January 1969, 86–93.

13. See Mauricio Tapia Rodríguez, *Código Civil, 1855–2005. Evolución y perspectivas* (Santiago: Editorial Jurídica de Chile, 2005).

14. Sierra, "Nuevos derechos para la mujer," 86–93.

15. See, for instance, Pierre Martory, "La revolución de las mujeres," *Paula*, September 1971, 88–93; Cecilia Domeyko, "Quiénes y cómo fueron. Las pioneras de la emancipación de las chilenas," *Paula*, March 1973, 70–75; Amelia Celis, "La mujer de mañana," *Paula*, January 1968, 33; and Amanda Puz, "El trabajo. ¿Un nuevo destino para la mujer chilena?" *Paula*, August 1972, 87–91.

16. *Tribuna* (Santiago), October 15, 1971. Simone de Beauvoir published the renowned *The Second Sex* in 1949.

17. *Paula* published a story on Beauvoir and women's rights in July 1972. The anonymous author discusses *The Second Sex*, patriarchy, socioeconomic change, marriage, maternity, and related issues. The rather even-handed (if not sympathetic) piece, which amounts to a survey of Beauvoir's thought and work, concludes by encapsulating Beauvoir's call for young women (part of a generational upheaval at hand) to assume leadership in the struggle against "the slavery of half of humanity." See Anonymous, "Porque la mujer es un ser oprimido," *Paula*, July 1972, 90–97.

18. Anonymous, "La victoria tiene nombre de mujer," *Vea*, July 2, 1970, 20.

19. Consult the *El Siglo* editions of July 2–3, 1970. Also see editions on those dates for *Puro Chile, La Tercera, La Segunda, La Nación*, and *El Mercurio*, all published in Santiago.

20. Salvador Allende, *La historia que estamos escribiendo: El presidente Allende en Antofagasta* (Santiago: Consejería de Difusión de la Presidencia de la República, 1972), 204. Shortly before his election, Allende identified mothers essentially as familial sentries, desperately staving off drugs and other maladies in defense of their children and their homes. *El Siglo*, October 12, 1970.

21. Marcela Otero, "La mujer chilena: Su larga marcha hacia la liberación," *Mayoría*, November 1971), 11–13. Little more than a year later, the Marxist *Mayoría*

discussed "feminine liberation" and the "breaking of *machismo*." The periodical cast "feminine liberation" as women's incorporation into various forms of "social service," including work in education and public-beautification projects, on behalf of Allende's socialist program. When describing women, the article refers to them as "mothers, sisters, daughters, and companions [*compañeras*]"—not citizens or individuals. *Mayoría*, December 1972, 13.

22. Quoted in Heidi Tinsman, "Good Wives and Unfaithful Men: Gender Negotiations and Sexual Conflicts in the Chilean Agrarian Reform, 1964–1973," *Hispanic American Historical Review* 81, nos. 3–4 (2011): 600; Virginia Vidal, *La emancipación de la mujer chilena* (Santiago: Editorial Quimantú, 1972), 49–52.

23. Anonymous, "Mujeres encabritadas," *Ramona*, February 1973, 19.

24. Ibid., 20. Again, the woman—even the liberated woman—exists in relation to the man, and feminism, Allende implies, makes for a better female companion. Also see Power, *Right-Wing Women in Chile*, 8.

25. Armand Mattelart and Michèle Mattelart, *La mujer chilena en una nueva sociedad: Un estudio exploratorio acerca de la situación e imagen de la mujer en Chile* (Santiago: Editorial del Pacífico, 1968), 30–34, 209–11. Amid a dominant Marxist discourse that emphasized domesticity and motherhood, UP women were just such a pressure group that lobbied the Allende government to address their pressing concerns. For instance, they pushed UP to establish the National Secretariat of Women (Secretaría Nacional de la Mujer, SNM) in September 1972. Its work focused on aiding working women—through such means as food programs and communal laundries—who were "conscious of their role" in UP's project, but its reach and efficacy were limited due to funding problems in tough economic times. Paula Fontaine, "Vamos mujer . . ." *Paloma* 1, no. 16 (June 1973): 106–9; Power, *Right-Wing Women in Chile*, 9.

26. *El Siglo*, June 3, 1971. On Christian Democracy and the Mothers' Centers, see Power, *Right-Wing Women in Chile*. The Mothers' Centers became a microcosm of political struggle between the Christian Democrats and ascendant Marxists. Michèle Mattelart, "La mujer y la línea de masa de la burguesía: El caso de Chile," in *La mujer en América Latina*, ed. María del Carmen Elu de Leñero (Mexico City: Secretaría de Educación Pública, 1975), 144; Power, *Right-Wing Women in Chile*, 117.

27. *Punto Final*, "La mujer chilena en la transición al socialismo," supplement to no. 133, June 22, 1971.

28. *Lolita* first appeared in Spanish translation in 1959.

29. Constanza Vergara, "Las Lolitas," *Paula*, September 1968, 52–59. The article includes a priest's rather negative assessment of the sexually charged "Lolita" phenomenon.

30. "La virginidad," *Paula*, April 1970, "Documento Official" supplement, 1.

31. Ibid., 3. For a "Confidential Document," the virginity discussion was tame compared to *Paula* articles that came with no such "parents only" caveat. For instance, a few months after the "Confidential Document" on virginity appeared, frequent *Paula* contributor Isabel Allende reflected (in detail) on the history of the

orgy from ancient times to the sexual revolution of the 1960s. Isabel Allende, "La orgía: Un antiguo pasatiempo," *Paula*, November 1970, 109–11.

32. Cecilia Domeyko, "La vida erótica de la mujer," *Paula*, June 1973, 86–88.

33. Ibid., 93.

34. Early-century anarchists in Chile and elsewhere were among the most revolutionary of all revolutionaries in matters related to gender and sexual liberation. Elizabeth Quay Hutchison, *Labors Appropriate to Their Sex: Gender, Labor, and Politics in Urban Chile, 1900–1930* (Durham, NC: Duke University Press, 2001), 88–89. For classical Marxist thought on these matters, consult Friedrich Engels, *The Origin of the Family, Private Property, and the State* (New York: International Publishers, 1942); Vladimir I. Lenin, *The Emancipation of Women: From the Writings of V. I. Lenin* (New York: International Publishers, 1966); and Wendy Z. Goldman, *Women, the State, and Revolution: Soviet Family Policy and Social Life, 1917–1936* (Cambridge: Cambridge University Press, 1993).

35. *Clarín* (Santiago), September 20, 1970.

36. Anonymous, "Sexo: no es gozo todo lo que se gime," *Mayoría*, January 26, 1972, 6–7.

37. See Tinsman, "Good Wives and Unfaithful Men," and Rosemblatt, *Gendered Compromises*.

38. Anonymous, "El ángulo de los padres: ¿Qué hacer ante la libertad sexual de nuestros hijos?" *Ramona*, July 1972, 16–19. Also see Lucho Abarca, "El adolescente chileno se desnuda ante el amor," *Ramona*, May 1972, 31–34.

39. "Patricia Politzer, "El sexo a tres velocidades," *Ramona*, February 1973, 14–19. See Alfonso Salgado, " 'A Small Revolution': Family, Sex, and the Communist Youth of Chile during the Allende Years (1970–1973)," *Twentieth Century Communism* 8 (Spring 2015): 66–67. *Ramona* also featured a multipart series on various forms of contraception, including "traditional methods," such as vaginal washes with a water-vinegar solution, as well as intrauterine devices. Consult *Ramona*, April 1973, 75–78.

40. Anonymous, "El amor hasta las últimas consecuencias," *Onda*, March 17, 1972, 14. In addition, consult "Bueno, ¿y el amor? . . . ¿es libre? . . . ¿o no?" *Onda*, February 14, 1973, 20–3. Such is the subtext of *Onda* articles on contraception as well. See, for example, the two-article series "La Anticoncepción," *Onda*, November 9, 1972), 56–57, and *Onda*, November 23, 1972, 56–57.

41. Also see Anonymous, "El ángulo de los padres: ¿Qué hacer ante la libertad sexual de nuestros hijos?" *Ramona*, July 1972, 16–19, and ¿Cómo es el universitario comunista?" *Ramona*, June 1972, 27.

42. Juan Carlos Moraga, interview by author, Santiago, May 2006.

43. *El Mercurio*, March 25, 1968.

44. La virginidad," *Paula*, April 1970, "Documento Official" Supplement, 5–6. The Church, though bound by the long-held practice of opposing birth control, nevertheless became more flexible in Chile amid the transnational sexual revolution. In light of high abortion rates and persistent poverty, some Chilean clerics embraced

Pope Pius XII's allowance in 1951 for natural forms of birth control, primarily the rhythm method, in specific contexts. In 1968, the Vatican's encyclical "On Human Life" made clear that all non-natural birth-control methods were sinful. Yet, a year earlier the Chilean episcopate circulated a declaration that identified a "demographic problem" and high abortion rates, both of which could be addressed through a more tolerant birth-control policy. Pieper-Mooney, *Politics of Motherhood*, 71–77.

45. Armand Mattelart, *¿Adónde va el control de la natalidad?* (Santiago: Editorial Universitaria, 1967), 165.

46. Pieper-Mooney, *Politics of Motherhood*, 39–52.

47. On sexual education, see Pieper-Mooney, *Politics of Motherhood*, 109–10; and M. Francoise Hall, "Male Attitudes to Family Planning Education in Santiago, Chile," *Journal of Biosocial Science* 3 (1971): 403–16. For views in the media, see the *El Siglo* editions of February 17, 24, and 25 and March 2, 1968; Anonymous, "Información sexual" and "La masturbación," *Onda*, October 29, 1971, 42–44; "El orgasmo," *Onda*, March 1972, 50–51; the series on sexual education in the government-owned *La Nación*, October 5, 9, and 10, 1971; Anonymous, "La cátedra del sexo," *Vea*, January 1970, 6–7; Anonymous, "Kama Sutra," *Ramona*, February 1973, 30–31; Malú Sierra, "En el colegio aprenden lo que es el amor," *Paula*, February 1970, 74–79; and Amanda Puz, "La educación sexual de nuestros niños," *Paula*, August 1970, "Confidential Document," n.p. The Ministry of Education also published various documents pertaining to the state of, and proposals for, sexual education in schools. For example, consult Anonymous, "Para una programa de educación sexual," *Revista de Educación* 27 (June 1970): 31–57; "Programa vida familiar y educación sexual," *Revista de Educación* 35 (April 1971): 34–40; and Anonymous, "Tareas de la educación sexual," *Revista de Educación* 35 (April 1971): 108–12. Also see Hernán Romero, *Sexo y educación sexual* (Santiago: Calderón y Cía, 1970).

48. Anonymous, "El aborto. ¿Un castigo para chilenos de segunda clase?" *Ramona*, February 1972, 24–28. According to a study by the Mattelarts, working women in the countryside during the late 1960s were less likely to use contraception, much less have a great deal of knowledge about it, than any other social constituency questioned by the sociologists' in their sample of one hundred females. A plurality of those who did use contraception relied on the birth-control pill, followed by the cervical ring. Such methods were acquired at local hospitals and at Mothers' Centers. Condom use, meanwhile, was scant across the board. The sociologists did not include data on urban women. Armand and Michèle Mattelart, *La mujer chilena*, 91–93.

49. Consult *El Siglo*, April 22, 1968; and *Tribuna*, April 9 and October 11, 1971. *Paula* balanced concerns about women's health, moral considerations, and legal questions. See the series "¿Aborto legal o control de la natalidad?" *Paula*, January 1970, 14–16; *Paula*, January 1970, 10–12; and *Paula*, February 1970, 10–11; Amanda Puz, "La mafia del aborto y sus víctimas," *Paula*, July 1971, 94–99; Ismael Espinosa, "Un aborto clandestino," *Paula*, August 1972, 88–95, 114–17; Amanda Puz,

"El aborto y el difícil camino de la legalización," *Paula,* February 1973, 68–75; and the letters to the editor section titled "Las lectoras polemizan sobre la legalización del aborto," *Paula,* May, 1973, 87–89, 108–13.

50. Pieper-Mooney, *Politics of Motherhood,* 110. While abortion became legal in the early 1930s in cases where pregnancy endangered women's lives, the Pinochet dictatorship banned all abortion in the late 1980s. Pinochet's edict prevailed until early 2017, when legislators approved abortion under three circumstances: danger to a mother's health, fetal inviability, and pregnancy resulting from rape.

51. Ibid., 44–52. Some leftists lashed out against "foreign" family planning strategies and practices that sought to limit population growth. In one 1968 editorial, the Communist daily *El Siglo* quoted a Yugoslavian diplomat who, when addressing Western Europe and the United States, noted, "You, the capitalists, refuse to plan the economy but plan populations so as to adapt it to [capitalism's] defects. We, on the other hand, want to adapt the economy for our population." *El Siglo,* February 9, 1968. Many on the Left came to see family planning in Chile as a foreign plot, with health officials acting as willing agents for the Rockefeller Foundation and other international family-planning groups. Pieper-Mooney, *Politics of Motherhood,* 95–96.

52. See Tinsman, *Partners in Conflict*; Florencia E. Mallon, *"Barbudos,* Warriors, and *Rotos"*: The MIR, Masculinity, and Power in the Chilean Agrarian Reform, 1965-74," in *Changing Men and Masculinities in Latin America,* ed. Matthew Gutmann (Durham, NC: Duke University Press, 2003), 182–83; and Pieper-Mooney, *Politics of Motherhood.* For earlier decades, consult Klubock, *Contested Communities,* and Rosemblatt, *Gendered Compromises.* The question of masculinity appeared in the media with some regularity. Consult, for example, M. Elena Gertner, "El hombre chileno: positivo y negativo," *Paula,* March 1971, 49–51; Elide Balocchi and Luisa Ulibarri, "Machismo sin careta," *Ahora,* September 28, 1971, 41–43; and Rodrigo Quijada, "¿Dominio masculino en Chile?" *Paula,* February 1972, 34–35.

53. Anonymous, "Homosexuales a la ofensiva," *Paloma,* May 1973, 9; *El Siglo,* March 1, 1968; Anonymous, "Homosexualismo ¿vicio o enfermedad?" *Paloma,* November 1972, 38–41; and Anonymous, "Homosexuales a cara abierta," *Ahora,* April 27, 1971, 12–14. In 1954, sodomy—construed as a fundamental aspect of male homosexuality—became illegal in Chile, and it continued to be so until the late 1990s. Under the "Law of Antisocial Status," approved during the presidency of Carlos Ibáñez del Campo, the mentally ill (referred to in the law as *locos,* or "crazies") and vagabonds joined male homosexuals in facing a minimum of five years in prison if found guilty of "antisocial" behavior. Claudia Dides, Arturo Márquez, Alejandro Guajardo, and Lidia Casas, *Chile: Panorama de sexualidad y derechos humanos* (Santiago, Chile, and Rio de Janeiro, Brazil: Centro Latinoamericano de Sexualidad y Derechos Humanos, 2007), 72–73.

54. Anonymous, "El sangriento fin de los homosexuales," *Ahora,* October 5, 1971, 22–23. Other articles on homosexuality in Marxist publications include: "La homosexualidad," *Onda,* August 18, 1972, 58–59; "La homosexualidad es así,"

Ramona, October 1972, 38–39; and "Nidales de perversión de menores," *Vea*, January 8, 1970, 15–16. The magazine *Paula* also ran numerous stories on the subject. See, for example, "Gay Power: La revolución alegre de los homosexuales norteamericanos," *Paula*, October 1970), 42–45, and "El homosexualismo: enemigo temible de nuestros hijos," *Paula*, April 1970, "Confidential Document," no page numbers. Meanwhile, there was a striking silence in the media regarding lesbianism, which, in its own way, conceivably could be construed as a "danger" to normative conceptions of masculinity, with men being erased from the sexual equation outright.

55. *La Nación*, October 5, 1971.

56. *Las Noticias de Última Hora* (Santiago), October 8, 1971.

57. Víctor Hugo Robles and Alejandra Sarda, "History in the Making: The Homosexual Liberation Movement in Chile," *NACLA Report on the Americas* 21 no. 4 (1998): 36.

58. *La Segunda*, March 12, 2004.

59. Ibid.

60. *El Mercurio*, July 10, 1969. One study noted that smoking marijuana was on the rise in high schools as of 1967. *El Mercurio*, September 16, 1971.

61. Ibid.

62. *Clarín*, July 7, 1969. Also consult the *Clarín* editions of July 8 and 11. In the former, *Clarín* blames well-to-do young people's indolence and the aloof parenting of the socioeconomically well positioned (*gente bien*) for the unfolding marijuana "scandal."

63. Hernán Cereceda Bravo, *Rompiendo silencio: El acusado del 93* (Santiago: Editorial Pretor, 1998), 71–76. Cereceda published the book in response to his dismissal in 1993 from his post as a prosecutor for the Supreme Court. He further described his role in anti-marijuana efforts in *La Segunda*, March 12, 2004.

64. *Clarín*, July 11, 1969.

65. *El Mercurio*, September 16, 1971.

66. Republic of Chile, Chamber of Deputies. Ordinary Legislative Session No. 23 (July 22, 1969), 2109–110.

67. "Aprueba reglamento que fija estupefacientes y drogas que producen estado de dependencia," Ministerio de Salud Pública, Decretos, vol. 10, no. 459, July 22, 1969, ARNAD, Santiago, Chile. Also see articles 319A and 391B in *Código Penal: Edición oficial: Al 31 de Marzo de 1970, aprobada por Decreto No. 536, de 2 de Abril de 1971 del Ministerio de Justicia* (Santiago: Editorial Jurídica de Chile, 1970), 90. Other measures followed, including requirements placed on laboratories and pharmacies to closely monitor their inventories of "pharmaceuticals that cause dependency." See "Aprueba reglamento sobre productos farmacéuticos que causan dependencia," Ministerio de Salud Pública, Decretos, vol. 1, no. 4, January 2, 1970, ARNAD, Santiago, Chile.

68. Anonymous, "Hippies místicos . . . un primo de los Kennedy . . . todos juntos y revueltos en la playa," *Onda*, February 1973, 33–34.

69. Gary Fritz, interview by author, Charleston, IL, June 2007.

70. Patricia Richard, Ana María Viveros, and Liana Ortiz, ¿*Fuma marihuana el estudiante chileno?* (Santiago: Ediciones Nueva Universidad, 1972), 30.

71. Lana D. Harrison, Michael Backenheimer, and James A. Inciardi, "Cannabis use in the United States: Implications for Policy," in *Cannabisbeleid in Duitsland, Frankrijk en de Verenigde Staten,* ed. Peter Cohen and Arjan Sas, (Amsterdam: Centrum voor Drugsonderzoek, Universiteit van Amsterdam, 1996), 181.

72. Richard et al., ¿*Fuma marihuana el estudiante chileno?*, 30–41. Richard and her colleagues used somewhat vague terms to describe the class standings of the respondents' families. Their parents' "upper class" professions included being a "big businessman" or manager of a large company, while an "upper-middle class" professional would be a university professor or in another well-placed white-collar vocation. Being a small businessman, a civil servant or having a desk job with limited authority would classify one as "lower-middle class." To be "lower class" would, for the most part, entail blue-collar work. A more limited study of 734 students in a single *liceo* in Greater Santiago found that 27 percent had smoked marijuana at least once. The survey also found that 29 percent said they would smoke marijuana if the opportunity arose. Some investigators believed that up to 60 percent of adolescents had smoked marijuana at least once. Anonymous, "La escalada de una droga," *Vea,* January 29, 1971, 1–3. Also see *El Mercurio,* November 8, 1970. *Vea* also reported that marijuana also was a problem in a girls' *liceo* in the southern city of Concepción, where a "scandal" erupted when fifteen students were found smoking marijuana provided by a male friend. Investigators learned that the marijuana had been taken to Concepción from Parque Forestal in Santiago, known for such activity. Wolrad Klopp, "Marihuana en colegio de niñas," *Vea,* August 27, 1970, 20–21.

73. Richard et al., ¿*Fuma marihuana el estudiante chileno?*, 47, 87, 123. Also see Armando Roa, *La marihuana: Aspectos clínico y antropológico* (Santiago: Editorial Universitaria, 1971).

74. *Clarín,* October 3, 1970.

75. "La muerte al acecho: fiebre de marihuana en el Forestal," *Vea,* October 9, 1970, 16–17.

76. *Clarín,* September 30, 1970.

77. María Teresa Larraín, "Las drogas le hacen decir que este mundo es una buena mierda," *Ramona,* November 1971, 11–12. For articles with similar stories and overtones in other youth-focused periodicals, see "Yo fui marihuanero," *Onda,* October 1, 1971, 44–45; and Manolo Olalquiaga "Drogas . . . ¿para qué?" *Ritmo de la Juventud,* April 1971, 75–77.

78. *El Mercurio,* July 11, 1969; María Yolanda González, "La marihuana . . . ¿pasaporte a la muerte?" *Ritmo de la Juventud,* July 1970, 16–19.

79. Anonymous, "El alucinante mundo de las drogas," *Vea,* February 12, 1970, 1–2; *El Mercurio,* April 14, 1968, and January 21, 1968. Also consult "La fatídica huella de las drogas," *Vea,* February 19, 1970, 1–2. Cocaine, too, was the subject of some concern. Consult, for example, *La Huella,* the Radical Party's periodical: "Boites: el 'toque' no es de 'queda,'" *La Huella,* November 1971, 19–21.

80. *Clarín*, September 28, 1971.

81. Juan Pablo Orrego, interview by author, Santiago, August 2007; Gómez Ainslie, author interview.

82. *Clarín*, September 28, 1971; and *El Mercurio*, September 28, 1971. Other cases are described in the *La Segunda* editions of October 1, 11, and 16, 1971.

83. Javier Martínez, "Las drogas vuelan en valija diplomática," *Punto Final*, June 22, 1971, 10–11.

84. Gary Fritz, personal correspondence with author, September 2009.

85. Fritz, author interview.

86. Ibid.; Orrego, author interview; Oscar Ortiz, interview by author, Santiago, June 2003; Gómez Ainslie, author interview.

87. Isabel Allende, "LSD: La droga que empieza a alucinar a los chilenos," *Paula*, (March 1968), 62–65, 109–10.

88. In one instance, the media reported a raid at a hotel in the port city of Valparaíso, where police said they found adolescent females dancing nude for Central American sailors, all of whom were enjoying marijuana and unspecified "hallucinogens." The drugs reportedly served to "soften up" and embolden the young dancers. *Clarín*, July 5, 1969.

89. "El peligroso mundo de la Quinta Normal," *Vea*, June 25, 1970, 8–9. Also see "Fiesta pública con marihuana," *Vea*, June 22, 1970, 12.

90. *Clarín*, October 4, 1971.

91. "La marihuana invade Chile," *Vea*, April 16, 1970, 3–4. Manson's image and the sociopathic-marihuanero construct often surfaced in the media as components of more broadly cast anticounterculture discourses. Attention to Manson was merely one angle from which Chileans assessed drug use outside their country. Consult, for instance, the *El Mercurio* editions of January 4, 8, and 14, and February 13, 1968. On moves by the Nixon administration to stem drug use in the United States, see *El Mercurio*, September 10, 1971.

92. The appellation "Nueva Canción" came out of the 1967 "Encuentro de la Canción Protesta," a gathering of Marxist musicians (from eighty countries) in Cuba. The Chilean movement adopted the term. Jan Fairley, "La Nueva Canción Latinoamericana," *Bulletin of Latin American Research* 3, no. 2 (1984): 108.

93. Fabio Salas Zúñiga, *La primavera terrestre: Cartografías del rock chileno y la Nueva Canción chilena* (Santiago: Cuarto Propio, 2003), 109. The tariff also provided some protection to criollo rock. By the end of the 1970s, the tariff had fallen to 10 percent under Pinochet's neoliberal project, which opened Chilean markets to foreign producers.

94. Folklorism, as a mainstream urban phenomenon, has roots in the 1920s and 1930s, becoming an instrument of cultural politics across the sociopolitical landscape. See Patrick Barr-Melej, *Reforming Chile, Cultural Politics, Nationalism, and the Rise of the Middle Class* (Chapel Hill: University of North Carolina Press, 2001), chapters 4–5. Also consult J. Patrice McSherry, *Chilean New Song: The Political Power of Music, 1960s–1973* (Philadelphia: Temple University Press, 2015); Fairley, "La

Nueva Canción Latinoamericana"; and Ignacio Ramos Rodillo, "Música típica, folkore de proyección y Nueva Canción. Versiones de la identidad nacional bajo el desarrollismo en Chile, décadas de 1920 a 1973," *Revista NEUMA* 2, no. 2 (2011): 121.

95. The independence-era hero, who was murdered by political opponents in 1818, remains vivid in Chilean collective memory. The Manuel Rodríguez Patriotic Front, for example, appeared in 1983 as part of an armed resistance movement during the military regime of Augusto Pinochet. It was affiliated with the then-illegal Communist Party.

96. Anonymous, "Violeta Parra, el arte contra el sistema," *Punto Final*, August 1971, 14–15.

97. Folkloric *peñas*—ephemeral as well as permanent ones—sprouted up around Santiago in the late 1960s, with close ties to labor unions, workers, and leftist politics. One *peña*, for example, convened on May Day 1968 to honor the Central Workers' Union (CUT). *El Siglo*, April 2, 1968.

98. Joan Baez was a strong supporter of Allende and visited the country in 1972. Marxists praised her commitment to "music as a form of struggle," linking Baez's folk music to Nueva Canción and properly revolutionary culture. Evelyn Mesquida, "Joan Baez," *Ramona*, November 1971, 28–29. Baez, moreover, declared to young Chileans, "Mr. Allende is the best thing that has happened to Chile." Nora Massignotti, "Mr. Allende is the best thing that has happened to Chile," *Ramona*, September 1972), 14–17. Also see "Joan Baez en Chile," *Mayoría*, October 1971, 9.

99. *El Siglo*, November 15, 1970. Also, alongside such artists as Isabel Parra (Violeta's Parra's daughter and Ángel's sister), Jara traveled to Cuba in 1972 for an international gathering of fifty musicians based on principles similar to those of the East German confab. *El Siglo*, October 4, 1972.

100. *El Siglo*, December 10, 1972.

101. Orrego, author interview; Carlos Lowry, telephone interview by author, October 2007. Orrego was the bass player for Los Blops. Lowry co-organized Piedra Roja and got to know many musicians, including those of Los Blops, while in high school in Santiago.

102. Carol A. Hess, *Representing the Good Neighbor: Music, Difference, and the Pan American Dream* (Oxford: Oxford University Press, 2013), 174.

103. David Ponce, *Prueba de sonido: Primeras historias del rock en Chile, 1956–1984* (Santiago: Ediciones B, 2008), 43.

104. Salas, *La primavera terrestre*, 28–31.

105. Ibid., 27–30.

106. Fabio Salas Zúñiga, *El grito del amor: Una actualizada historia temática del rock* (LOM Ediciones 1998), 195; Tito Escárate, *Frutos del país: Historia de rock chileno* (Santiago: Triunfo, 1994), 8–9. On Beatlemania in Chile, see Benjamín Torrejón, ed., *Los Beatles y las chilenas* (Santiago: Sourir, 1966); and Sergio Pastene Ortega, "Chillones por los chascones: La Beatlemania en Chile, 1962–1970," Baccalaureate thesis, Pontifical Catholic University of Chile, 2006. Los Picapiedras recorded much of the music for *New Love* under the name "Los Vips." They were forced to

employ the temporary moniker because the film was to be distributed internationally and cartoon producer Hanna-Barbera held international copyrights to the name "Los Picapiedras" (The Flintstones).

107. Luz María Vargas, "*Chascones* 'Made in Chile': Los Jockers," *Ritmo de la Juventud*, (February 1967), 10–11.

108. Alex Fiori, "El hábito no hace al monje," *Ritmo de la Juventud*, October 1967, 2–3; *El Siglo*, December 3, 1970.

109. Ponce, *Prueba de sonido*, 87–90.

110. *El Siglo*, December 3, 1970.

111. Fabio Salas Zúñiga, *Utopía: Antología lírica del rock chileno, 1967–1990* (Santiago: Bravo y Allende Editores, 1993), 19.

112. *El Siglo*, November 20, 1970.

113. *Las Noticias de Última Hora*, November 6, 1970, and October 31, 1970. The theater department also presented the anti-imperialist "Viet Rock" (1966). Ibid., May 17, 1970.

114. Luis Pradenas, *Teatro en Chile: Huellas y trayectorias, siglos XVI-XX* (Santiago: LOM Ediciones, 2006), 293; Julio Durán Cerda, *Teatro chileno contemporáneo* (Mexico City: Aguilar, 1970), 17.

115. Los Beat 4, "Self-Made Man," *El Degenéresis*, 1971, RCA/CML-2853.

116. This notion is evident in the Communist press coverage of "El degenéresis." See *El Siglo*, November 26, 1970.

117. Most notable are such groups as Congreso, Kissing Spell, Congregación, Lágrima Seca, Los Trapos, Los Ripios, and Vidrios Quebrados.

118. Salas, *La primavera terrestre*, 89.

119. *La Estrella* (Valparaíso), October 31, 1964.

120. Tito Escárate, *Canción telepática: Rock en Chile* (Santiago: LOM Ediciones, 1999), 186–89.

121. Interview with Mario Mutis in *Piedra Roja*, documentary film. Directed by Gary Fritz, produced by Ann Fritz and Gary Fritz, 2011.

122. Escárate, *Canción telepática*, 190.

123. Lowry, author interview.

124. Escárate, *Canción telepática*, 195.

125. Ibid., 195–96. Country Joe kept the masters and stored them appropriately for conservation. They presumably remain in his possession. Los Jaivas retained a poor copy.

126. Stock, *Los caminos que se abren*, 74.

127. Escárate, *Canción telepática*, 196.

128. Anonymous, "Un concierto 'hippie' de Los Jaivas," *Novedades*, December 1971), 24–27.

129. Anonymous, " 'Jaivas 'para la exportación,' " *Ramona*, August 1972, 34–35.

130. Los Jaivas, "Todos Juntos," *Todos Juntos*, 1972, IRT.

131. Stock, *Los caminos que se abren*, 74.

132. Patricia Politzer, "¡Estos sí son pájaros raros! Los Jaivas 'vuelan,'" *Ramona*, (January 1973), 12–16.

133. Orrego, author interview.

134. Interview with Juan Pablo Orrego in *Piedra Roja*.

135. In its inaugural call for artists, DICAP stipulated a number of requirements, including for songs to have "social content." *Las Noticias de Última Hora*, May 5, 1969.

136. Patricio Reyes, interview by author, Santiago, August 2004.

137. Orrego, author interview.

138. Ponce, *Prueba de sonido*, 128.

139. Interview with Eduardo Gatti in *Piedra Roja*.

140. Los Blops, *Blops*, Discoteca del Cantar Popular (DICAP), Chile, 1970, Catalog No. DCP-04.

141. Orrego, author interview.

142. Ibid.

143. Salas, *La primavera terrestre*, 92.

144. "Blops: Una burbuja que reinventa la música," *Onda*, November 1971, 35–38.

145. Isabel Allende, "Los Blops. Una extraña comunidad musical," *Paula*, June 1971, 50–53.

146. Orrego, author interview.

147. *La Segunda* (Santiago), March 13, 1970.

148. Interview with Denise in *Piedra Roja*.

149. "EVOL," *Aguaturbia*, vol. 2, Aguaturbia, 1970, Arena.

150. Francisco Leal, "'Aguaturbia' y sus experiencias en USA," *Onda*, January 1973, 34.

151. Fabio Salas Zúñiga, *Aguaturbia: Una banda chilena del rock* (Santiago: Bravo y Allende Editores, 2006), 39–40, 65.

152. Lowry, author interview. Soon after the festival, Lowry organized a Los Blops concert at his high school, the private Grange School, which Gatti had attended.

153. Orrego, author interview; Interview with Eduardo Gatti in *Piedra Roja*.

154. Orrego, author interview.

155. Interview with Mario Mutis in *Piedra Roja*.

156. Lowry, author interview.

157. Fritz, author interview.

158. *La Segunda*, March 12, 2004; *La Época* (Santiago), June 12, 1994; Interview with Denise Puleghini in *Piedra Roja*.

159. Interview with Mario Soza in *Piedra Roja*.

160. See César Albornoz, "Los sonidos del golpe," in *1973: La vida cotidiana de un año crucial*, ed. Claudio Rolle (Santiago: Planeta, 2003), 161–96.

161. Mattelart and Mattelart, *Juventud chilena*, 174–75.

162. Consult *El Musiquero*, October–December 1970.

Chapter Four

1. Anonymous, "Hair en Chile: Hippies desnudos cantan en la Eve," *Novedades*, January 1972, 1–6.

2. Patricia Politzer, "El show que desnuda por E° 500 cuan fuera de onda y de época estan ciertos burgueses," *Ramona*, February 1972, 18–20.

3. Pink Lizard, telephone interview by author, June 2007.

4. See Alejo Carpentier, *La música en Cuba* (Mexico City: Fondo de Cultura Económica, 1946).

5. Gary Fritz, interview by author, Charleston, IL, June 2007.

6. Oscar Ortiz, interview by author, Santiago, June 2003.

7. *Clarín* (Santiago), September 26, 1970; *El Mercurio* (Santiago), October 5, 1970.

8. Carlos Lowry, telephone interview by author, October 2007.

9. *El Mercurio*, October 14, 1970.

10. Anonymous, "Woodstock: El festival hippie más grande del mundo," *Ritmo de la Juventud*, May 1970, 19. Abruzzi presided over two deaths, two births, and some 2,500 drug-related incidents. "Woodstock: Ten Years Later," *People*, August 1979, 22–27.

11. Juan Ehrmann, "Canciones y anarquía," *Ercilla*, October 1970, 72–73.

12. Ibid., 73.

13. Abraham Santibañez, "La cruzada de los hippies," *Ercilla*, November 1970, 36–37.

14. Consult *El Mercurio*, October 12, 1970, and *Las Noticias de Última Hora* (Santiago), October 14, 1970, for other tie-ins involving counterculture and Manson.

15. Anonymous, "Nueva Massacre Hippie," *Vea*, February 1970, 7–8.

16. *El Mercurio*, October 30, 1970. *Paula* struck a similar tone in a 1972 article on *hippismo*, larceny, rebelliousness, and Scotland Yard's attempt to crack down on hippie delinquency. See "Hippies ingleses ya tienen un manual para aprender a vivir sin hacer nada," *Paula*, February 1972, 25–26.

17. *El Siglo*, October 23 and 25, 1970.

18. Fritz, author interview.

19. Lowry, author interview. Lowry studied at The Grange.

20. Consult "The Doors," *Ritmo de la Juventud*, June 1970, 22–23; "Los Beatles pueden separarse," *Ramona*, November 1971, 7–9; and Ricardo García, "¿Quién ocupará el trono vacío de Los Beatles?" *Ramona*, May 1972, 34–37.

21. See *Ritmo de la Juventud*, March–April, 1971.

22. Pablo Aguilera, "La marihuana, Alicia, y otras 'yerbas'," *Onda*, August 31, 1972, 24–27. The exploits of British hippies, beyond the happenings on the Isle of Wight, also appeared in Santiago's press. The glossy *Paula*, for instance, expressed interest in understanding better how London hippies meet their material needs despite shunning work. Shoplifting was one option, the magazine noted sarcastically. See "Hippies ingleses ya tienen un manual," 25–26.

23. Amanda Puz, "Cómo se vive en una comunidad hippie," *Paula*, March 1972, 74–79, 111.

24. See Camilo Trumper, *Ephemeral Histories: Public Art, Politics, and the Struggle for the Streets in Chile* (Berkeley: University of California Press, 2016).

25. Jorge Gómez Ainslie, telephone interview by author, October 2007.

26. Lowry, author interview; Patricio Reyes, interview by author, Santiago, August 2004.

27. Consult *Paula*, March 1972, 6. The Communist press admitted that women of all classes were interested and drawn to new clothing styles, including the miniskirt. *El Siglo* (Santiago), March 20, 1968. Also see Pía Montalva, *Morir un poco: Moda y sociedad en Chile, 1960–1976* (Santiago: Editorial Sudamericana, 2004).

28. *Clarín*, July 8, 1969. "High" becomes *"jai"* when Spanish spelling rules are applied.

29. Interviews with Mario Mutis and Carlos Corales in *Piedra Roja*, documentary film. Directed by Gary Fritz, produced by Ann Fritz and Gary Fritz, 2011. The Caupolicán Theater, located on San Diego Street in Santiago's downtown, also saw rock concerts, including visits by Los Jaivas, in the early seventies.

30. Lucho Abarca and Juan E. Forch, *Viaje por la juventud* (Santiago: Quimantú, 1972), 9–10.

31. Abarca and Forch, *Viaje por la juventud*, 12–13.

32. Interview with Eduardo Gatti in *Piedra Roja*.

33. Anonymous, "El festival de droga y sexo," *Vea*, October 16, 1970, 6.

34. Interview with Jorge Gómez Ainslie in the documentary *Piedra Roja*.

35. Jaime Román, interview by author, Santiago, June 2003.

36. Gómez Ainslie, author interview.

37. Allen Ginsberg and Louis Ginsberg, *Family Business: Selected Letters Between a Father and Son*, ed. Michael Schumacher (New York: Bloomsburg, 2011), 129. On Chilean poetry of the 1960s and early 1970s, see, for instance, Javier Campos, *La joven poesía chilena del período 1961–1973* (Concepción: Ediciones Literatura Americana Reunida, 1987), and Ricardo Yamal, *La poesía chilena actual (1960–1984) y la crítica* (Concepción: Ediciones Literatura Americana Reunida, 1988).

38. *La Nación* (Santiago), online edition, August 26, 2007; *La Nación*, May 25, 2003. Consult Juan Andrés Piña, *Historia del teatro en Chile, 1941–1990* (Santiago: Taurus, 2014).

39. César Albornoz, "El tiempo del volar de las palomas," in *Música popular en América Latina: Actas del II Congreso Latinoamericano, International Association for the Study of Popular Music*, ed. Rodrigo Torres, (Santiago: Fondo de Desarrollo de las Artes y la Cultura, 1999), 314.

40. Oscar Ortiz, interview by author, Santiago, June 2003; Felipe Solar and Andrés Pérez, *Anarquistas: Presencia libertaria en Chile* (Santiago: RIL Editores, 2008), 217–220.

41. Ortiz, author interview.

42. Juan Pablo Orrego, interview by author, Santiago, August 2007; Pía Figueroa Edwards, interview by author, Santiago, March 2004; Ortiz, author interview; and Gómez Ainslie, author interview.

43. María Yolanda González, "Macondo . . . un mundo aparte en Santiago," *Ritmo de la Juventud,* May 1972, 46.

44. Ibid., 46.

45. Ibid., 47.

46. Ibid., 47.

47. Ibid., 49.

48. *Ritmo* also ran a story that compared favorably the artistic creativity going on in the barrio to that of Soho in London and the artists on the banks of Paris's Seine River. *Ritmo de la Juventud,* July 1972, 46–51.

49. Román, author interview; Ortiz, author interview.

50. Ortiz, author interview.

51. Gómez Ainslie, author interview.

52. Lowry, author interview.

53. *Puro Chile* (Santiago), October 4, 1971. *Puro Chile* had strong ties to UP.

54. *El Siglo,* November 24, 1970.

55. *El Mercurio,* November 27, 1970.

Chapter Five

1. Interview with Malucha Pinto in *Piedra Roja,* documentary film. Directed by Gary Fritz, produced by Ann Fritz and Gary Fritz, 2011. Pinto descends from a founding father of the Chilean Republic, Francisco Antonio Pinto, and her father was the renowned and award-winning economist Aníbal Pinto.

2. *El Mercurio* (Santiago), October 15, 1970.

3. Ibid.

4. *La Nación* (Santiago), October 16, 1970.

5. *Clarín* (Santiago), October 14, 1970. Also see the socialist *Las Noticias de Última Hora* (Santiago), October 13, 1970 (not to be confused with the conservative *Las Últimas Noticias,* published by the *El Mercurio* crowd). Pareto served in the Chamber of Deputies for twenty years before becoming Intendant of Santiago during the early 1990s. He then returned to the Chamber of Deputies, becoming its president in 2001.

6. *La Nación,* October 12, 1970.

7. Jorge Gómez Ainslie, telephone interview by author, October 2007; *Las Últimas Noticias,* February 3, 2004.

8. *El Mercurio,* October 14, 1970.

9. Anonymous, without title, *Ercilla* 36, October 20–27, 1970. Also see *La Nación,* October 19, 1970.

10. *La Nación,* October 16, 1970.

11. Gómez Ainslie, author interview.

12. Ibid.

13. A useful treatment of youth cultures and moral panic is Ulf Boëthius, "Youth, the Media, and Moral Panics," in *Youth Culture in Late Modernity,* ed. Johan Furnas and Groan Bolin (London: Sage Publications, 1995), 39–57.

14. *Clarín*, October 13, 1970.

15. *El Mercurio*, October 14, 1970.

16. Ibid.

17. *Clarín*, October 15, 1970. Also consult *Las Noticias de Última Hora*, October 14, 1970.

18. *El Mercurio*, October 14, 1970.

19. Ibid., November 29, 1970.

20. Interview with Charlie Alvarado in *Piedra Roja*. Pink Lizard noted, "There were also a fair number of young people who were beginning to experiment with alternate lifestyles, which, in some sense, involved living on the streets, but there was a very positive air about it. There was a lot of excitement and sense of renewal and awakening and doing different things, so living on the street seemed to be a cool thing to do rather than a depressing thing to do. It was an all-night scene, in other words." Pink Lizard, telephone interview by author, June 2007.

21. *Puro Chile* (Santiago), October 14, 1970.

22. *El Mercurio*, October 14, 1970.

23. *La Nación*, October 14, 1970.

24. *El Sur* (Concepción), October 15, 1970. The charge of homosexuality seems to have come out of nowhere.

25. *La Nación*, October 14, 1970.

26. Archivo Nacional de la Administración (Santiago), Ministerio de Educación Pública, Decretos, No. 106 (October 19, 1970); *Diario Oficial de la República de Chile* (Santiago), No. 27,797 (November 14, 1970). Members of the commission, chaired by Deputy Roberto Muñoz Barra, included the education minister, Máximo Pacheco, representatives from police and the judiciary, and a psychiatrist. Also see *Clarín*, October 15, 1970.

27. *El Siglo*, December 16, 1970, and *El Mercurio*, October 21, 1970.

28. Anonymous, "La escalada de una droga," *Vea*, January 1971, 1.

29. *El Siglo*, October 14, 1970.

30. *Clarín*, October 13, 1970; Gary Fritz, interview by author, Charleston, IL, June 2007; Carlos Lowry, telephone interview by author, October 2007.

31. Anonymous, "El festival de droga y sexo," *Vea*, October 16, 1970), 6–7.

32. *Clarín*, October 14, 1970.

33. Gómez Ainslie, author interview.

34. Interview with Denise in *Piedra Roja*.

35. Gómez Ainslie, author interview.

36. *El Mercurio*, October 14 and 18, 1970; Anonymous, "Las candentes 'Piedras Rojas,'" *Ercilla*, October 20–27, 1970, 14; *Las Noticias de Última Hora*, October 13, 1970.

37. Anonymous, "El festival de droga y sexo," 6–7.

38. Interview with Denise in *Piedra Roja*.

39. *El Mercurio*, October 18, 1970.

40. *Clarín*, October 14, 1970.

41. Pink Lizard, author interview; Fritz, author interview; Lowry, author interview.

42. Gómez Ainslie, author interview.

43. Anonymous, "El festival de droga y sexo," 6.

44. *La Tercera*, October 11, 1970; Antonio Díaz Oliva, *Piedra Roja: El mito del Woodstock chileno* (Santiago: RIL Editores, 2010), 38–39, 172.

45. *La Nación*, October 15, 1970. Also see *Clarín*, October 14, 1970.

46. *La Nación*, October 12, 1970.

47. *El Siglo* (Santiago), October 17, 1970.

48. Gómez Ainslie, author interview; Interviews with Jorge Gómez Ainslie and Mario Soza in *Piedra Roja*.

49. Interview with Carlos Varela in *Piedra Roja*.

50. Eduardo Yentzen Peric, *La voz de los setenta: Un testimonio sobre la resistencia cultural a la dictadura, 1975–1982* (Santiago: self-published, 2014), 9–10. A cadet in the late 1960s, Yentzen talks of Saturday rumbles against hippies as if they were regularly scheduled events for the military youths.

51. Interview with Carlos Varela in *Piedra Roja*.

52. Isabel Allende, "A través de los impertinentes," *Paula*, September 1968, 120.

53. *El Siglo*, March 14, 1968.

54. *El Mercurio*, January 3, 1968. Later that year, when apparently asked by a fascinated reader where one could get in touch with hippies, the newspaper directed the inquirer to the United States and Europe, without mentioning the existence of any hippies in Chile. *El Mercurio*, August 11, 1968.

55. *El Siglo*, October 13, 1970.

56. Ibid.

57. *El Mercurio*, October 16, 1970.

58. *El Siglo*, October 14, 1970.

59. *El Siglo*, October 22, 1970.

60. *Las Noticias de Última Hora*, October 13, 1970.

61. *Las Noticias de Última Hora*, October 13, 1970.

62. *El Siglo*, October 15, 1970.

63. *Las Noticias de Última Hora*, October 13, 1970.

64. *El Siglo*, October 14, 1970; *Clarín*, October 13, 1970.

65. Federico Gana, "Providencia: ¿Tontódromo o fascistódromo?" *Ahora*, December 1971, 31–32.

66. Ibid., 34.

67. Ibid., 36.

68. Vania Bambirra, "La mujer chilena en la transición al socialismo," *Punto Final*, June 1971, 7–8.

69. Florencia Mallon, "*Barbudos*, Warriors, and *Rotos*: The MIR, Masculinity, and Power in the Chilean Agrarian Reform, 1965–74," in *Changing Men and Masculinities in Latin America*, ed. Matthew Gutmann (Durham, NC: Duke University Press, 2003), 182–83. See also Heidi Tinsman, *Partners in Conflict: The Politics of Gender,*

Sexuality, and Labor in the Chilean Agrarian Reform, 1950–1973 (Durham, NC: Duke University Press, 2002).

70. *Clarín*, October 7, 1970.

71. *El Siglo*, October 7, 1972.

72. *Tribuna*, August 22, 1972.

73. *El Siglo*, October 7, 1972.

74. *Tribuna*, August 22, 1972.

75. *El Siglo*, October 6, 1972. Del Campo became a leading television journalist during post-dictatorship democratization in the early 1990s.

76. Anonymous, *Patria y Libertad*, April 1971, 5.

77. Juan Pablo Orrego, interview by author, Santiago, August 2007; Gómez Ainslie, author interview.

78. Anonymous, "Contra el hippismo decadente: Brigada Ramona Parra," *Plan: Política Latinoamericana Nueva* 4, no. 54 (October–November 1970): cover. The Socialist Youth had the Brigada Elmo Catalán.

79. *El Mercurio*, October 14, 1971.

80. Ibid.

81. Salvador Allende, "Missions and Tasks of Youth and Agrarian Reform," in *The Salvador Allende Reader*, ed. James Cockroft (Melbourne: Ocean Press, 2000), 67.

82. *El Mercurio*, October 13, 1970.

83. Ibid., October 14, 1970.

84. Ibid., October 16, 1971.

85. Ibid., October 19, 1970.

86. Ibid., October 18, 1970.

87. Ibid., October 16, 1970.

88. Ibid., September 28, 1971.

89. *Tribuna*, October 1, 1971.

90. *El Mercurio*, September 10, 1971. The first Spanish translation of *The Theory of the Leisure Class* appeared in 1944, published by the Fondo de Cultura Económica in Mexico City.

91. *La Nación*, October 18, 1970. The newspaper recommended to its readers a book written by the Spaniard Guillermo Díaz-Plaja, *Los paraísos perdidos: La actitud "hippy" en la historia* (Barcelona: Seix Barral, 1970), which describes the international hippista movement and other "countercultural" movements in history. *La Nación*, October 19, 1970.

92. *La Nación*, October 21, 1970. The article's headline, "The Hippie: Psychopath, Coward, and Disloyal," blows Taibo's statements out of proportion but most certainly caught the eyes of readers.

93. See Lillian Guerra, *Visions of Power in Cuba: Revolution, Redemption, and Resistance, 1959–1971* (Chapel Hill: University of North Carolina Press, 2012); Carrie Hamilton, *Sexual Revolutions in Cuba: Passion, Politics, and Memory* (Chapel Hill: University of North Carolina Press, 2012); Linda S. Howe, *Transgression and Conformity: Cuban Writers and Artists After the Revolution* (Madison: University of

Wisconsin Press, 2004); and Abel Sierra Madero, "'El trabajo os hará hombres': Masculinización nacional, trabajo forzado y control social en Cuba durante los años sesenta," *Cuban Studies* 44 (2016): 309–49. Castro expressed many of the same frustrations toward young people as did principal political actors in Chile and elsewhere during the late sixties and seventies. He complained in 1972, for instance, that young Cubans "are willing to do anything except study hard." Quoted in Julie Marie Bunck, *Fidel Castro and the Quest for a Revolutionary Culture in Cuba* (University Park: Penn State University Press, 1994), 53.

Chapter Six

1. María Ester Lezaeta, interview by author, Santiago, May 2006.

2. Silo (Mario Luis Rodríguez Cobos), interview by author, Tunquén, Chile, June 2005.

3. H. Van Doren, *Silo y la liberación* (Santiago: Transmutación, 1971), 31; Silo, author interview.

4. Silo, author interview.

5. The moniker "Silo" stems from Rodríguez's tall, narrow physique. While family and childhood friends coined and used the nickname, some Siloists later perceived another connotation: Silo as a granary of ideas. Mario Gómez López, "¡Exclusivo!" *Ramona*, October 29, 1971, 49; Julián Burgos, interview by author, Santiago, March 2004.

6. Silo, *Recopilación de opiniones, comentarios y conferencias, 1969–1995* (Santiago: Virtual Ediciones, 1996), 10–13.

7. Ibid., 12–14.

8. Donald H. Bishop, ed., *Chinese Thought: An Introduction* (New Delhi: Motilal Banarasidass, 1985), 450–51.

9. Gómez, "¡Exclusivo!" 46.

10. Ibid., 49.

11. On the *Cordobazo*, consult James Brennan, *The Labor Wars in Córdoba, 1955–1976: Ideology, Work, and Labor Politics in an Argentine Industrial City* (Cambridge: Harvard University Press, 1998), and Juan Carlos Cena, *El cordobazo: Una rebelión popular* (Buenos Aires: La Rosa Blindada, 2000).

12. Gómez, "¡Exclusivo!" 49.

13. Ibid.

14. Mario Gómez López, interview by author, Santiago, June 2005.

15. Silo, author interview.

16. Poder Joven produced other books, including *Jaque al Mesías* (1970) and *Siloismo: Doctrina, práctica, vocabulario* (1971), published in Santiago by Transmutación.

17. Six editions appeared between May and September of 1971. Runs typically were in the 3,000-copy range. Pía Figueroa Edwards, interview by author, Santiago, March 2004.

18. H. Van Doren, *Manual del Poder Joven* (Santiago: Transmutación, 1971), 5.

19. See Ernesto Guevara, "Socialism and Man in Cuba," in *The Che Guevara Reader*, edited by David Deutschmann (New York: Ocean Press, 2005), 212–30.

20. Van Doren, *Manual del Poder Joven*, 29.

21. Ibid.

22. See Michel Foucault, "About the Beginning of the Hermeneutics of the Self: Two Lectures at Dartmouth," *Political Theory* 21, no. 2 (May 1993): 198–227.

23. Silo, author interview.

24. Van Doren, *Manual del Poder Joven*, 31–33.

25. Ibid., 45, 49.

26. Silo, author interview.

27. Ibid.

28. Van Doren, *Manual del Poder Joven*, 57–58.

29. Figueroa, author interview.

30. Van Doren, *Silo y la liberación*, 33–34.

31. Ibid., 34–55.

32. Ibid., 14.

33. H. Van Doren, *Exordio del Poder Joven* (Santiago: Transmutación, 1971), 7–9.

34. Ibid., 11–13, 31.

35. Ibid., 34–35.

36. Silo, author interview.

37. H. Van Doren, *Meditación Trascendental* (Santiago: Transmutación, 1973), http://siloteca.org/hvd/wpfb-file/doren-h-van-meditacion-trascendental-pdf/ (accessed May 14, 2014).

38. Ibid.

39. Silo, author interview.

40. Luis Fernando Lira, interview by author, Santiago, June 2005.

41. Figueroa, author interview.

42. Ibid.; Julián Burgos, author interview, Santiago, March 2004.

43. Silo, author interview.

44. Gómez, "¡Exclusivo!" 49.

45. Figueroa, author interview.

46. María Eliana Astaburuaga, interview by author, Santiago, March 2004.

47. Bibhuti Baruah, *Buddhist Sects and Sectarianism* (Delhi: Sarup and Sons, 2008), 101.

48. Walpola Rahula, cited in Gail Presbey, Karsten Struhl, and Richard Olsen, eds., *The Philosophical Quest: A Cross-Cultural Reader* (New York: McGraw-Hill, 1999), 179.

49. Peter DeShazo, *Urban Workers and Labor Unions in Chile, 1902–1927* (Madison: University of Wisconsin Press, 1983), 91.

50. Ibid., 201. Also see Raymond B. Craib, "Students, Anarchists and Categories of Persecution in Chile, 1920," *A Contracorriente* 8, no. 1 (Fall 2010): 22–60.

51. Felipe Solar and Andrés Pérez, *Anarquistas: Presencia libertaria en Chile* (Santiago: RIL Editores, 2008), 65–66.

52. Ibid., 221–31.

53. Consult Elizabeth Quay Hutchison, *Labors Appropriate to Their Sex: Gender, Labor, and Politics in Urban Chile, 1900–1930* (Durham, NC: Duke University Press, 2001), and José Moya, "Italians in Buenos Aires' Anarchist Movement: Gender Ideology and Women's Participation, 1890–1910," in *Women, Gender, and Transnational Lives: Italian Women around the World,* edited by Donna R. Gabaccia and Franca Iacovetta (Toronto: University of Toronto Press, 2002).

54. Pierre-Joseph Proudhon, "What is Government?" in *General Idea of the Revolution in the Nineteenth Century,* trans. John Beverly Robinson (London: Freedom Press, 1923), 293–94.

55. Solar and Pérez, *Anarquistas,* 69–74.

56. Silo, author interview.

57. Ibid.

58. Figueroa, author interview. Her first encounter with Siloism came at her friend's *quinceañera.* There, a young man told Figueroa of Poder Joven and later supplied her with a list of some thirty readings, which included books by Marcuse and Gurdjieff.

59. For a comprehensive treatment of the Frankfurt School, see Martin Jay, *The Dialectical Imagination: A History of the Frankfurt School and the Institute of Social Research, 1923–1950* (Berkeley: University of California Press, 1973).

60. See Herbert Marcuse, "On Hedonism," in *Negations: Essays in Critical Theory,* trans. Jeremy J. Shapiro (Boston: Beacon Press, 1968).

61. Consult Herbert Marcuse, *Eros and Civilization: A Philosophical Inquiry into Freud* (Boston: Beacon Press, 1955). On Marcuse, see Douglass Kellner, *Herbert Marcuse and the Crisis of Marxism* (London: Macmillan, 1984), and Barry Katz, *Herbert Marcuse and the Art of Liberation* (London: Verso, 1982). For Marcusean thought in Latin American contexts, consult Francisco López Cámara, *La cultura del 68: Reich y Marcuse* (Cuernavaca, Mexico: Universidad Nacional Autónoma de México, 1989); Rosendo Bolívar Meza, *Tendencias actuales de la izquierda en México: El hombre unidimensional y la teoría crítica de Herbert Marcuse* (Iztapalapa: Universidad Autónoma Metropolitana, 1988); and Américo Martín, *Marcuse y Venezuela* (Caracas: Cuadernos Rocinante, 1969).

62. See Herbert Marcuse, *One-Dimensional Man* (Boston: Beacon Press, 1964).

63. Martin Jay, *Marxism and Totality: The Adventures of a Concept from Lukács to Habermas* (Berkeley: University of California Press, 1984), 220–21.

64. Carlos Maldonado, "Marcuse y el Poder Joven" in *¿Lenin o Marcuse?,* edited by Carlos Maldonado and Sergio Vuskovic (Santiago: Impresora Horizonte, 1970), 9

65. Sergio Vuskovic, "¿Lenin o Marcuse?" in *¿Lenin o Marcuse?,* 30.

66. Maldonado, "Marcuse y el Poder Joven," 18–20.

67. Vuskovic, "¿Lenin o Marcuse?", 26.

68. Douglas Kellner, *Herbert Marcuse and the Crisis of Marxism* (Berkeley: University of California Press), 81. Marcuse and Fromm did not always see eye-to-eye, with the former doubting the latter's revolutionary zeal.

69. Silo, author interview.

70. Erich Fromm, *The Fear of Freedom* (London: Routledge & Kegan Paul, 1942), 158; italics in original. The original German title translates best as *Escape from Freedom*; it was altered for the first English edition. Fromm's writings also include *The Heart of Man: Its Genius for Good and Evil* (London: Routledge & Kegan Paul, 1964); and *The Revolution of Hope: Toward a Humanized Technology* (New York: Bantam, 1968). On Fromm, consult Daniel Burston, *The Legacy of Erich Fromm* (Cambridge, MA: Harvard University Press, 1991); and Florentina Moreno, *Hombre y sociedad en el pensamiento de Erich Fromm* (Mexico City: Fondo de Cultura Económica, 1981).

71. See Erich Fromm, *Humanismo socialista*, trans. Eduardo Goligorsky (Buenos Aires: Paidós, 1966).

72. Erich Fromm, *Marx's Concept of Man*, and Marx, *Economic and Philosophical Manuscripts*, trans. T. B. Bottomore (New York: Frederick Ungar Publishing, 1961), 63.

73. Tony Judt, *Reappraisals: Reflections on the Forgotten Twentieth Century* (New York: Penguin, 2008), 108.

74. Tomás Moulian, "El marxismo en Chile: Producción y utilización" (Faculdad Latinoamericana de Ciencias Sociales [FLACSO], Santiago, Working Paper No. 7, 1991), 138.

75. Ibid., 118, 125.

76. Joaquín Fermandois, *La revolución inconclusa: La izquierda chilena y el gobierno de la Unidad Popular* (Santiago: Centro de Estudios Públicos, 2013), 253.

77. Néstor Kohan, *Marx en su (tercer) mundo: Hacia un socialismo no colonizado* (Buenos Aires: Editorial Biblos, 1998), 49–50.

78. Figueroa, author interview; Burgos, author interview; Oscar Ortiz, interview by author, Santiago, June 2003.

79. The sexual philosophies of Marcuse and Reich are taken up in Paul Robinson, *The Sexual Radicals: Wilhelm Reich, Geza Roheim, and Herbert Marcuse* (London: Maurice Temple Smith Ltd., 1970). Also see Wilhelm Reich, *The Discovery of the Orgone: The Function of the Orgasm* (New York: Orgone Institute Press, n.d.); and Reich, *People in Trouble* (New York: Farrar, Straus, and Giroux, 1976). Studies of Reich include Myron Sharaf, *Fury on Earth: A Biography of Wilhelm Reich* (New York: St. Martin's, 1983); and Jean-Michel Palmier, *Wilhelm Reich: Ensayo sobre el nacimiento del freudo-marxismo* (Barcelona: Anagrama, 1970).

80. Marcuse, *Eros and Civilization*, 218.

81. On esotericism's revival in the sixties and seventies, see Edward Tiryakian, "Toward a Sociology of Esoteric Culture," *American Journal of Sociology* 78, no. 3 (November 1972): 257–80.

82. Although Spanish translations of Gurdjieff's more important writings were not readily available until the late 1970s, Chileans read his work in other languages. Oscar Ortiz, author interview.

83. G. I. Gurdjieff's most remembered works are *Beelzebub's Tales to His Grandson: An Objectively Impartial Criticism of the Life of Man* (New York: Dutton, 1978); and *Life is Real Only Then, When "I Am"* (New York: Dutton, 1982). On Gurdjieff, see Jacob Needleman and George Baker, eds., *Gurdjieff: Essays and Reflections on the Man and His Teaching* (New York: Continuum, 1996); and Sophia Wellbeloved, *Gurdjieff: The Key Concepts* (London: Routledge, 2002).

84. Consult Oscar Ichazo, *Interviews with Oscar Ichazo* (New York: Arica Institute Press, 1982).

85. Juan Pablo Orrego, interview by author, Santiago, August 2007.

86. A critical work on the subject is Michel Foucault, *Discipline and Punish: The Birth of the Prison* (New York: Vintage Books, 1995). The original French edition appeared in 1975.

87. *La Tercera* (Santiago), April 26, 1969.

88. *Los Andes* (Mendoza), May 5, 1969.

89. *La Segunda* (Santiago), May 7, 1969; *El Mercurio*, May 18, 1969.

90. *El Mercurio* (Santiago), May 7, 1969. Also see *La Tercera*, May 7, 1969.

91. *La Tercera*, May 8, 1969.

92. Ibid.

93. As a former Poder Joven member explained, the circle represents totality, without a beginning and without an end, while the points of the triangle represent the cultural, the psychological, and the social elements of Siloist thought. It bears some resemblance to the anarchist symbol. Luis Felipe García, interview by author, Santiago, June 2005.

94. *Clarín* (Santiago), October 1, 1971; *Puro Chile* (Santiago), October 1, 1971; *La Nación*, October 1, 1971; *Las Noticias de Última Hora* (Santiago), October 1, 1971.

95. *El Mercurio* (Santiago), October 1, 1971.

96. Ibid., October 6, 1971.

97. *La Nación* (Santiago), October 5, 1971.

98. Figueroa, author interview.

99. *El Siglo* (Santiago), October 7, 1971; *La Segunda*, October 7, 1971.

100. *El Siglo*, October 10, 1971; *El Sur*, October 6, 1971; *Puro Chile*, October 6, 1971.

101. Later in October, the Marxist *Puro Chile* suggested that Silo was behind the disappearance of four more young women. No follow-up appeared. *Puro Chile*, October 23, 1971.

102. *Puro Chile*, October 9, 1971; *El Sur* (Concepción), October 13, 1971; *El Mercurio*, October 8, 1971; *La Nación*, October 10, 1971; *Tribuna* (Santiago), October 15, 1971; *El Correo de Valdivia* (Valdivia), August 31, 1971.

103. *El Sur*, October 7–8, 1971.

104. *Clarín* (Santiago), October 6, 1971. *Puro Chile* wrote that the young women worshiped Silo. *Puro Chile*, October 8, 1971.

105. *Clarín*, October 1, 1971.

106. *Puro Chile*, October 9, 1971.

107. *Tribuna,* October 7 and 9, 1971.

108. *Puro Chile,* October 25, 1971.

109. *El Siglo,* October 10, 1971.

110. *Clarín,* October 7, 1971.

111. Ibid., October 8, 1971.

112. Ibid.

113. Ibid., October 14, 1971. There are no reports of what later happened to "Chanita" or her terrified mother.

114. Figueroa, author interview; Astaburuaga, author interview.

115. *La Segunda,* October 9, 1971.

116. *Clarín,* October 12, 1971.

117. *La Tercera,* March 9, 1972.

118. *El Mercurio,* October 4, 1971.

119. Other elements of UP, including the Radical Party and the Unitary Popular Action Movement (MAPU), also were harshly critical of Poder Joven. See the Radicals' *La Huella* (Santiago) 1, no. 2 (November 1971): 30–31, and MAPU's *De Frente* (Santiago) 1, no. 14 (November 1972): 8–9.

120. *El Siglo,* October 13, 1971. Calling itself "Zero Group" ("Grupo Cero"), a small group of students from the Pontifical Catholic University and University of Chile also invoked Manson when addressing Siloism. Formed specifically to combat Poder Joven, Zero Group told of Siloist brainwashing and odd rituals, including one involving nudity and red-hot pokers, all of which posed a direct threat to "the family and Western culture." The group was short lived and received limited publicity. María Yolanda González, "¿Qué es el 'Grupo O?'" *Ritmo de la Juventud,* October 21, 1971, 22–25.

121. *Puro Chile,* October 10, 1971.

122. *El Siglo,* October 13, 1971

123. Silo, author interview.

124. Anonymous, "Poder Joven ¿y eso, qué es?" *Ahora,* July 1971, 6–7.

125. "Silo: Poder Joven ¿contra quién?" *Onda,* September 1971, 54–55.

126. Ibid., 55.

127. Anonymous, "Silo: estupidez y fascismo," *Mayoría,* October 20, 1971, 25.

128. Anonymous, "'Yo soy la mujer del jefe de Silo'," *Novedades,* October 1971, 14. Von Ehrenberg's marital status (and the fact that he had a young daughter) did nothing to mitigate either left- or right-wing criticism of his apparently antifamily pursuits; neither did Silo's marriage in 1971. Von Ehrenberg did not respond to the author's request for an interview before his death in 2013.

129. Silo, author interview.

130. María Luisa Señoret, "Contra el hippismo decadente: Brigada Ramona Parra," *Plan* 4, no. 54 (November 1970): n.p.; Anonymous, "Todos Contra Silo," *Ahora,* October 26, 1971, 20. The brigade's principles appear in the short manifesto *La revolución chilena no la para nadie* (Santiago: n.p., 1971). Ramona Parra was a nineteen-year-old revolutionary shot dead by police, along with five others, during

a labor demonstration in Santiago in January 1946. The magazine *Ramona* took its name from Ramona Parra.

131. Burgos, author interview; Astaburuaga, author interview.

132. Anonymous, "Todos contra Silo," 20.

133. Ibid., 21.

134. Ibid., 20.

135. *El Siglo*, October 14, 1971.

136. Anonymous, "Todos contra Silo," 20.

137. *El Mercurio*, October 4, 1971.

138. Ibid.

139. Ibid.

140. Anonymous, "Silo, negocio de la abominación," *Qué Pasa* 26 (October 14, 1971), 11.

141. *El Mercurio*, October 16, 1971.

142. Ibid.

143. Burgos, author interview.

144. *El Mercurio*, October 4, 1971.

145. *La Prensa* (Santiago), October 9, 1971. Also see *Tribuna*, October 13, 1971.

146. *Tribuna*, October 11, 1971.

147. Ibid., October 14, 1971.

148. Ibid., October 28, 1971.

149. *El Mercurio*, October 8, 1971; *Tribuna*, October 11, 1971.

150. *El Mercurio*, October 18, 1971.

151. See, for instance, Anonymous, "Los engaños del Poder Joven," *Punto Final* 139 (September 14, 1971).

152. Figueroa, author interview.

153. Peter Winn, "The Furies of the Andes: Violence and Terror in the Chilean Revolution and Counterrevolution," in *A Century of Revolution: Insurgent and Counterinsurgent Violence During Latin America's Long Cold War*, edited by Greg Grandin and Gil Joseph, 246–47 (Durham: Duke University Press, 2010).

154. Enrique Fernández, "Tiempo del ocio," *Punto Final*, April 27, 1971.

155. On the question of the MIR's New Leftism, see Eugenia Palieraki, *¡La revolución ya viene! El Mir chileno en los años sesenta* (Santiago: LOM, 2014).

156. Ernesto Guevara, *Che Guevara Reader: Writings on Politics and Revolution*, edited by David Deutschmann (North Melbourne: Ocean Press, 2004), 223

157. Van Doren, *Manual del Poder Joven*, 30.

158. Tamara Vidaurrázaga Aránguiz, "¿El hombre nuevo? Moral revolucionaria guevarista y militancia femenina. El caso del MIR," *Revista Nomadías* 15 (July 2012): 69–89.

159. Greg Grandin, *The Last Colonial Massacre: Latin America in the Cold War* (Chicago: University of Chicago Press, 2004), 15.

160. Silo, author interview.

161. Luis Fernando Lira, author interview.

162. Gómez, "¡Exclusivo!" 49. In 2005, Silo expressed doubt that he used such a blunt word but noted that the sentiment applied. Silo, author interview.

163. Silo, author interview.

Chapter Seven

1. *Descomedidos y chascones*, film directed by Carlos Flores, (Santiago: Department of Film, University of Chile, 1973).

2. *El Mercurio* (Santiago), October 19, 1970.

3. Ibid., October 21, 1970.

4. Ibid., October 10, 1970.

5. *El Siglo* (Santiago), November 16 and 18, 1972. The current events magazine *Vea* summed up the 1972 FESES election: it was a "student war." See Raquel Correa, "Guerra estudiantil," *Vea*, September 28, 1972, 12–13.

6. UP hailed the resounding reelection of Communist Alejandro Rojas as FECh president in November 1970 as a sign that a majority of the country's youth was united with Allende. It was an exaggeration but nevertheless made for catchy headlines two months after UP's victory. See *El Mercurio*, November 25, 1970, and *El Siglo*, November 25–26, 1970.

7. PDC figure Edgardo Boeninger, also of Frei's faction, was reelected rector of the University of Chile in mid-1971—a blow to the UP. The MIR called Boeninger's win "a grave problem for a government that wants to transform Chilean society in a socialist direction." Anonymous, "La 'U' a contrapelo," *Punto Final*, June 1971, 27. Also see Hernán Lavín Cerda, "Lucha frontal en la Universidad de Chile," *Ahora*, November 23, 1971, 2–4.

8. Yungue went on to become a lawyer and important PDC figure, was imprisoned by the post-Allende military government, won a seat in the Chamber of Deputies in 1989, and served as ambassador to Costa Rica in the early 2000s under President Ricardo Lagos.

9. Juventud Demócrata Cristiana, *La Democracia Cristiana y la Revolución en Libertad* (Santiago: Ediciones Rebeldía, 1965), 3–5, 35.

10. Juventud Demócrata Cristiana, *¡A terminar con los momios, estén donde estén!* (Santiago: no publisher, 1969), n.p.

11. Juventud Demócrata Cristiana, *¿Qué es la JDC?* (Santiago: JDC Departamento de Formación, 1969), 3–5, 7–9, 37–39.

12. *El Mercurio*, October 11, 1968. The JDC declared in early 1968 that it would organize those in the PDC "who have the strong will to break from the capitalist system and from the classes that support it." *El Siglo*, January 13, 1968.

13. See *El Mercurio*, March 14, 1968.

14. "¿Independencia o indiferencia?" *Alerta! La posición de una juventud firme*, September 1972, 3.

15. "Multitudinaria concertación organizada por la Juventud Nacional de Providencia," *Alerta! La posición de una juventud firme*, October 1972, n.p. Jarpa's

Tribuna was a big fan of Yungue's victory in October 1971, calling his approximately 50 percent share of the student vote an important part of the "democratic" push to "defeat totalitarianism" (Allende's UP). *Tribuna* (Santiago), October 8, 1971.

16. The construction helmet, or hardhat, had transnational symbolism as a sign of the "everyday man" resisting radicalism. In the United States, blue-collar "hardhats" would attack antiwar protestors, for instance. See Penny W. Lewis, *Hardhats, Hippies, and Hawks: The Vietnam Antiwar Movement as Myth and Memory* (Ithaca, NY: Cornell University Press, 2013).

17. Anonymous, "Mito y realidad del Comando Rolando Matus," *Alerta! La posición de una juventud firme*, October 1972, 14.

18. Anonymous, "La reconstrucción de Chile," *Alerta! La posición de una juventud firme*, October 1972, 15.

19. *El Mercurio*, October 1, 1970.

20. "Presencia juvenil de Patria y Libertad," *Patria y Libertad*, 1972, 6–7. Also see Pablo Rodríguez Grez, *Manifiesto Nacionalista*, 3rd ed. (Santiago: SOPECH Impresores, 1973), and Secretaría General de Propaganda, Frente Nacionalista Patria y Libertad, "Somos la única alternativa," internal document, 1973.

21. See Brian Loveman and Thomas Davies, eds., *The Politics of Antipolitics: The Military in Latin America* (Lanham, MD: Rowman and Littlefield, 1997).

22. *Descomedidos y chascones*. UPI is United Press International, a U.S.-based media conglomerate; CUT is the Central Workers' Union, a powerful federation of unions; and FLN is the National Liberation Front, which comprised numerous socialist and communist grassroots groups and neighborhood committees. LSD, of course, is the hallucinogen lysergic acid diethylamide.

23. Ibid.

24. Interview with Eduardo Gatti in *Piedra Roja*, documentary film, directed by Gary Fritz, produced by Ann Fritz and Gary Fritz, 2011.

25. See Tamara Vidaurrázaga Aránguiz, "¿El hombre nuevo? Moral revolucionaria guevarista y militancia femenina. El caso del MIR," *Revista Nomadías* 15 (July 2012): 69–89.

26. María Elena Hurtado, "Una puerta se abrió para nosotras," *Paloma*, September 1973, 105–9.

27. Liliana Viola, *Los discursos del poder* (Buenos Aires: Grupo Editorial Norma, 2000), 105.

28. *Las Noticias de Última Hora* (Santiago), October 19, 1970.

29. Salvador Allende, *Abrirán las grandes alamedas: Discursos* (Santiago: LOM, 2003), 74.

30. Anonymous, "¡Cabros! Somos el motor de Chile," *Ramona*, July 1972, 23, 26.

31. Salvador Allende, "Educación para la democracia," in *El gobierno popular*, edited by Centro de Estudios Latinoamericanos Salvador Allende (Tlaxcala, Mexico: Universidad Autónoma de Tlaxcala, 1990), 67.

32. Francisco Rivera Tobar, "Construir la patria nueva. Los trabajos voluntarios en la Universidad Técnica del Estado (Chile, 1964–1973)," *La Cañada*, 3 (2012): 217–20.

33. *El Siglo,* October 21, 1972.

34. Coordinador Nacional de Trabajos Voluntarios, "Declaración del coordinador nacional juvenil de los trabajos voluntarios," in *La juventud junto a su pueblo construye el Chile Nuevo* (Santiago: Impresora Horizonte, 1971), n.p.

35. Luis Corvalán, *El gobierno de Salvador Allende* (Santiago: LOM, 2003), 167.

36. *Brecha* (Santiago), 1971, no volume, number or month; Rivera, "Construir la patria nueva," 215.

37. Rivera, "Construir la patria nueva," 215. See *El Siglo,* March 3, 1972.

38. Anonymous, "Por la patria todo," *Onda,* January 17, 1973, 52–53. For a sample of other activities conducted by CUT youths, see *La Nación* (Santiago) March 15, 1972, and *El Siglo,* March 5, 1972.

39. Anonymous, "Las manos jóvenes construyen Chile," *Mayoría,* January 19, 1972, 24–25.

40. Oscar Ortiz, interview by author, Santiago, June 2003.

41. Consult Jorge Rojas Flores, "Los estudiantes secundarios bajo la Unidad Popular, 1970–1973," *Revista Historia,* 42, no. 2 (December 2009): 471–503; Robert Austin, *The State, Literacy, and Popular Education in Chile* (Lanham, MD: Lexington Books, 2003); and Joseph Farrell, *The National Unified School in Allende's Chile: The Role of Education in the Destruction of a Revolution* (Vancouver: University of British Columbia Press, 1986).

42. Allende, "Educación para la democracia," 67.

43. Ministry of Education, Republic of Chile, "Panorama de la educación chilena a través del mensaje del presidente de la república," *Revista de Educación* 39 (May 1972): 27.

44. Centro de Estudios Latinoamericanos Salvador Allende, ed., "Educación para la democracia," in *El gobierno popular* (Tlaxcala, Mexico: Universidad Autónoma de Tlaxcala, 1990), 67.

45. Anonymous, "Los jóvenes adquieren responsabilidades," *Onda,* November 25, 1971, 66–67.

46. Anonymous, "FECh: La casa de la cultura, la cultural de la casa," *Onda,* June 23, 1972, 44–45.

47. Anonymous, "Los jóvenes opinan y discuten de política," *Onda,* October 26, 1972, 24.

48. *Descomedidos y chascones.*

49. "Opposite to what the MIR thinks, we are not waiting for a single confrontation, and it will not be an armed one obligatorily," Marín noted in mid-1971. Anonymous, "JJ.CC. hacia el hombre nuevo," *Ahora,* June 8, 1971, 14.

50. On the general history of the JS, see Jorge Valle and José Díaz, *Federación de la Juventud Socialista: Apuntes históricos. 1935–1973* (Santiago: Ediciones Documentas, 1987).

51. Federación Juvenil Socialista, *Informe a la XX conferencia nacional de la Federación Juvenil Socialista, celebrada en Concepción en 1971* (no publisher), 9–10, 14–15. The declaration came at a national conference of socialist youth groups, linked to

the JS in the form of the Federation of Socialist Youth. Also see Carlos Lorca Tobar, *Informe al pleno nacional de la Juventud Socialista, 4 de junio de 1972* (no publisher); and *El Siglo*, October 3, 1971.

52. Federación Juvenil Socialista, *Informe a la XX conferencia*, 15.

53. *Descomedidos y chascones*.

54. Recent scholarship on the Jota includes the collection by Rolando Álvarez and Manuel Loyola, *Un trébol de cuatro hojas: Las juventudes comunistas de Chile en el siglo XX* (Santiago: Ariadna, 2014); and Alfonso Salgado, " 'A Small Revolution': Family, Sex, and the Communist Youth of Chile during the Allende Years (1970–1973)," *Twentieth Century Communism: A Journal of International History* 8 (Spring 2015): 62–88.

55. Marín died of cancer in 2005 before we could hold our scheduled interview.

56. *Clarín* (Santiago), September 20, 1970; Secretaría General, Juventudes Comunistas de Chile, *Luchar, trabajar, estudiar por la patria y la revolución* (Santiago, no publisher, 1972); *El Siglo*, November 22 and 25, 1970. The Communist newspaper noted that some 5,000 Jota members had registered for trabajos slated for January and February 1970. Also see *El Siglo*, October 15, 1972, and Juan Carlos Arriagada, "Los trabajos voluntarios de la juventud," *Principios* 30, no. 137 (January–February, 1971): 46–53.

57. *El Siglo*, November 22, 1970.

58. Anonymous, "JJ.CC."; Cherie Zalaquett, *Chilenas en armas: Testimonios e historia de mujeres militares y guerrilleras subversivas* (Santiago: Catalonia, 2009), 178.

59. On the aesthetic and discursive qualities of BRP muralism, see Camilo Trumper, *Ephemeral Histories: Public Art, Politics, and the Struggle for the Streets in Chile* (Berkeley: University of California Press, 2016); Nelly Richard, *Margins and Institutions: Art in Chile Since 1973*, Special Issue of *Art & Text* (May–July 1986).

60. *El Siglo*, December 16, 1970.

61. *Las Noticias de Última Hora*, March 7–8, 1972.

62. *El Siglo*, November 27, 1972.

63. Ibid., December 3, 1970.

64. Ibid., December 16, 1970.

65. María Eliana Astaburuaga, interview by author, Santiago, March 2004; Pía Figueroa Edwards, interview by author, Santiago, March 2004.

66. *Puro Chile* (Santiago), October 25, 1971.

67. *Descomedidos y chascones*.

68. *Chicago Tribune*, March 10, 1972. I thank Sebastián Hurtado Torres for passing along this article.

69. See Alice Nelson, *Political Bodies: Gender, History, and the Struggle for Narrative Power in Recent Chilean Literature* (Lewisburg: Bucknell University Press, 2002); Lyman L Johnson, ed., *Death, Dismemberment, and Memory: Body Politics in Latin America* (Albuquerque: University of New Mexico Press, 2004); and Julia Tuñón, *Enjualar los cuerpos: Normativas decimonónicas y feminidad en México* (Mexico City: El Colegio de México, 2008).

70. Interview with Mario Soza in *Piedra Roja*, documentary film.

71. Ortiz, author interview.

72. *El Mercurio*, March 11, 1968.

73. Constanza Vergara, "¿Todavia prefiere los hombres de pelo corto?" *Paula*, March 1971, 69–70.

74. Anonymous, "El pelo largo," *Ramona*, April 1972, 42.

75. See Víctor Hugo Robles, "History in the Making: The Homosexual Liberation Movement in Chile," *NACLA Report on the Americas* 31, no. 4 (1998); Robles, *Bandera hueca: Historia del movimiento homosexual de Chile* (Santiago: Editorial Arcis, 2008); and Claudio Acevedo and Eduardo Elgueta, "El discurso homofóbico en la prensa izquierdista durante la Unidad Popular," *Revista Izquierdas* 2, no. 3 (April 2009): 1–12.

76. "Yippie" referred to association with the Youth International Party, a radical, anti-imperialist, and countercultural group with no formal membership. It relished public theatricality and confrontation.

77. Anonymous, "La revolución peluda," *Ahora*, September 21, 1971, 42–44.

78. Anonymous, "La minifalda y el pelo largo. ¿Un impedimento para estudiar?" *Paula*, June 1971, 31.

79. Anonymous, "Ministerio de Educación autoriza el pantalón femenino para ir a clases," *Paula*, June 1971, 30.

80. Anonymous, "La minifalda y el pelo largo," 31.

81. *El Mercurio*, March 3, 1972. Also see the March 6 edition.

82. *El Sur* (Concepción), March 7, 1972.

83. Ibid.

84. Anonymous, "El asunto peludo," *Onda*, March 1972, 42–43.

85. Anonymous, "Tanta bulla por unos pelitos de más," *Ramona*, March 1972, 18–20.

86. Ibid., 20.

87. Mario Gómez López, "Sí a las melenas en los países socialistas," *Ramona*, March 1972, 22–24.

88. *El Siglo*, October 16, 1970.

89. The subject of youth culture in the Soviet bloc exposes the influence of Western cultural trends and efforts by socialist states to manage them. See William Jay Risch, ed., *Youth and Rock in the Soviet Bloc: Youth Cultures, Music, and the State in Russia and Eastern Europe* (Lanham, MD: Lexington, 2014).

90. Florencia Mallon, "*Barbudos*, Warriors, and *Rotos*: The MIR, Masculinity, and Power in the Chilean Agrarian Reform, 1965–74," in *Changing Men and Masculinities in Latin America*, edited by Matthew Gutmann (Durham, NC: Duke University Press, 2003), 180–81.

91. Juan Carlos Moraga, interview by author, Santiago, May 12–13, 2006. Moraga later became general secretary of the JS in 1979, in exile, upon the invitation of Altamirano.

92. *El Siglo*, March 7 and 11, 1972.

93. Ibid., March 8, 1972.

94. Ibid., March 11, 1972.

Chapter Eight

1. Enrique Lafourcade, *Palomita Blanca*, 39th ed. (Santiago: Zig-Zag, 2002), 8. The publishing powerhouse Editorial Zig-Zag published the first edition and has released most all of the novel's subsequent editions.

2. Ibid., 9.

3. Ibid., 17.

4. Ibid., 17.

5. Ibid., 24–30.

6. Ibid., 31.

7. Ibid., 35–37.

8. Ibid., 45–46.

9. Ibid., 53.

10. Ibid., 60–61.

11. Ibid., 62–63.

12. Ibid., 69.

13. Ibid., 81–82.

14. Ibid., 94–98.

15. Ibid., 100.

16. Ibid., 103.

17. Ibid., 124–25.

18. Ibid., 127.

19. Ibid., 116.

20. Ibid., 137–45.

21. Viaux and another conspiring general, Camilo Valenzuela, were later tried and found guilty of attempting a coup. Viaux also was convicted of kidnapping, escaping a murder charge. He was released in August 1973 and moved to Paraguay before returning to Chile. He died in 2005.

22. Lafourcade, *Palomita Blanca*, 149–55.

23. Ibid., 156–59.

24. Roberto Bolaño, *Nocturno de Chile* (New York: Vintage Español, 2000), 117–18.

25. Pía Figueroa Edwards, interview by author, Santiago, March 2004; Julián Burgos, interview by author, Santiago, March 2004.

26. *El Periodista* (Santiago), November 5, 2004.

27. Recent syllabi from high schools across the country—such as the Liceo Marta Donoso (Talca) and Colegio Sofía Infante Hurtado (Maipú, Greater Santiago)—demonstrate this predilection.

28. On Heidegger's *Dasein*, see *A Companion to Heidegger*, edited by Hubert L. Dreyfus and Mark A. Wrathall (Malden, MA: Blackwell, 2005), and M. J. Inwood, *Heidegger* (Oxford: Oxford University Press, 1997).

29. Meanwhile, the Christian Democrats barely appear in *Palomita Blanca*, and moderates seemingly are falling away, consigned to the role of spectators despite the importance of the Christian Democratic congressional vote October 1970 that bestowed the presidency on Allende after the Marxist struck a deal with the party, guaranteeing that Allende's road to socialism would remain within the boundaries of Chilean law.

30. *Tribuna* (Santiago), October 28, 1971.

31. Some who worked on *Palomita Blanca* had contributed to Álvaro Covacevich's 1968 film, *New Love*. Sergio Trabucco, a well-known Chilean film producer, acted in the latter and was the assistant director for the former.

32. Francisco Leal, "*Palomita Blanca* emprendió el vuelo," *Onda*, May 8, 1973, 51.

33. Consult Valeria de los Ríos, ed., *El cine de Raúl Ruiz: Fantasmas, simulacros y artificios*, (Santiago: Uqbar Editores, 2010); and Michael Goddard, *The Cinema of Raúl Ruiz: Impossible Cartographies* (London: Wallflower Press, 2013).

Epilogue

1. *Comisión Interamericana de Derechos Humanos, Informe Anual 1974: Comunicaciones dirigidas a la Comisión* (Organization of American States, Case No. 1799, December 1974).

2. Jorge Gómez Ainslie, telephone interview by author, October 2007.

3. Oscar Ortiz, interview by author, Santiago, June 2003. Consult Oscar Ortiz, *Nuevas crónicas anarquistas de la subversión olvidada* (Santiago: Editorial La Simienta, 2008).

4. On Pisagua, see Lessie Jo Frazier, *Salt in the Sand: Memory, Violence, and the Nation-State in Chile, 1890 to the Present* (Durham, NC: Duke University Press, 2007).

5. *Comisión Interamericana de Derechos Humanos.*

6. Ibid.

7. Ibid.

8. Luis Fernando Lira, interview by author, Santiago, June 2005.

9. Ibid. Silo concurred. Silo (Mario Luis Rodríguez Cobos), interview by author, Tunquén, Chile, June 2005.

10. Jaime Román, interview by author, Santiago, June 2003.

11. See the chapter "Children of the Dictatorship" in Pamela Constable and Arturo Valenzuela, *A Nation of Enemies: Chile Under Pinochet* (New York: Norton, 1993).

12. I borrow "politics of antipolitics" from Thomas Davies and Brian Loveman, eds., *The Politics of Antipolitics: The Military in Latin America* (Lanham, MD: Rowman and Littlefield, 1997).

13. Verónica Valdivia, Rolando Álvarez, and Julio Pinto, *Su revolución contra nuestra revolución: Izquierdas y derechas en el Chile de Pinochet, 1973–1981* (Santiago: LOM, 2006), 70–86.

14. Gobierno de Chile, Secretaría Nacional de la Juventud, *El General Pinochet se reúne con la juventud: Textos de los discursos en el primer aniversario de la Secretaría Nacional de la Juventud* (Santiago: Secretaría Nacional de la Juventud, 1974), 11.

15. Gobierno de Chile, Secretaría Nacional de la Juventud, *La junta de gobierno se dirige a la juventud* (Santiago: Secretaría Nacional de la Juventud, 1974), 10.

16. Pía Figueroa Edwards, interview by author, Santiago, March 2004.

17. Silo estimated in 1990 that about 100,000 Chileans supported the Humanist movement. Graciela Romero, "Los aletazos de Silo," *Paula*, October 1990, 90. Figueroa became the sub-secretary for the environment (and thus one of the highest-ranking women in government) during the presidency of Christian Democrat Patricio Aylwin (1990–1994) and subsequently ran unsuccessfully for a Senate seat from Santiago as the PH candidate. In 1990, moreover, voters in the working-class municipality of Peñalolén, part of the Santiago's metropolitan area, elected PH candidate and former Poder Joven member Laura Rodríguez to the Chamber of Deputies—the only Humanist to hold elective office at the national level. She died before finishing her first four-year term.

18. Figueroa, author interview; Silo, author interview.

19. See José Luis Acevedo, *El futuro ha llegado: Una mirada humanista* (Santiago: Ediciones Chile-América, 1991).

20. *Los Andes* (Mendoza, Argentina), May 4, 2004.

21. *Las Últimas Noticias* (Santiago), September 7, 2003.

22. Gómez Ainslie, author interview.

Index

Note: Images are indicated by page numbers in *italics*.

www.ingramcontent.com/pod-product-compliance
Lightning Source LLC
Chambersburg PA
CBHW032306221125
35799CB00029B/1347